Reviewing Chemistry

With Sample Examinations

Revised Edition

Peter E. Demmin
Chairman, Science Department
Amherst Central High School
Amherst, New York

When ordering this book, please specify:
either **R 496 P** *or* REVIEWING CHEMISTRY

AMSCO SCHOOL PUBLICATIONS, INC.
315 Hudson Street / New York, N.Y. 10013

NOTE TO STUDENTS:

Text and diagrams that are marked with a large asterisk (✳) are tested only in Part II of the examinations.

NOTE TO THE TEACHER:

The books of this series—*Reviewing Biology, Reviewing Earth Science, Reviewing Chemistry,* and *Reviewing Physics*—offer an innovative format that comprehensively reviews and supplements the study of science as it is usually taught at the high school level. Each book is readily correlated with the standard textbooks for this level. The series is specifically geared to the needs of students who want to refresh their memory and review the material in preparation for final exams.

Reviewing Chemistry contains a review of the one-year introductory chemistry course for college-bound students. The material is divided into eleven units, each of which is subdivided into major topic sections. The book is abundantly illustrated with clearly labeled drawings and diagrams that illuminate and reinforce the subject matter. Important science terms are boldfaced and are defined in the text. Other terms that may be unfamiliar to students are italicized for emphasis. In addition, the large work-text format makes *Reviewing Chemistry* easy for students to read.

Within each unit are several sets of multiple-choice questions that test students' knowledge and reasoning while provoking thought. Questions are often accompanied by diagrams that aid in reviewing and testing the materials. The more than 700 questions found in the text can be used for topic review throughout the year, as well as for final exams and homework assignments.

A section called Laboratory Activities follows the eleven topic units. This special section reviews the skills that all students should master in the course of completing one year of chemistry instruction at this level. *Reviewing Chemistry* also contains a complete set of Reference Tables and a guide to how to use them. There is a full Glossary, where students can find concise definitions of significant scientific terms. The extensive Index should be used by students to locate fuller text discussions of chemical terms and concepts. Exams at the back of the book can be used for extra practice and review.

Newly added to this revised edition of *Reviewing Chemistry* are eleven special end-of-book features that explore current controversial issues in chemical science, technology, and society. Reading comprehension, free response, and research questions presented at the end of each feature encourage students to evaluate the issues, and to make their own decisions about the impact of science and technology on society, the environment, and their lives.

The author wishes to acknowledge the helpful contributions of the following consultants in the preparation of this book: Saul L. Geffner, Former Chairman, Department of Physical Sciences, Forest Hills High School, New York City; Paul Cohen, Assistant Principal, Science, Franklin Delano Roosevelt High School, New York City; and George Akst, High School Science Department Chairperson, Syosset High School, Syosset, New York.

Cover Photos: (Background shot) Amino Acid, Comstock Inc., William Marin Jr.; DNA Molecule, Comstock Inc., Mike & Carol Werner; Natural Elements and Atoms, Superstock, Kogi Kitagawa.

ISBN 0-87720-124-2

Contents

Unit 10: Applications of Chemical Principles

Unit 11: Nuclear Chemistry

Unit 12: Laboratory Activities

Science, Technology, and Society

UNIT 1 Matter and Energy

Chemistry is the study of the nature of matter and the changes that matter undergoes. The term *matter* applies to anything that has mass and volume. Much work in chemistry is concerned with learning about and controlling chemical changes in matter and the accompanying changes in energy.

CLASSIFICATION OF MATTER

Matter exists in a seemingly infinite variety of forms. Thus, it is convenient, and in many cases necessary, to organize the different forms of matter in some useful way. In chemistry, matter is usually divided into two broad classes—substances and mixtures of substances.

Substances.
A **substance** is any variety or sample of matter for which all specimens or components have identical composition and identical properties. For example, all samples of a particular substance are homogeneous, or made up of the same material (identical composition). They also have the same heat of vaporization, melting point, and boiling point (identical properties). Properties are related to the composition of a substance and can be used to identify the substance.

An **element** is a substance that cannot be decomposed by chemical change. It cannot be broken down into simpler components by ordinary chemical means.

A **compound** is a substance that is composed of two or more elements chemically combined in a definite ratio. Compounds have a fixed composition by mass and by relative numbers of atoms. Unlike elements, compounds can be decomposed by chemical change.

Mixtures of Substances.
A **mixture** consists of two or more substances. The composition by mass of a mixture can be varied. **Solutions** are *homogeneous* mixtures. For example, table salt dissolved in water is a solution. Although the total amount of salt dissolved can vary, equal parts of the water will contain the same amount of salt. Other mixtures, such as sand in water, are *heterogeneous*. In such a mixture, most of the sand lies on the bottom of the container.

ENERGY

Energy is defined as the capacity to do work. Work is done whenever a force is used to change the position or motion of an object. All forms of matter contain **potential energy**, which is stored energy. When this stored energy is released, it becomes **kinetic energy**, or moving energy, and can do work.

Energy is associated with all chemical changes, and different forms of energy are identified with different changes. Some forms of energy are heat, light, electricity, nuclear energy, and chemical energy. Energy can be converted from one form to another, but energy can never be destroyed.

Energy and Chemical Change.
Chemical change almost always involves the breaking and forming of chemical bonds. In the course of a chemical change, energy is either absorbed or released. Energy is always absorbed (stored) by molecules when chemical bonds are broken. Energy is always released (liberated) when chemical bonds are formed.

Most chemical reactions involve a series of steps, during which some bonds are broken and other bonds are formed. When the net result of bond breaking and bond formation is the liberation of energy, the reaction is described as **exothermic**. In exothermic reactions, energy is released. In an exothermic reaction, the environment outside the reaction acquires energy, often in the form of heat or light.

When the net result of bond breaking and bond formation is the absorption of energy, the reaction is said to be **endothermic**. In endothermic reactions, the environment outside the reaction loses energy.

Measurement of Energy.

Heat. The form of energy most often associated with chemical change is heat. Heat energy, or heat, is measured in calories and kilocalories. A **calorie** is the amount of heat needed to raise the temperature of 1 gram of water 1C°. A **kilocalorie** is equal to 1,000 calories. Heat energy can be represented as

$$\text{calories} = g_{H_2O} \times \Delta t$$

Temperature. Temperature is a measure of the average kinetic energy of the particles that make up a body. Recall that **kinetic energy** is energy associated with the movement of particles. For all samples of matter at the same temperature, therefore, the average kinetic energy of their particles is the same.

A thermometer is used to measure temperature. The calibration markings on a thermometer are based on two fixed points—the freezing point of water (0°C) and the boiling point of water (100°C). (Note that 0 degrees on this scale is an arbitrary designation and does not refer to a zero quantity.)

Another temperature scale frequently used in science is the **Kelvin**, or **absolute**, **scale**. On this scale, the zero point represents the temperature associated with zero kinetic energy. This temperature is called **absolute zero**.

The Kelvin scale is calibrated in units called **kelvins**. A temperature change of 1 kelvin represents the same change in temperature as 1 Celsius degree. Thus, 0°C equals 273 K (273 kelvins), and 100°C equals 373 K (373 kelvins). Absolute zero equals 0 kelvins or -273°C. To convert from Celsius degrees to kelvins, use

$$C° + 273 = K$$

PHASES OF MATTER AND PHASE CHANGE

Matter exists in three phases—solid, liquid, and gas. These phases are often represented by the symbols (s), (ℓ), and (g). A **solid** sample has its own shape and volume, while a **liquid** sample takes the shape, but not necessarily the volume, of its container. A sample of matter in the **gas** phase takes the shape and the volume of its container.

When matter changes from one phase to another, changes in energy also occur. The warming curve, shown in Figure 1-1, illustrates the endothermic nature of melting (also called fusion) and boiling. The opposite processes, freezing (solidification) and condensation, are exothermic. Note that temperature remains constant (unchanged) throughout the time interval that a phase change is occurring.

In part 1 of the curve (see the number in a circle), the temperature changes during the warming of the solid phase and the curve rises. At t_1, the change of phase from solid to liquid begins and continues throughout part 2 to t_2. Thus, at any time between t_1 and t_2, both solid and liquid phases are present. Note that the temperature during this period remains constant and the curve is flat. Time t_2 represents the point at which all the solid has changed to liquid. Beyond this point, the temperature starts to increase and the curve again rises. Part 3 of the curve represents the warming of the liquid phase. At t_3, the change

of phase from liquid to gas begins. Throughout part 4, both liquid and gas phases are present, the temperature again remains constant, and the curve is flat. At t_4, all the liquid has changed to gas, the temperature starts to rise once more, and the curve continues to rise.

QUESTIONS

1. The number of calories of heat energy released when 20 grams of water are cooled from 20°C to 10°C is (1) 10 (2) 20 (3) 200 (4) 400

2. Of the following kinds of matter, which is most likely to be heterogeneous? (1) a compound (2) a mixture (3) an element (4) a pure substance

3. When 40 calories of heat are added to 4 grams of water at 10°C, the resulting temperature will be (1) 5°C (2) 20°C (3) 40°C (4) 15°C

4. When the temperature of a system increases by 20 Celsius degrees, the corresponding temperature change on the Kelvin scale is (1) $+20$ (2) -20 (3) $+293$ (4) -253

5. Any sample of a compound (1) can consist of one element (2) is homogeneous (3) can have a varied chemical composition (4) can be decomposed by a physical change

6. Which Kelvin temperature is equivalent to 20°C? (1) 20 K (2) 253 K (3) 273 K (4) 293 K

7. A true solution is best described as a (1) heterogeneous compound (2) homogeneous compound (3) heterogeneous mixture (4) homogeneous mixture

8. Which formula represents a mixture? (1) NaCl(aq) (2) NaCl(s) (3) $H_2O(\ell)$ (4) $H_2O(s)$

9. Which change of phase is exothermic? (1) gas to liquid (2) solid to liquid (3) solid to gas (4) liquid to gas

10. The normal boiling point of water is equal to (1) 173 K (2) 273 K (3) 373 K (4) 473 K

11. Which of the following best describes exothermic chemical reactions? (1) They never release heat. (2) They always release heat. (3) They never occur spontaneously. (4) They always occur spontaneously.

12. Which substance cannot be decomposed by a chemical change? (1) mercury(II) oxide (2) potassium chlorate (3) water (4) copper

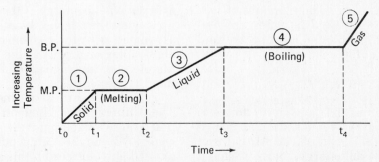

Figure 1-1. Warming Curve. If read from right to left, this curve would illustrate a cooling curve.

Base your answers to questions 13 and 14 on the following graph, which represents the uniform heating of a water sample at standard pressure, starting at a temperature below 0°C.

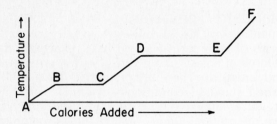

13. The number of calories required to vaporize the entire sample of water at its boiling point is represented by the interval between (1) A and B (2) E and F (3) C and D (4) D and E

14. If 5 grams of water undergo a temperature change from C to D, the total energy absorbed is (1) 80 calories (2) 100 calories (3) 180 calories (4) 500 calories

15. How many calories of heat energy are released when 50 grams of water are cooled from 70°C to 60°C? (1) 10 calories (2) 50 calories (3) 500 calories (4) 1,000 calories

16. If 10.0 grams of water at 20°C absorb 100 calories of heat, the temperature of the water will be increased by (1) 2C° (2) 5C° (3) 10C° (4) 30C°

17. The melting point of ice on the Kelvin scale is (1) 0 K (2) 32 K (3) 80 K (4) 273 K

18. A substance that has a definite shape and a definite volume at STP is (1) NaCl(aq) (2) Cl_2(g) (3) $CCl_4(\ell)$ (4) $AlCl_3$(s)

19. What is the maximum mass of water that can be heated from 25°C to 30°C by the addition of 300 calories of heat? (1) 3,000 grams (2) 300 grams (3) 60 grams (4) 10 grams

THE GAS PHASE

The statements of observed regularities in the behavior of gases are known collectively as the **gas laws**. Each of the gas laws is expressed as a verbal statement and by a mathematical statement. The gas laws are summarized in Table 1-1 on page 5.

Boyle's Law.
Boyle's law, developed in the 17th century, states that at constant temperature, the volume of a given mass of gas varies inversely with the pressure exerted on it.

The mathematical statement of Boyle's law is shown below.

$$P_1V_1 = P_2V_2 \qquad \text{or} \qquad \frac{V_1}{V_2} = \frac{P_2}{P_1}$$

Boyle's law can therefore be stated thus: For a given sample of gas at constant temperature, the product of its pressure and volume is a constant. This is stated mathematically as:

$$PV = k$$

Sample Problems

1. At 1 atmosphere, a cylinder with a movable piston contains 2,000 mL of gas. If the pressure is increased to 5 atmospheres and the temperature remains unchanged, what is the new volume of the gas?

$$P_1V_1 = P_2V_2$$

$$(1 \text{ atm})(2000 \text{ mL}) = (5 \text{ atm})(V_2)$$

$$\frac{(1 \text{ atm})(2000 \text{ mL})}{5 \text{ atm}} = V_2$$

$$400 \text{ mL} = V_2$$

2. At 3 atmospheres pressure, the volume of a gas is 1,200 mL. What pressure is required to reduce the volume of the gas to 300 mL without changing the temperature?

$$P_1V_1 = P_2V_2$$

$$(3 \text{ atm})(1200 \text{ mL}) = P_2 (300 \text{ mL})$$

$$\frac{(3 \text{ atm})(1200 \text{ mL})}{300 \text{ mL}} = P_2$$

$$12 \text{ atm} = P_2$$

Charles' Law.
Charles' law states that at constant pressure, the volume of a given mass of gas varies directly with the Kelvin (absolute) temperature.

The mathematical statement of Charles' law is shown below.

$$\frac{V_1}{V_2} = \frac{T_1}{T_2}$$

The statement of Charles' law specifies that under constant pressure, the volume of a gas, originally measured at 0°C, decreases by $\frac{1}{273}$ of its volume for each decrease of 1C°. Thus, when the temperature has decreased by 273C°, the volume of the gas will theoretically be zero. This accounts for the fact that the zero point on the Kelvin scale is 273C° below the Celsius zero. As a practical matter, all gases become liquids before reaching -273°C, at which point the gas laws no longer apply.

Sample Problem

At 40°C, the volume of a gas is 50.0 mL. At constant pressure, what is the new volume of the gas if the temperature is decreased to 20°C?

$$\frac{V_1}{V_2} = \frac{T_1(K)}{T_2(K)}$$

$$\frac{50.0 \text{ mL}}{V_2} = \frac{40°C + 273}{20°C + 273}$$

$$\frac{50.0 \text{ mL}}{V_2} = \frac{313 \text{ K}}{293 \text{ K}}$$

$$313 \text{ K} \times V_2 = 293 \text{ K} \times 50.0 \text{ mL}$$

$$V_2 = 50.0 \text{ mL} \times \frac{293 \text{ K}}{313 \text{ K}}$$

$$V_2 = 46.8 \text{ mL}$$

* Combined Gas Laws.

Changes in volume, pressure, and temperature usually occur simultaneously. For calculations involving such changes, Boyle's law and Charles' law can be combined into one expression:

$$\frac{P_1 V_1}{T_1} = \frac{P_2 V_2}{T_2}$$

P_1, V_1, and T_1 are the original conditions of pressure, volume, and Kelvin temperature; P_2, V_2, and T_2 are the values of the final conditions. Note that for Boyle's and Charles' laws individually, as well as for the combined law, the mass of the gas involved (the number of particles) must remain constant.

Dalton's Law.

In a mixture of gases that do not react, each gas exerts the same pressure as if it were alone in a given volume. According to Dalton's law of partial pressures, the total pressure of a mixture of gases (P_T), at constant temperature, equals the sum of the individual, or partial, pressures (P_1, P_2, . . .):

$$P_T = P_1 + P_2 + \cdots$$

* Graham's Law.

Since the molecules of a gas, unlike the molecules of a solid or a liquid, have no fixed volume, they tend to spread out, or diffuse. The rate at which gas molecules diffuse depends upon the mass and temperature of the gas. At the same temperature and pressure, light molecules diffuse more rapidly than do heavy molecules. Graham related the rates of diffusion of different gases (r_1 and r_2), at the same condi-

tions, to their molecular masses (m_1 and m_2), using the equation:

$$\frac{r_1}{r_2} = \sqrt{\frac{m_2}{m_1}}$$

Standard Temperature and Pressure.

Quantities of gas samples are usually given in terms of volume instead of mass. However, the volume of a gas sample varies with temperature and pressure. Therefore, scientists have established standard conditions of temperature and pressure, known as **STP**, that are used in giving volume measurements. Standard temperature is 0°C, or 273 K. Standard pressure is 760 mm of mercury (760 torr), or 1 atmosphere (atm).

* Sample Problem

At 0°C and 1 atm (STP), the volume of a gas is 1,000 mL. If the temperature is increased to 25°C and the pressure is doubled, what is the new volume of the gas?

Solution: First convert the temperature from Celsius to Kelvin.

$$0°C = 273 \text{ K}; 25°C = 273 + 25 = 298 \text{ K}$$

Then: $\dfrac{P_1 V_1}{T_1} = \dfrac{P_2 V_2}{T_2}$

$$\frac{(1 \text{ atm})(1000 \text{ mL})}{273} = \frac{(2 \text{ atm})(V_2)}{298}$$

$$V_2 = \frac{(1 \text{ atm})(1000 \text{ mL})(298)}{(2 \text{ atm})(273)}$$

$$V_2 = 546 \text{ mL}$$

Avogadro's Hypothesis.

An explanation for some properties of gases was offered by Avogadro in 1811. He proposed that equal volumes of all gases measured at the same temperature and pressure contain the same number of particles. Even though these particles may have different masses and molecular dimensions, they effectively occupy the same amount of space.

Laboratory observations have determined that, at the same temperature and pressure, 32.0 grams of oxygen occupy the same space as do 2.0 grams of hydrogen, 20.2 grams of neon, and 39.9 grams of argon. These four samples contain the same number of molecules. Note that a molecule of argon is about 20 times heavier than a molecule of hydrogen (39.9:2). Each of these quantities is equivalent to 1 **mole**, or 1 **gram molecular mass** of the substance (see pages 29 and 30).

Experiments show that the volume of each of the samples of oxygen, hydrogen, and argon at STP is 22.4 liters. This quantity, 22.4 liters, is called the volume of one mole of a gas at STP, or simply, the **molar volume**. Note that as conditions

Note to Students: Text and diagrams that are marked with a large asterisk (*) are tested only in Part II of the examinations.

Table 1-1. The Gas Laws

Law	Verbal Statement	Mathematical Statement
Boyle's law	At constant temperature, the volume (V) of a given mass of gas varies inversely with the pressure (P).	$PV = k$ or $P_1 V_1 = P_2 V_2$
Charles' law	At constant pressure, the volume of a given mass of gas varies directly with the Kelvin (absolute) temperatures.	$\dfrac{V_1}{V_2} = \dfrac{T_1}{T_2}$
Dalton's law	The total pressure of a gas mixture (P_T) is equal to the sum of the individual pressures of the gases in the mixture (called partial pressures).	$P_T = P_1 + P_2$
✷ Graham's law	Under the same conditions of temperature and pressure, gases diffuse at rates (r_1 and r_2) that are inversely proportional to the square roots of their molecular masses (m_1 and m_2).	$\dfrac{r_1}{r_2} = \sqrt{\dfrac{m_2}{m_1}}$

of temperature and pressure change, the volume of each of these samples will change to conform to Boyle's and Charles' laws.

Kinetic-Molecular Theory of Gases.
The behavior of gases, as described in the gas laws, is accounted for by the **kinetic-molecular theory**. This theory, also called a model, is only an approximation. Like any model, it is only as good as its ability to predict behavior under new conditions.

The kinetic-molecular theory includes the following assumptions about the nature of gases:

1. Gases are composed of individual particles called **molecules** that are in continuous, random motion. The particles move in straight lines until they collide with one another or with the walls of their container, whereupon they move off in new directions.

2. Collisions between gas particles may result in a transfer of energy between particles, but the total energy of the system remains constant.

3. The volume of the gas particles themselves is negligibly small compared with the volume of the space in which the gas particles are contained.

4. There are no attractive forces between the particles of a gas.

5. The average kinetic energy of the particles is proportional to the Kelvin (absolute) temperature of the gas, but not all of the particles in a given gas sample have the same kinetic energy.

Deviations from the Gas Laws.
The gas laws and the conditions assumed in the kinetic-molecular theory are oversimplifications of the natural world. Thus, the behavior of real gases shows deviations from the behavior described by the gas laws.

A gas that conforms strictly to the model of the gas laws is called an *ideal gas*. However, no real gas is ideal under all conditions of temperature and pressure. Deviations occur because molecules of real gases do have some volume and do exert some force of attraction for one another. These deviations become significant when the space between gas particles is decreased, for example, at relatively high pressures and at very low temperatures. Under these conditions, the velocities of gaseous molecules diminish, thus permitting the forces of attraction between molecules to become more effective.

QUESTIONS

1. Compared to a 1-mole sample of hydrogen at 273 K and 1 atmosphere, a 1-mole sample of hydrogen at 298 K and 1 atmosphere contains (1) more molecules (2) fewer molecules (3) molecules with higher average kinetic energy (4) molecules with lower average kinetic energy

Base your answers to questions 2–6 on the following diagram, which represents a movable piston and a cylinder. The cylinder contains 1,000 mL of gas G at STP.

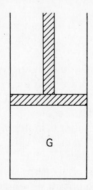

2. If the temperature remains constant and the pressure on gas G is increased to 4 atmospheres, the new volume of gas G will be (1) 250 mL (2) 500 mL (3) 2,000 mL (4) 4,000 mL

3. If the pressure remains constant and the temperature of gas G is raised to 273°C, the piston will move until the new volume of gas G becomes (1) 273 mL (2) 500 mL (3) 2,000 mL (4) 273,000 mL

4. If the pressure remains constant and the temperature of gas G is raised to 273°C, the volume of the sample will (1) increase (2) decrease (3) remain the same

5. If the pressure remains constant and the temperature of gas G is raised to 273°C, the mass of the sample will (1) increase (2) decrease (3) remain the same

6. If more molecules of gas G are added to the system at constant temperature and pressure, the volume of the system will (1) increase (2) decrease (3) remain the same

7. A sample of neon gas at STP has a mass of 10.0 grams. The quantity of neon in the sample is (1) 0.5 molecule (2) 0.5 liter (3) 0.5 milliliter (4) 0.5 mole

8. Which sample of oxygen at STP represents the greatest mass? (1) one mole (2) one gram (3) one liter (4) one milligram

9. Which system contains molecules with the same average kinetic energy as the molecules in 10.0 grams of carbon dioxide at 10°C? (1) 10 grams of CO_2 at 40°C (2) 20 grams of CO_2 at 0°C (3) 20 grams of CO_2 at 20°C (4) 40 grams of CO_2 at 10°C

10. Which conditions of pressure and temperature are represented by STP? (1) 1 atm and 0 K (2) 273 atm and 273 K (3) 1 atm and 0°C (4) 273 atm and 0°C

11. Which of the following is a principle of the kinetic-molecular theory? (1) Molecules of a gas bond together following collisions. (2) As temperature decreases, gas molecules maintain constant velocities. (3) Strong forces of attraction exist between molecules of a gas. (4) The distances between molecules of a gas are much greater than the diameters of the molecules.

12. Under which conditions do real gases most closely approach ideal behavior? (1) high temperature and low pressure (2) low temperature and low pressure (3) high temperature and high pressure (4) low temperature and high pressure

13. At STP, 2.0 liters of helium gas, He, contain the same number of molecules as (1) 1.0 liter of $O_2(g)$ (2) 2.0 liters of $O_2(g)$ (3) 1.5 liters of $O_2(g)$ (4) 4.0 liters of $O_2(g)$

14. Which sample of hydrogen gas at STP occupies the largest volume? (1) 1 mole (2) 1 gram (3) 2 liters (4) 2 moles

15. One mole of an ideal gas occupies a volume of 22.4 liters at (1) 273 K and 760 torr (2) 273 K and 0 torr (3) 760°C and 273 torr (4) 0°C and 273 torr

16. The number of molecules in 16 grams of oxygen is the same as the number of molecules in (1) 2 grams of hydrogen (2) 2 grams of helium (3) 4 grams of hydrogen (4) 4 grams of helium

17. Equal volumes of all gases at the same temperature and pressure contain an equal number of (1) electrons (2) protons (3) molecules (4) atoms

18. At standard temperature, 1.0 liter of $O_2(g)$ at 760 torr contains the same number of molecules as (1) 2.0 liters of $O_2(g)$ at 380 torr (2) 2.0 liters of $O_2(g)$ at 760 torr (3) 0.50 liter of $O_2(g)$ at 380 torr (4) 0.50 liter of $O_2(g)$ at 760 torr

19. As 1 mole of a gas at STP is compressed, the number of molecules (1) decreases (2) increases (3) remains the same

20. Which change is most closely associated with an increase in the average kinetic energy of the molecules of a sample of $N_2(g)$? (1) a change in pressure from 1 atm to 0.5 atm (2) a change in volume from 2 liters to 1 liter (3) a change in temperature from 20°C to 30°C (4) a change in temperature from 30°C to 20°C

Base your answers to questions 21–24 on the following graphs.

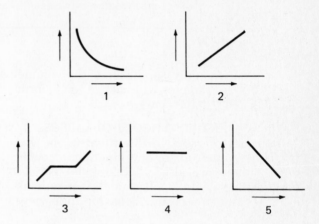

21. Which graph best represents how the volume of a given mass of a gas varies with increasing temperature at constant pressure? (1) 1 (2) 2 (3) 3 (4) 5

22. Which graph best represents temperature in a system that undergoes a temperature change and a phase change as heat is added at a constant rate? (1) 1 (2) 2 (3) 3 (4) 4

23. Which graph best represents the temperature in a pure water system as heat is removed at a constant rate between 80°C and 20°C? (1) 1 (2) 2 (3) 3 (4) 5

24. Which graph best represents the mass of a sample of gas as pressure increases at constant temperature? (1) 5 (2) 2 (3) 3 (4) 4

25. A sealed flask contains 1 molecule of hydrogen for every 3 molecules of nitrogen at 20°C. If the total pressure is 400 torr, the partial pressure of the hydrogen is (1) 100 torr (2) 200 torr (3) 300 torr (4) 400 torr

26. A 1-liter flask contains two gases at a total pressure of 3.0 atmospheres. If the partial pressure of one of the gases is 0.5 atmosphere, then the partial pressure of the other gas must be (1) 1.0 atm (2) 2.5 atm (3) 1.5 atm (4) 0.50 atm

THE LIQUID PHASE

A sample of any liquid has a fixed volume, but the liquid takes the shape of its container. Particles of a liquid have no regular arrangement and are in constant, random motion.

Vapor Pressure.

The term *vapor* is frequently used to refer to the gas phase of a substance that is normally a liquid or solid at room temperature. In a closed system, the vapor (gas) arising from the liquid exerts a pressure, called the **vapor pressure**, which increases as the temperature of the liquid is raised. Vapor pressure has a specific value for each substance at any given temperature.

Evaporation and Boiling.

The process by which a liquid changes to a gas is called **evaporation**. Evaporation tends to take place at all temperatures at the surface of a liquid. In an open container, evaporation continues until all the liquid is vaporized.

A liquid will boil at the temperature at which its vapor pressure equals the external pressure acting on the surface of the liquid. The **normal boiling point** of a liquid is the temperature at which the vapor pressure of the liquid equals 1 atmosphere. The bubbles in a boiling liquid are made up of the gas phase of the substance being boiled. These gas molecules "push aside" some of the liquid to make room for themselves. Unless otherwise stated, a reference to the "boiling point" of a substance means the normal boiling point, or the boiling point at 1 atmosphere.

Heat of Vaporization.

The amount of energy required to vaporize a unit mass of a liquid at its boiling temperature and 1 atmosphere is called **heat of vaporization**. When the unit is 1 mole, the amount of energy is called the *molar heat of vaporization*. Usually, heat of vaporization is given for the liquid-to-gas phase change at the normal boiling point. The energy involved in phase change is used to overcome the forces of attraction between particles and does not increase their average kinetic energy. Thus, there is no increase in temperature during a phase change. (Refer again to Figure 1-1 on page 2.)

THE SOLID PHASE

A sample of any solid has a fixed shape and volume. All true solids have crystalline structures. The particles that make up **crystals** are arranged in a regular geometric pattern that repeats itself. Certain materials are considered to be solids, but are actually supercooled liquids. That is, they are liquids that have been cooled below certain temperatures without crystallizing. Glass and some plastics are examples of such materials. They do not have crystalline structures.

The **normal melting point** of a solid or the **normal freezing point** of a liquid is the temperature at which the phase change takes place at 1 atmosphere pressure. A melting point can be determined from cooling curves, which are obtained experimentally.

The amount of energy required to change a unit mass of a solid to a liquid at its melting temperature is called **heat of fusion**. When the quantity melted is 1 mole, the amount of energy is called the *molar heat of fusion*.

Sublimation is a change from the solid phase directly to the gas phase without an apparent intervening liquid phase. The **heat of sublimation** is the amount of energy required to accomplish this phase change. Solids that sublime have high vapor pressures and low intermolecular attractions. Examples of solids that sublime at room temperature are solid carbon dioxide (dry ice), solid iodine, and naphthalene.

QUESTIONS

1. The term *fusion* refers to (1) warming only (2) condensation only (3) melting only (4) condensation and melting

2. In a closed system, as temperature increases, the vapor pressure of a confined liquid (1) increases (2) decreases (3) remains the same

3. When heat energy is lost by a pure substance at its freezing point with no change in temperature, its potential energy (1) decreases (2) increases (3) remains the same

4. When a substance is melting at constant temperature, its potential energy (1) is increasing (2) is decreasing (3) remains the same

5. The change in phase from a solid to a liquid is (1) melting (2) sublimation (3) evaporation (4) condensation

6. Which change of phase represents sublimation? (1) solid to liquid (2) solid to gas (3) liquid to gas (4) liquid to solid

7. The phase change most similar to boiling is (1) melting (2) sublimation (3) evaporation (4) condensation

8. As temperature increases, the vapor pressure of water (1) increases (2) decreases (3) remains the same

9. The heat of fusion for ice is 80 calories per gram. Adding 80 calories of heat to 1 gram of ice at STP will cause the ice to (1) increase in temperature (2) decrease in temperature (3) change to water at a higher temperature (4) change to water at the same temperature

10. Solid substances are most likely to sublime if they have (1) high vapor pressures and strong intermolecular attractions (2) high vapor pressures and weak intermolecular attractions (3) low vapor pressures and strong intermolecular attractions (4) low vapor pressures and weak intermolecular attractions

11. At 1 atmosphere, which substance will sublime when heated? (1) $CO_2(s)$ (2) $H_2O(\ell)$ (3) $CH_4(g)$ (4) $HCl(aq)$

12. As heat is applied to a piece of ice at 0°C, the temperature of the ice initially (1) decreases (2) increases (3) remains the same

13. Burning is an example of a change that is (1) physical (2) chemical (3) endothermic (4) nuclear

14. Which change involves the largest number of calories? (1) heating 100 grams of water from 90°C to 99°C (2) heating 10 grams of water from 1°C to 98°C (3) cooling 50 grams of water from 90°C to 80°C (4) cooling 100 grams of water from 90°C to 70°C

15. If the Celsius temperature of a gas at constant pressure is increased from 10°C to 20°C, the volume is (1) doubled (2) halved (3) increased but not doubled (4) decreased but not halved

16. Standard temperature and pressure (STP) are equal to (1) 273°C and 760 atmospheres (2) 0°C and 760 atmospheres (3) 0°C and 760 torr (4) 0°C and 1 torr

17. As the Celsius temperature is increased, the volume of a mole of gas at constant pressure (1) decreases (2) increases (3) remains the same

18. As the Celsius temperature is decreased, the molar mass of a sample of oxygen at constant pressure (1) decreases (2) increases (3) remains the same

19. Based on Reference Table O (see page 110), if water is boiling at 50°C, the external pressure is (1) 92.5 torr (2) 0.5 atm (3) 40 torr (4) 2 atm

20. With increasing temperature and decreasing pressure, the value of Avogadro's number (1) decreases (2) increases (3) remains the same

21. The relationship between the volume of a gas and the number of molecules it contains was developed by (1) Boyle (2) Charles (3) Dalton (4) Avogadro

22. As the external pressure acting on a liquid increases, the boiling temperature of the liquid (1) decreases (2) increases (3) remains the same

23. The change from the solid phase directly to the gas phase is called (1) sublimation (2) evaporation (3) boiling (4) freezing

24. As the number of particles of a gas increases at constant volume and temperature, the pressure of the gas (1) decreases (2) increases (3) remains the same

UNIT 2 Atomic Structure

ATOMS

Historical Background.

The ancient Greeks had two theories concerning the nature of matter, both based on philosophical beliefs rather than on scientific studies. According to the **continuous theory**, a sample of matter could be divided and subdivided into smaller and smaller parts indefinitely. Each part, no matter how small, would retain the characteristics of the original sample. According to the **discontinuous theory**, all matter is made up of tiny particles, or **atoms**, which could not be broken down into smaller particles.

The first modern atomic theory was developed in the early 1800s by the English chemist John Dalton. Dalton's theory was based on laws of chemistry established by scientific experiments and observations. In Dalton's theory, as in the discontinuous theory of the ancient Greeks, the atom was considered to be a solid, indivisible particle.

With the discovery of electrons in the late 1890s, the accepted model of the atom as a solid particle began to change. It is now known that atoms are made up of many different kinds of smaller particles.

Subatomic Particles.

The three major kinds of particles in an atom are electrons, protons, and neutrons.

The **electron** is the fundamental unit of negative charge in an atom. The mass of an electron, which equals $\frac{1}{1836}$ the mass of a proton, is negligibly small.

The **proton** is the fundamental unit of positive charge in an atom. Its mass is approximately 1 atomic mass unit (amu).

The **neutron** has zero charge. Its mass is also approximately 1 amu, but is slightly greater than the mass of a proton. It is sometimes helpful to think of a neutron as a particle formed by the combination of a proton and an electron.

Characteristics of the three major subatomic particles are given in Table 2-1.

Because protons and neutrons are found in the nucleus of atoms, they are called **nucleons**. These are the only particles that have been found in a stable nucleus. However, many other particles, such as *positrons* and *mesons*, have been observed during experiments involving nuclear disintegration.

Structure of Atoms.

In 1911, Ernest Rutherford showed that the positive charge and mass of an atom are concentrated in the very small, dense nucleus, and that most of the atom is empty space.

Rutherford developed this model of the atom after conducting experiments in which he bombarded very thin gold foil with a beam of positively charged particles called *alpha particles*. Most of the alpha particles passed straight through the foil without being deflected, indicating that there is mostly empty space in atoms. A few of the alpha particles were deflected at angles of more than 90°. These deflections occurred when the positively charged alpha particles came near the positively charged nuclei and were repelled by the like electrical charges.

Differences Between Atoms.

A major principle of the atomic theory states that atoms of different elements are different. They have different chemical and physical properties, which can be attributed to differences in the number of protons and neutrons, and in the number and arrangement of electrons.

Atomic Numbers. The **atomic number** of an atom is equal to the number of protons in its nucleus. Since an atom has no net charge, the atomic number also equals the number of electrons. The number of protons in the nucleus distinguishes one element from another and identifies a particular element.

Mass Numbers and Isotopes. The **mass number** of an atom is equal to the number of protons plus the neutrons in its nucleus. Every atom of a particular element has the same number of protons,

Table 2-1. Subatomic Particles

| Particle | Symbol | | Mass | Charge |
	In General Use	In Nuclear Equations		
Electron	e^-	$_{-1}^{0}e$	1/1836 amu	−1
Proton	p	$_{1}^{1}H$	1 amu	+1
Neutron	n	$_{0}^{1}n$	1 amu	0

but the number of neutrons may differ. These different forms of an element having the same number of protons but a different number of neutrons are called **isotopes**. Thus, while all atoms of an element have the same atomic number, their mass numbers can vary.

The mass number of an atom can be written as a number following the name of the element, for example, carbon-12. The atomic number and mass number of an atom are also shown by a subscript and superscript preceding the chemical symbol for the element, as in $^{12}_{6}C$ and $^{14}_{6}C$.

In $^{12}_{6}C$, note that:

1. The mass number, or the number of nucleons (protons + neutrons), is 12.

2. The atomic number, or the number of protons (equal to the number of electrons), is 6.

3. The number of neutrons (mass number − atomic number) is $12 - 6 = 6$.

In $^{14}_{6}C$, note that:

1. The mass number is 14.

2. The atomic number is 6.

3. The number of neutrons is 8.

The number of neutrons in an atom can be found by subtracting the atomic number from the mass number.

Atomic Mass.   The mass of a neutral atom is measured in **atomic mass units** (**amu**), which are based on the mass of the carbon-12 atom. By definition, the mass of the carbon-12 atom is 12.000 amu, and 1 amu equals $\frac{1}{12}$ the mass of a carbon-12 atom.

Isotopes and Average Atomic Mass.   Most elements occur in nature as mixtures of isotopes. In general, the atomic mass for an element given in tables is an average atomic mass that is the average of the masses of the naturally occurring isotopes of the element. For example, most chlorine exists as two isotopes, chlorine-35 and chlorine-37. About 75 percent of naturally occurring chlorine is chlorine-35. Most other chlorine atoms, about 25 percent, are chlorine-37. The weighted average atomic mass given for chlorine in reference tables is 35.453 amu, or 35.5 amu.

Gram Atomic Mass.   A sample of an element with a mass in grams numerically equal to the atomic mass is a **gram atomic mass**. For example, 12 grams of carbon, 16 grams of oxygen, and 32 grams of sulfur are equal to 1 gram atomic mass of each element. One gram atomic mass of an element contains 6.02×10^{23} atoms. This is Avogadro's number (see page 29).

The Bohr Model of the Atom.   Niels

Bohr developed a model of the atom in which electrons are described as revolving around the nucleus in concentric circular orbits, or shells (see Figure 2-1). The shells, at increasing distances from the nucleus, are designated by the letters *K*, *L*, *M*, *N*, *O*, *P*, and *Q*, or by the numbers 1 through 7. The energy of the electrons in the shells increases with distance from the nucleus; that is, the electrons nearest the nucleus have the lowest energy, while those most distant have the highest energy.

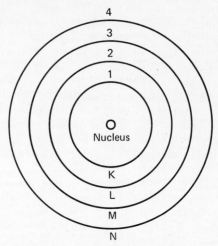

Figure 2-1. The Bohr atom.

Quanta and Spectral Lines.   When all

the electrons of an atom are at their lowest energy levels, the atom is said to be in the **ground state**. When an electron absorbs energy and moves to a higher energy level, the atom is said to be in an **excited state**, which is unstable. When the electron falls from a higher energy level to a lower energy level, it gives off energy.

Electrons absorb and give off energy only in discrete amounts called **quanta**. An electron can move from one energy level to a higher energy level only by absorbing a quantum of energy equal to the difference in energy between the two levels. When an electron falls from a higher to a lower energy level, it gives off a quantum of energy equal to the difference in energy between the two levels.

When the electrons of an atom in the excited state return to the ground state, they give off energy in the form of radiant energy of specific frequencies, or colors. By viewing radiation from various sources with a spectroscope, scientists have found that each element produces a characteristic set of **spectral lines** by which it can be identified.

Orbital Model of the Atom.   Much of the

Bohr model of the atom was based on analysis of the emission of energy by hydrogen atoms. Careful analysis of energy emission by atoms of other elements revealed flaws in the Bohr model and

Table 2-2. Subshells and Orbitals

Energy sublevels	Orbitals
7s	○
6p	○○○
5d	○○○○○
4f	○○○○○○○
6s	○
5p	○○○
4d	○○○○○
5s	○
4p	○○○
3d	○○○○○
4s	○
3p	○○○
3s	○
2p	○○○
2s	○
1s	○

resulted in the development of the orbital model of the atom. In the orbital model, the locations of electrons are described in terms of the average regions of most probable electron location. These regions, called **orbitals**, differ in size, shape, and orientation in space from the circular orbits of the Bohr atom.

Arrangement of Electrons.

In the orbital model, the positions of electrons are represented by **quantum numbers**. The electron shells proposed by Bohr became the **principal energy levels** of the orbital model. Each principal energy level is represented by a **principal quantum number** (n), which is the same as the shell designation in the Bohr model. For any atom in the ground state, the number of energy levels that have at least one electron is equal to the number of the period of the element in the periodic table.

Sublevels. The principal energy levels of the orbital model are divided into **sublevels**. The number of possible sublevels in each principal energy level is equal to the principal quantum number for that energy level. Thus, the first principal energy level has one sublevel, the second principal energy level has two sublevels, and so on. The sublevels are designated s, p, d, and f. The s sublevel has the lowest energy in that energy level, while the f sublevel has the highest. In an atom in the ground state, no principal energy level has more than four occupied sublevels.

Sublevels contain one or more orbitals (see Table 2-2). Each orbital has a different spatial orientation and can accommodate one or two electrons. Electrons behave like tiny magnets spinning on their axes. When two electrons occupy the same orbital, they have opposite spin.

Table 2-3 shows the distribution of electrons in principal energy levels 1 through 4.

Electron Configuration. The electron configuration of an atom describes the arrangement of electrons in principal energy levels, sublevels, and orbitals. Beginning with the hydrogen atom, and in order of atomic number, the electron configurations of the atoms of each element can be built up by adding one electron at a time according to the following rules.

1. Any orbital can accommodate one or two electrons (if two, the electrons have opposite spins).

2. An added electron is placed in the unfilled orbital of the lowest energy.

3. Within a given sublevel, a second electron is not added to an orbital until each orbital in the sublevel contains one electron.

4. Only the s sublevel or the s and p sublevels (four orbitals for a maximum of eight electrons) can be occupied in the outermost energy level of any atom.

Table 2-3 also shows the order in which electron levels fill. Beginning with the lowest energy, $1s$ to $2s$ to $2p$ to $3s$ to $3p$ to $4s$ to $3d$, which has

Table 2-3. Electron Arrangement

Principal Quantum Number (n)	Number of Permitted Sublevels (n)	Symbol	Number of Orbitals		Electron Capacity	
			Total (n^2)	By Sublevel	Total $(2n^2)$	By Sublevel
1	one	s	one	—	2	2
2	two	s, p	four	(1 + 3)	8	(2 + 6)
3	three	s, p, d	nine	(1 + 3 + 5)	18	(2 + 6 + 10)
4	four	s, p, d, f	sixteen	(1 + 3 + 5 + 7)	32	(2 + 6 + 10 + 14)

lower energy than $4p$. Again, $4d$ has lower energy than $5p$. Then $5p$ to $6s$.

The electron configuration of an atom can be written out as shown below. The principal energy levels, sublevels, and numbers of electrons are each specified. For example, the electron configuration of magnesium ($_{12}$Mg) is written as:

principal energy level $\nearrow 1s^2 2s^2 2p^6 3s^2 \leftarrow$ number of electrons — sublevel

A simplified electron configuration can be written as 2-8-2, which indicates the number of electrons in the principal energy levels, K-L-M.

Sometimes, for atoms with many electrons, it is convenient to represent the arrangement of inner electrons by referring to the last preceding noble gas in the periodic table. For example, the electron configuration for $_{56}$Ba is:

$$[1s^2 2s^2 2p^6 3s^2 3p^6 3d^{10} 4s^2 4p^6 4d^{10} 5s^2 5p^6]6s^2$$

xenon core

Thus, the simplified electron configuration for $_{56}$Ba may be written as:

$$[\text{Xe core}]6s^2$$

The term "Xe core" refers to the configuration of 54 electrons as found in an atom of the noble gas xenon, $_{54}$Xe.

Valence Electrons.
The electrons found in the outermost principal energy level of an atom are the **valence electrons**. The remainder of the atom—its nucleus and other electrons—is the **core**, or **kernel**, of the atom. Most of the chemical properties of an atom are related to the valence electrons.

Electron-dot symbols are used to represent valence electrons. The electron configuration for an atom gives the correct number of valence electrons, generally not more than eight. Examples of electron-dot diagrams are shown in Figure 2-2.

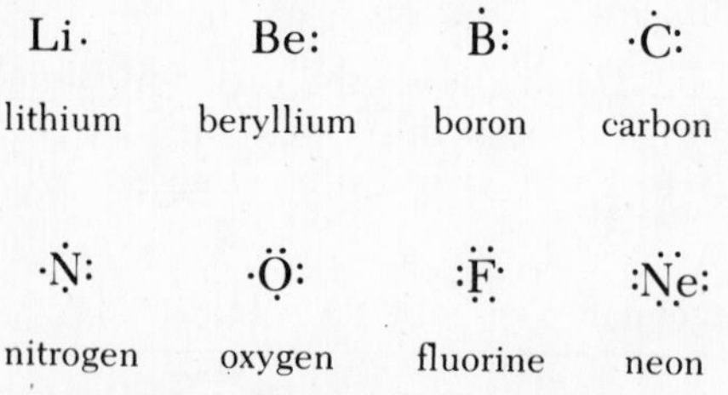

Li·   Be: Ḃ: ·Ċ·

lithium   beryllium   boron   carbon

·N̈·   ·Ö·   :F̈·   :N̈e:

nitrogen   oxygen   fluorine   neon

Figure 2-2. Electron-dot diagrams.

Note that electrons are often paired to reflect their arrangement within the orbitals of the s and p sublevels. In these diagrams, the chemical symbol for an atom represents the kernel.

Ionization Energy.
The amount of energy required to remove the most loosely bound electron from an atom in the gas phase is called the **ionization energy** (IE).

$$M(g) + IE \rightarrow M^+(g) + e^-$$

The **second ionization energy** refers to the amount of energy needed to remove the second most loosely bound electron. Removal of the outermost electron of an atom requires the least amount of energy because the attractive force of the positively charged nucleus is least. Removal of the electron nearest the nucleus requires the greatest amount of energy because the attractive force of the nucleus is greatest. Thus, beginning with the outermost electron, each successive ionization energy is greater than the previous one. In Table K of the Reference Tables (see page 108), first ionization energies are expressed in kcal/mole of atoms. These energies can also be expressed in electron-volts per atom. Ionization energies are used to compare certain chemical properties of elements, such as chemical reactivity.

QUESTIONS

1. What is the maximum number of electrons that can occupy the second principal energy level? (1) 6 (2) 8 (3) 18 (4) 32

2. Compared to an atom of $^{12}_6$C, an atom of $^{14}_6$C has (1) more protons (2) fewer protons (3) more neutrons (4) fewer neutrons

3. The characteristic bright-line spectrum of an element is produced when electrons (1) fall back to lower energy levels (2) are gained by a neutral atom (3) are emitted by the nucleus as beta particles (4) move to higher energy levels

4. How many electrons would be indicated in the electron-dot diagram of an atom with the electron configuration $1s^2 2s^2 2p^6 3s^2 3p^4$? (1) 2 (2) 4 (3) 6 (4) 16

5. If atom X is represented by $^{12}_6$X and atom Y is represented by $^{14}_6$Y, then X and Y are (1) isotopes of the same element (2) isotopes of different elements (3) ions of the same element (4) ions of different elements

6. When an atom goes from the excited state to the ground state, the total energy of the atom (1) decreases (2) increases (3) remains the same

7. Which of the following represents the electron configuration of an atom in the excited state? (1) $1s^1 2s^1$ (2) $1s^2 2s^2 2p^1$ (3) $1s^2 2s^2 2p^5$ (4) $1s^2 2s^2 2p^6 3s^1$

8. A sample of element X contains 90% ^{35}X atoms, 8% ^{37}X atoms, and 2% ^{38}X atoms. The average isotopic mass is closest to (1) 32 (2) 35 (3) 37 (4) 38

9. The atomic number of an atom is always equal to the total number of (1) neutrons in the nucleus (2) protons in the nucleus (3) neutrons plus protons in the atom (4) protons plus electrons in the atom

12

10. Which principal energy level can hold a maximum of 18 electrons? (1) 5 (2) 2 (3) 3 (4) 4

11. Which is the correct electron-dot representation of an atom of sulfur in the ground state?

(1) S: (2) ·S:

(3) ·S: (4) :S:

12. The total number of d orbitals in the third principal energy level is (1) 1 (2) 5 (3) 3 (4) 7

13. The "kernel" usually includes all parts of the atom except the (1) neutrons (2) protons (3) valence electrons (4) orbital electrons

14. The amount of energy required to remove the most loosely bound electron from an atom in the gaseous phase is called (1) kinetic energy (2) potential energy (3) ionization energy (4) electron affinity

15. What is the total number of electrons in an atom with an atomic number of 13 and a mass number of 27? (1) 13 (2) 14 (3) 27 (4) 40

16. What is the maximum number of sublevels in the third principal energy level? (1) 1 (2) 2 (3) 3 (4) 4

17. The number of valence electrons in an atom with an electron configuration of $1s^2 2s^2 2p^6 3s^2 3p^4$ is (1) 6 (2) 2 (3) 16 (4) 4

18. Which two particles have approximately the same mass? (1) neutron and electron (2) neutron and deuteron (3) proton and neutron (4) proton and electron

19. Which diagram correctly represents an atom of fluorine in an excited state?

20. The mass number of an atom is equal to the number of (1) neutrons, only (2) protons, only (3) neutrons plus protons (4) electrons plus protons

21. In an atom, the s sublevel has (1) 1 orbital (2) 5 orbitals (3) 3 orbitals (4) 7 orbitals

22. An atom of $^{226}_{88}Rn$ contains (1) 88 protons and 138 neutrons (2) 88 protons and 138 electrons (3) 88 electrons and 226 neutrons (4) 88 electrons and 226 protons

23. What is the maximum number of electrons that can occupy an orbital? (1) 1 (2) 2 (3) 3 (4) 6

24. Which electron configuration contains three half-filled orbitals? (1) $1s^2 2s^2 2p^6$ (2) $1s^2 2s^2 2p^5$ (3) $1s^2 2s^2 2p^3$ (4) $1s^2 2s^2 2p^4$

NATURAL RADIOACTIVITY

Radioactivity is the spontaneous disintegration of the nucleus of certain atoms with the emission of particles and radiant energy to form other, more stable atoms. The transformation of one element into another as a result of nuclear disintegration is called **transmutation**. Among the elements with atomic numbers from 1 to 83, there are some that have both stable isotopes and radioactive isotopes (**radioisotopes**). For elements with atomic numbers greater than 83, there are no stable isotopes; all are radioactive.

Decay Products. Three major products are emitted by the decay of naturally occurring radioactive isotopes—alpha particles, beta particles, and gamma radiation.

An **alpha particle**, produced by **alpha decay**, is the nucleus of a helium atom, ^4_2He. It contains two neutrons and two protons. In nuclear equations for alpha decay, alpha particles appear as products. The following example shows the alpha decay of radium-226 to radon-222.

$$^{226}_{88}Ra \rightarrow {}^{222}_{86}Rn + {}^4_2He$$

Nuclear equations are balanced when the number of nucleons (mass number) represented as reactants is equal to the number of nucleons represented as products, thus maintaining conservation of mass. Charge is maintained when the sum of the atomic numbers of the reactants is equal to the sum of the atomic numbers of the products.

Beta decay occurs when a **beta particle** is emitted from a nucleus. A beta particle has the properties of a high-speed electron and is represented in nuclear equations by the symbol $_{-1}^{0}e$.

The radioactive isotope thorium-234 is a beta emitter.

$$^{234}_{90}Th \rightarrow {}^{234}_{91}Pa + {}^{0}_{-1}e$$

Like alpha decay, beta decay is accompanied by transmutation of the original isotope into an isotope of another element. The product of the decay of thorium-234 is protactinium-234. In beta decay, the atomic number increases by 1, while the mass number remains unchanged. The process can be considered to be the breakdown of a neutron to an electron (which is emitted) and a proton (which increases the atomic number). Thus, there is one less neutron in the nucleus, but there is one more proton. Therefore, the mass number remains unchanged.

Gamma radiation is another product of radioactive decay. Gamma rays, which are similar to high-energy X rays, are not particles and do not have mass or charge. Since the presence of gamma rays does not affect the balancing of nuclear equations, the symbol for gamma rays is rarely used in equations.

The products of radioactive decay can be separated from each other by the application of an electric or magnetic field to the path of the emanations. In an electric field, positively charged alpha particles are deflected toward the negative electrode, while negatively charged beta particles are deflected toward the positive electrode. In a magnetic field, alpha and beta particles move toward opposite poles. Since gamma rays have no charge, they are not affected by either electric or magnetic fields.

Studies of radioactive decay make use of the ionizing, fluorescent, and photographic effects of radioactivity.

Half-Life of Radioactive Isotopes.
The **half-life** of a radioactive isotope is the time required for one-half of the nuclei in a given sample of that isotope to undergo radioactive decay. The half-lives of selected radioactive isotopes are given in Table H of the Reference Tables (see page 107). The half-life period can vary from a fraction of a second to billions of years. The isotope iodine-131 has a half-life of about 8 days. As a 1-gram sample of iodine-131 decays, the quantity of iodine present changes according to Table 2-4.

Table 2-4. Half-Life of Iodine-131

Day	Mass of ^{131}I Remaining
0	1.00 gram
8	0.500 gram
16	0.250 gram
24	0.125 gram

QUESTIONS

1. An original sample of a radioisotope had a mass of 10 grams. After 2 days, 5 grams of the radioisotope remained unchanged. What is the half-life of this radioisotope? (1) 1 day (2) 2 days (3) 5 days (4) 4 days

2. In the equation $^{32}_{15}P \rightarrow ^{32}_{16}S + X$, the particle represented by X is (1) $^{4}_{2}He$ (2) $^{1}_{0}n$ (3) $^{2}_{1}H$ (4) $_{-1}^{0}e$

3. The structure of an alpha particle is the same as a (1) lithium atom (2) neon atom (3) hydrogen nucleus (4) helium nucleus

4. Based on Table H of the Reference Tables (see page 107), what is the number of hours required for potassium-42 to undergo three half-life periods? (1) 6.2 hours (2) 12.4 hours (3) 24.8 hours (4) 37.2 hours

5. Which nuclear emission moving through an electric field would be deflected toward the positive electrode? (1) alpha particle (2) beta particle (3) gamma radiation (4) proton

6. Gamma rays are most similar to (1) positively charged hydrogen nuclei (2) positively charged helium nuclei (3) high-energy X rays (4) high-speed electrons

7. An 80-gram sample of a radioisotope decayed to 10 grams after 24 days. What was the total number of grams of the original sample that remained unchanged after the first 8 days? (1) 60 (2) 20 (3) 30 (4) 40

Unit 3 Bonding

THE NATURE OF CHEMICAL BONDING

A **chemical bond** is the attractive force that holds atoms together. It results from the simultaneous attraction of a pair of electrons to the nuclei of two atoms. Although some bonds are formed through the sharing of electrons by the nuclei of two atoms, other bonds are formed through the transfer of electrons from one atom to the other.

Energy Changes and Bonding.

Changes in energy generally result from the forming or breaking of chemical bonds. Chemical energy is potential, or stored, energy that is associated with the attractive forces between the electrons and nuclei of atoms.

When a chemical bond is formed, energy, usually in the form of heat, is released. When a chemical bond is broken, energy is absorbed. During the formation of a chemical bond between two atoms, electrons move to a lower energy state. To break a bond and return each atom to its original unbonded state, energy must be added to the system. As the system absorbs energy, the electrons move to higher energy levels.

In general, a system that is at a lower energy level is more stable and less likely to change than is a similar system at a higher energy level. Chemical changes are more likely to occur in a system when those changes lead to a lower energy condition, a condition in which less chemical energy is stored.

Electronegativity.

Electrons play the major role in the formation of chemical bonds. The differences in attractive forces between the positively charged nuclei of different atoms and negatively charged electrons help to explain many observations associated with chemical change. The **electronegativity** of an atom is a measure of its ability to attract the electron pair that forms a bond between it and another atom.

The Pauling scale of electronegativity is an arbitrary scale that can be used to help predict bond characteristics. On this scale, nonmetals generally have high values, with fluorine assigned the highest value of 4.0. Metals have lower values, with cesium and francium assigned the lowest value of 0.7. Electronegativity values are listed in Reference Table K (see page 108).

Electronegativity values have no units and do not measure the reactivity of an element. Instead, they give a relative measure of the strength of the attractive force that an atom has for the electrons involved in bond formation.

BONDS BETWEEN ATOMS

There are two main types of chemical bonds—ionic and covalent. When electrons are transferred from one atom to another, ionic bonds are formed. When electrons are shared between atoms, covalent bonds are formed.

When atoms of elements combine, their electron structures become more like the stable electron structure of one of the noble gases.

Ionic Bonds

An **ionic bond** is formed when one or more electrons are transferred from one atom to another. In general, the atom with lower electronegativity, a metal, gives up one or more electrons and thus acquires a positive charge. It becomes a positive ion, or **cation**. The atom with higher electronegativity, a nonmetal, gains one or more electrons and becomes negatively charged. It becomes a negative ion, or **anion**. Each kind of atom loses or gains electrons so that it achieves the stable noble gas electron configuration (see Figure 3-1). The force of attraction between oppositely charged ions is the ionic bond.

$$Na^{\cdot} + \overset{\times}{\underset{\times\times}{\times Cl \times}} \longrightarrow [Na]^{+} + \left[\overset{\cdot\times}{\underset{\times\times}{\times Cl \times}}\right]^{-}$$

| 2-8-1 | 2-8-7 | 2-8 (neon) | 2-8-8 (argon) |

Figure 3-1. Electron transfer to form ions with noble gas electron structures.

Ionic solids have characteristic properties based on their structure. Because of the strong force of attraction between the oppositely charged ions, ionic solids have high melting points and high boiling points, high heats of fusion and high heats of vaporization. Ionic solids also have low vapor pressures.

Under certain conditions, ionic solids conduct an electric current. For a substance to be a conductor of electricity, ions must be present and they must be mobile (free to move from place to place). When ionic solids are melted (fused) or dissolved in water, the force of attraction between the oppositely charged ions is overcome, and the ions become mobile. Thus, ionic solids, when melted or when in solution, will conduct an electric current.

In an ionic solid, the ions are held in relatively fixed positions by the force of electrostatic attraction between ions of opposite charge. An ionic solid is characterized by a regular geometric arrangement of oppositely charged ions, called a **crystal**. No molecules are present in ionic solids. Each positive ion is strongly attracted to a group of nearby negative ions. Each negative ion is attracted to a similar group of positive ions. Thus, solid sodium chloride, as a typical ionic solid, is crystalline. It exists as a regular geometric arrangement of Na^+ cations and Cl^- anions, with no identifiable molecules of NaCl (see Figure 3-2).

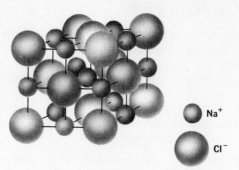

Figure 3-2. An ionic crystal.

Covalent Bonds.
Atoms can bond together to form molecules by sharing electrons. This force of attraction is called a **covalent bond**. A *single* covalent bond is formed by the sharing of one pair of electrons by two atoms (see Figure 3-3a). A *double* covalent bond involves two shared pairs of electrons (see Figure 3-3b), while a *triple* covalent bond is formed by three shared pairs of electrons (see Figure 3-3c).

When both electrons of a shared pair are donated by the same atom, the resulting bond is called a **coordinate covalent bond** (see Figure 3-3d).

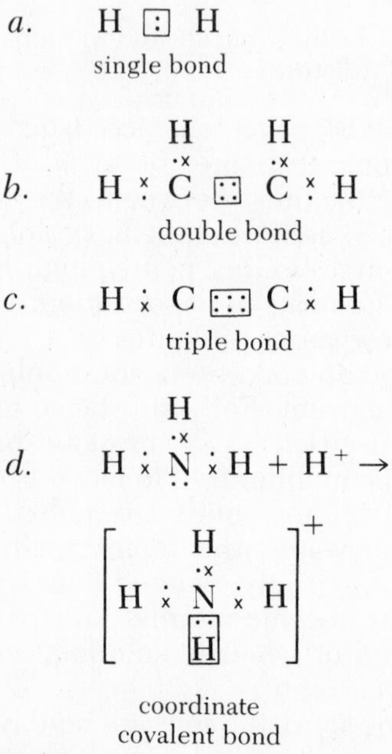

a. H ⊡ H
single bond

b. H ˟ C ⊡ C ˟ H
double bond

c. H ˟ C ⠿ C ˟ H
triple bond

d. H ˟ N ˟ H + H^+ →

[H
H ˟ N ˟ H
H]⁺

coordinate
covalent bond

Figure 3-3. Covalent bonds.

Polarity. In a covalent bond between atoms of the same element, the electron pair that forms the bond is shared equally by the two atoms. Since both atoms have the same electronegativity, they both exert the same attractive force for the shared electrons. Such bonds are said to be **nonpolar covalent bonds**.

When atoms of different elements share an electron pair, the electrons are not shared equally. The atom that has the higher electronegativity exerts the stronger attractive force on the shared electrons. As the electrons are attracted toward this atom and away from the other atom, a bond with some polarity forms. The bond is a **polar covalent bond** because there is a negative region near the atom with the higher electronegativity and a positive region near the atom with the lower electronegativity.

Directional Nature of Covalent Bonds. Recall that in the ionic solid sodium chloride each sodium ion (Na^+) is surrounded by six chloride ions (Cl^-). The Na^+ ion is attracted equally to all six Cl^- ions. Ionic bonds are said to be *nondirectional*; that is, the positive ion is attracted equally in all directions to its neighboring negative ions.

By contrast, covalent bonds are said to be *directional*; that is, the electrons are concentrated only in certain regions of space determined by the boundary orbitals. This arrangement gives the molecule a definite shape and helps determine the properties of the molecule. Note that, in a water molecule, the bonding *p* orbitals explain the asymmetrical (unbalanced) shape of the molecule. The molecule is "bent" (see Figure 3-4).

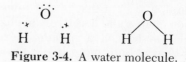

Figure 3-4. A water molecule.

Bond Character.
Differences in the electronegativity of the two atoms in a chemical bond indicate the character of the bond. A difference in electronegativity equal to or greater than 1.7 indicates that the bond is predominantly ionic. A difference in electronegativity of less than 1.7 indicates that the bond is predominantly covalent. Bonds that are nearly 100 percent ionic are characterized by a transfer of electrons to form positive and negative ions (see Figure 3-5).

There are many exceptions in predicting bond type based upon electronegativity differences alone. For example, chemical bonds in the hydrides of active metals, such as LiH and NaH, have electronegativity differences of less than 1.7, but are predominantly ionic in character.

Molecules and Molecular Substances.
Molecules are discrete particles formed by covalently bonded atoms. They may also be defined as the smallest particles of an element or compound capable of independent motion.

The Rule of Eight. In many molecules, the electrons of the atoms are arranged so that each atom

16

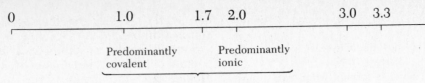

Bond character

Figure 3-5. Electronegativity differences.

achieves the electron configuration of a noble gas with eight electrons in the outermost shell. This is known as the *rule of eight,* or the *octet rule.*

Figure 3-6 shows the arrangement of electrons in some common molecules. The shared pair of electrons in a chemical bond belongs to both of the atoms joined by the bond.

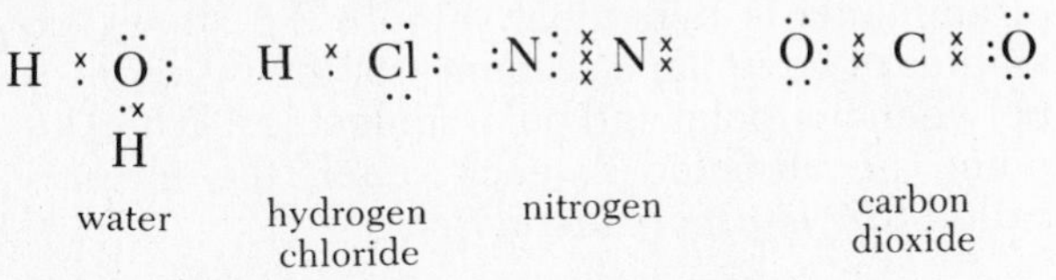

H ⚬ Ö: H ⚬ Cl: :N ⚬ N ⚬   Ö: ⚬ C ⚬ :Ö
⚬
H

water   hydrogen   nitrogen   carbon
           chloride   dioxide

Figure 3-6. Electron arrangements.

Properties of Molecular Substances. Molecular substances exist in all three phases, depending on the strength of the attractive forces between the molecules. In general, the strongest forces of attraction are found in compounds that are solid under ordinary temperatures and pressures. Compared to ionic and metallic solids, molecular solids are softer, they are poorer conductors of heat and electricity, and they have lower melting points.

Network Solids.
Certain substances consist of covalently bonded atoms linked in a network that extends throughout a large sample. No simple, discrete particles can be identified, and there is no evidence of the existence of molecules in these substances. Since these substances are always solids at ordinary temperatures, they are called **network solids.** Examples include diamond (C), silicon carbide (SiC), and silicon dioxide (SiO_2).

Network solids are hard, are usually poor conductors of heat and electricity, and have high melting points.

Metallic Bonds.
Metals are substances that have a luster and are good conductors of heat and electricity. Metals also have low ionization energies. A metal consists of a regular geometric arrangement of positive ions located at specific sites in a crystal lattice. The positive ions are said to be immersed in a "sea" of electrons. These electrons can be considered as belonging to the whole crystal rather than to individual ions (or atoms) and are said to be *mobile.* The area showing the arrangement of the shared electrons (the electron cloud) in a metal is called a **metallic bond.** The mobility of the electrons accounts for the properties of metals and distinguishes metallic bonds from ionic and covalent bonds.

QUESTIONS

1. When an ionic bond is formed, the atom that transfers its valence electron is the atom that has the (1) higher electronegativity value (2) lower atomic number (3) higher atomic mass (4) lower ionization energy

2. When an ionic bond is formed, the atom that transfers its valence electron becomes an ion with (1) positive charge and more protons (2) positive charge and no change in the number of protons (3) negative charge and more protons (4) negative charge and no change in the number of protons

3. What type of bond is found in copper metal? (1) ionic (2) covalent (3) metallic (4) van der Waals

4. The bonding in network solids is (1) ionic (2) covalent (3) metallic (4) van der Waals

5. In potassium hydrogen carbonate, $KHCO_3$, the bonds are (1) ionic, only (2) covalent, only (3) both ionic and covalent (4) both covalent and metallic

6. When potassium and chlorine form a chemical compound, energy is (1) released and ionic bonds are formed (2) released and covalent bonds are formed (3) absorbed and ionic bonds are formed (4) absorbed and covalent bonds are formed

7. Which substance, in its solid phase, contains positive ions distributed in a diffuse cloud of electrons? (1) N_2 (2) C (3) Mg (4) CO_2

8. If a pure substance is a good conductor of electricity in both its solid and its liquid phases, the bonding in the substance is predominantly (1) ionic (2) metallic (3) polar covalent (4) nonpolar covalent

9. If a pure substance is a good conductor of electricity in both its liquid phase and in aqueous solution, but not in its solid phase, it is probably a(n) (1) metallic element (2) nonmetallic element (3) ionic compound (4) covalent compound

10. Which compound best illustrates ionic bonding? (1) CCl_4 (2) $MgCl_2$ (3) H_2O (4) CO_2

11. Which type of solid generally has the lowest melting point? (1) molecular (2) metallic (3) ionic (4) network

12. Which sample of HCl most readily conducts electricity? (1) HCl(s) (2) HCl(ℓ) (3) HCl(g) (4) HCl(aq)

13. An atom that loses or gains one or more electrons becomes (1) an ion (2) an isotope (3) a molecule (4) an electrolyte

14. Which is a characteristic of ionic solids? (1) They conduct electricity. (2) They have high vapor pressures. (3) They have high melting points. (4) They are very malleable.

15. The carbon atoms in a diamond are held together

The Nature of Chemical Bonding

by (1) metallic bonds (2) hydrogen bonds (3) ionic bonds (4) covalent bonds

16. Which element is most likely to exist as a network solid? (1) C (2) K (3) He (4) Na

17. Which kind of bond is formed when two atoms share electrons to form a molecule? (1) ionic (2) metallic (3) electrovalent (4) covalent

18. Which type of bonding is usually exhibited when the electronegativity difference between two atoms is 1.2? (1) ionic (2) metallic (3) network (4) covalent

19. The solid formed by water when it freezes is (1) ionic (2) network (3) metallic (4) molecular

20. Which molecule contains a nonpolar covalent bond?

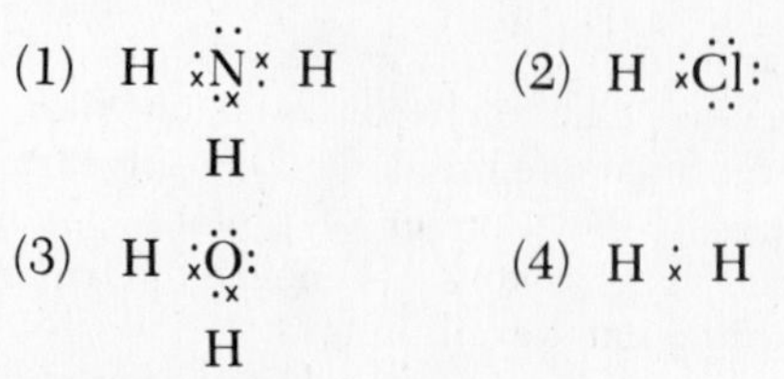

(1) H $\ddot{\times}$N$\ddot{\times}$ H   (2) H $\ddot{\times}$Cl$\ddot{:}$

      H

(3) H $\ddot{\times}$O$\ddot{:}$ (4) H $\times$ H

      H

ATTRACTIONS BETWEEN MOLECULES

Forces of attraction exist between molecules. These forces account for the existence of molecular solids and molecular liquids. If there were no attractive forces between molecules, the molecules would spread out, and all substances would be gases, even at very low temperatures.

Dipoles. A molecule that is polar is called a **dipole**. In dipoles, the distribution of electrical charge is asymmetrical; that is, the centers of positive and negative charge are located at different parts of the molecule. For example, in hydrogen chloride, HCl (g), the greater electronegativity of chlorine pulls the electron pair away from hydrogen, moving it closer to the chlorine (see Figure 3-7). This creates a kind of electrical imbalance.

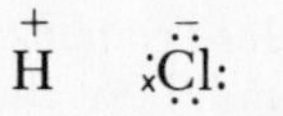

$$\overset{+}{H} \quad \overset{-}{\ddot{C}l:}$$

Figure 3-7. A hydrogen chloride molecule.

A molecule composed of only two atoms is a dipole if the bond between the atoms is polar. Hydrogen chloride, HCl (g), and hydrogen fluoride, HF (g), are examples of two-atom molecules that are dipoles.

Depending on their shapes, molecules composed of more than two atoms may be nonpolar even though the individual bonds are polar. If the shape of the molecule is such that the polar bonds are distributed symmetrically, then the electric charges cancel one another and the molecule is not a dipole. If the polar bonds are distributed asymmetrically, the electric charges do not cancel

one another, and the molecule exhibits polarity and is a dipole.

Some examples of symmetrical molecules that contain polar bonds but are not dipoles are carbon dioxide (CO_2), methane (CH_4), and carbon tetrachloride (CCl_4). The linear shape of the CO_2 and the tetrahedral shape of CH_4 and CCl_4 cancel the charges in the molecule. This accounts for the absence of polarity, even though the C—O, C—H, and C—Cl bonds are polar.

All dipoles have polar bonds, but the distribution of these bonds and the arrangement of their electrons are asymmetrical. Water (H_2O) and ammonia (NH_3) are dipoles. The molecular shape of water is described as "bent." The shape of ammonia is pyramidal. Figure 3-8 shows examples of how shape accounts for the differences between nonpolar and polar molecules. When dipoles are attracted to each other, the force is called *dipole-dipole attraction*.

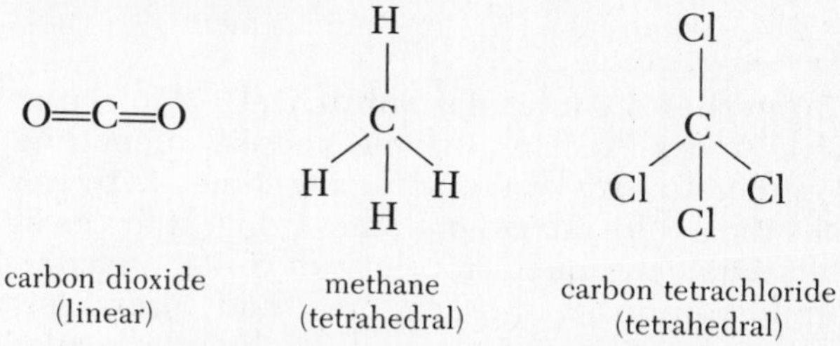

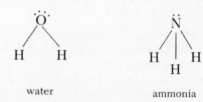

carbon dioxide (linear)   methane (tetrahedral)   carbon tetrachloride (tetrahedral)

a. Symmetrical molecules (nonpolar)

water   ammonia

b. Asymmetrical molecules (polar)

Figure 3-8. Shape in nonpolar and polar molecules.

Hydrogen Bonding. A special type of dipole-dipole attraction exists between some molecules that contain hydrogen atoms. When a hydrogen atom is bonded to a small, highly electronegative atom, the shared electron pair is attracted to the more electronegative atom so strongly that only a very small share of the charge remains with the hydrogen. The hydrogen behaves as if it were a bare proton. With this uneven distribution of electrons, the hydrogen side of the molecule has a positive charge, while the opposite side has a negative charge. The hydrogen atom end of the molecule is then strongly attracted to the highly electronegative atom of a neighboring molecule. This "bridge" of attractive force between molecules, shown by the dashed lines, is called a **hydrogen bond** (see Figure 3-9).

Hydrogen bonding accounts for certain characteristic properties of the substances in which it

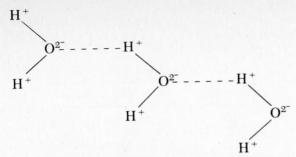

Figure 3-9. Hydrogen bonding in water.

is found. Among these properties is an increased boiling point. For example, H_2O has a relatively high boiling point compared with its related compounds, H_2S, H_2Se, and H_2Te. The high boiling point suggests that water is not a simple molecule as its formula H_2O indicates. Rather, because of hydrogen bonding, water molecules join together to form more complex units that could be expressed as $[H_2O]_x$. Since additional energy is now required to break the hydrogen bonds, water boils at a higher temperature than it normally would if a simple molecule of water (H_2O) were present. Hydrogen bonding is also present in compounds in which hydrogen is bonded to atoms of fluorine or nitrogen, which are small atoms that have high electronegativity.

Van der Waals Forces.
Weak forces of attraction, called **van der Waals forces**, exist between nonpolar molecules when they are crowded together as in solids, liquids, and gases under high pressure. Small nonpolar molecules, such as H_2, He, and O_2, exist in the liquid and solid phases under conditions of low temperature and high pressure because of the van der Waals forces between the molecules.

When nonpolar molecules such as those in gases approach one another, their electrons interact, or shift, to produce temporary oppositely charged regions. These weak attractions are van der Waals forces, which hold the molecules together with sufficient strength to influence boiling points and melting points of gases (when they are solid).

The strength of van der Waals forces increases with increasing molecular size. This increase is caused by the presence of more electrons in larger molecules. Trends in boiling point in a series of analogous compounds, such as the alkane series of hydrocarbons, can be accounted for in terms of differences in van der Waals forces.

Molecule-Ion Attraction.
When some polar solvents are mixed with some ionic solids, interactions between the solvent molecules and the ions cause the ions of the solid to become dissolved in the solvent. A solution is formed as the crystal lattice of the ionic solid is destroyed.

Water is the polar solvent most commonly used to dissolve ionic compounds. When an ionic solid is dissolved in water, the water molecules sur-

round each ion and pull it out of its fixed position. This process is called **hydration** of ions. In the process, the negative ions of the ionic solid are attracted to the positive ends of the water molecules, while the positive ions are attracted to the negative ends of the water molecules. Other polar solvents that dissolve many ionic compounds are alcohol and ammonia.

QUESTIONS

1. Why is NH_3 classified as a polar molecule? (1) It is a gas at STP. (2) N—H bonds are nonpolar. (3) Nitrogen and hydrogen are both nonmetals. (4) NH_3 molecules have asymmetrical charge distributions.
2. Which molecule is not a dipole? (1) HF (2) H_2O (3) NH_3 (4) CH_4
3. Which molecule is a dipole? (1) H_2 (2) N_2 (3) CH_4 (4) HF
4. Which statement best explains why carbon tetrachloride (CCl_4) is nonpolar? (1) Each carbon-chloride bond is polar. (2) Carbon and chlorine are both nonmetals. (3) Carbon tetrachloride is an organic compound. (4) The carbon tetrachloride molecule is symmetrical.
5. Which term applies to the attraction between nonpolar molecules? (1) hydrogen bonding (2) ionic bonding (3) covalent bonding (4) van der Waals forces
6. Which term applies to the forces of attraction between any polar molecules? (1) dipole attraction (2) electrovalent bonding (3) hydrogen bonding (4) van der Waals forces
7. The weakest van der Waals forces exist between molecules of (1) C_2H_6 (2) C_3H_8 (3) C_4H_{10} (4) C_5H_{12}
8. Molecule-ion attractions are found in (1) Cu(s) (2) CO(g) (3) $KBr(\ell)$ (4) NaCl(aq)
9. Hydrogen bonds are strongest between the molecules of (1) $HF(\ell)$ (2) $HCl(\ell)$ (3) $HBr(\ell)$ (4) $HI(\ell)$
10. Helium may be liquefied at low temperature and high pressure primarily because of (1) hydrogen bonding (2) covalent bonds (3) van der Waals forces (4) ionic attraction
11. The process in which water molecules surround ions in solution is called (1) van der Waals forces (2) hydration (3) hydrogen bonding (4) dipole bonding
12. Under similar conditions, van der Waals forces are strongest in (1) $He(\ell)$ (2) $Ne(\ell)$ (3) $Ar(\ell)$ (4) $Kr(\ell)$

CHEMICAL FORMULAS

A chemical formula is a qualitative and quantitative description of the composition of a pure substance, either an element or a compound. In a formula, the symbol for an element represents one atom of that element. The formula for a compound is represented by the symbols of the component atoms and subscripts that show the number of each kind of atom. For example, K_2SO_4 is the formula for the compound potassium sulfate, which contains three kinds of atoms: potassium (K), sulfur (S), and oxygen (O). The formula also specifies that the ratio of these atoms is two K to one S to four O.

A **molecular formula** shows the total number of atoms of each element found in one molecule of the compound. An **empirical formula** represents the simplest whole-number ratio in which the atoms combine to form a compound. For example, benzene has the molecular formula C_6H_6 and the empirical formula CH. Empirical formulas are also used to represent ionic solids. For example, sodium chloride is represented as NaCl. There is no molecular formula because there are no individual molecules of the substance.

Binary Compounds.

Binary compounds are made up of atoms of two different elements. In binary compounds containing a metal and a nonmetal, the metallic element is usuallly named and written first. The name of the nonmetal ends in -*ide*. The empirical formulas for most of these compounds can be determined from a consideration of the structure of the valence electrons. Metals typically have one, two, or three valence electrons that are transferred when an ionic bond is formed. Nonmetals typically gain one, two, or three electrons to fill vacancies in their valence shells. The formulas for these compounds are written so as to maintain conservation of charge (charge is not lost). Table 3-1 shows the names and formulas for some binary chlorides and sulfides.

Table 3-1. Binary Compounds

Formula	Ions		Name
KCl	K^+	Cl^-	potassium chloride
$CaCl_2$	Ca^{2+}	Cl^-	calcium chloride
$AlCl_3$	Al^{3+}	Cl^-	aluminum chloride
Na_2S	Na^+	S^{2-}	sodium sulfide
BaS	Ba^{2+}	S^{2-}	barium sulfide
Al_2S_3	Al^{3+}	S^{2-}	aluminum sulfide

When two nonmetals form a compound, the name of the less electronegative element is usually written first. The name of the compound ends in -*ide*. Some examples include carbon dioxide (CO_2), sulfur trioxide (SO_3), and carbon tetrachloride (CCl_4).

The Stock system can also be used to name compounds based on the *apparent* charge (oxidation number, see page 55) of the less electronegative element. In the Stock system, a Roman numeral immediately following the symbol or name of the element is used to indicate the oxidation number. Table 3-2 gives the names and

formulas of several oxides of nitrogen using the Stock system.

Table 3-2. Oxides of Nitrogen

Formula	Stock Name
N_2O	nitrogen (I) oxide
NO	nitrogen (II) oxide
N_2O_3	nitrogen (III) oxide
NO_2	nitrogen (IV) oxide
N_2O_5	nitrogen (V) oxide

Ternary Compounds.

Ternary compounds are made up of three kinds of atoms. The most common ternary compounds have metallic positive ions bonded to polyatomic negative ions. In general, the polyatomic negative ions contain oxygen atoms and one other kind of atom, usually a nonmetal. An example is sodium carbonate, Na_2CO_3, where two Na^+ ions are bonded to one CO_3^{2-} ion.

The names of ternary compounds most often end in -*ite* or -*ate*. Subscripts are used in these empirical formulas to show the simplest whole number ratio of ions and atoms. When a subscript is applied to a polyatomic ion, parentheses are placed around the formula for the ion. Many polyatomic ions are listed in Table F of the Reference Tables (see page 107). The use of poly-atomic ions in formulas is illustrated in Table 3-3.

Table 3-3. Ternary Compounds

Formula	Ions		Name
$NaNO_3$	Na^+	NO_3^-	sodium nitrate
$Mg(NO_3)_2$	Mg^{2+}	NO_3^-	magnesium nitrate
$Al(NO_3)_3$	Al^{3+}	NO_3^-	aluminum nitrate

Metals with Multiple Oxidation Numbers.

The Stock system is also used to name compounds of metals that have more than one possible ionic charge. The charge, or oxidation number, is shown by a Roman numeral immediately following the name of the metal. Iron and copper are two common metals that have more than one oxidation number. Table 3-4 shows how the Stock system is used in specifying compounds of these elements.

Table 3-4. The Stock System

Formula	Ions		Stock Name
$Fe(NO_3)_2$	Fe^{2+}	NO_3^-	iron (II) nitrate
$Fe(NO_3)_3$	Fe^{3+}	NO_3^-	iron (III) nitrate
CuCl	Cu^+	Cl^-	copper (I) chloride
$CuCl_2$	Cu^{2+}	Cl^-	copper (II) chloride

Naming Acids.

Acids are frequently used in chemical reactions and will be discussed fully in Unit 7. Binary acids contain hydrogen and a nonmetal. The names of binary acids have the form hydro ___ -ic acid, such as hydrochloric acid for the water solution of hydrogen chloride. Ternary acids contain hydrogen bonded covalently to a polyatomic ion. The names of ternary acids generally follow the pattern shown below for increasing numbers of oxygen atoms or increasing oxidation numbers of the named nonmetal.

Naming Ternary Acids	Examples	
hypo- ___ -ous	Hypochlorous acid	(HClO)
___ -ous	Chlorous acid	($HClO_2$)
___ -ic	Chloric acid	($HClO_3$)
per- ___ -ic	Perchloric acid	($HClO_4$)

CHEMICAL REACTIONS

Equations.

A chemical equation describes starting substances (reactants) and products of a chemical reaction. The equation also represents the qualitative and quantitative changes in bonding (arrangement of atoms) and energy that take place in a chemical reaction.

In an equation, it is often desirable to indicate the phase of the reactants and products. Phase symbols are given below.

Phase	Symbol
solid	(s)
liquid	(ℓ)
gas	(g)
aqueous (water solution)	(aq)

The energy changes associated with a reaction may also be written in the equation. Thus, the equation that follows shows that two molecules (or moles) of hydrogen gas react with one molecule (or mole) of oxygen gas to form two molecules (or moles) of liquid water and that heat is given off by the reaction. (Recall that a mole is Avogadro's number of particles and has a mass in grams equal to the molecular mass.)

$$2H_2(g) + O_2(g) \rightarrow 2H_2O(\ell) + heat$$

Balanced chemical equations illustrate the principles of conservation of mass and conservation of charge. Coefficients are used before the formulas for each reactant and product showing the ratio of molecules (or moles) in the reaction.

Types of Chemical Reactions.

Many simple chemical reactions can be classified as one of four types shown in Table 3-5.

Table 3-5. Types of Chemical Reactions

Type of Reaction	Description/Typical Equation
Synthesis	Atoms of elements combine to form a compound. $$4Fe + 3O_2 \rightarrow 2Fe_2O_3$$
Decomposition (analysis)	Compound is broken down into its component elements or a simpler compound. $$2HgO \rightarrow 2Hg + O_2$$ $$2KClO_3 \rightarrow 2KCl + 3O_2$$
Single replacement	Element reacts with a compound to set free a different element and form a new compound. $$Cu + 2AgNO_3 \rightarrow Cu(NO_3)_2 + 2Ag$$
Double replacement	Two compounds react (usually in water solution) to produce two new compounds. $$Ca(OH)_2 + H_2SO_4 \rightarrow 2HOH + CaSO_4$$

The equations for these reactions can usually be balanced by inspection, or trial-and-error. This method involves choosing small, whole-number coefficients so that the number of atoms of each element shown as reactants is equal to the number of atoms of that element shown as product. (The balancing of more complex equations is discussed in Unit 8.)

QUESTIONS

1. Which compound has the empirical formula P_2O_5? (1) potassium (II) oxide (2) potassium (V) oxide (3) phosphorus (II) oxide (4) phosphorus (V) oxide

2. What is the correct name for the compound with the formula NH_4NO_2? (1) ammonium nitride (2) ammonium nitrite (3) ammonia nitrate (4) ammonium nitrate

3. Given the balanced equation:

$$2Na + 2H_2O \rightarrow 2X + H_2$$

What is the correct formula for the product represented by the letter X? (1) NaO (2) Na_2O (3) NaOH (4) Na_2OH

The Nature of Chemical Bonding

4. What is the correct formula of potassium hydride? (1) KH (2) KH_2 (3) KOH (4) $K(OH)_2$

5. When the equation $NH_3 + O_2 \rightarrow HNO_3 + H_2O$ is completely balanced using smallest whole numbers, the coefficient of O_2 would be (1) 1 (2) 2 (3) 3 (4) 4

6. What is the name of the calcium salt of sulfuric acid? (1) calcium thiosulfate (2) calcium sulfate (3) calcium sulfide (4) calcium sulfite

7. What is the formula of nitrogen (I) oxide? (1) NO (2) N_2O (3) NO_2 (4) N_2O_4

8. Which represents both an empirical and a molecular formula? (1) P_2O_5 (2) N_2O_4 (3) C_3H_6 (4) $C_6H_{12}O_6$

9. Which is the correct formula for nitrogen (IV) oxide? (1) NO (2) NO_2 (3) NO_3 (4) NO_4

10. Which is an empirical formula? (1) C_2H_2 (2) C_2H_4 (3) Al_2Cl_6 (4) K_2O

11. When the equation $C_2H_4 + O_2 \rightarrow CO_2 + H_2O$ is completely balanced using smallest whole numbers, the coefficient of O_2 would be (1) 1 (2) 2 (3) 3 (4) 4

4 The Periodic Table

ORIGINS OF THE PERIODIC TABLE

By the early 1800s, study of the elements had produced a large collection of observations about their physical properties and chemical behavior. It was known that certain elements had similar properties. When the elements were listed in order of increasing atomic mass, the similarities recurred at definite intervals. In other words, the similarities recurred periodically and were called *regularities*.

An early periodic law proposed by the Russian chemist Dimitri Mendeleev expressed the regularities as a periodic function of atomic mass. Using this principle, Mendeleev developed the first version of the periodic table in 1869. Although this was a brilliant contribution to chemistry, it left many questions unanswered.

As a result of the work of Henry Moseley, a British physicist, we now know that it is more accurate to describe the regularities in physical and chemical properties as periodic functions of atomic number. This revised version of Mendeleev's law is known as the **modern periodic law**. Scientists also recognize that the chemical similarities among certain elements are due to similarities in the configurations (number and arrangement) of their valence electrons.

STRUCTURE OF THE PERIODIC TABLE

In the modern periodic table, the elements are placed in order of increasing atomic number. They are arranged in vertical columns and horizontal rows.

Groups.
Elements with similar valence electron configurations fall into vertical columns known as **groups**, or **families**. For example, chlorine and fluorine, both with seven valence electrons, are in the same group called the *halogens*. These elements and other members of the group show similar properties because the arrangements of their valence electrons are similar. The characteristics of different groups are discussed later in the chapter.

Periods.
Elements whose valence electrons have the same principal quantum number (the outermost principal energy level that contains electrons) fall in horizontal rows known as **periods**, or **series**. Many properties of the elements change systematically through a period. For example, in Period 2 (second horizontal row), note

the progression from active metal to metalloid (Li, Be, B) followed by a similar progression from least active nonmetal to most active nonmetal (C, N, O, F). N, O, and F are diatomic molecules (N_2, O_2, and F_2). There are seven periods in the modern periodic table. For each element, the number of the period in which it is found corresponds to the principal quantum number of its valence electrons.

Trends in Properties.
Although the chemical behavior of elements within a period varies because of variations in the electron configurations of the elements, certain generalizations about trends in properties within a period are significant. These trends are a function of increasing atomic number and changing valence electron configuration.

Covalent Atomic Radius.
Atoms have no specific boundaries. It is therefore convenient to describe the sizes of atoms as they approach one another. The **covalent atomic radius**, or atomic radius, is one-half the distance between the nuclei of atoms that are joined together by a covalent bond in the solid phase. The relation between covalent atomic radius and atomic number can be interpreted in terms of nuclear charge and in terms of the arrangement of electrons in the orbitals of atoms. Atomic radii are usually measured in Angstrom units (Å). One Angstrom is equal to 10^{-10} meter.

For all elements within a period, the valence electrons (the electrons in the outermost energy level) are arranged around a kernel that contains the same number of energy levels. However, the number of valence electrons and the total number of protons in the nucleus are different for each element.

As elements are considered from left to right, the atomic number (protons or electrons) increases. Thus, within a period, nuclear charge increases because of the increasing number of protons in the atoms. This increase in positive charge causes the electrons to be attracted more closely to the nucleus. That is, the nucleus is not shielded sufficiently from the added electron repulsions. The increased attraction between the negative electrons and the positive nucleus is greater than any repulsion between the added electron and the other valence electrons. Thus, within a period, as atomic number increases, the covalent atomic radius decreases.

For all elements within a group, the atoms of each successive member have a larger kernel containing more filled energy levels, and the valence electrons are located at successively greater distances from the nucleus. The charge of the nucleus is shielded more and more as energy levels are added to successive members of the group. Thus, within a group, as atomic number increases, the covalent atomic radius increases.

The values for the atomic radii of metals are based on the distance between two bonded atoms in the solid state. For nonmetals, for the distance between two nonbonded atoms, the values given are the van der Waals radii. Reference Table P (see page 111) shows the radii of atoms.

Ionic Radius. When atoms form ions and acquire a charge, they gain or lose one or more electrons. The change in the number of electrons produces a corresponding change in the size of the electron cloud—the **ionic radius**. Since metal atoms become ions by losing electrons, the radii of these positive metal ions are smaller than the radii of the corresponding atoms in the ground state. This is because the loss of an electron reduces the repulsive forces, and the electron cloud shrinks. Nonmetal atoms become ions by gaining electrons. Therefore, the radii of negative nonmetal ions are larger than the radii of the corresponding atoms in the ground state. This is because more electrons increase the repulsive forces, and the electron cloud expands.

Trends in the properties of elements within periods and within groups are summarized in Table 4-1.

Table 4-1. Trends in Properties Within Periods and Groups

Within a period, as atomic number increases:

covalent atomic radius	decreases
ionization energy	increases
electronegativity	increases
metallic character	decreases

Within a group, as atomic number increases:

covalent atomic radius	increases
ionization energy	decreases
electronegativity	decreases
metallic character	increases

Classes of Elements.

Elements are classified as **metals**, **nonmetals**, or **metalloids**. More than three-fourths of the elements are metals, approximately twenty are nonmetals, and the remaining few are metalloids.

In the periodic table, metallic properties are most pronounced in the elements found in the lower left corner. Thus, the Group 1 (alkali metal) family represents the most active metals. Nonmetallic properties are most pronounced in the elements in the upper right corner. Thus, the Group 17 (halogen) family represents the most active nonmetals. Metalloids are found just to the right of the heavy black dividing line between metals and nonmetals, which begins between boron and aluminum and proceeds stepwise down and to the right across groups 13 [IIIA] through 16 [VIA].

Metals. All metals are solid at room temperature except mercury, which is a liquid. Metals generally have a metallic, silvery luster. Metals are malleable (they can be hammered into thin sheets) and ductile (they can be drawn into thin wires). They form chemical bonds in such a way that their valence electrons are relatively mobile (the electrons do not belong to a particular atom). This type of bonding, called **metallic bonding**, makes metals good conductors of heat and electricity. Metals have low ionization energies and low electronegativities; thus, they often act as electron donors in chemical reactions.

Nonmetals. Nonmetals are quite different from metals. Nonmetals tend to be gases, molecular solids, or network solids. In the solid phase, nonmetals are brittle, they lack a luster, and they are poor conductors of heat and electricity. When nonmetals bond together, the bonds tend to be predominantly covalent in character. Because of their high ionization energies, nonmetals tend to act as electron acceptors in ionic compounds. They are highly electronegative.

Metalloids. A few elements have properties that are intermediate between those of metals and nonmetals. These elements are known as metalloids, or **semimetals**. Metalloids tend to form bonds that are partially ionic and partially covalent in character. The best-known metalloid is probably silicon, a semiconductor that is widely used in computers. Boron, arsenic, and tellurium are also metalloids.

QUESTIONS

1. More than two-thirds of the elements of the periodic table are (1) metalloids (2) metals (3) nonmetals (4) noble gases
2. The elements in the modern periodic table are arranged in order of increasing (1) atomic number (2) atomic mass (3) ionic radius (4) oxidation state
3. The atomic number of a metalloid in Period 4 is (1) 22 (2) 33 (3) 35 (4) 72
4. Which of the following has the highest first ionization energy? (1) Li (2) Na (3) K (4) Rb
5. Which of the following is the most active? (1) neon (2) boron (3) beryllium (4) lithium
6. Which is an active nonmetal? (1) F (2) Na (3) Si (4) Kr
7. Within a period, the element with the lowest first ionization energy is found in Group (1) 1 (2) 18 (3) 17 (4) 14
8. Which of the following has the greatest tendency to gain electrons? (1) phosphorus (2) carbon (3) chlorine (4) boron

9. Which of the following has the least tendency to gain electrons? (1) fluorine (2) iodine (3) bromine (4) chlorine

10. The increase in atomic radius of each successive element within a group is primarily due to an increase in the number of (1) neutrons in the nucleus (2) electrons in the outermost shell (3) unpaired electrons (4) principal energy levels

11. The element found in Group 13 (IIIA) and in Period 2 is (1) Be (2) Mg (3) B (4) Al

12. Elements that have properties of both metals and nonmetals are called (1) alkali metals (2) metalloids (3) transition elements (4) halogens

13. According to the modern periodic table, the chemical properties of elements are periodic functions of their (1) ionic charges (2) oxidation states (3) atomic numbers (4) mass numbers

14. Two properties of most nonmetals are (1) low ionization energy and electrical conductivity (2) high ionization energy and poor electrical conductivity (3) low ionization energy and poor electrical conductivity (4) high ionization energy and good electrical conductivity

15. Atoms of metallic elements tend to (1) gain electrons and form negative ions (2) gain electrons and form positive ions (3) lose electrons and form negative ions (4) lose electrons and form positive ions

16. Which is the best example of a metalloid? (1) sodium (2) strontium (3) silicon (4) sulfur

17. Which of the following is the most active nonmetal? (1) sodium (2) magnesium (3) chlorine (4) argon

18. Which of the following has the most metallic character? (1) bromine (2) chlorine (3) fluorine (4) iodine

19. Which element exhibits both metallic and nonmetallic properties? (1) boron (2) barium (3) potassium (4) argon

20. Which of the following is most likely to be malleable? (1) gold (2) hydrogen (3) sulfur (4) radon

21. Which period contains three elements that commonly exist as diatomic molecules at STP? (1) Period 1 (2) Period 2 (3) Period 6 (4) Period 7

22. Elements in the same period all have the same number of (1) protons (2) neutrons (3) valence electrons (4) occupied principal energy levels

23. Elements in the same period all have the same number of (1) kernel electrons (2) isotopes (3) half-filled orbitals (4) occupied sublevels

24. The element in Period 3 with the most metallic character is (1) sodium (2) aluminum (3) silicon (4) phosphorus

25. Within a period, as atomic number increases, ionization energy generally (1) increases (2) decreases (3) remains the same

26. Within a period, as atomic number increases, the number of valence electrons (1) increases (2) decreases (3) remains the same

27. Within a period, as atomic number increases, electrical conductivity in the solid state generally (1) increases (2) decreases (3) remains the same

28. As the elements of Period 2 are considered from left to right, there is a decrease in (1) ionization energy (2) atomic mass (3) metallic character (4) nonmetallic character

29. The element in Period 2 with the largest atomic radius is (1) a halogen (2) a noble gas (3) an alkali metal (4) an alkaline earth metal

30. The element in Period 3 with the lowest first ionization energy is (1) an alkali metal (2) an alkaline earth metal (3) a halogen (4) a noble gas

31. Which element is a member of the halogen family? (1) K (2) B (3) I (4) S

32. The S^{2-} ion differs from the S^0 atom in that the S^{2-} ion has a (1) smaller radius and fewer electrons (2) smaller radius and more electrons (3) larger radius and fewer electrons (4) larger radius and more electrons

33. One reason that fluorine has a higher ionization energy than oxygen is that fluorine has a (1) smaller nuclear charge (2) larger nuclear charge (3) smaller number of neutrons (4) greater number of neutrons

34. A property of most nonmetals in the solid state is that they are (1) brittle (2) malleable (3) good conductors of electricity (4) good conductors of heat

35. An Angstrom unit is equal to (1) 10^{10} cm (2) 10^{-8} cm (3) 10^{10} m (4) 10^{-8} m

36. In the periodic table, elements in the same group, or vertical column, have similar (1) atomic masses (2) principal quantum numbers (3) valence electron configurations (4) covalent atomic radii

37. In the periodic table, elements in the same period, or horizontal row, have the same (1) first ionization energy (2) electronegativity (3) valence electron configuration (4) number of occupied principal energy levels

CHEMICAL PROPERTIES WITHIN GROUPS

The elements in the periodic table are divided into 18 (or 8) groups on the basis of their electron configurations. Each group is assigned a group number. Under the recently adopted system used in this book, group numbers are Arabic numerals from 1 to 18. The group at the extreme left of the periodic table is Group 1, the group to its right is Group 2, and so on through Group 18.

In the system commonly used in the past, groups are designated by a combination of Roman numerals and letters. The periodic table in this book (see pages 112–113) gives both the new (18) and old (8) group designations.

Similarities Within Groups.
Within each group, the elements exhibit related chemical and physical properties. As stated previously, the similarities in properties within a group are associated with similarities in the number of valence electrons.

The similarity in chemical properties within a group is reflected in the types of compounds formed by members of the group and is illustrated by their formulas. For example, the elements in

Group 1 form chlorides with the general formula MCl and oxides with the general formula M_2O, where M represents any member of the group. Elements in Group 2 form chlorides with the general formula MCl_2 and oxides with the general formula MO.

The properties of elements in a group generally change progressively with increasing atomic number. Properties of the members of a group can be compared in terms of bonding, electronegativity, atomic size, and electron configuration.

Anomalies (exceptions) in the properties of elements within a group do occur. For example, in Group 13 (IIIA), boron does not form an ion as do other members of the group. The anomalies occur most frequently among the elements in Period 2 because in these atoms the valence electrons are relatively close to the nucleus and the two kernel electrons (the two electrons in the $1s$ sublevel) provide a relatively small shielding effect; that is, the added repulsions provided by the two electrons are small.

In general, as the atomic number increases within a group, the radius of the atoms increases and the ionization energy of the elements decreases. There is a corresponding decrease in electronegativity with increasing atomic number. The decreases in ionization energy and electronegativity are due to: (1) the increased distance of the valence electrons from the nucleus, and (2) the increased shielding effect produced as a newly occupied energy level is added with each successive member of the group. Consistent with these changes in ionization energy and electronegativity, each successive element within a group has increasingly metallic properties.

Groups 1 [IA] and 2 [IIA].

Groups 1 and 2 include the most reactive metals. Recall that members of Group 1 are called the **alkali metals**. (Hydrogen is not considered an alkali metal.) Members of Group 2 are called the **alkaline earth metals**. The Group 1 and Group 2 metals react with water to form bases (alkalies), which will be discussed in Unit 7. Because of their reactivity, these elements do not occur in nature in the uncombined state; that is, they occur only in chemical compounds. The elements in both groups undergo reduction to form the uncombined (free) metal by electrolysis of their fused compounds (see page 62).

In the elements of Groups 1 and 2, the valence shells are nearly empty. In the ground state, each element in Group 1 has one electron in its valence s orbital, while each element in Group 2 has two electrons in its valence s orbital. The elements in these groups form only ionic compounds because of their low ionization energies and electronegativities. They lose electrons readily, forming positive ions (cations) and relatively stable ionic compounds.

For metals, high reactivity is related to low ionization energy. In Groups 1 and 2, ionization energy tends to increase with decreasing atomic number. In the same period, each Group 1 metal is more reactive than the metal in Group 2. For example, sodium is more reactive than magnesium and potassium is more reactive than calcium.

Groups 3 [IIIB] through 11 [IB].

The elements of Groups 3 through 11 are known as the **transition elements**. They are all metals with unfilled d orbitals; that is, orbitals in various stages of completion. Remember that the d orbital of an energy level fills only after the s orbital of the next higher energy level has been filled. Thus, in going from Ca to Sc, the twenty-first electron begins to fill the $3d$ orbital rather than the $4p$. The elements of Group 12, which complete the d orbitals, show somewhat different properties.

Because electrons from the two outermost sublevels may be involved in a chemical reaction, transition elements generally exhibit multiple positive ionic charges and oxidation states. Thus, in Cr, $3d$ and $4s$ electrons are used in compound formation. Compounds of the transition elements, such as Cr, are often intensely colored yellow or orange both in the solid state and in aqueous solution.

Groups 13 [IIIA] and 14 [IVA].

In the ground state, the members of Group 13 have one electron in their valence p orbitals and a filled s orbital. Thus, one or three electrons are used in compound formation. The lighter members of this group form oxides with the general formula X_2O_3. The heaviest member, Tl, forms Tl_2O. Therefore, both p and s orbitals are used in compound formation. All the members of Group 13 are metals except for the first member, boron, which is a metalloid.

The members of Group 14 each have two electrons in their valence p orbital. Carbon, the first member, is a nonmetal, and silicon, the second member, is a metalloid. The rest are metals.

Groups 15 [VA] and 16 [VIA].

With increasing atomic number, the members of Group 15 show a marked progression in properties from nonmetallic to metallic. Nitrogen and phosphorus, the first and second members of the group, are typical nonmetals; arsenic, the third member, is a metalloid; and antimony and bismuth are metallic both in appearance and in properties. In general, within a group, the reactivity of nonmetals decreases with increasing atomic number.

The element nitrogen is relatively unreactive at room temperature because of the high energy of activation associated with most of its reactions (see page 39). Nitrogen exists as a diatomic molecule with a triple bond between the two atoms. The high energy required to break the triple bond explains the relative inactivity of elemental nitrogen. However, many nitrogen compounds are unstable, which makes them useful in explosives.

Nitrogen forms many organic compounds, including proteins, which are essential to living things.

At room temperature, elemental phosphorus exists as a molecule with four phosphorus atoms, P_4. It is more reactive than nitrogen. In nature, phosphorus usually occurs in the form of phosphates, PO_4^{3-}, which are essential components of living things. For example, calcium phosphate is a constituent of bones and teeth; phosphate groups are present in DNA and RNA molecules.

The elements in Group 16 also show a marked progression from nonmetallic to metallic properties with increasing atomic number. Oxygen, sulfur, and selenium are nonmetals; tellurium is a metalloid; polonium shows definite metallic properties.

Oxygen is extremely reactive, forming compounds with most other elements. Molecular oxygen, which is a by-product of photosynthesis, makes up about 20 percent of the atmosphere by volume. Because of its high electronegativity, oxygen in compounds always shows a negative oxidation state, except when combined with fluorine, which has the highest electronegativity.

Phosphorus, oxygen, and sulfur exhibit different forms, or **allotropes**. An element can have allotropic forms if at least two different numbers of atoms of that element can bond together to form molecules. The different allotropic forms of an element have different chemical and physical properties. For example, oxygen exists as ordinary atmospheric oxygen, $O_2(g)$, and as ozone, $O_3(g)$. Ozone is a highly reactive form that is produced from O_2 during the electrical discharges associated with thunderstorms.

Group 17 [VIIA].

Group 17 is known as the **halogen family**. Even though the metallic character of the elements within the group increases with increasing atomic number, none of the elements in the group is a metal. The halogens are all highly reactive and occur in nature only in compounds.

The elements in Group 17 have relatively high electronegativities. Fluorine has the highest electronegativity of any element. In compounds, it always shows a negative oxidation state. The other elements in the group may exhibit positive oxidation states in combination with more electronegative elements, for example, Cl_2O. The ease with which halogens show positive oxidation states increases with increasing atomic number.

Among the halogens, the physical forms of the free elements at room temperature vary with increasing atomic number. At room temperature, fluorine and chlorine are gases, bromine is a liquid, and iodine is a solid. The change in physical form is a result of increased van der Waals forces between molecules (see page 19).

Uncombined (free) halogens can be produced in the laboratory by chemical or electrolytic oxidation, which removes one of the electrons from the negative halide ion (anion).

Group 18 [O].

The elements of Group 18 are monatomic gases known as the **noble gases**. The electron configuration of each of these elements has what is called the "inert gas" structure. With the exception of helium, the atoms of these elements have filled s and p sublevels, resulting in an exceptionally stable electron configuration (s^2p^6). Helium has a single energy level that can accommodate only two electrons ($1s^2$). With this energy level filled, helium is even more stable than the other members of the group.

The Group 18 elements are sometimes called the *rare gases* or *inert gases*. However, the term "inert" is no longer strictly applicable because compounds of krypton, xenon, and radon with fluorine and oxygen have been produced in the laboratory.

QUESTIONS

1. Which of the following pairs exhibits the most similar chemical properties? (1) Mg and S (2) Ca and Br (3) Mg and Ca (4) S and Cl

2. An aqueous solution of a salt of chlorine and element X, XCl, has an intense color. Element X is most likely (1) an alkaline earth metal (2) a halogen (3) a transition metal (4) an alkali metal

3. Which element is an alkaline earth metal? (1) Ba (2) Zn (3) Li (4) Pb

4. Which group contains elements whose atoms in the ground state have a total of five electrons in their outermost p sublevel? (1) noble gases (2) metalloids (3) halogens (4) alkaline earth metals

5. The most active nonmetals are members of Group (1) 1 (2) 13 (3) 15 (4) 17

6. Which element exists as diatomic molecules at STP? (1) nitrogen (2) argon (3) uranium (4) rubidium

7. Which compound produces a bright yellow solution when dissolved in water? (1) KNO_3 (2) K_2CrO_4 (3) KOH (4) K_3PO_4

8. Which group of elements usually forms oxides with the general formula X_2O_3? (1) 1 (2) 2 (3) 13 (4) 14

9. How many electrons are found in the valence shell of an alkaline earth metal in the ground state? (1) 1 (2) 2 (3) 3 (4) 4

10. Which group is known as the noble gases? (1) 1 (2) 2 (3) 16 (4) 18

11. In which group are all of the elements solids at STP? (1) 14 (2) 15 (3) 16 (4) 17

12. A white anhydrous (dry) powder that dissolves in water to form a blue aqueous solution is most likely to be (1) Na_2SO_4 (2) $BaSO_4$ (3) $CuSO_4$ (4) $CaSO_4$

13. Which element occurs in nature only in compounds? (1) Au (2) Na (3) Ne (4) Ag

14. Which symbol represents an alkaline earth metal? (1) Na (2) Mg (3) Ne (4) Ag

15. The element in Group 1 whose isotopes are all radioactive is (1) Fr (2) Cs (3) Rb (4) Li

16. As the elements in Group 2 are considered from beryllium to radium, the degree of metallic activity (1) increases and atomic radius increases (2) increases and atomic radius decreases (3) decreases and atomic radius increases (4) decreases and atomic radius decreases

17. If X represents an element from Group 1, the formula of its oxide is (1) XO (2) X_2O (3) XO_2 (4) X_2O_3

18. The alkali metals are found in Group (1) 1 (2) 2 (3) 15 (4) 17

19. Which element has no stable isotopes? (1) O (2) S (3) Po (4) Te

20. Within a group, as atomic number increases, electronegativity generally (1) increases (2) decreases (3) remains the same

21. Within a group, as atomic radius increases, ionization energy generally (1) increases (2) decreases (3) remains the same

22. Which of the following noble gases has the lowest normal boiling point? (1) Ne (2) Ar (3) Kr (4) Xe

23. Which of the following is the atomic number of a transition metal? (1) 20 (2) 27 (3) 33 (4) 35

24. Ozone is an allotropic form of the element (1) oxygen (2) phosphorus (3) sulfur (4) carbon

25. Which of the following elements is most likely to form a compound with radon? (1) iodine (2) fluorine (3) sodium (4) calcium

26. As the elements are considered from the top to the bottom of Group 15, which sequence in properties occurs?
(1) metal → metalloid → nonmetal
(2) metal → nonmetal → metalloid
(3) metalloid → metal → nonmetal
(4) nonmetal → metalloid → metal

27. Which element exhibits a crystalline structure at STP? (1) fluorine (2) chlorine (3) bromine (4) iodine

28. Which group contains elements with a total of four electrons in the outermost principal energy level? (1) 1 (2) 18 (3) 16 (4) 14

29. Which electron configurations represent the first two elements in Group 17? (1) 2-1 and 2-2 (2) 2-2 and 2-3 (3) 2-7 and 2-8-7 (4) 2-8 and 2-8-7

30. Which is the electron configuration of a transition element? (1) 2-2 (2) 2-8-2 (3) 2-8-8-2 (4) 2-8-9-2

UNIT 5 The Mathematics of Chemistry

THE MOLE CONCEPT

Chemists need accurate and reliable methods for measuring the amounts of substances they work with; they often need to know the relative numbers of atoms and molecules used in an experiment. Since very large numbers of such particles may be involved, they are counted indirectly by using the masses of substances. This indirect method of counting is possible because, for practical purposes, all atoms of a given element have the same mass.

Atomic Mass.

The atomic mass of each element is defined in relation to the mass of a carbon-12 atom, which is assigned an atomic mass of 12.0. The mass of an atom is expressed in atomic mass units (amu). Atomic mass is discussed in Unit 2 (see page 10).

The need to express the masses of elements in laboratory quantities led to the concept of gram atomic mass. One **gram atomic mass**, or **gram-atom**, of an element is the atomic mass of that element in grams. For example, hydrogen has an atomic mass of 1, so 1 gram-atom of hydrogen has a mass of 1 gram. Carbon-12 has an atomic mass of 12, so 1 gram-atom of carbon-12 has a mass of 12 grams.

Avogadro's Number.

For each element, the ratio of its atomic mass to its gram atomic mass is the same. Thus, one gram atomic mass of all elements must have the same number of atoms. The number of atoms in 1 gram atomic mass of any element is approximately 6.02×10^{23}. This number is called **Avogadro's number** in honor of the Italian chemist, Amadeo Avogadro. Avogadro's number is sometimes abbreviated N_A.

Definition of a Mole.

The quantity represented by Avogadro's number of particles is called a **mole**. A mole is a fixed quantity, 6.02×10^{23}, just as a dozen is a fixed quantity, 12. One mole of an element, or 6.02×10^{23} atoms, is equal to the gram atomic mass of the element. The term "mole" is sometimes abbreviated *mol*.

Just as the gram atomic masses of different elements vary, so the mass of a mole varies from one element to another. For example, sodium has an atomic mass of 23. One gram atomic mass of sodium equals 23 grams, which also equals one mole of sodium atoms. Carbon, on the other hand, has an atomic mass of 12. One gram atomic mass of carbon equals 12 grams, which also equals one mole of carbon atoms. Both 23 grams of sodium and 12 grams of carbon contain 6.02×10^{23} atoms

because each quantity represents one mole of atoms.

Recall that atoms contain electrons, protons, and neutrons. A mole of atoms therefore contains $6.02 \times 10^{23} \times$ the number of these particles. A mole of Na atoms contains $11 \times 6.02 \times 10^{23}$ electrons, $11 \times 6.02 \times 10^{23}$ protons, and $12 \times 6.02 \times 10^{23}$ neutrons.

✳ You can solve problems involving mass, moles, and numbers of particles (atoms or molecules) by using the proper conversion factors. In elements, particles represent atoms, while in compounds, particles refer to molecules. To change from mass to moles, use grams/mole. To change from moles to number of molecules, use N_A/mole. Using the proper conversion factor not only provides the correct numerical answer, but also the correct unit. Following are some examples of conversion factors for sodium:

$$\text{Atomic mass:} \quad \frac{1 \text{ mole Na}}{6.02 \times 10^{23} \text{ atoms Na}}$$

$$\text{Moles:} \quad \frac{23 \text{ g Na}}{1 \text{ mole Na}}$$

$$\text{Mass:} \quad \frac{6.02 \times 10^{23} \text{ atoms Na}}{23 \text{ g Na}}$$

Sample Problems

1. How many moles are in 80 grams of calcium?

Solution: Since the atomic mass of calcium is 40, then 1 mole of calcium has a mass of 40 grams.

$$80 \text{ g Ca} \times \frac{1 \text{ mol Ca}}{40 \text{ g Ca}} = 2.0 \text{ mol Ca}$$

✳ **2.** How many molecules are there in 0.25 mole of pure water?

Solution: There are 6.02×10^{23} molecules per mole in any molecular substance. Thus, one-fourth of a mole would have one-fourth as many molecules. To find the answer, divide 6.02×10^{23} by 4, which equals 1.51×10^{23} molecules.

You can also solve the problem by using conversion factors:

$$0.25 \text{ mol } H_2O \times \frac{6.02 \times 10^{23} \text{ molecules } H_2O}{1 \text{ mol } H_2O}$$

$$= 1.51 \times 10^{23} \text{ molecules } H_2O$$

✳ **3.** If 8.0 grams of an element contain 0.25 mole, what is the gram atomic mass of that element?

One mole of an element corresponds to its gram atomic mass. Thus:

$$1 \, \cancel{mol} \times \frac{8 \text{ g}}{0.25 \, \cancel{mol}} = 32 \text{ g}$$

QUESTIONS

1. The number of moles in 2.16 grams of silver is (1) 2.00×10^{-2} (2) 4.59×10^{-2} (3) 2.00×10^{2} (4) 2.33×10^{2}

2. Which of the following represents 1 mole of calcium? (1) 23 liters (2) 22.4 grams (3) 6.02×10^{23} atoms (4) 3.01×10^{23} molecules

3. The atomic mass unit is defined as exactly (1) $\frac{1}{12}$ the mass of a carbon-12 atom (2) $\frac{1}{14}$ the mass of a nitrogen-14 atom (3) $\frac{1}{16}$ the mass of an oxygen-16 atom (4) the mass of a hydrogen atom

4. A 2-gram sample of which element contains the greatest number of atoms? (1) Al (2) Na (3) P (4) S

✷ 5. How many atoms are in 46.0 grams of sodium? (1) 3.01×10^{23} (2) 6.02×10^{23} (3) 12.0×10^{23} (4) 24.0×10^{23}

6. What is the mass, in atomic mass units, of an ion that contains 18 electrons, 15 protons, and 16 neutrons? (1) 49 amu (2) 33 amu (3) 31 amu (4) 15 amu

7. One atomic mass unit is most nearly equal to the mass of (1) the nucleus of a hydrogen atom (2) a carbon-12 atom (3) an oxygen molecule (4) 1,836 protons

✷ 8. Which sample contains the same number of atoms as 24 grams of carbon? (1) 80 g Ar (2) 24 g Mg (3) 10 g Ne (4) 4 g He

Formulas.
To determine the mass of one mole of a compound, you must know the chemical formula of the compound. Two kinds of chemical formulas are empirical formulas and molecular formulas.

Empirical and Molecular Formulas. A formula that gives the simplest whole-number ratio in which atoms combine is an **empirical formula**. Empirical formulas are used primarily for nonmolecular substances, including ionic substances and network solids. For example, sodium chloride is an ionic substance. Its empirical formula is NaCl. This empirical formula shows that sodium and chlorine ions combine in a one-to-one ratio in the compound.

Molecular formulas specify the exact number of each kind of atom in a molecule of a compound. For example, the molecular formula for glucose is $C_6H_{12}O_6$. One molecule of glucose contains 6 carbon atoms, 12 hydrogen atoms, and 6 oxygen atoms. Since not all compounds are molecular, not all compounds have molecular formulas.

Occasionally, the empirical and molecular formulas of a compound are the same. For example, the molecular formula of water, H_2O, is also the empirical formula because the ratio of hydrogen to oxygen, $2:1$, is expressed in its simplest whole-number form. More often, however, the empirical and molecular formulas of a compound are very different. The empirical and molecular formulas for several common compounds are given in Table 5-1. Note that several molecular formulas can be associated with the same empirical formula.

Table 5-1. Empirical and Molecular Formulas

Name	Empirical Formula	Molecular Formula
Benzene	CH	C_6H_6
Ethyne (acetylene)	CH	C_2H_2
Hydrogen peroxide	HO	H_2O_2
Ethane	CH_3	C_2H_6
Oxalic acid	HCO_2	$H_2C_2O_4$

Gram Formula Mass. The **gram formula mass** of a compound is the sum of the masses of all atoms in the empirical formula, with the result expressed in grams. For example, the gram formula mass of NaCl is equal to the mass of a sodium atom, 23, plus the mass of a chlorine atom, 35.5. Its gram formula mass is 58.5 grams.

The number of electrons in one Na atom is 11. A mole of Na atoms (23 g) contains $11 \times 6.02 \times 10^{23}$ electrons. Similarly, the number of electrons in one Cl atom is 17. A mole of Cl atoms (35.5 g) contains $17 \times 6.02 \times 10^{23}$ electrons. The total number of electrons in one mole (58.5 g) of NaCl is $11 \times 6.02 \times 10^{23}$ electrons + $17 \times 6.02 \times 10^{23}$ electrons, or $28 \times 6.02 \times 10^{23}$ electrons.

In the compound zinc sulfide, ZnS, one zinc atom is combined with one sulfur atom. Its gram formula mass is 97.4. A sample of this compound that contains 6.02×10^{23} zinc atoms also contains 6.02×10^{23} sulfur atoms. This sample has a mass of 97.4 grams. Thus, one mole of zinc sulfide contains one mole of zinc atoms and one mole of sulfur atoms, and its gram formula mass is 97.4 grams. In general, for any compound, its formula mass measured in grams is equal to one mole.

Gram Molecular Mass. The gram molecular mass of a compound is the sum of the masses of all atoms in the molecular formula, with the result expressed in grams. The gram molecular mass of glucose, $C_6H_{12}O_6$, is 180 $(6 \times 12) + (12 \times 1) + (6 \times 16)$. In practice, the terms "gram formula mass" and "gram molecular mass" are often used interchangeably.

QUESTIONS

1. Which compound has an empirical formula of CH_2O? (1) CH_3COOH (2) CH_3CH_2OH (3) $HCCOH$ (4) CH_3OH

2. Which of the following is an empirical formula? (1) C_4H_8 (2) C_2H_2 (3) H_2O_2 (4) HO

3. What is the empirical formula for the compound dinitrogen tetroxide? (1) NO_2 (2) N_2O_3 (3) N_2O (4) N_2O_5

4. A compound is found to contain 2 grams of hydrogen to each 16 grams of oxygen. What is the empirical formula for the compound? (1) HO (2) H_2O (3) H_2O_2 (4) HO_2

5. A compound contains 0.5 mole of sodium, 0.5 mole of nitrogen, and 1.0 mole of hydrogen. What is the empirical formula for this compound? (1) $NaNH$ (2) Na_2NH (3) $NaNH_2$ (4) NaN_2H_2

6. The empirical formula for a compound is CH. The molecular formula for this compound could be (1) CH_4 (2) C_2H_2 (3) C_2H_4 (4) C_3H_8

7. The empirical formula of a compound is C_2H_3, and its molecular mass is 54. The molecular formula for this compound is (1) C_2H_4 (2) C_4H_6 (3) C_4H_8 (4) C_6H_{10}

8. The gram molecular mass of CO_2 is the same as the gram molecular mass of (1) CO (2) SO_2 (3) C_2H_6 (4) C_3H_8

9. Which quantity is equivalent to 39 grams of LiF? (1) 1.0 mole (2) 2.0 moles (3) 0.5 mole (4) 1.5 moles

10. What is the gram formula mass of $CaSO_4 \cdot 2H_2O$? (1) 172 g (2) 154 g (3) 136 g (4) 118 g

11. What is the gram molecular mass of a compound if 5 moles of the compound have a mass of 100 grams? (1) 5 g (2) 20 g (3) 100 g (4) 500 g

12. A compound has an empirical formula of CH_2 and a molecular mass of 56. Its molecular formula is (1) C_2H_4 (2) C_3H_6 (3) C_4H_8 (4) C_5H_{10}

13. The empirical formula of a compound is CH_2 and its molecular mass is 70. What is the molecular formula of the compound? (1) C_2H_2 (2) C_2H_4 (3) C_4H_{10} (4) C_5H_{10}

14. Which is an empirical formula? (1) C_2H_2 (2) C_2H_4 (3) Al_2Cl_6 (4) K_2O

15. What is the molecular formula of a compound whose empirical formula is CH_2 and whose molecular mass is 42? (1) $HCOOH$ (2) C_2H_2O (3) C_3H_6 (4) C_3H_8

✳ 16. How many molecules are in 18.0 grams of water?
(1) 6.02×10^{23}
(2) $3 \times 18 \times 6.02 \times 10^{23}$
(3) $3 \times 6.02 \times 10^{23}$
(4) $18 \times 6.02 \times 10^{23}$

✳ 17. What is the total number of atoms in 18.0 grams of water?
(1) 6.02×10^{23}
(2) $3 \times 6.02 \times 10^{23}$
(3) $18.0 \times 6.02 \times 10^{23}$
(4) $3 \times 18 \times 6.02 \times 10^{23}$

✳ 18. What is the total number of electrons in 18.0 grams of water?
(1) 6.02×10^{23}
(2) $3 \times 6.02 \times 10^{23}$
(3) $10 \times 6.02 \times 10^{23}$
(4) $3 \times 10 \times 6.02 \times 10^{23}$

19. How many molecules are in 1 mole of ammonia, NH_3?
(1) 1×10^{23}
(2) 6.02×10^{23}
(3) 12×10^{23}
(4) 24.2×10^{23}

✳ 20. Which expression represents the number of atoms in 44 grams of carbon dioxide?
(1) $3(6.02 \times 10^{23})$
(2) $\dfrac{6.02 \times 10^{23}}{6}$
(3) $6(6.02 \times 10^{23})$
(4) $\dfrac{6.02 \times 10^{23}}{2}$

Molar Volume of a Gas. As a result of observations of the behavior of gases, Avogadro developed a hypothesis that states: *At the same conditions of temperature and pressure, equal volumes of all gases contain the same number of molecules.*

Since the space between molecules is very great compared to the actual size of the molecules, differences in molecular size do not make an appreciable difference in the total space occupied. Thus, at the same temperature and pressure, one mole of a heavy gas with large molecules, such as krypton (radius 2.18 Å, mass 131 amu) occupies the same volume as one mole of a light gas, such as helium (radius 1.22 Å, mass 4 amu).

Experiments show that the volume occupied by one mole of any gas at STP, its **molar volume**, is 22.4 liters.

Sample Problems

1. What is the volume of 2.5 moles of Ne at STP?

Solution: The volume of 1 mole of any gas at STP is 22.4 L. The problem can be solved by using the expression:

$$2.5 \;\text{mol Ne} \times \frac{22.4 \text{ L Ne}}{1 \text{ mol Ne}} = 56 \text{ L}$$

2. What is the mass of 12.0 L of CO_2 at STP?

Solution: The molecular mass of CO_2 is 44.0 g. The molar volume of CO_2 is 22.4 L. The problem can be solved by using the expression:

$$12.0 \text{ L } CO_2 \times \frac{1 \text{ mol } CO_2}{22.4 \text{ L } CO_2}$$

$$\times \frac{44.0 \text{ g } CO_2}{1 \text{ mol } CO_2} = 23.6 \text{ g } CO_2$$

3. How many molecules are in 5.0 L of CH_4 at STP?

Solution: There are 6.02×10^{23} molecules in 1 mole of any gas. The volume of 1 mole of any gas is 22.4 L at STP. The problem can be solved using the expression:

$$5.0 \text{ L } CH_4 \times \frac{1 \text{ mol } CH_4}{22.4 \text{ L } CH_4}$$

$$\times \frac{6.02 \times 10^{23} \text{ molecules } CH_4}{1 \text{ mol } CH_4}$$

$$= 1.34 \times 10^{23} \text{ molecules}$$

✳ Gas Density and Molecular Mass. Density is a physical property of gases that relates the mass of a gas to its volume. Or density = mass/volume. The density of a gas is usually stated in grams per liter. When the density is reported in grams per liter at STP, the mass of one mole of the gas—the molecular mass—can be determined. Similarly, the density of a gas at STP can be calculated from a known molecular mass. Calculations using gas density are somewhat inaccurate because all gases deviate from ideal behavior (see page 5). However, for most purposes, the inaccuracy is negligibly small.

The densities of several gases are listed in Reference Table C (see page 106).

✳ Sample Problems ────────

1. What is the density of $NO_{2(g)}$ at STP?

Solution: The molecular mass of NO_2 is 46. Thus, one mole of NO_2 has a mass of 46 g and occupies a volume of 22.4 L at STP. The problem can be solved by using the expression:

$$\frac{46 \text{ g } NO_2}{1 \text{ mol } NO_2} \times \frac{1 \text{ mol } NO_2}{22.4 \text{ L } NO_2} = 2.05 \text{ g/L}$$

2. What is the molecular mass of a gas whose density is observed to be 2.32 g/L at STP?

Solution: One mole of the gas will occupy 22.4 L. The mass of one liter is given as 2.32 g. The problem can be solved by using the expression:

$$\frac{2.32 \text{ g}}{1 \text{ L}} \times \frac{22.4 \text{ L}}{1 \text{ mol}} = 52.0 \text{ g/mol}$$

QUESTIONS

1. Which quantity of N_2 gas has a volume of 11.2 liters at STP? (1) 1.0 mole (2) 2.0 moles (3) 14.0 grams (4) 28.0 grams

✳ 2. What is the gram molecular mass of a gas with a density of 1.78 grams per liter at STP? (1) 17.8 g (2) 22.4 g (3) 39.9 g (4) 79.6 g

✳ 3. The gram molecular mass of a given gas is 44.0 grams. What is its density at STP? (1) 0.509 g/L (2) 1.43 g/L (3) 1.96 g/L (4) 2.84 g/L

4. What is the volume of 4.00 moles of N_2 gas at STP? (1) 11.2 L (2) 22.4 L (3) 44.8 L (4) 89.6 L

5. Based on Reference Table C (see page 106), which gas a greater density at STP than air at STP? (1) H_2 (2) NH_3 (3) Cl_2 (4) CH_4

✳ 6. If the density of a gas at STP is 2.50 grams per liter, what is the gram molecular mass of the gas? (1) 2.50 (2) 22.4 (3) 56.0 (4) 89.6

7. A 2.00-gram sample of helium gas at STP will occupy (1) 11.2 L (2) 22.4 L (3) 33.6 L (4) 44.8 L

✳ 8. The density of a gas is 2.0 grams per liter at STP. Its molecular mass is approximately (1) 67 (2) 45 (3) 22 (4) 8

Calculating Percent Composition.

The percent by mass of each element in a compound can be calculated by using the gram atomic mass of the element and the formula mass. The percent by mass of each element in a compound is calculated by the formula:

$$\frac{\text{percent}}{\text{mass}} = \frac{\text{atomic mass of element}}{\text{formula mass of compound}} \times 100$$

Sample Problem ────────

What is the percent by mass of each element in ammonium sulfate, $(NH_4)_2SO_4$?

Solution: Find the atomic mass of each element in the compound. Calculate the total atomic masses. Then determine the formula mass of the compound.

2 N atoms: $2 \times 14.0 =$	28.0
8 H atoms: $8 \times 1.01 =$	8.08
1 S atom: $1 \times 32.1 =$	32.1
4 O atoms: $4 \times 16.0 =$	64.0
Total formula mass	132.18

The formula mass of ammonium sulfate is rounded off to 132 grams. The percent by mass of each element can be calculated by the preceding formula.

$$\%N: \frac{28.0}{132} \times 100 = 21.2\%$$

$$\%H: \frac{8.08}{132} \times 100 = 6.12\%$$

$$\%S: \frac{32.1}{132} \times 100 = 24.3\%$$

$$\%O: \frac{64.0}{132} \times 100 = 48.5\%$$

The values for percent by mass should total 100%. As a result of rounding off, however, some small differences may occur.

Hydrated Salts. Some solid compounds contain water molecules bonded directly to the solid crystal. These compounds are called **hydrated salts,** or **hydrates.** Hydrated cupric sulfate is an example. Its formula is $CuSO_4 \cdot 5H_2O$. The percent of water in a hydrated salt can be calculated from its formula by using the atomic masses of all the components of the salt.

Sample Problem

What is the percent of water in hydrated copper (II) sulfate?

Solution: Find the formula mass for hydrated copper (II) sulfate.

1 Cu		63.5
1 S		32.1
4 O	(4 × 16)	64.0
5 H_2O	(5 × 18)	90.0
		249.6

Note that the formula mass of the hydrate includes the mass of 5 moles of water. From the formula for percent mass:

$$\frac{90.0}{249.6} \times 100 = 36.1\% \text{ water}$$

* Calculating Empirical Formulas.

Just as the percent composition of a compound can be calculated if the empirical formula is known, the empirical formula can be calculated if the percent composition is known. This is the reverse of the procedure used in calculating percent composition.

* Sample Problems

1. Laboratory analysis shows that a certain hydrocarbon consists of 14.3% hydrogen and 85.7% carbon by mass. What is the empirical formula of the compound?

Solution: If the compound contains 14.3% hydrogen and 85.7% carbon by mass, then 100 grams of the compound contain 14.3 grams of hydrogen and 85.7 grams of carbon. The number of moles of each element per 100 grams of compound can be calculated by using the expressions:

$$14.3 \text{ g H} \times \frac{1 \text{ mol H}}{1.01 \text{ g H}} = 14.15 \text{ mol H}$$

$$85.7 \text{ g C} \times \frac{1 \text{ mol C}}{12.0 \text{ g C}} = 7.14 \text{ mol C}$$

The results can be expressed in the format of a chemical formula as $C_{7.14}H_{14.2}$. This formula is not an empirical formula because it does not express a whole-number ratio. A simpler ratio of atoms (the empirical formula) is obtained by dividing each of the subscripts by the smaller of the two:

$$\frac{C_{7.14}}{7.14} \quad \frac{H_{14.2}}{7.14} = C_1H_2 \text{ or } CH_2$$

2. Laboratory analysis shows that a certain compound consists of 40% calcium, 12% carbon, and 48% oxygen by mass. What is the empirical formula of the compound?

Solution: A sample of 100 grams of the compound contains 40 grams of calcium, 12 grams of carbon, and 48 grams of oxygen. The number of moles of each element can be found by using the expressions:

$$40 \text{ g Ca} \times \frac{1 \text{ mol Ca}}{40.1 \text{ g Ca}} = 1.0 \text{ mole Ca}$$

$$12 \text{ g C} \times \frac{1 \text{ mol C}}{12.0 \text{ g C}} = 1.0 \text{ mole C}$$

$$48 \text{ g O} \times \frac{1 \text{ mol O}}{16 \text{ g O}} = 3.0 \text{ moles O}$$

For every mole of calcium and carbon, there are three moles of oxygen. This relationship is expressed by the formula $CaCO_3$, which is the empirical formula.

3. An oxide of chromium is analyzed in the laboratory and is found to contain 68.6% Cr and 31.4% O by mass. (*a*) Find the number of moles of each element in 100 grams of this compound. (*b*) Find the empirical formula for the compound.

$$(a) \quad 68.6 \text{ g Cr} \times \frac{1 \text{ mol Cr}}{52.0 \text{ g Cr}} = 1.32 \text{ mol Cr}$$

$$31.4 \text{ g O} \times \frac{1 \text{ mol O}}{16.0 \text{ g O}} = 1.97 \text{ mol O}$$

(*b*) The molar ratio of the two elements is 1.32 : 1.97. Divide these two numbers by the smaller of the two:

$$\frac{Cr_{1.32}}{1.32} \quad \frac{O_{1.96}}{1.32} = Cr_1O_{1.5}$$

Doubling both numbers gives the smallest whole-number values for both elements, Cr_2O_3, which is the empirical formula for the compound.

QUESTIONS

1. What is the percent by mass of oxygen in Fe_2O_3? (1) 2.3% (2) 30% (3) 56% (4) 70%
2. The mass ratio of sulfur to oxygen in sulfur dioxide is (1) 1:1 (2) 1:2 (3) 2:3 (4) 3:2
3. What is the total mass of iron in 1 mole of Fe_2O_3? (1) 160 g (2) 112 g (3) 72 g (4) 56 g

4. What is the ratio by mass of carbon to hydrogen in the compound C_2H_6? (1) 6:2 (2) 2:6 (3) 1:4 (4) 4:1

✳ 5. A compound is found to contain 85.6% carbon and 14.4% hydrogen. What is its empirical formula? (1) CH (2) CH_2 (3) C_2H (4) C_2H_2

6. The percentage by mass of hydrogen in H_3PO_4 is equal to (1) $\frac{1}{98} \times 100$ (2) $\frac{3}{98} \times 100$ (3) $\frac{98}{3} \times 100$ (4) $\frac{98}{1} \times 100$

7. In the compound $Pb_3(OH)_2(CO_3)_2$, the element that is present in the greatest percentage by mass is (1) Pb (2) O (3) H (4) C

8. As a sample of $Na_2CO_3 \cdot 10H_2O$ is heated in an open crucible, the mass of the contents of the crucible (1) increases (2) decreases (3) remains the same

9. A 10-gram sample of a hydrate was heated until all the water of hydration was driven off. The mass of the anhydrous product remaining was 8.0 grams. What is the percent by mass of water in the hydrate? (1) 12.5% (2) 20% (3) 25% (4) 80%

10. A 60-gram sample of $LiCl \cdot H_2O$ is heated in an open crucible until all the water has been driven off. What is the mass of LiCl that remains in the crucible? (1) 18 g (2) 24 g (3) 42 g (4) 60 g

11. What is the maximum number of grams of potassium that can be obtained from 100 grams of $KHCO_3$? (1) 19 g (2) 39 g (3) 58 g (4) 100 g

STOICHIOMETRY

Stoichiometry is the study of the quantitative relationships in chemical equations. In solving stoichiometric problems, it is often convenient to use mole relationships.

Problems Involving Equations.

A balanced chemical equation represents the relative numbers of atoms, molecules, or moles of each substance consumed or produced in a reaction. The equation for the reaction of iron with oxygen,

$$4Fe(s) + 3O_2(g) \rightarrow 2Fe_2O_3(s)$$

can mean that 4 atoms of iron react with 3 molecules of oxygen to produce 2 molecules of iron (III) oxide. It can also mean that 4 moles of iron combine with 3 moles of oxygen to form 2 moles of iron (III) oxide.

The quantitative relationships shown by balanced chemical equations can be used to determine the quantities of reactants (starting substances) consumed and products formed in a given reaction.

Sample Problems

Sample problems 1–5 are based on the equation

$$2CH_3OH(\ell) + 3O_2(g) \rightarrow 2CO_2(g) + 4H_2O(\ell)$$

1. What mass of $H_2O(\ell)$ is produced when 8.0 g of $CH_3OH(\ell)$ are burned in excess $O_2(g)$?

The equation shows that 4 moles of H_2O are produced from 2 moles of CH_3OH. One mole of CH_3OH equals 32 grams, and 8 grams of CH_3OH are equivalent to 0.25 mole. Thus, 0.25 mole of CH_3OH forms 0.50 mole of H_2O, or 9 grams. Or,

$$8.0 \text{ g } CH_3OH \times \frac{1 \text{ mol } CH_3OH}{32.0 \text{ g } CH_3OH}$$

$$\times \frac{4 \text{ mol } H_2O}{2 \text{ mol } CH_3OH} \times \frac{18 \text{ g } H_2O}{1 \text{ mol } H_2O} = 9.0 \text{ g } H_2O$$

2. At STP, what volume of $O_2(g)$ is consumed when 24 g of $CH_3OH(\ell)$ are burned?

Every 2 moles of CH_3OH react with 3 moles of O_2. One mole of CH_3OH equals 32 grams, and 24 grams of CH_3OH are equivalent to 0.75 mole. Thus, 0.75 mole of CH_3OH reacts with 1.13 moles of O_2. Since there are 22.4 liters of O_2/mole, the volume of O_2 is 22.4 × 1.13 or 25.2 liters. Or,

$$24.0 \text{ g } CH_3OH \times \frac{1 \text{ mol } CH_3OH}{32.0 \text{ g } CH_3OH}$$

$$\times \frac{3 \text{ mol } O_2}{2 \text{ mol } CH_3OH} \times \frac{22.4 \text{ L } O_2}{1 \text{ mol } O_2} = 25.2 \text{ L } O_2$$

3. At STP, what volume of CO_2 is produced when 5 L of O_2 are consumed?

$$5.0 \text{ L } O_2 \times \frac{1 \text{ mol } O_2}{22.4 \text{ L } O_2} \times \frac{2 \text{ mol } CO_2}{3 \text{ mol } O_2}$$

$$\times \frac{22.4 \text{ L } CO_2}{1 \text{ mol } CO_2} = 3.3 \text{ L } CO_2$$

Note that the coefficients of a balanced chemical equation also express the relative volumes of the gaseous participants in a chemical reaction. This is because the accepted molar volume for every gas is the same, 22.4 L at STP.

4. How many molecules of H_2O are produced when 16 g of CH_3OH are consumed?

$$8.0 \text{ g } CH_3OH \times \frac{1 \text{ mol } CH_3OH}{32 \text{ g } CH_3OH}$$

$$\times \frac{4 \text{ mol } H_2O}{2 \text{ mol } CH_3OH}$$

$$\times \frac{6.0 \times 10^{23} \text{ molecules } H_2O}{1 \text{ mol } H_2O}$$

$$= 3.0 \times 10^{23} \text{ molecules } H_2O$$

5. How many moles of CH_3OH are consumed when 1.5×10^{23} molecules of H_2O are produced?

$$1.5 \times 10^{23} \text{ molecules } H_2O \times \frac{1 \text{ mol } H_2O}{6.0 \times 10^{23}}$$

$$\times \frac{2 \text{ mol } CH_3OH}{4 \text{ mol } H_2O} = 0.125 \text{ mol } CH_3OH$$

1. Given the reaction: $2CO + O_2 \rightarrow 2CO_2$. What is the minimum number of moles of O_2 required to produce 1 mole of CO_2? (1) 1.0 (2) 2.0 (3) 0.25 (4) 0.50

2. Given the reaction:

$$3PbCl_2 + Al_2(SO_4)_3 \rightarrow 3PbSO_4 + 2AlCl_3$$

How many moles of $PbSO_4$ are formed when 0.150 mole of $Al_2(SO_4)_3$ is consumed? (1) 0.050 (2) 0.150 (3) 0.45 (4) 0.60

✳ 3. Given the reaction:

$$2C_2H_6 + 7O_2 \rightarrow 4CO_2 + 6H_2O$$

How many moles of CO_2 are produced when 30.0 grams of C_2H_6 are burned completely? (1) 1.0 (2) 2.0 (3) 8.0 (4) 4.0

✳ 4. What mass of oxygen is produced by the decomposition of 3.0 moles of water:

$$2H_2O \rightarrow 2H_2 + O_2$$

(1) 1.5 g (2) 32 g (3) 36 g (4) 48 g

5. Given the reaction: $N_2 + 3H_2 \rightarrow 2NH_3$. If 14 grams of N_2 are consumed in the reaction, what is the mass of H_2 consumed? (1) 6.0 g (2) 2.0 g (3) 3.0 g (4) 4.0 g

6. Given the reaction:

$$C_2H_4 + 3O_2 \rightarrow 2CO_2 + 2H_2O$$

What volume of CO_2 is produced when 15.0 liters of O_2 are consumed? (1) 10.0 L (2) 15.0 L (3) 22.5 L (4) 45.0 L

7. Given the reaction:

$$4NH_3 + 5O_2 \rightarrow 4NO + 6H_2O$$

What volume of O_2 is required to produce 80.0 L of $NO(g)$? (1) 5.0 L (2) 64.0 L (3) 80.0 L (4) 100.0 L

8. Given the reaction:

$$Ca + 2H_2O \rightarrow Ca(OH)_2 + H_2$$

How many moles of H_2O are needed to react exactly with 2.0 moles of Ca? (1) 1.0 (2) 2.0 (3) 0.50 (4) 4.0

✳ 9. Given the reaction: $N_2 + 3H_2 \rightarrow 2NH_3$. How many grams of H_2 are needed to produce exactly 1 mole of ammonia? (1) 1 g (2) 2 g (3) 3 g (4) 4 g

10. Given the reaction:

$$2NaOH + H_2SO_4 \rightarrow Na_2SO_4 + 2H_2O$$

What is the total number of moles of NaOH needed to react completely with 2 moles of H_2SO_4? (1) 1 (2) 2 (3) 0.5 (4) 4

11. Given the reaction:

$$2Na + 2H_2O \rightarrow 2NaOH + H_2$$

What is the total number of moles of hydrogen produced when 4 moles of sodium react completely? (1) 1 (2) 2 (3) 3 (4) 4

12. Given the reaction:

$$3Fe + 4H_2O \rightarrow Fe_3O_4 + 4H_2$$

What volume of H_2 is produced when 36.0 grams of H_2O are consumed? (1) 89.6 L (2) 44.8 L (3) 33.6 L (4) 22.4 L

13. Given the reaction: $2H_2 + O_2 \rightarrow 2H_2O$. What mass of oxygen will combine with 3.0 grams of hydrogen to produce water? (1) 1.5 g (2) 0.37 g (3) 6.0 g (4) 24 g

SOLUTIONS

Nature of Solutions.
A **solution** is a homogeneous mixture of two or more substances that are usually present in unequal amounts. The substance present in greater amount in the solution is the **solvent**, and the substance or substances present in lesser amounts are **solutes**. The solvent is generally a liquid, while the solute may be a solid, liquid, or gas. True solutions are transparent. The solute particles are either ionic or molecular in size and cannot be separated from the solvent by filtration.

When a homogeneous mixture contains particles large enough to reflect a beam of light, the mixture is referred to as a **colloid**. Colloids are not transparent. Homogenized milk is an example of a colloid.

When two liquids can mix to form a solution, they are said to be **miscible** in each other. Ethyl alcohol and water are miscible in all proportions. Oil and water are **immiscible**—they will not mix to form a solution.

Solutions, like other mixtures, may vary in composition. However, a solution must be homogeneous, with the solute dispersed uniformly throughout the solvent. Thus, equal volumes of a solution have the same composition.

The amount of solute that will dissolve in a solvent varies, depending on the nature of both substances and on the temperature of the system. If there is very little solute compared to the amount of solvent, the solution is said to be **dilute**. If the amount of solute is large compared to the amount of solvent, the solution is said to be **concentrated**.

Solutions can also be described as saturated, unsaturated, or supersaturated. A **saturated solution** contains all the solute it can hold at a given temperature. An **unsaturated solution** contains less solute than it can hold under the existing conditions. Additional solute can be added to an unsaturated solution until saturation is reached. Under certain conditions, a solution may contain more solute than would normally produce a saturated solution. Such a solution is said to be a **supersaturated solution** and contains more solute than it can ordinarily hold at a given temperature. A supersaturated solution is not stable. Addition of solute to a supersaturated solution will cause all the excess solute to crystallize and precipitate out of solution. An abrupt shock to the solution may also cause crystallization and precipitation of the excess solute.

Reference Table D (see page 106) shows solute capacity in saturated solutions of several substances. When the concentration and temperature characteristics of a solution coincide with its solubility curve, the solution is saturated. Solutions that place above the curve are supersaturated, while those that fall below the curve are unsaturated.

Molarity.

The concentration of a solution is often expressed in terms of molarity. **Molarity** (M) is the number of moles of solute per liter of solution. Thus, 1 liter of 0.50 M solution of sodium nitrate ($NaNO_3$) contains 0.50 mole $NaNO_3$ plus enough water to produce exactly 1 liter of solution. (Unless otherwise stated, solutions are aqueous; that is, water is the solvent.)

Numerical problems involving molarity typically include information about two of the following three quantities: moles (or mass) of solute, volume of solution, and molarity of the solution. The quantity about which information is not given is the "unknown."

Molarity is used to express solution concentration when quantities of solution are intended to be measured with volumetric equipment, such as burets, pipettes, graduated cylinders, or volumetric flasks.

* Molality.

The relationship between the number of moles of solute and the mass of solvent is expressed by another unit of concentration, called molality. The **molality** (m) of a solution is the number of moles of solute per kilogram of solvent. A 1 m solution has 1 mole of solute dissolved in 1,000 g of solvent.

Sample Problems _____

1. What is the molarity of a solution that contains 25.0 g of KNO_3 in 0.500 L of solution?

Solution: Find the molar mass of KNO_3:

$$(1)(39) + (1)(14) + (3)(16) = 101$$

A 1.0 M KNO_3 solution contains the gram molar mass (101 g) per liter of solution. A solution that contains 25 g/0.50 L has the same concentration as 50 g/L. If a 1 M solution contains 101 g/L, then a solution with 50 g/L is $\frac{50}{101} = 0.5$ M.

The problem can be solved by using the expression:

$$\frac{25.0 \text{ g } KNO_3}{0.500 \text{ L solution}} \times \frac{1 \text{ mol } KNO_3}{101 \text{ g } KNO_3}$$

$$= \frac{0.50 \text{ mol } KNO_3}{1 \text{ L solution}}$$

The molarity of the solution is 0.50 M.

2. What volume of 1.25 M solution can be produced using 73.0 g HCl?

Solution: Find the molar mass of HCl:

$$(1)(1) + (1)(35.5) = 36.5$$

$$73.0 \text{ g HCl} \times \frac{1 \text{ mol HCl}}{36.5 \text{ g HCl}} \times \frac{1 \text{ L solution}}{1.25 \text{ mol HCl}}$$

$$= 1.60 \text{ liters of solution}$$

3. What mass of $MgCl_2$ is required to prepare 100 mL of 0.750 M solution?

Solution: Find the molar mass of $MgCl_2$:

$$(1)(24.3) + (2)(35.5) = 95.3$$

Since molarity is given in liters, 100 mL must be converted to liters:

$$100 \text{ mL solution} \times \frac{1 \text{ L solution}}{1000 \text{ mL solution}}$$

$$= 0.1 \text{ L solution}$$

The problem can be solved by using the expression:

$$0.1 \text{ L solution} \times \frac{.750 \text{ mol } MgCl_2}{1 \text{ L solution}}$$

$$\times \frac{95.3 \text{ g } MgCl_2}{1 \text{ mol } MgCl_2} = 7.15 \text{ g } MgCl_2$$

✳ 4. A sugar solution is prepared by adding 90.0 grams of glucose ($C_6H_{12}O_6$) to 500 mL of distilled water. What is the molality of the solution? (The molar mass of glucose is 180.)

Solution: Molality $= \dfrac{\text{moles solute}}{\text{kg solvent}}$

Use conversion factors to change 90 g glucose to moles and 500 mL water to kilograms. The density of water is 1 g/mL:

$$\frac{90 \text{ g glucose}}{500 \text{ mL } H_2O} \times \frac{1 \text{ mol glucose}}{180 \text{ g glucose}}$$

$$\times \frac{1000 \text{ mL } H_2O}{1 \text{ kg } H_2O} = \frac{1 \text{ mole glucose}}{\text{kg water}}$$

$$= 1 \text{ m solution}$$

* Concentration by Percent Mass.

The concentration of a solution can also be expressed as the mass of solute per 100 grams of solution. Thus, an aqueous solution that is 10% H_2SO_4 by mass contains 10 grams of H_2SO_4 dissolved in 90 grams of water, resulting in 100 grams of solution.

* Sample Problems _____

1. What is the mass of NaCl in 40 grams of 10% salt solution?

Solution: In a 10% solution, there are 10 grams

36

of NaCl per 100 grams of solution. The problem can be solved by using the expression:

$$40 \text{ g solution} \times \frac{10 \text{ g NaCl}}{100 \text{ g solution}} = 4.0 \text{ g NaCl}$$

2. What is the mass of the solvent in 60 grams of 30% alcohol solution?

Solution: In a 30% alcohol solution, there are 30 grams of alcohol and 70 grams of solvent per 100 grams of solution. The problem can be solved by using the expression:

$$60 \text{ g solution} \times \frac{70 \text{ g solvent}}{100 \text{ g solution}} = 42 \text{ g solvent}$$

3. What mass of 20% aqueous solution can be produced using 80 grams of sugar as the solute?

Solution: In a 20% solution, there are 20 grams of sugar per 100 grams of solution. The problem can be solved by using the expression:

$$80 \text{ g sugar} \times \frac{100 \text{ g solution}}{20 \text{ g sugar}} = 400 \text{ g solution}$$

QUESTIONS

1. How many moles of H_2SO_4 are needed to prepare 5 L of a 2.0 M solution of H_2SO_4? (1) 2.5 moles (2) 5.0 moles (3) 10 moles (4) 20 moles

2. What is the mass of KCl in 1.0 L of 0.2 M solution? (1) 7.46 g (2) 14.9 g (3) 22.4 g (4) 29.8 g

3. What is the molarity of a solution that contains 20 g $CaBr_2$ in 0.50 L of solution? (1) 0.50 M (2) 2.0 M (3) 0.10 M (4) 0.20 M

4. What is the mass of solute in 500 mL of 1.0 M CH_3COOH? (1) 30 g (2) 60 g (3) 90 g (4) 120 g

5. What is the molarity of a solution that contains 10 g of NaOH in 500 mL of solution? (1) 1.0 M (2) 0.50 M (3) 0.25 M (4) 0.10 M

6. How many moles of $AgNO_3$ are found in 500 mL of a 5.0 M solution of $AgNO_3$? (1) 2.5 moles (2) 5.0 moles (3) 10 moles (4) 170 moles

7. What is the molarity of a solution that contains 80 g of NaOH in 4.0 liters of solution? (1) 0.50 M (2) 2.0 M (3) 8.0 M (4) 20.0 M

8. If 0.50 liter of a 12 M solution is diluted to 1.0 liter, what is the molarity of the new solution? (1) 2.4 M (2) 6.0 M (3) 12.0 M (4) 24.0 M

9. What is the molarity of a solution of KNO_3 (molecular mass = 101) that contains 404 grams of KNO_3 in 2.0 liters of solution? (1) 1.0 (2) 2.0 (3) 0.50 (4) 4.0

10. A 5% solution of potassium chloride contains 5 grams of solid dissolved in a quantity of water that is equal to (1) 100 grams (2) 100 moles (3) 95 grams (4) 95 moles

11. In 10 grams of a 5% salt solution, the mass of salt is (1) 0.5 gram (2) 0.2 gram (3) 95 grams (4) 9.5 grams

* Colligative Properties of Solutions.

Many properties of solutions are different from the properties of the pure solvents because of the presence of dissolved solute particles. Seawater, for example, is a solution of water and various dissolved salts. It freezes at a lower temperature than does pure water. Such variations depend on the relative number of solute particles rather than on the nature of the particles. Properties that vary with the number, rather than the nature, of solute particles are called **colligative properties**. Boiling point, freezing point, vapor pressure, and osmotic pressure are colligative properties of solutions.

* Boiling Point and Freezing Point Changes.

The presence of a nonvolatile solute raises the boiling point of the solvent by an amount that is proportional to the concentration of the dissolved solute particles. One mole of dissolved particles per 1,000 grams of water (a 1-molal solution) raises the boiling point of water by 0.52C°, called the **molal boiling point elevation constant** (see Reference Table A, page 105).

Similarly, the presence of a solute lowers the freezing point of the solvent by an amount that is proportional to the concentration of dissolved solute particles. One mole of particles per 1,000 grams of water (a 1-molal solution) lowers the freezing point of water by 1.86C°, called the **molal freezing point depression constant** (see Reference Table A, page 105).

Thus, a solution of one mole of sugar dissolved in one kilogram of water has a boiling point of 100.52°C—slightly greater than the boiling point of pure water—and a freezing point of −1.86°C— slightly lower than the freezing point of pure water.

* Electrolyte Solutions.

Substances whose aqueous solutions will conduct electric current are called **electrolytes** (see page 48). Electrolytes tend to dissociate in solution, forming positive ions (cations) and negative ions (anions). Because these charged particles are mobile, they allow the solution to conduct electric current. Because of the tendency of electrolytes to dissociate, an electrolyte solution contains more solute particles than does a nonelectrolyte solution of the same molality, because each ion acts as a separate particle in the solution. Thus, for equal concentrations, an electrolyte has a greater effect on the elevation of the boiling point and on the depression of the freezing point of a solution than does a nonelectrolyte of the same molality. The greater the total concentration of ions, the lower the freezing point and the higher the boiling point of the solution.

* QUESTIONS

1. Compared to pure water, a 1.0 m solution of NaCl will have a

(1) higher boiling point and a higher freezing point
(2) higher boiling point and a lower freezing point
(3) lower boiling point and a higher freezing point
(4) lower boiling point and a lower freezing point

2. Which 0.1 molal solution has the lowest freezing point? (1) $C_6H_{12}O_6$ (2) $(NH_4)_2SO_4$ (3) KBr (4) $CuSO_4$

3. Which 0.1 molal solution has the highest freezing point? (1) $C_6H_{12}O_6$ (2) $(NH_4)_2SO_4$ (3) KBr (4) $CuSO_4$

4. A 1-kilogram sample of water will have the highest freezing point when it contains (1) 1×10^{17} dissolved particles (2) 1×10^{19} dissolved particles (3) 1×10^{21} dissolved particles (4) 1×10^{23} dissolved particles

5. Which solution will freeze at the *lowest* temperature? (1) 1 mole of sugar in 500 g of water (2) 1 mole of sugar in 1,000 g of water (3) 2 moles of sugar in 500 g of water (4) 2 moles of sugar in 1,000 g of water

CALORIMETRY

✳ Calorimeters.
Most chemical reactions liberate energy or consume energy due to the making and breaking of chemical bonds. The amount of energy released or absorbed in a chemical reaction can be measured with a device called a **calorimeter**. A calorimeter is insulated to prevent heat exchange with the environment. Within the calorimeter, the reaction occurs in a sealed vessel that is surrounded by water. If the reaction releases energy, the temperature of the water rises. If the reaction absorbs energy, the temperature of the water falls.

Calories.
The amount of energy released or absorbed in chemical reactions is measured in units called calories. A **calorie** is the amount of heat needed to raise the temperature of 1 gram of water 1C°. One thousand calories is a **kilocalorie** (kcal).

The number of calories of energy lost or gained in a chemical reaction (Q) can be calculated by the following equation:

$$Q = (\Delta t)(M_w)$$

where Δt is the change in temperature (C°) of the water within the calorimeter, and M_w is the mass of the water within the calorimeter, in grams.

Heat of Fusion.
Energy changes are also associated with phase changes. Energy is required to change a solid to a liquid or a liquid to a gas. The **heat of fusion** is the amount of energy needed to melt 1 gram of a solid at its melting point. The **heat of vaporization** is the amount of energy needed to vaporize 1 gram of a liquid at its boiling point.

Energy is released when a liquid is frozen or when a gas is liquefied. The energy released during freezing (solidification) is numerically equal to the heat of fusion for the solid. The energy released during liquefaction is numerically equal to the heat of vaporization for the liquid.

Sample Problem
How much energy is required to raise the temperature of 100 grams of water from 20°C to 30°C?

Solution: The problem can be solved by using the formula:

$$Q = (\Delta t)(M_w)$$

$$Q = (10)(100) = 1,000 \text{ calories}$$

QUESTIONS

1. The temperature of a sample of water is changed from 15°C to 25°C by the addition of 500 calories. What is the mass of the water? (1) 10 g (2) 50 g (3) 100 g (4) 5,000 g

2. A sample of water is heated from 10°C to 15°C by the addition of 30 calories of heat. What is the mass of the water? (1) 5 g (2) 6 g (3) 30 g (4) 150 g

3. A 5-gram sample of water is heated so that its temperature increases from 10°C to 15°C. The total amount of heat energy absorbed by the water is (1) 25 calories (2) 20 calories (3) 15 calories (4) 5 calories

4. The number of calories needed to raise the temperature of 100 grams of water 10C° is the same as the number of calories needed to raise the temperature of 1,000 grams of water (1) 1C° (2) 0.1C° (3) 10C° (4) 100C°

✳ 5. How many calories are needed to change 100 grams of ice at 0°C to water at 0°C? (The heat of fusion of water = 80 cal/gram.) (1) 0.80 (2) 80 (3) 800 (4) 8,000

6. If 15 calories of heat energy are added to 1 gram of water at 20°C, the resulting temperature of the water will be (1) −10°C (2) 5°C (3) 35°C (4) 50°C

7. When a sample of 25 grams of water is cooled from 20°C to 10°C, the number of calories of heat energy released is (1) 10 (2) 25 (3) 200 (4) 250

8. When a 5-gram sample of a substance is burned in a calorimeter, 3 kilocalories (3,000 calories) of energy are released. The energy released per gram of substance is (1) 600 calories (2) 1,700 calories (3) 5,000 calories (4) 15,000 calories

✳ 9. According to Reference Table I (see page 108), how many calories are released when 2 moles of NaOH(s) are dissolved in water? (1) 5.3 kcal (2) 10.6 kcal (3) 13.8 kcal (4) 21.2 kcal

10. When any substance solidifies, each gram of the substance loses an amount of energy equal to its heat of (1) fusion (2) reaction (3) sublimation (4) vaporization

UNIT 6 Kinetics and Equilibrium

KINETICS

Chemical kinetics is concerned with the rates at which chemical reactions occur and the physical mechanisms, or pathways, along which they proceed.

The speed, or *rate*, at which a reaction occurs can be measured experimentally. Rates are expressed in terms of the quantity of product produced or reactant consumed per unit of time. The rate of reaction may also be expressed in terms of the decrease in reactant concentration (molarity) per unit time.

The *mechanism* of a chemical reaction is the sequence of intermediate reactions that make up the overall reaction. The number of intermediate steps depends on the individual reaction. Chemical equations generally show only the overall process, or net reaction, not the intermediate steps and products.

Energy in Chemical Reactions.
All chemical reactions involve changes in potential and kinetic energy. Recall that chemical energy—the energy stored in chemical bonds—is a form of potential energy. **Enthalpy** is a measure of the potential energy stored in the chemical bonds of the reactants and products in a chemical reaction.

Heat of Reaction. The **heat**, or enthalpy, **of reaction**, ΔH, is the difference in heat content (H) between the products and reactants of a chemical reaction. ΔH is often expressed in kilocalories/mol.

$$\Delta H = H_{products} - H_{reactants}$$

When energy is released by a reaction, the potential energy of the products is less than the potential energy of the reactants. Such a reaction is said to be **exothermic**. In an exothermic reaction, ΔH is negative. When energy is absorbed by a reaction, the potential energy of the products is greater than the potential energy of the reactants. Such a reaction is said to be **endothermic**. In an endothermic reaction, ΔH is positive.

Energy changes are sometimes included in a chemical equation along with reactants and products. It is necessary to specify the phase of the reactants and products when ΔH is indicated for a chemical change because phase changes themselves involve energy changes. For example, the formation of $NO_2(g)$ from its elements is endothermic. The equation for the reaction can be shown in two ways:

$$8.1 \text{ kcal} + \tfrac{1}{2}N_2(g) + O_2(g) \rightarrow NO_2(g)$$

$$\tfrac{1}{2}N_2(g) + O_2(g) \rightarrow NO_2(g) \quad \Delta H = 8.1 \text{ kcal/mol}$$

If $NO_2(s)$ were the product, the value of ΔH would be different because energy is involved in the change from gas to solid.

The exothermic reaction for the formation of NaCl(s) from its elements can be represented by either of the following equations:

$$Na(s) + \tfrac{1}{2}Cl_2(g) \rightarrow NaCl(s) + 98.2 \text{ kcal}$$

$$Na(s) + \tfrac{1}{2}Cl_2(g) \rightarrow NaCl(s)$$

$$\Delta H = -98.2 \text{ kcal/mol}$$

Activation Energy. All chemical reactions, whether exothermic or endothermic, require an initial input of energy to proceed. The minimum energy required to initiate a chemical reaction is called the **activation energy**. The activation energy provides colliding molecules with enough energy for an effective collision, that is, a collision in which reactants are converted into products.

When activation energy is supplied to the reactants, the resulting collisions produce a short-lived intermediate species that has the properties of a molecule. This intermediate species is called an **activation complex**. Most activated complexes cannot be isolated from reacting mixtures.

Potential Energy Diagrams. The relationship between the activation energy of a reaction and the change in enthalpy for that reaction can be shown graphically in a **potential energy diagram**. As shown in Figure 6-1 on page 40, reading from left to right, in an exothermic reaction, the potential energy of the reactants is greater than the potential energy of the products. Reading from right to left, in an endothermic reaction, the potential energy of the products is greater than the potential energy of the reactants.

Observe that in both exothermic and endothermic reactions, the potential energy of the intermediate phase, the activated complex, is greater than the potential energy of either reactants or products. Note, also, how the presence of a catalyst provides another pathway for the reaction with *lower* activation energy. In the diagram, the vertical distance from the reactants to the crest of the curve is the activation energy; the vertical distance from the reactants to the products is the change in enthalpy, or heat of reaction (ΔH). The horizontal axis is called the reaction

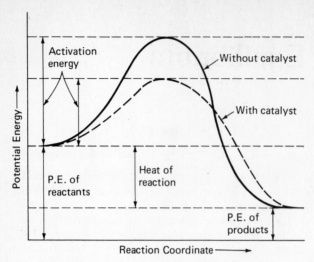

Figure 6-1. A potential energy diagram.

coordinate, which represents the progress of the reaction or the passage of time during the reaction.

Factors That Affect Reaction Rate.

Chemical reactions occur when atoms, ions, or molecules collide and produce different substances. The rate of chemical reaction is determined by the rate of these collisions and by the fraction of the collisions that is effective in producing new species. The rate and effectiveness of the collisions are affected by the nature of the reactants, their concentrations, the temperature of the system, the surface area of contact, and the presence or absence of catalysts.

Nature of Reactants. In chemical reactions, chemical bonds are broken and new bonds are formed. The nature of the bonds in the reactants is an important factor in determining reaction rate. Reactions that require few changes in bond arrangement proceed more rapidly than do those that require many changes. Reactions of ionic compounds in water solutions proceed almost instantaneously because the oppositely charged mobile ions are randomly distributed and readily attracted to one another. Reactions that require the breaking of covalent bonds usually proceed slowly at ordinary temperatures.

Concentration of Reactants. An increase in concentration of one or more of the reactants generally increases the rate of a reaction because of the increased frequency of collisions between reacting particles. A decrease in concentration of one or more of the reactants generally produces a corresponding decrease in the reaction rate. Because the compression of a gas effectively increases the concentration of the gas (the same number of particles is made to fit into a smaller volume), an increase in pressure generally results in an increase in the reaction rate between gases.

Temperature. As discussed in Unit 1 (page 1), temperature is a measure of the average kinetic energy of the particles in a system. The greater the kinetic energy, the higher is the temperature and the greater is the velocity of the particles in the system. As particle velocity increases, both the rate and effectiveness of the collisions increase. Thus, increasing the temperature increases the reaction rate, while decreasing the temperature decreases the reaction rate.

Surface Area. The extent of the area of contact between reacting substances is important in heterogeneous reaction systems—that is, where reactions take place between more than one phase. Increasing the surface area of the reactants increases the number of particles that are exposed to contact with other reactants. An increase in surface area effectively increases the number of particle collisions. For example, a given mass of sawdust will burn much more rapidly than a log of the same mass because the sawdust has a much larger surface area for contact with oxygen. Any method of increasing the surface area of a reactant, such as cutting, grinding, or spraying, will increase the rate of reaction. In homogeneous (one-phase) systems, such as solutions or mixtures of gases, there is no observable surface of contact between phases.

Catalysis. A catalyst is a substance that increases the rate of a reaction without itself being permanently altered chemically by the overall reaction. Catalysts do not initiate chemical reactions; they merely increase the rate of reactions that would normally occur. Catalysts provide a new reaction pathway that has a lower activation energy. Thus, more particles have the energy necessary for an effective collision.

QUESTIONS

1. Based on Reference Table I (see page 108), which reaction has a positive heat of reaction?
(1) $CH_4(g) + 2O_2(g) \rightarrow CO_2(g) + 2H_2O(\ell)$
(2) $CO(g) + \frac{1}{2}O_2(g) \rightarrow CO_2(g)$
(3) $NH_4Cl(s) \xrightarrow{H_2O} NH_4^+(aq) + Cl^-(aq)$
(4) $H^+(aq) + OH^-(aq) \rightarrow H_2O(\ell)$

2. Based on Reference Table I (see page 108), which of the following reactions releases the greatest amount of energy?
(1) $CH_4(g) + 2O_2(g) \rightarrow CO_2(g) + 2H_2O(\ell)$
(2) $CO(g) + \frac{1}{2}O_2(g) \rightarrow CO_2(g)$
(3) $C_8H_{18}(\ell) + \frac{25}{2}O_2(g) \rightarrow 8CO_2(g) + 9H_2O(\ell)$
(4) $C_6H_{12}O_6(s) + 6O_2(g) \rightarrow 6CO_2(g) + 6H_2O(\ell)$

3. Which potential energy diagram represents the following reaction?

$$A + heat \rightarrow B$$

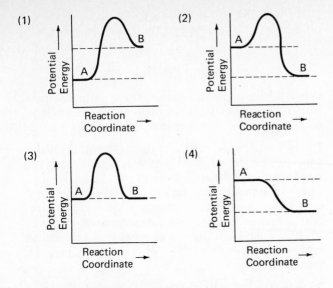

(1)   (2)   (3)   (4)

4. Based on Reference Table G (see page 107), how many kilocalories of heat are produced when 0.5 mole of MgO(s) is formed from its elements? (1) 63.1 (2) 71.9 (3) 143.8 (4) 287.6

Base your answers to questions 5–8 on the accompanying potential energy diagram.

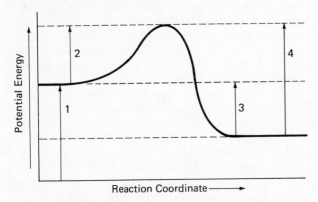

5. The activation energy for the reverse reaction is represented by interval (1) 1 (2) 2 (3) 3 (4) 4
6. The heat of reaction (ΔH) is represented by (1) 1 (2) 2 (3) 3 (4) 4
7. The interval 1 represents the (1) catalyzed energy (2) potential energy of the reactants (3) activation energy of the reverse reaction (4) free energy change for the forward reaction
8. Interval 1 minus interval 3 represents the (1) potential energy of the catalyst (2) potential energy of the products (3) heat of reaction (4) activation energy

9. In a gas phase system at constant temperature, an increase in pressure will (1) increase the activation energy (2) decrease the activation energy (3) increase the reaction rate (4) decrease the reaction rate
10. Which phrase best describes the following reaction?

$$H_2O(\ell) + \text{energy} \rightarrow H_2(g) + \tfrac{1}{2}O_2(g)$$

(1) exothermic, releasing energy (2) exothermic, absorbing energy (3) endothermic, releasing energy (4) endothermic, absorbing energy
11. In a reversible reaction, the difference between the activation energy of the forward reaction and the activation energy of the reverse reaction is equal to the (1) activation complex (2) heat of reaction (3) potential energy of reactants (4) potential energy of products

Base your answers to questions 12 and 13 on the potential energy diagram below.

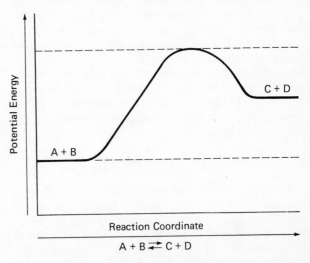

A + B ⇌ C + D

12. Compared to the potential energy of the activated complex of the forward reaction, the potential energy of the activated complex of the reverse reaction is (1) less (2) greater (3) the same
13. Compared to the activation energy of the forward reaction, the activation energy of the reverse reaction is (1) less (2) greater (3) the same

14. In a chemical reaction, the difference in potential energy between the products and the reactants is equal to (1) ΔS (2) ΔG (3) ΔH (4) ΔT
15. For any chemical reaction, the heat of reaction is equal to the (1) heat content of products minus the heat content of reactants (2) heat content of reactants minus the heat content of products (3) entropy of products minus entropy of reactants (4) entropy of reactants minus entropy of products
16. Which of the following does *not* affect reaction rate? (1) nature of products (2) temperature (3) catalysts (4) concentration of reactants
17. When a catalyst lowers the activation energy of a reaction, the rate of both the forward and reverse reactions (1) increases (2) decreases (3) remains the same
18. The addition of a catalyst to a reaction changes the potential energy of the (1) products (2) reactants (3) catalyst (4) activated complexes
19. Which change may occur when a catalyst is added to a reaction system? (1) Activation energy for reaction decreases. (2) The potential energy of the reac-

tants increases.   (3) The potential energy of the products decreases.   (4) The heat of the reaction decreases.
20.   In the equilibrium system

$$A(g) + 2B(g) + heat \leftrightarrows AB_2(g)$$

the rate of the forward reaction will increase if there is   (1) an increase in pressure   (2) an increase in the volume of the reaction vessel   (3) a decrease in pressure   (4) a decrease in the concentration of $A(g)$
21.   As the average kinetic energy in a reaction system decreases, the rate of reaction   (1) increases   (2) decreases   (3) remains the same
22.   An increase in temperature increases the rate of a chemical reaction because the   (1) activation energy increases   (2) activation energy decreases   (3) number of molecular collisions increases   (4) number of molecular collisions decreases
23.   As the temperature in a reaction system increases, the number of effective collisions between reactant particles   (1) first increases, then decreases   (2) decreases, only   (3) first decreases, then increases   (4) increases, only

EQUILIBRIUM

Many chemical reactions are reversible; that is, the reactants can be converted into the products and the products can be converted into the reactants. In reversible reactions, the concentrations of reactants and products eventually reach an equilibrium. At **equilibrium**, the opposing reactions are in a state of balance, both occurring at the same rate.

Chemical equilibria are described as *dynamic* because even at equilibrium, changes are still occurring. The interaction of the particles of the reactants in one direction is balanced by the interaction of the particles of the products in the opposite direction. In reversible reactions, equilibrium can be reached either from the forward direction or from the reverse direction.

The point at which equilibrium is reached varies with the reaction. In some cases, the amounts of reactants and products may be nearly equal at equilibrium. In other situations, equilibrium may be reached when only a small quantity of reactants remains or when only a small quantity of product has formed. Thus, at equilibrium, although the concentrations of reactants and products may *not* be equal, the rates of the opposing reactions are always equal.

In a system that has reached equilibrium, the composition of the equilibrium mixture (the point of equilibrium) will be affected by changes in temperature, pressure, or concentration of any of the components. When an equilibrium is disturbed, or displaced, by such changes, the rates of the opposing reactions will no longer be equal. The forward and reverse reactions then proceed toward a new and different equilibrium point where there are different concentrations of each component.

Phase Change Equilibrium.   In general, phase changes are reversible. For example:

$$gas \rightleftarrows liquid$$

$$liquid \rightleftarrows solid$$

When a phase change is reversible, a **phase equilibrium** is set up. Phase equilibria are dependent on temperature and pressure.

Gases in Liquids.   In a closed system, equilibrium can be established between a gas dissolved in a liquid and the undissolved gas above the liquid. The equilibrium between the dissolved and undissolved phases is affected by temperature and pressure. As temperature increases, the solubility of gases in liquids decreases. As pressure increases, the solubility of gases in liquids increases.

Solution Equilibrium.   The solubility of a given solute in a given solvent is defined as the maximum mass of that solute that can be dissolved in a given quantity of the solute under specified conditions.

Solids in Liquids.   When a solid solute is present in excess in a solution—that is, when there is more solute present than can dissolve in the volume of solvent at some fixed temperature—an equilibrium may develop between the dissolved and undissolved solute. Some particles of the solid solute go into solution, while some of the dissolved solute crystallizes and precipitates out of solution. When such an equilibrium develops, the solution is said to be **saturated** with respect to the solute. When the concentration of solute is less than the equilibrium value, the solution is said to be **unsaturated**.

It is sometimes possible to prepare a solution that contains more solute than the equilibrium value. Such solutions, which are said to be **supersaturated**, are unstable. A supersaturated solution, however, cannot exist in contact with the undissolved solute without precipitating the excess solute from solution.

For most solid-in-liquid solutions, the solubility of the solid solute in the liquid solvent increases as temperature increases.

Solubility Curves.   Reference Table D (see page 106) shows the solubility curves of various substances over a temperature range of 0° to 100°C. Note that solubility is given in grams of solute per 100 grams of water. From such information, it is possible to determine which proposed mixture of solute and solvent will be unsaturated, saturated, or supersaturated.

For example, from the solubility curve of KNO_3, note that about 50 grams will dissolve in 100 grams of water at 32°C. This is the composition of the *saturated* solution at 32°C. Any quantity of KNO_3 *less* than 50 grams will also dissolve in 100 grams of H_2O at that temperature, but the solution is *unsaturated.* This means that the solution can dissolve additional KNO_3 solid. If a saturated KNO_3 solution at 32°C is cooled to 10°, the excess solute (about 28 grams) will precipitate. Under certain conditions and with certain solutes, for example with sodium acetate, cooling the saturated solution does *not* precipitate the excess solid. The excess solid remains dissolved, and the solution is *supersaturated.*

QUESTIONS

Questions 1–9 are based on Reference Table D (see page 106).

1. A solution contains 90 grams of salt dissolved in 100 grams of water at 40°C. The solution could be an unsaturated solution of (1) KCl (2) KNO_3 (3) NaCl (4) $NaNO_3$

2. Which of the following substances is most soluble (in grams per 100 g of water) at 60°C? (1) NH_4Cl (2) KCl (3) NaCl (4) NH_3

3. Which saturated solution is most concentrated at 20°C? (1) KI (2) KNO_3 (3) $NaNO_3$ (4) SO_2

4. At 10°C, a saturated solution is formed when 23 grams of a particular substance are dissolved in 100 grams of water. This substance could be (1) $NaNO_3$ (2) KNO_3 (3) NH_4Cl (4) KCl

5. What mass of KNO_3 is needed to saturate 50 grams of water at 70°C? (1) 130 grams (2) 69 grams (3) 45 grams (4) 22.5 grams

6. What is the approximate difference between the masses of $KClO_3$ and KNO_3 that will dissolve to form saturated solutions in 100 grams of water at 40°C? (1) 16 grams (2) 22 grams (3) 46 grams (4) 62 grams

7. A solution contains 70 grams of $NaNO_3$ in 100 grams of water at 10°C. What additional mass of $NaNO_3$ is required to saturate this solution? (1) 9 grams (2) 20 grams (3) 60 grams (4) 70 grams

8. As temperature increases from 30°C to 40°C, the solubility of KNO_3 in 100 grams of water increases by approximately (1) 5 grams (2) 10 grams (3) 15 grams (4) 25 grams

9. What mass of sodium chloride is required to saturate 500 grams of water at 50°C? (1) 38 grams (2) 50 grams (3) 190 grams (4) 500 grams

Chemical Equilibrium.
In a chemical reaction that has reached equilibrium, reactants are converted to products at the same rate that products are reconverted to reactants—forward and reverse reactions occur at the same rate. When a chemical system is at equilibrium, its observable physical properties, such as color, pressure, and temperature, remain unchanged.

Law of Chemical Equilibrium. For a reaction at equilibrium, the ratio of the product of the molar concentrations of the substances on the right side of the equation to the product of the molar concentrations of the substances on the left side of the equation, each raised to the power of its coefficient in the balanced reaction, is a constant. The system at equilibrium can be represented by the following general equation:

$$aA + bB \rightleftarrows cC + dD$$

The equilibrium constant K_{eq} or K can then be expressed in the general form:

$$K_{eq} = \frac{[C]^c[D]^d}{[A]^a[B]^b}$$

In this expression, note that the products are found in the numerator and the reactants are the denominator. The bracketed terms represent concentrations measured in moles per liter. The coefficients from the balanced equation (the moles of the components) are the exponents for each concentration term.

In calculating the equilibrium constant, the only terms that are used are those whose concentrations are variable, usually gases and solutes in water solutions. Since the concentration of a solid or a pure liquid is not variable, values for species in these phases do not appear in equilibrium constant calculations. In reality, these values are constant and do not affect the calculations.

The magnitude of K_{eq} is used to predict the extent to which a chemical reaction will proceed. A large value for K indicates that the system at equilibrium favors the formation of products. A small value for K indicates that the system at equilibrium favors the formation of reactants.

The equilibrium constants for other kinds of equilibria, to be discussed later, have special symbols and names (see Table 6-1).

✳ Solubility Product Constant. The equilibrium constant for a dissolved (dissociated) salt in

Table 6-1. Equilibrium Constants

Symbol	Kind of Reaction	Example
K_a	Ionization of a weak acid	$HNO_2 \rightleftarrows H^+(aq) + NO_2^-(aq)$
K_b	Ionization of a weak base	$NH_3 + HOH \rightleftarrows NH_4^+(aq) + OH^-(aq)$
K_{sp}	Dissociation of a nearly insoluble salt	$AgCl(s) \rightleftarrows Ag^+(aq) + Cl^-(aq)$
K_w	Ion product for water (self-ionization of water)	$HOH + HOH \rightleftarrows H_3O^+(aq) + OH^-(aq)$

equilibrium with its undissolved (undissociated) form is known as the **solubility product constant**. This constant, which is given the symbol K_{sp}, is applied to water solutions of slightly soluble or nearly insoluble salts. The more soluble the substance, the larger is the value of K_{sp}. As with all equilibrium constants, the value of K_{sp} depends on the temperature. Since most salts have increased solubility at higher temperatures, their K_{sp} values increase with temperature.

The dissociation reaction is considered to be the forward reaction, and the precipitation reaction is considered to be the reverse reaction. For example, in a saturated solution of ZnS,

$$ZnS(s) \rightleftarrows Zn^{2+}(aq) + S^{2-}(aq)$$

the dissociation of ZnS is the forward reaction, while the precipitation of solid ZnS from solution is the reverse reaction.

Following the law of chemical equilibrium,

$$K_{eq} = \frac{[Zn^{2+}][S^{2-}]}{[ZnS]}$$

Since the concentration of the solid [ZnS] is constant, the value of the denominator is constant. Thus, it is incorporated into the value of the solubility product constant (see page 43). The expression can be simplified to:

$$K_{sp} = [Zn^{2+}][S^{2-}]$$

Thus, the solubility product constant, K_{sp}, is equal to the product of the concentrations of the dissociated ions. Again, the brackets signify molar concentrations.

The magnitude of K_{sp} is used to compare the solubilities of substances that are not very soluble in water. The K_{sp} value increases with increasing solubility. The solubility product constants for various compounds are given in Reference Table M (see page 109).

QUESTIONS

1. Which is the correct equilibrium expression for the following system?

$$A(g) + B(g) \rightleftarrows C(g) + D(g)$$

(1) $K = [C][D]$

(2) $K = \dfrac{[C][D]}{[A][B]}$

(3) $K = \dfrac{[C] + [D]}{[A] + [B]}$

(4) $K = \dfrac{[A] + [B]}{[C] + [D]}$

2. Which is the correct equilibrium expression for the following system?

$$H_2(g) + I_2(g) \rightleftarrows 2HI(g)$$

(1) $K = \dfrac{[HI]^2}{[H_2][I_2]}$

(2) $K = \dfrac{[HI]^2}{[2H][2I]}$

(3) $K = \dfrac{[H_2][I_2]}{[HI]^2}$

(4) $K = \dfrac{[HI]^2}{[H][I]}$

3. Which is the correct equilibrium expression for the following system?

$$2A(g) + B(s) \rightleftarrows 3C(g)$$

(1) $K = \dfrac{[C]^3}{2[A]^2[B]}$

(2) $K = \dfrac{[C]^3}{[A]^2}$

(3) $K = \dfrac{[C]^3}{[A]^2 + [B]}$

(4) $K = \dfrac{[C]^3}{[2A][B]}$

4. For the equilibrium system

$$H_2(g) + \tfrac{1}{2}O_2(g) \rightleftarrows H_2O(g) + heat$$

the value of the equilibrium constant can be changed by (1) changing the pressure (2) changing the temperature (3) adding more O_2 (4) adding a catalyst

5. When a system is at equilibrium, the concentrations of the reactants (1) increase (2) decrease (3) remain the same

✲ 6. For the solubility equilibrium system

$$AgCl(s) \rightleftarrows Ag^+(aq) + Cl^-(aq)$$

the equilibrium constant will change when there is an increase in the (1) concentration of Ag^+ ions (2) pressure (3) concentration of Cl^- ions (4) temperature

7. In any chemical system that has reached equilibrium (1) the forward reaction stops (2) the reverse reaction stops (3) the concentrations of products and reactants are equal (4) the rates of the forward and reverse reactions are equal

8. Which pair represents the substances formed in the reverse reaction for the equilibrium expression

$$K = \frac{[X][Y]}{[A][B]}$$

(1) A and B (2) A and X (3) B and Y (4) X and Y

✲ 9. Based on Reference Table M (see page 109), at 25°C, which salt is less soluble than AgBr? (1) Li_2CO_3 (2) AgCl (3) $BaSO_4$ (4) $PbCO_3$

✲ 10. Based on Reference Table M (see page 109), in a saturated solution of $PbCrO_4$ at 1 atmosphere and 298 K, the product of $[Pb^{2+}]$ and $[CrO_4^{2-}]$ is equal to (1) 2.8×10^{-13} (2) 1.3×10^{-7} (3) 1.8×10^{14} (4) 1.8×10^{-7}

✲ 11. Which is the solubility product constant expression for the following system?

$$Mg(OH)_2(s) \rightleftarrows Mg^{2+}(aq) + 2OH^-(aq)$$

(1) $[Mg^{2+}][2OH^-]$

(2) $[Mg^{2+}] + 2[OH^-]$

(3) $[Mg^{2+}][OH^-]^2$

(4) $[Mg^{2+}] + [OH^-]$

✲ 12. When AgBr(s) dissolves in water, what is the ratio of Ag^+ ions to Br^- ions?

(1) $1:1$

(2) $\dfrac{7.7 \times 10^{-13}}{1.0 \times 10^{-14}}$

(3) $\dfrac{7.7 \times 10^{-13}}{7.7 \times 10^{-1}}$

(4) $\dfrac{7.7 \times 10^{-13}}{1.0 \times 10^{-7}}$

13. For the reaction A + B $\leftrightharpoons$ AB, the greatest amount of AB would be produced if the equilibrium constant of the reaction was to be (1) 1×10^{-5} (2) 1×10^{-1} (3) 1×10^1 (4) 1×10^5

14. Which reaction has the equilibrium expression

$$K = \frac{[A][B]^2}{[AB_2]}$$

(1) $AB_2(g) \rightleftarrows A(g) + 2B(g)$
(2) $2AB(g) \rightleftarrows A(g) + B_2(g)$
(3) $A(g) + 2B(g) \rightleftarrows AB_2(g)$
(4) $A(g) + B_2(g) \rightleftarrows 2AB(g)$

15. Given the system

$$2O_3(g) \rightleftarrows 3O_2(g) \qquad (K_{eq} = 2.5 \times 10^{23})$$

At equilibrium, the concentrations of O_3 and O_2 are (1) constant (2) increasing (3) decreasing

✱ 16. Based on Reference Table M (see page 109), which salt forms a saturated solution that is most dilute? (1) AgCl (2) $BaSO_4$ (3) $CaSO_4$ (4) $PbCrO_4$

Le Chatelier's Principle.

When a system at equilibrium is disturbed, the rates of the opposing reactions change so that they are no longer equal. These reactions then proceed toward a new equilibrium with new and different concentrations and other properties. Disturbances to systems in equilibrium are sometimes referred to as "stresses." According to Le Chatelier's principle, when a system at equilibrium is subjected to a stress, the system will shift so as to relieve the stress and move toward a new equilibrium.

The following factors affect systems at equilibrium:

Concentration. Increasing the concentration of one substance in an equilibrium system causes the system to shift so that some of this increased quantity is consumed. Conversely, removal of a substance from an equilibrium system causes the system to shift so that more of that substance is formed. In both cases, a new equilibrium will eventually be established.

Pressure. Changes in pressure affect equilibrium systems containing gases. An increase in pressure causes a shift in the equilibrium in the direction favoring the formation of fewer moles of gas. A decrease in pressure causes a shift in the equilibrium in the direction favoring the formation of more moles of gas. A change in pressure has no effect on a system in which the number of moles of gas molecules does not change:

$$H_2(g) + Cl_2(g) \rightleftarrows 2HCl(g)$$

Temperature. In a system at equilibrium, an increase in temperature increases the rates of both the forward and reverse reactions. However, any temperature increase has a greater effect on the reaction with the higher activation energy. In equilibrium systems, the endothermic reaction has the greater energy of activation. Thus, an increase in temperature favors the endothermic change.

Catalysis. Addition of a catalyst to a system at equilibrium increases the rates of both opposing reactions equally. There is no net change in equilibrium concentrations. The presence of a catalyst may cause equilibrium to be reached more quickly, but it does not change the point of equilibrium.

The Haber Process.

Le Chatelier's principle is employed in the Haber process for the commercial preparation of ammonia gas (see page 79). Note the reaction that occurs:

$$N_2(g) + 3H_2(g) \rightleftarrows 2NH_3(g) + 22 \text{ kcal}$$

Effect of Concentration. As indicated previously, an increase in concentration of the reactants in an equilibrium is offset by shifting the equilibrium toward the formation of more products. Thus, increasing the concentrations of N_2 and H_2 drives the equilibrium to the right. If enough NH_3 is formed, the rate of the reverse reaction—the decomposition of NH_3—is favored. In actual practice, NH_3 is removed so that the rate of the reverse reaction decreases.

Effect of Pressure. In the Haber process, reactants and product are gaseous. An increase in pressure favors the formation of fewer moles of gas. Note that 4 moles of reactants produce 2 moles of product. Thus, an increase in pressure favors formation of product, while a decrease in pressure favors reactants. A change in pressure in an equilibrium system has no effect when the numbers of moles do not change. Thus, increased pressure favors the formation of ammonia.

Effect of Temperature. Recall that temperature increases reaction rate. This means that, in an equilibrium, an increase in temperature favors both the forward and reverse reactions. As noted previously, the effect is greater on the reaction with the greater activation energy. Thus, in an endothermic change such as the Haber process, increasing the temperature favors the formation of reactants. A temperature is selected that increases the rate of formation of products while minimizing the reverse reaction.

Effect of Catalysts. In the Haber process, suitable catalysts are used so that equilibrium can be reached quickly.

✱ The Common Ion Effect.

The solubility of a slightly soluble salt is decreased in the presence of a solution that contains a common ion, that is, an ion that appears in both the salt and the solution.

The solubility equilibrium

$$BaSO_4(s) \rightleftarrows Ba^{2+}(aq) + SO_4^{2-}(aq)$$

is decreased by the addition of either $Ba^{2+}(aq)$

Kinetics and Equilibrium

ions or SO_4^{2-} (aq) ions from a source other than $BaSO_4$. For example, the addition of $BaCl_2$ as a solid or as a water solution introduces the common ion Ba^{2+} (aq) to this equilibrium system. This favors the reverse reaction, causing precipitation of $BaSO_4$(s). Thus, the solubility of $BaSO_4$ is decreased by the addition of the Ba^{2+} (aq) ion, an ion common to both the original $BaSO_4$ and the added $BaCl_2$. Addition of Na_2SO_4 would have a similar effect—in this case, the common ion would be SO_4^{2-} (aq).

QUESTIONS

1. In the equilibrium system

$$2SO_2(g) + O_2(g) \rightleftarrows 2SO_3(g) + heat$$

the concentration of SO_3 may be increased by (1) increasing the concentration of SO_2 (2) decreasing the concentration of SO_2 (3) increasing the temperature (4) decreasing the concentration of O_2

2. Given the reaction at constant temperature:

$$CO_2(s) \rightleftarrows CO_2(g)$$

As pressure increases, the amount of CO_2(g) present (1) increases (2) decreases (3) remains the same

3. Given the reaction at equilibrium:

$$H_2(g) + Cl_2(g) \rightleftarrows 2HCl(g) + heat$$

The equilibrium will shift to the left when there is an increase in (1) temperature (2) pressure (3) H_2 concentration (4) Cl_2 concentration

4. Given the reaction at equilibrium:

$$A(g) + B(g) \rightleftarrows C(g) + D(g)$$

At constant temperature and pressure, an increase in the concentration of A(g) causes (1) an increase in the concentration of B(g) (2) a decrease in the concentration of B(g) (3) a decrease in the concentration of C(g) (4) a decrease in the concentration of D(g)

5. Given the reaction at equilibrium:

$$H_2(g) + Cl_2(g) \rightleftarrows 2HCl(g) + heat$$

The equilibrium will shift to the right when there is an increase in (1) temperature (2) pressure (3) concentration of H_2(g) (4) concentration of HCl(g)

∗ 6. Given the equilibrium:

$$AgCl(s) \rightleftarrows Ag^+(aq) + Cl^-(aq)$$

The addition of KCl to this system will cause a shift in the equilibrium to the (1) left, and the concentration of Ag^+(aq) ions will increase (2) right, and the concentration of Ag^+(aq) ions will increase (3) left, and the concentration of Ag^+(aq) ions will decrease (4) right, and the concentration of Ag^+(aq) ions will decrease

7. Which of the following equilibrium systems at constant temperature will shift to the right if the pressure is increased?

(1) $2H_2(g) + O_2(g) \rightleftarrows 2H_2O(g)$
(2) $2SO_3(g) \rightleftarrows 2SO_2(g) + O_2(g)$
(3) $2NO(g) \rightleftarrows N_2(g) + O_2(g)$
(4) $2CO_2(g) \rightleftarrows 2CO(g) + O_2(g)$

8. For a system at equilibrium, a catalyst (1) increases the rate of forward reaction only (2) increases the rate of reverse reaction only (3) increases the rates of forward and reverse reactions equally (4) increases the activation energy

9. In the Haber process,

$$N_2(g) + 3H_2(g) \rightleftarrows 2NH_3(g) + 22 \text{ kcal}$$

a larger yield of NH_3 is obtained when (1) temperature and pressure are decreased (2) temperature and pressure are increased (3) temperature is increased and pressure is decreased (4) temperature is decreased and pressure is increased

∗ SPONTANEOUS REACTIONS

A **spontaneous reaction** is one that occurs in nature under a given set of conditions. For example, iron rusts only when exposed to moisture and air. Under these conditions, iron continues to rust.

Two fundamental tendencies in nature provide the driving force for spontaneous chemical change. Reactions proceed when the products possess a lower energy (enthalpy) state and/or a more random, or disordered, state.

∗ Energy Changes.
At constant temperature and pressure, a system tends to undergo chemical change when it can move from a higher energy state to a lower energy state. Exothermic reactions proceed from a higher to a lower energy state with an overall decrease in enthalpy (stored energy). The amount of energy lost is represented by a negative ΔH. Thus, most spontaneous reactions are exothermic. Endothermic reactions proceed from a lower to a higher energy state with an overall increase in enthalpy (positive ΔH). Endothermic reactions may occur spontaneously when the temperature is increased above a certain point. Thus, the change in enthalpy alone does not determine whether a reaction will or will not occur spontaneously.

∗ Entropy Changes.
Entropy is a measure of the lack of organization in a system. Entropy is often referred to as randomness or disorder. It is related to the number of different ways in which the components of a system can arrange themselves. The solid phase, as in a crystal, is more ordered than the liquid phase. The component parts occupy fixed positions in the crystal lattice. The liquid phase is more ordered than the gas phase, where the arrangement of particles is more random than in any other phase.

Entropy is defined so that as the disorder in a system increases, its entropy increases. An increase in entropy during a phase change means that, in its final state, the system is more disordered than in its initial state. High entropy is favored by high temperatures.

At constant temperature, a system tends to change spontaneously so that in its final state the system has higher entropy than in its initial state. Thus, a system tends to change spontaneously from a state of greater order to a state of lesser order. For chemical systems, this change in entropy is represented quantitatively as ΔS. An increase in randomness has a positive value for ΔS.

* Predicting Spontaneous Reactions.

For any chemical system, the net effect of its tendency toward minimum energy and maximum entropy is called its **free energy change**. Free energy change, ΔG, is the difference between energy change (ΔH) and entropy change (ΔS). T is the Kelvin temperature.

$$\Delta G = \Delta H - T\Delta S$$

For a change to be spontaneous, its net free energy change (ΔG) must be negative. A system at equilibrium has no net driving force. The rate of forward reaction equals the rate of the reverse reaction. Hence, its free energy change is zero.

* QUESTIONS

1. Which change represents an increase in the entropy of a system?
(1) $NaCl(s) \rightarrow NaCl(aq)$
(2) $H_2O(\ell) \rightarrow H_2O(s)$
(3) $CO_2(g) \rightarrow CO_2(s)$
(4) $C_2H_5OH(g) \rightarrow C_2H_5OH(\ell)$
2. The ΔG of a chemical reaction refers to the change in (1) entropy (2) state (3) activation energy (4) free energy
3. Based on Reference Table G (see page 107), which compound forms spontaneously from its elements? (1) ethene (2) ethane (3) nitrogen (II) oxide (4) nitrogen (IV) oxide
4. For a chemical reaction, the free energy change, ΔG, is equal to (1) $\Delta H + T\Delta S$ (2) $\Delta H - T\Delta S$ (3) $T\Delta H + \Delta S$ (4) $T\Delta S - \Delta H$
5. The free energy change, ΔG, must be negative when (1) ΔH is positive and ΔS is positive (2) ΔH is positive and ΔS is negative (3) ΔH is negative and ΔS is positive (4) ΔH is negative and ΔS is negative
6. A chemical reaction will always occur spontaneously if the reaction has a (1) negative ΔG (2) positive ΔG (3) negative ΔH (4) positive ΔH
7. Which statement is true if the free energy change (ΔG) of a reaction is zero? (1) The rate of the forward reaction is zero. (2) The rate of the reverse reaction is zero. (3) The reaction is approaching equilibrium. (4) The reaction is at equilibrium.
8. Based on Reference Table G (see page 107), why does the reaction $K(s) + \frac{1}{2}Cl_2(g) \rightarrow KCl(s)$ occur spontaneously? (1) ΔS is positive (2) ΔS is negative (3) ΔG is positive (4) ΔG is negative
9. As a liquid solidifies at a given temperature and pressure, the degree of randomness of the system (1) increases (2) decreases (3) remains the same
10. At equilibrium:
(1) $\Delta H = 0$ (2) $\Delta S = 0$
(3) $\Delta G = 0$ (4) $\Delta H = \Delta S$

UNIT 7 Acids and Bases

ELECTROLYTES

An **electrolyte** is a substance that dissolves in water to form a solution that conducts an electric current. Water itself is a very weak electrolyte—pure water conducts electricity very poorly.

Characteristics of Electrolytes.
In 1887, the Swedish chemist Svante Arrhenius noted that all ionic compounds and many polar covalent compounds are electrolytes. He found that these substances dissociate, or ionize, to some extent in aqueous solution. The mobility of the dissociated ions permits the solution to conduct electricity. As noted in Unit 5 (page 37), electrolytes, because of their tendency to ionize, affect the colligative properties of aqueous solutions more strongly than do nonelectrolytes.

Dissociation Constants. An equilibrium expression can be written for the dissociation of an electrolyte AB.

$$AB \rightleftarrows A^+ + B^-$$

$$K = \frac{[A]^+[B]^-}{[AB]}$$

If AB is a strong electrolyte, the concentration of the undissociated AB is very small, and the value of K becomes very large, approaching infinity. Thus, dissociation constants are meaningful only for weak electrolytes. For weak electrolytes, the ratio of the product of the ionic concentrations to the undissociated form, at a fixed temperature, equals the **dissociation constant**, written K_d.

Acids, Bases, and Salts.
Most electrolytes can be classified as acids, bases, or salts. Arrhenius defined an **acid** as an electrolyte that yields hydrogen ions (H^+) as the only **cation** (positively charged ion) in aqueous solution. He defined a **base** as an electrolyte that yields hydroxide ions (OH^-) as the only **anion** (negatively charged ion) in an aqueous solution. **Salts** are ionic compounds that dissociate to form cations other than H^+ and anions other than OH^-. Since salts dissociate completely, they are strong electrolytes. Acids and bases, however, can be either strong or weak electrolytes, depending on the particular compound.

ACIDS

The term *acid* can be defined in more than one way. Before Arrhenius' findings, the definition of an acid was largely an **operational definition**—one based on observed characteristics, without interpretation of empirical evidence.

Characteristics of Acids.
The operational definition of acids was based on the following characteristics:

1. Acids in water solution conduct electricity. The degree of conductivity varies from one acid to another. Acids whose aqueous solutions are good conductors of electricity are strong acids; they are strong electrolytes. Acids whose aqueous solutions are poor conductors of electricity are weak acids; they are weak electrolytes.

2. Acids react with the metals below hydrogen in the "Table of Standard Electrode Potentials," Reference Table N (see page 110) to produce hydrogen gas. For example,

$$Mg(s) + 2HCl(aq) \rightarrow MgCl_2(aq) + H_2(g)$$

Acids that are also oxidizing agents, such as sulfuric acid, evolve hydrogen only in dilute solutions.

3. Acids cause reversible color changes in substances called **acid-base indicators**. Phenolphthalein and litmus are two such indicators. Litmus becomes red in acid solution; phenolphthalein becomes colorless.

4. Acids react with hydroxide compounds to form water and a salt. This type of reaction is referred to as **neutralization**. The following reaction is a neutralization reaction:

$$2KOH + H_2SO_4 \rightarrow K_2SO_4 + 2H_2O$$

5. Dilute water solutions of acids have a sour taste. *CAUTION: Although this property, like the others, can be confirmed experimentally, you should NEVER taste laboratory chemicals.* Sour taste in foods is due to the presence of acids: acetic acid is present in vinegar, citric acid is found in citrus fruits, and lactic acid is responsible for the sour taste of yogurt, sour milk, and sour cream.

The Arrhenius Theory of Acids.
According to Arrhenius' theory, the characteristic properties of acids are due to the formation of hydrogen ions. In general, the intensity of acidic properties increases as the hydrogen ion concentration increases. A strong acid is one that dissociates completely in solution; a weak acid is one that dissociates only partially. Arrhenius' definition applies only to aqueous solutions.

The Brönsted-Lowry Theory of Acids.
Brönsted and Lowry, in the 1920s, offered a definition of acids that expanded the definition pre-

sented by Arrhenius. Their definition includes nonaqueous as well as aqueous solutions. A Brönsted-Lowry acid is any species (molecular or ionic) that can donate a proton to another species. In this context, "proton" refers to the nucleus of a hydrogen atom. All substances that are Arrhenius acids are also acids according to the Brönsted-Lowry definition, but not all Brönsted-Lowry acids are Arrhenius acids. For example, in the reaction

$$NH_3 + H_2O \rightarrow NH_4^+ + OH^-$$

the water molecule donates a proton to the ammonia. Thus, in this case, water acts as an acid according to the Brönsted-Lowry definition. However, according to the Arrhenius definition, water would not be considered an acid because hydrogen ions were not the positive ions produced by the reaction.

The Brönsted-Lowry definition of an acid is a **conceptual definition**, one based on interpretation of observations and on empirical evidence. (An **operational definition** is based only on observations and does not include any interpretation or explanation.)

According to the Brönsted-Lowry theory, free hydrogen ions (protons) do not exist in solution. Instead, in aqueous solution, the H^+ (proton) bonds with a water molecule to form a hydrated proton called a **hydronium ion**, H_3O^+ (see Figure 7-1).

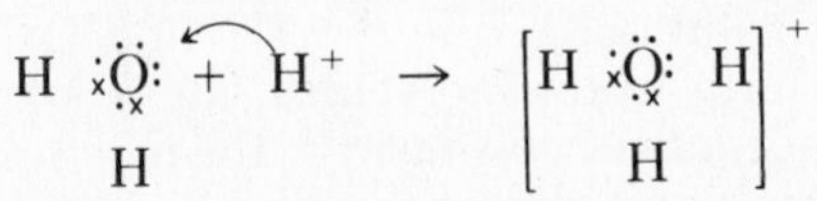

Figure 7-1. Formation of a hydronium ion, H_3O^+.

BASES

Like acids, bases can be defined both operationally and conceptually.

Characteristics of Bases.
Laboratory observations of the properties of basic (alkaline) substances led to an operational definition that includes the following characteristics:

1. Bases in water solution conduct electricity. Bases whose aqueous solutions conduct electricity relatively well are referred to as strong bases; they are also strong electrolytes. Bases whose aqueous solutions are poor conductors of electricity are referred to as weak bases; they are also weak electrolytes.

2. Bases cause reversible color changes in acid-base indicators. Litmus becomes blue in basic solutions, while phenolphthalein turns pink.

3. Bases react with acids in neutralization reactions to form water and a salt.

4. Bases in aqueous solution are slippery to the touch. *CAUTION: Strong bases have a caus-*

tic action on the skin and can be especially harmful to eye tissue.

The Arrhenius Theory of Bases.
Arrhenius defined a base as a substance that yields hydroxide ions as the only negative ions in aqueous solution. Only hydroxide compounds can be Arrhenius bases. The characteristic properties of bases just described are due to the presence of the hydroxide ion. A strong base is one that dissociates completely in solution; a weak base is one that dissociates only partially in solution.

The Brönsted-Lowry Theory of Bases.
According to the conceptual definition of the Brönsted-Lowry theory, a base is any species that can accept a proton. By this definition, many chemical species in addition to hydroxides can act as bases, including many species that have an unshared electron pair. For example, NH_3 has an unshared electron pair and can accept a proton (H^+) to form NH_4^+ (see Figure 7-2).

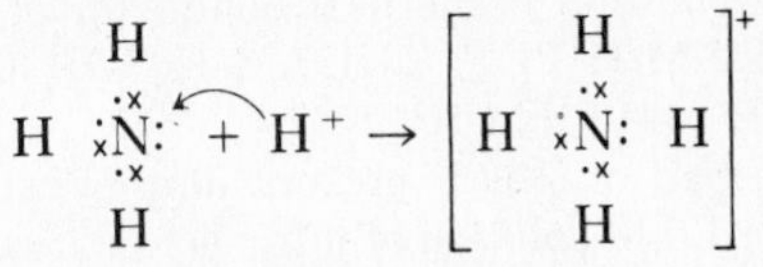

Figure 7-2. NH_3 is a base.

AMPHOTERIC SUBSTANCES

An **amphoteric**, or **amphiprotic**, **substance** is one that can act either as an acid or as a base, depending on the degree of acidity or alkalinity of the solution. For example, HCO_3^- acts as an acid and will lose a proton in a basic solution, according to the reaction

$$HCO_3^- + OH^- \rightleftarrows CO_3^{2-} + H_2O$$

In an acidic solution, however, HCO_3^- acts as a base and will accept a proton, according to the reaction

$$HCO_3^- + H^+ \rightleftarrows H_2O + CO_2$$

You can determine whether or not a species is amphoteric by referring to Reference Table L (see page 109). An ion, such as HS^-, that appears both in the acid column and in the base column is amphoteric.

QUESTIONS

1. A solution that contains hydrogen ions as the only positive ions is classified as (1) acidic (2) basic (3) anionic (4) cationic

2. Compared to a solution of a strong acid, a solution of a weak acid of the same molarity has a (1) lower concentration of acid molecules (2) higher concen-

tration of anions (3) lower concentration of cations (4) lower concentration of water

3. What are the two Brönsted-Lowry acids in the following reaction?

$$HPO_4^{2-} + H_2O \rightleftarrows PO_4^{3-} + H_3O^+$$

(1) HPO_4^{2-} and PO_4^{3-} (2) HPO_4^{2-} and H_3O^+ (3) H_2O and H_3O^+ (4) H_2O and PO_4^{3-}

4. What is a difference between solutions of a weak acid and a strong acid of equal concentrations? (1) The strong acid is more concentrated. (2) The weak acid does not turn litmus red. (3) The weak acid does not conduct electricity. (4) The strong acid has more hydronium ions per liter.

Questions 5–9 are based on Reference Table L (see page 109).

5. A gas whose water solution is basic is (1) CO_2 (2) SO_2 (3) NH_3 (4) HCl

6. Which compound is a strong electrolyte? (1) CH_3COOH (2) H_2S (3) $C_6H_{12}O_6$ (4) HNO_3

7. Which solution is the best conductor of electricity? (1) 1.0 M H_3PO_4 (2) 1.0 M H_2SO_4 (3) 1.0 M CH_3COOH (4) 1.0 M HF

8. Which pair of ions is present in greatest concentration in a 1.0 M solution of nitric acid in water? (1) $H_2NO_3^+$ and NO_3^- (2) H_3O^+ and NO_3^- (3) $H_2NO_3^+$ and OH^- (4) NO_2^- and OH^-

9. Which aqueous solution has the highest concentration of H_3O^+ ions? (1) 1 M H_2SO_4 (2) 1 M CH_3COOH (3) 1 M NH_3 (4) 1 M NaOH

10. Which group of the periodic table contains elements whose hydroxides are strong bases? (1) 1 (2) 13 (3) 15 (4) 17

11. Which formula represents a hydrated proton? (1) H_2O (2) H_3O^+ (3) H_2 (4) OH^-

12. When additional HCl(g) dissolves in a 0.010 M aqueous solution of HCl, the concentration of H_3O^+ in the solution (1) increases (2) decreases (3) remains the same

13. Any solution that contains dissociated ions (1) is acidic (2) is alkaline (3) conducts electricity (4) has a negligible vapor pressure

14. How many moles of ions are produced when one mole of $(NH_4)_2SO_4$ dissolves in water? (1) 1 (2) 2 (3) 3 (4) 6

Questions 15–18 are based on Reference Table L (see page 109).

15. Which acid produces the fewest ions when dissolved in 1.0 M water solution? (1) HI (2) HF (3) H_2S (4) H_3PO_4

16. In which reaction does water act as a Brönsted-Lowry acid?
(1) $NH_3 + H_2O \rightarrow NH_4^+ + OH^-$
(2) $HCl + H_2O \rightarrow H_3O^+ + Cl^-$
(3) $Ca(HCO_3)_2 \rightarrow CaCO_3 + H_2O + CO_2$
(4) $CuSO_4 + 5H_2O \rightarrow CuSO_4 \cdot 5H_2O$

17. Which is the weakest Brönsted-Lowry acid? (1) $H_2PO_4^-$ (2) HSO_4^- (3) HSO_3^- (4) HCO_3^-

18. Which ion is amphiprotic? (1) Br^-(aq) (2) HS^-(aq) (3) S^{2-}(aq) (4) CO_3^{2-}(aq)

19. In the reaction $H_2O + H_2O \rightleftarrows H_3O^+ + OH^-$, the water is acting as (1) a proton acceptor, only (2) a proton donor, only (3) both a proton acceptor and a proton donor (4) neither a proton acceptor nor a proton donor

ACID-BASE REACTIONS

Neutralization. In a **neutralization reaction**, one mole of H^+ from an acid combines with one mole of OH^- from a base to form water. This is the actual neutralization reaction. In addition, one mole of anions (negative ions) from the acid combines with one mole of cations (positive ions) from the base to form a salt (see page 51).

Consider the reaction between KOH and HCl:

$$KOH + HCl \rightleftarrows KCl + H_2O$$

$$base + acid \rightleftarrows salt + water$$

This reaction can also be represented by an ionic equation:

$$K^+(aq) + OH^-(aq) + H^+(aq) + Cl^-(aq)$$
$$\rightleftarrows K^+(aq) + Cl^-(aq) + H_2O$$

All of the reactants are present as ions in an aqueous solution. While the H^+ and OH^- ions react to form water molecules, the K^+ and Cl^- ions do not actually take part in the reaction. They appear on both sides of the equation and are referred to as "spectator ions."

Acid-Base Titrations. The concentration, or molarity, of an acid or base can be determined by a technique called **titration**. To find the molarity of an acid by titration, a base of known concentration is added to a specific volume of the acid until neutralization occurs. The solution of known concentration is called the **standard solution**. The volume of standard base needed for neutralization is measured precisely.

The point at which neutralization occurs, called the *end point* of titration, can be detected by appropriate indicators or by observation of temperature change or by a change in electrical conductivity.

The concentration of an unknown base can be determined in a similar manner by titration with a standard acid.

Two indicators commonly used in titration are litmus and phenolphthalein. Litmus is blue in base and red in acid. Phenolphthalein is pink in base and colorless in acid.

Calculation of the molarity of a solution of unknown concentration is based on the molar relationships of the substances involved in the reaction.

50

1. Neutralization is observed when 26.0 mL of standard 0.50 M HCl(aq) is mixed with 39.0 mL of NaOH(aq) of unknown concentration. What is the concentration of the NaOH solution?

Solution: Write the equation for the reaction:

$$HCl + NaOH \rightarrow HOH + NaCl$$

Observed volumes (in liters)	Known concentration of standard solution	Mole ratio from equation		

$$\frac{Standard\ solution}{Unknown\ solution}$$

$$\frac{0.026\ \cancel{L}\ HCl}{0.039\ \cancel{L}\ NaOH} \times \frac{0.50\ mol\ HCl}{1\ L\ HCl} \times \frac{1\ \cancel{mol}\ NaOH}{1\ \cancel{mol}\ HCl} = \frac{0.33}{L}\ mol\ NaOH(aq) = 0.33\ molar$$

2. Standard hydrochloric acid is used to determine the concentration of a solution of barium hydroxide. At neutralization, 36.0 mL of 0.10 M HCl(aq) reacts with 20.0 mL of Ba(OH)$_2$(aq). What is the concentration of the Ba(OH)$_2$ solution?

Solution: Note that 2 moles of HCl react with 1 mole of Ba(OH)$_2$.

$$2HCl + Ba(OH)_2 \rightarrow 2HOH + BaCl_2$$

$$\frac{Volume\ of\ standard\ solution}{Volume\ of\ unknown\ solution} \qquad \frac{Known\ concentration}{of\ standard\ solution} \qquad \frac{Mole\ ratio}{from\ equation}$$

$$\frac{0.036\ \cancel{L}\ HCl}{0.020\ \cancel{L}\ Ba(OH)_2} \times \frac{0.10\ mol\ HCl}{1\ L\ HCl} \times \frac{1\ \cancel{mol}\ Ba(OH)_2}{2\ \cancel{mol}\ HCl} = 0.090\ M\ Ba(OH)_2(aq)$$

3. What volume of 2 M HNO$_3$ is needed to neutralize 40 mL of 5 M NaOH?

Solution: Write the equation for the reaction.

$$HNO_3 + NaOH \rightarrow HOH + NaNO_3$$

$$0.040\ \cancel{L\ NaOH} \times \frac{5.0\ \cancel{mol\ NaOH}}{1\ \cancel{L\ NaOH}} \times \frac{1\ \cancel{mol\ HNO_3}}{1\ \cancel{mol\ NaOH}} \times \frac{1\ L\ HNO_3}{2\ \cancel{mol\ HNO_3}} = 0.10\ L\ HNO_3$$

4. What volume of 0.1 M H$_2$SO$_4$ is needed to neutralize 100 mL of 0.5 M KOH?

Solution: Write the equation for the reaction.

$$H_2SO_4 + 2KOH \rightarrow HOH + K_2SO_4$$

$$0.100\ \cancel{L\ KOH} \times \frac{0.500\ \cancel{mol\ KOH}}{1\ \cancel{L\ KOH}} \times \frac{1\ \cancel{mol\ H_2SO_4}}{2\ \cancel{mol\ KOH}} \times \frac{1\ L\ H_2SO_4}{0.100\ \cancel{mol\ H_2SO_4}} = 0.250\ L\ H_2SO_4$$

Salts and Hydrolysis Reactions.

A salt is an ionic compound that contains positive ions other than H$^+$ and negative ions other than OH$^-$. Most salts are strong electrolytes and dissociate completely in water. The ions of some salts react with water to form acidic or basic solutions.

Ammonium chloride, NH$_4$Cl, dissolves in water to form NH$_4^+$ and Cl$^-$ ions. The ammonium ion tends to react with water, removing OH$^-$ ions, according to the equilibrium

$$NH_4^+ + H_2O \rightleftarrows NH_3 + H_3O^+$$

The resulting solution contains hydronium ions and is therefore slightly acidic.

Sodium acetate, CH$_3$COONa, dissolves in water to form Na$^+$ and CH$_3$COO$^-$ ions. The acetate ion tends to react slightly with water, re-moving H$^+$ ions, according to the equilibrium

$$CH_3COO^- + H_2O \rightleftarrows CH_3COOH + OH^-$$

The resulting solution contains hydroxide ions, and is therefore slightly basic.

A reaction in which a salt reacts with water to form a solution that is acidic or basic is called **hydrolysis**. During hydrolysis, the water equilibrium (H$_2$O $\rightleftarrows$ H$^+$ + OH$^-$) is upset, producing either excess H$^+$ (H$_3$O$^+$) ions or OH$^-$ ions.

Ions associated with strong acids and bases do not hydrolyze in aqueous solution. Thus, the ions SO$_4^{2-}$, NO$_3^-$, Cl$^-$, K$^+$, and Na$^+$ do not react with water molecules in aqueous solution and do not affect the acidity or alkalinity of the solution. Anions, such as acetate and phosphate, that are associated with weak acids produce basic solutions when their salts are dissolved in water. Cations, such as NH_4^+, that are associated with weak bases produce acidic solutions when their salts are dissolved in water.

Salts can be regarded as having been derived from parent acids and bases in neutralization reactions. The alkalinity or acidity of a salt solution can be predicted according to the general rules in Table 7-1.

Table 7-1. Hydrolysis of Salt Solutions

The Salt From a	Produces a Solution That Is	Example of Salt
strong acid and weak base	acidic	NH_4Cl
weak acid and strong base	basic	CH_3COONa
strong acid and strong base	neutral	$NaCl$
weak acid and weak base	not easily predicted	CH_3COONH_4

Conjugate Acid-Base Pairs.

According to the Brönsted-Lowry theory, acid-base reactions involve the transfer of a proton from the acid to the base. Such reactions are reversible.

For the proton transfer to occur, the acid must have a proton that can be donated, and the base must have an unshared electron pair that can accept the proton. In an acid-base reaction, the proton from the acid bonds to the unshared electron pair of the base, forming a coordinate covalent bond (see page 49).

When an acid donates a proton in an acid-base reaction, the acid becomes a base. Thus, in HCl, the loss of a proton (H^+) forms Cl^-, which can only accept a proton and act as a base. The original acid and the newly formed base are a **conjugate pair**. The presence of a transferable proton is the only difference between the acid and its conjugate base.

In each acid-base reaction, there are two acid-base conjugate pairs.

$$HCl + H_2O \rightleftharpoons H_3O^+ + Cl^-$$

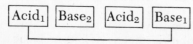
Acid₁ Base₂ Acid₂ Base₁

Acid₁ and base₁ are a conjugate pair, and acid₂ and base₂ are a conjugate pair. An acid-base reaction can be summarized as:

$$Acid_1 + Base_2 \rightleftharpoons Acid_2 + Base_1$$

The strongest acids have the weakest conjugate bases, and the strongest bases have the weakest conjugate acids.

In a Brönsted-Lowry acid-base reaction, the stronger acid (of Acid₁ and Acid₂) donates its proton to the stronger base (of Base₁ and Base₂). In other words,

$$\left(\begin{array}{c}\text{Stronger}\\\text{Acid}\end{array}\right) + \left(\begin{array}{c}\text{Stronger}\\\text{Base}\end{array}\right) \text{ forms}$$

$$\left(\begin{array}{c}\text{Weaker}\\\text{Acid}\end{array}\right) + \left(\begin{array}{c}\text{Weaker}\\\text{Base}\end{array}\right)$$

When applied to Reference Table L (see page 109), it can be seen that any acid (on the left) can donate a proton to any base (on the right) that is located below the conjugate base of that acid.

The equations below are taken from Reference Table L.

$$HSO_4^- \rightarrow H^+ + SO_4^{2-}$$

$$HNO_2 \rightarrow H^+ + NO_2^-$$

$$HF \rightarrow H^+ + F^-$$

$$H_2S \rightarrow H^+ + HS^-$$

HNO_2, an acid, can donate protons to F^- or HS^-. Both are stronger bases than NO_2^-, the conjugate of HNO_2. HNO_2 cannot donate protons to SO_4^{2-} because SO_4^{2-} is a weaker base than NO_2^-.

QUESTIONS

1. How many moles of KOH are needed to neutralize 1.5 moles of H_2SO_4? (1) 0.75 (2) 1.5 (3) 3.0 (4) 6.0
2. What volume of 0.80 M HCl will exactly neutralize 100 mL of 0.40 M KOH? (1) 20 mL (2) 50 mL (3) 80 mL (4) 200 mL
3. An aqueous solution of $Al_2(SO_4)_3$ contains (1) H_3O^+ ions, only (2) OH^- ions, only (3) both H_3O^+ and OH^- ions (4) neither H_3O^+ nor OH^- ions
4. If exactly 5.0 mL of an aqueous HNO_3 solution will neutralize 15 mL of 2.0 M NaOH, what is the molarity of the HNO_3 solution? (1) 0.50 (2) 0.67 (3) 3.0 (4) 6.0
5. What volume of 0.25 M HCl is needed to neutralize 20 mL of 0.10 M $Ba(OH)_2$? (1) 8.0 mL (2) 16 mL (3) 20 mL (4) 50 mL
6. Which salt will hydrolyze in water solution to produce a basic solution? (1) $NaNO_2$ (2) KNO_3 (3) $CaCl_2$ (4) $MgSO_4$
7. What volume of 1.5 M H_2SO_4 is needed to neutralize 1.5 L of 4.0 M NaOH? (1) 0.50 L (2) 2.0 L (3) 8.0 L (4) 4.0 L
8. As more KOH is added to a KOH solution, the number of moles of HCl needed to neutralize the KOH solution (1) increases (2) decreases (3) remains the same
9. In the neutralization reaction between HCl and NaOH, the spectator ions are (1) H^+ and OH^- (2) Cl^- and OH^- (3) Na^+ and H^+ (4) Na^+ and Cl^-
10. How many moles of H_2SO_4 can be neutralized by

0.1 L of 0.50 M NaOH? (1) 0.025 (2) 0.25 (3) 0.50 (4) 1.0

11. What volume of 5.0 M NaOH is needed to neutralize 40 mL of 2.0 M HCl? (1) 8.0 mL (2) 10 mL (3) 16 mL (4) 40 mL

12. In the reaction

$$H_3PO_4 + 20H^- \rightarrow HPO_4^{2-} + 2H_2O$$

the number of moles of protons donated by one mole of phosphoric acid is (1) 1 (2) 2 (3) 3 (4) 4

13. Which is the conjugate acid of HSO_4^-? (1) H_2SO_4 (2) OH^- (3) H_3O^+ (4) SO_4^{2-}

14. Which is the conjugate base of the HSO_3^- ion? (1) H_2SO_3 (2) OH^- (3) SO_3^{2-} (4) S^{2-}

15. Which Brönsted-Lowry acid has a conjugate base that has amphoteric properties? (1) HCl (2) HNO_3 (3) H_3O^+ (4) HSO_4^-

16. Which best describes a difference between any Brönsted-Lowry acid and its conjugate base? (1) The acid has one more electron. (2) The acid has one more proton. (3) The acid has one less electron. (4) The acid has one less proton.

17. Which neutralization yields a mixture of products that is acidic? (1) HCl + $Al(OH)_3$ (2) HCl + KOH (3) HNO_3 + NaOH (4) CH_3COOH + NaOH

18. An aqueous solution of NaCl and an aqueous solution of HCl are similar in that both solutions (1) contain H_3O^+ ions (2) are strongly alkaline (3) turn blue litmus paper red (4) are neutral

19. An aqueous solution of $NaCH_3COO$ is alkaline because the solution contains more (1) acetate ions than water molecules (2) sodium ions than water molecules (3) hydronium ions than hydroxide ions (4) hydroxide ions than hydronium ions

IONIZATION CONSTANTS

Ionization Constants of Acids.

The relative strength of an electrolyte depends on the extent to which it dissociates in solution. The greater the dissociation, the stronger is the electrolyte. The smaller the dissociation, the weaker is the electrolyte. Refer to the dissociation constant for a weak electrolyte on page 48. When the weak electrolyte is a weak acid, the equilibrium constant is referred to as the **ionization constant**, abbreviated as K_a. For the weak acid HA:

$$K_a = \frac{[H]^+[A]^-}{[HA]}$$

Ionization constants are used to compare the relative strengths of acids. The ionization constants of common acids are given in Reference Table L (see page 109). The smaller the value of K_a, the weaker is the acid.

Ionization of Water.

Pure water ionizes slightly, forming equal quantities of hydrogen ions and hydroxide ions.

$$H_2O \rightleftarrows H^+ + OH^-$$

The equilibrium expression for the dissociation reaction is

$$\frac{[H]^+[OH]^-}{[H_2O]} = K = 1.8 \times 10^{-16}$$

The concentration of $[H_2O]$ is constant, however, and equals 55.5 moles. Therefore:

$$\frac{[H]^+[OH]^-}{55.5} = 1.8 \times 10^{-16}$$

$$\text{or} \quad K_w = [H]^+[OH]^- = 1.0 \times 10^{-14}$$

Because the hydrogen ion and hydroxide ion concentrations are equal, the solution is neutral. That is, the solution is neither acidic nor basic.

In all aqueous solutions, whether acidic, basic, or neutral, the product of the concentration of hydrogen ions multiplied by the concentration of hydroxide ions is equal to K_w.

$$[H]^+[OH]^- = K_w = 1.0 \times 10^{-14} \text{ (at 298 K)}$$

In pure water, the hydrogen ion and hydroxide ion concentrations are equal.

$$[H]^+ = 1.0 \times 10^{-7} \text{ and } [OH]^- = 1.0 \times 10^{-7}$$

In an acidic solution, however, the hydrogen ion concentration is greater, while in a basic solution, the hydroxide ion concentration is greater. Since the value of K_w is constant (the product $[H]^+ \times [OH]^-$ is constant), an increase in the concentration of one of these ions means that there is a corresponding decrease in the concentration of the other.

pH. The acidity or alkalinity of a solution is measured in terms of its hydrogen ion concentration. The equilibrium concentration of hydrogen ions in pure water is 1.0×10^{-7}. If the concentration of hydrogen ions exceeds the equilibrium concentration (for example, 1.0×10^{-6}), then the solution is acidic. If the concentration of hydrogen ions is less than 1.0×10^{-7} (for example, 1.0×10^{-8}), then the solution is basic.

The **pH** of a solution is defined as the negative logarithm of the hydrogen ion concentration.

$$pH = -(\log [H]^+)$$
$$[H]^+ = 10^{-(pH)}$$

Therefore, if the hydrogen ion concentration is 1.0×10^{-4} mole/liter, the pH is 4; if the pH is 8, the hydrogen ion concentration is 1.0×10^{-8} mole/liter. Since the hydrogen ion concentration of pure water is 1.0×10^{-7}, the pH of pure water is 7. A pH lower than 7 is acidic, and a pH higher than 7 is basic.

The measurement of $[H]^+$ and pH applies to any water solution, even basic solutions, since any water solution contains some H^+ ions. When a solution has $[OH]^-$ of 10^{-3}, it is basic. To calculate its $[H]^+$ and pH, use K_w.

$$K_w = [H]^+[OH]^- = 1.0 \times 10^{-14}$$

$$[H]^+ = \frac{1.0 \times 10^{-14}}{10^{-3}}$$

$$= 1.0 \times 10^{-11}$$

Thus, pH = 11.

Because the pH scale is *logarithmic*, the difference in acidity between integral (whole-number) values is not constant. A solution with a pH of 1 is not twice as acidic as one with a pH of 2; it is ten times as acidic. A solution with a pH of 1 is one hundred times more acidic than a solution with a pH of 3.

QUESTIONS

1. The K_w value for a sample of water will most likely change when there is an increase in (1) temperature (2) pressure (3) the concentration of hydrogen ions (4) the concentration of hydroxide ions

2. Equal volumes of 0.1 M solutions of KOH and HNO_3 are mixed. The pH of the resulting solution is closest to (1) 7 (2) 11 (3) 3 (4) 14

3. When additional solid NaCl is added to an aqueous solution of NaCl, the pH of the solution (1) increases (2) decreases (3) remains the same

4. A 0.1 M HCl solution differs from a 0.1 M NaOH solution in that the HCl solution (1) has a lower pH (2) turns litmus blue (3) contains fewer H_3O^+ ions (4) will not conduct electricity

5. Which pH value describes the most acidic solution? (1) 4 (2) 2 (3) 10 (4) 14

6. If the concentration of hydroxide ions in a solution is 1×10^{-5} moles per liter, this solution is (1) acidic and has a pH of 5 (2) acidic and has a pH of 9 (3) basic and has a pH of 5 (4) basic and has a pH of 9

7. The hydroxide ion concentration in a 0.001 M NaOH solution is (1) less than 10^{-3} mole/liter (2) equal to 1×10^{-3} mole/liter (3) greater than 1×10^{-3} mole/liter

8. Which of the following is true of HCl and NaOH solutions of equal concentrations? (1) They have the same pH. (2) They have the same K_w. (3) They both turn blue litmus red. (4) They have equal concentrations of hydronium ions.

9. What is the H_3O^+ concentration of a solution that has an $[OH]^-$ of 1×10^{-3} M? (1) 1×10^{-3} M (2) 1×10^{-7} M (3) 1×10^{-11} M (4) 1×10^{-14} M

10. The ionization constant (K_a) of HF is 6.7×10^{-4}. Which is true in a 0.1 M solution of this acid? (1) [HF] is greater than $[H]^+ \times [F]^-$. (2) [HF] is less than $[H]^+ \times [F]^-$. (3) [HF] is equal to $[H]^+ \times [F]^-$.

11. The pH of a 0.1 M CH_3COOH solution is (1) less than 1 (2) greater than 1 but less than 7 (3) equal to 7 (4) greater than 7

12. What is the pH of an aqueous solution of $C_6H_{12}O_6$? (1) 1 (2) 7 (3) 11 (4) 14

13. A sample of pure water contains (1) neither OH^- ions nor H_3O^+ ions (2) equal concentrations of OH^- and H_3O^+ ions (3) a larger concentration of H_3O^+ than OH^- ions (4) a smaller concentration of H_3O^+ ions than OH^- ions

14. Which of the following ionizes to the *least* extent at 298 K? (1) HF (2) HNO_2 (3) H_2S (4) H_2O

UNIT 8 Redox Reactions and Electrochemistry

OXIDATION AND REDUCTION

In many chemical reactions, electrons are removed from some particles (atoms or ions) and are transferred to other particles. Such reactions are called **oxidation-reduction**, or **redox**, **reactions**.

In the reaction

$$2Na(s) + Cl_2(g) \rightarrow 2NaCl(s)$$

each sodium atom loses a valence electron, becoming a positive ion with a charge of $1+$. At the same time, each chlorine atom gains an electron, becoming a negative ion with a charge of $1-$. In such reactions, particles that lose electrons are said to be *oxidized*, while other particles that gain electrons are said to be *reduced*. In this case, the sodium atoms in Na(s) are oxidized, and the chlorine atoms in chlorine gas are reduced. Oxidation and reduction always occur together. If the particles in one substance are being oxidized, particles in another must be reduced.

Oxidizing and Reducing Agents.

In the reaction between sodium atoms and chlorine atoms, a sodium atom, by giving off (losing) an electron, causes a chlorine atom to be reduced. Therefore, sodium is said to act as a **reducing agent**. A chlorine atom, on the other hand, gains an electron and acts as an **oxidizing agent**. Some species may act as oxidizing agents in one reaction and reducing agents in another.

Because oxidizing agents take on (gain) electrons, oxidizing agents themselves are reduced during the course of a redox reaction. Similarly, reducing agents give off (lose) electrons and are oxidized.

Oxidation Numbers.

Oxidation number is the charge of an ion or the apparent charge of an atom in a compound. Oxidation numbers are assigned according to certain rules (see Table 8-1). Oxidation numbers generally range from -3 to $+7$, including zero.

For the purposes of redox reactions, oxidation is also defined as an increase in oxidation number, and reduction is also defined as a decrease in oxidation number.

Sample Problems

1. What is the oxidation number of Cl in $HClO_4$ (perchloric acid)?

Solution: Referring to Table 8-1, write the *known* oxidation numbers above the symbols of the elements. Be sure to multiply the oxidation

Table 8-1. Assigning Oxidation Numbers

Kind of Particle	Oxidation Number	Examples
Uncombined elements	0	H in H_2, S in S_8, O in O_3
Monatomic ions	Charge on ion	Ag^{+1} and S^{-2} in Ag_2S, Ba^{+2} and Cl^{-1} in $BaCl_2$, Cu^{+1} in $CuCl$, Cu^{+2} in $CuCl_2$
Group 1 metals (1+ ions)	+1	Na^{+1}, K^{+1}
Group 2 metals (2+ ions)	+2	Ca^{+2} in $Ca(OH)_2$, Mg^{+2} in $Mg(Cl)_2$

Oxygen
  Except in peroxides
  Except with fluorine
	-2
	-1
	$+2$
		O^{-2} in MgO, K_2SO_4
		O^{-1} in H_2O_2, BaO_2
		O^{+2} in OF_2

Hydrogen Except in metal hydrides	$+1$ -1	H^{+1} in HCl, $NaHCO_3$ H^{-1} in LiH, CaH_2
All other atoms	Maintain conservation of charge; electrons shared between two unlike atoms are arbitrarily assigned to the more electronegative atom.	In $MgSO_4$: Mg^{+2}, S^{+6}, O^{-2} In $(NH_4)_2CO_3$: H^{+1}, N^{-3}, C^{+4}, O^{-2}

Note:
    For a polyatomic ion, the oxidation numbers add up to the charge on that ion. SO_4^{2-}: $S^{+6} O_4^{-8}$; PO_4^{3-}: $P^{+5} O_4^{-8}$

    In a neutral molecule, the oxidation numbers add up to zero—the charge on the neutral molecule. CO_2^0: $C^{+4} O_2^{-4}$; H_2O^0: $H_2^{+1} O^{-2}$

number of the atom by the number of atoms in the compound.

$$\overset{+1}{H}\quad\overset{?}{Cl}\quad\overset{4(-2)}{O_4}$$

$$\overset{+1}{H}\quad\overset{?}{Cl}\quad\overset{-8}{O_4}$$

$$\left[\overset{+1}{H}\quad\overset{+7}{Cl}\quad\overset{-8}{O_4}\right]^0$$

Since the total of the oxidation numbers must add up to zero, the oxidation number of Cl is $+7$.

2. What is the oxidation number of Cr in $K_2Cr_2O_7$ (potassium dichromate)?

$$\overset{2(+1)}{K_2}\quad\overset{?}{Cr_2}\quad\overset{7(-2)}{O_7}$$

$$\overset{+2}{K_2}\quad\overset{2(+6)}{Cr_2}\quad\overset{-14}{O_7}$$

$$\left[\overset{+2}{K_2}\quad\overset{+12}{Cr_2}\quad\overset{-14}{O_7}\right]^0$$

The oxidation number of Cr is $+6$.

3. What are the oxidation numbers of N in NO, NO_2, N_2O, and $NaNO_3$?

NO: $\quad\overset{?}{N}\quad\overset{-2}{O}\qquad\overset{+2}{N}\quad\overset{-2}{O}$

$\left[\overset{+2}{N}\quad\overset{-2}{O}\right]^0\qquad$ N is $+2$.

NO_2: $\quad\overset{?}{N}\quad\overset{2(-2)}{O_2}\qquad\overset{+4}{N}\quad\overset{-4}{O_2}$

$\left[\overset{+4}{N}\quad\overset{-4}{O_2}\right]^0\qquad$ N is $+4$.

N_2O: $\quad\overset{?}{N_2}\quad\overset{-2}{O}\qquad\overset{2(+1)}{N}\quad\overset{-2}{O}$

$\left[\overset{+2}{N_2}\quad\overset{-2}{O}\right]^0\qquad$ N is $+1$.

$NaNO_3$: $\overset{+1}{Na}\quad\overset{?}{N}\quad\overset{3(-2)}{O_3}\qquad\overset{+1}{Na}\quad\overset{+5}{N}\quad\overset{-6}{O_3}$

$\left[\overset{+1}{Na}\quad\overset{+5}{N}\quad\overset{-6}{O_3}\right]^0\qquad$ N is 5.

4. What is the oxidation number of Mn in $KMnO_4$ (potassium permanganate)?

$$\overset{+1}{K}\quad\overset{?}{Mn}\quad\overset{4(-2)}{O_4}$$

$$\overset{+1}{K}\quad\overset{+7}{Mn}\quad\overset{-8}{O_4}$$

$$\left[\overset{+1}{K}\quad\overset{+7}{Mn}\quad\overset{-8}{O_4}\right]^0$$

The oxidation number of Mn is $+7$.

Electronic Equations.

Equations that show only the atoms oxidized and reduced and the transfer of electrons are called **electronic equations**. Electronic equations can be used to represent oxidation and reduction reactions. For example, the reaction of aluminum with chlorine gas

$$2Al + 3Cl_2 \rightarrow 2AlCl_3$$

can be represented by two electronic equations:

Oxidation: $Al^0 \rightarrow Al^{3+} + 3e^-$

Reduction: $Cl_2^0 + 2e^- \rightarrow 2Cl^-$

The electronic equation for the aluminum shows oxidation—aluminum loses electrons. The equation for the chlorine shows reduction—chlorine gains electrons.

Half-Reactions.

It is convenient to think of a redox reaction as consisting of two **half-reactions**. One half-reaction represents the loss of electrons (oxidation), while the other half-reaction represents the gain of electrons (reduction). Adding the two half-reactions together gives the complete oxidation-reduction reaction.

Consider the half-reactions

$$Al^0 \rightarrow Al^{3+} + 3e^-$$

$$Cl_2^0 + 2e^- \rightarrow 2Cl^-$$

Before the half-reactions can be added, it is first necessary to conserve charge. That is, the number of electrons lost must equal the number of electrons gained, or the total charge must equal zero. Multiplying the entire oxidation reaction by 2 and multiplying the entire reduction reaction by 3 and then adding both reactions gives the complete redox reaction.

$$2[Al^0 \rightarrow Al^{3+} + 3e^-]$$

$$3[Cl_2^0 + 2e^- \rightarrow 2Cl^-]$$

$$2Al + 3Cl_2 \rightarrow 2AlCl_3$$

Spectator ions—ions whose oxidation number remains unchanged during the course of a redox reaction—are generally not included in the half-reactions.

Many half-reactions are listed in Reference Table N (see page 110). When appropriate, half-reactions include ions and water. For example, the oxidation of ferrous ions by permanganate ions in acid solution is represented by the two half-reactions:

Oxidation: $5[Fe^{2+} \rightarrow Fe^{3+} + e^-]$

Reduction: $8H^+ + 5e^- + MnO_4^- \rightarrow Mn^{2+}$
$$+ 4H_2O$$

Adding the two half-reactions while conserving electrons gives

$5Fe^{2+} + 8H^+ + MnO_4^- \rightarrow 5Fe^{3+}$
$$+ Mn^{2+} + 4H_2O$$

1. In redox reactions, metals usually (1) act as reducing agents (2) share electrons (3) donate protons (4) acquire negative oxidation numbers
2. A bromine atom is changed to a bromide ion by (1) gaining an electron (2) losing an electron (3) gaining a proton (4) losing a proton
3. In the reaction

$$AgNO_3 + NaCl \rightarrow NaNO_3 + AgCl$$

silver is (1) oxidized only (2) reduced only (3) neither oxidized nor reduced (4) both oxidized and reduced
4. In the reaction

$$Zn + CuCl_2 \rightarrow ZnCl_2 + Cu$$

copper in $CuCl_2$ is (1) oxidized only (2) reduced only (3) neither oxidized nor reduced (4) both oxidized and reduced
5. In the reaction $Cl_2 + 2KBr \rightarrow Br_2 + 2KCl$ chlorine is (1) oxidized only (2) reduced only (3) neither oxidized nor reduced (4) both oxidized and reduced
6. In the reaction

$$Zn + Pb^{2+}(aq) \rightarrow Zn^{2+}(aq) + Pb$$

the Pb^{2+} ions (1) gain electrons (2) lose electrons (3) become cations (4) become anions
7. In the reaction $2K + Cl_2 \rightarrow 2KCl$ the species that is oxidized is (1) Cl^- (2) Cl_2 (3) K^0 (4) K^+
8. The half-reaction $Mg^{2+} + 2e^- \rightarrow Mg$ indicates that the (1) magnesium ion is being oxidized (2) magnesium ion is being reduced (3) magnesium atom is being oxidized (4) magnesium atom is being reduced
9. In the reaction

$$2NaCl + 3SO_3 \rightarrow Cl_2 + SO_2 + Na_2S_2O_7$$

the oxidation numbers of sulfur in SO_3 and SO_2 are (1) +2 and 0 (2) +6 and +4 (3) 0 and +4 (4) +4 and −4
10. In the half-reaction

$$HCOOH + 2H^+ + 2e^- \rightarrow HCHO + H_2O$$

the oxidation number of carbon changes from (1) +2 to +4 (2) 0 to +4 (3) +2 to 0 (4) 0 to +2
11. Which of the following is an oxidation-reduction reaction?
(1) $4Na + O_2 \rightarrow 2Na_2O$
(2) $2O_3 \rightarrow 3O_2$
(3) $AgNO_3 + NaCl \rightarrow AgCl + NaNO_3$
(4) $2KI \rightarrow K^+ + 2I^-$
12. The oxidation number of nitrogen is highest in (1) N_2 (2) NH_3 (3) NO_2 (4) N_2O
13. What is the oxidation number of carbon in $NaHCO_3$? (1) +6 (2) +2 (3) −4 (4) +4
14. Which of the following shows reduction?
(1) $S^{-2} + 2e^- \rightarrow S^0$
(2) $S^{-2} \rightarrow S^0 + 2e^-$
(3) $Mn^{+7} \rightarrow Mn^{+4} + 3e^-$
(4) $Mn^{+7} + 3e^- \rightarrow Mn^{+4}$

15. Which of the following is a redox reaction?
(1) $H^+ + OH^- \rightarrow H_2O$
(2) $2Br^- + Cl_2 \rightarrow 2Cl^- + Br_2$
(3) $H_2O + CO_2 \rightarrow H^+ + HCO_3^-$
(4) $HSO_4^- \rightarrow H^+ + SO_4^{2-}$
16. Which of the following is not an oxidation-reduction reaction?
(1) $2K + Cl_2 \rightarrow 2KCl$
(2) $2KClO_3 \rightarrow 2KCl + 3O_2$
(3) $KOH + HCl \rightarrow KCl + HOH$
(4) $2K + 2H_2O \rightarrow 2KOH + H_2$
17. In the reaction

$$Cu + 4HNO_3 \rightarrow Cu(NO_3)_2 + 2H_2O + 2NO_2$$

the oxidation number of oxygen (1) increases (2) decreases (3) remains the same
18. In the reaction

$$Cl_2 + 2KBr \rightarrow Br_2 + 2KCl$$

potassium is (1) oxidized only (2) reduced only (3) neither oxidized nor reduced (4) both oxidized and reduced
19. In an oxidation-reduction reaction, the reducing agent (1) loses electrons (2) gains electrons (3) donates protons (4) accepts protons

BALANCING SIMPLE REDOX EQUATIONS

In simple oxidation-reduction reactions, the equation can be balanced by inspection. Since charge is conserved in redox reactions, if the substance being oxidized loses 3 moles of electrons, the substance or substances being reduced must gain a total of 3 moles of electrons. For example, the following equation is not balanced:

$$Cu^0 + Ag^+ \rightarrow Cu^{2+} + Ag^0$$

As shown in the half-reactions below, copper, which is being oxidized, has lost 2 electrons, but silver, which is being reduced, has gained only 1 electron.

Oxidation: $Cu^0 \rightarrow Cu^{2+} + 2e^-$

Reduction: $Ag^+ + e^- \rightarrow Ag^0$

The charges will balance if Ag^+ is given a coefficient of 2:

$$Cu^0 + 2Ag^+ \rightarrow Cu^{2+} + 2Ag^0$$

In this reaction, note that 1 mole of Cu^0 has lost 2 moles of electrons to form 1 mole of Cu^{2+}. Similarly, 2 moles of Ag^+ have gained 2 moles of electrons to form 2 moles of Ag^0. Again, the number of moles of electrons has been conserved.

Synthesis and Decomposition Reactions.
Reactions in which elements combine to form compounds are known as **synthesis**. Reactions in which compounds are changed into their constituent elements or into simpler com-

pounds are known as **decomposition**, or **analysis**. In the equations for synthesis and decomposition reactions, the formulas for many elements are represented as single atoms, for example, K, Fe, and C. The formulas for some diatomic elements are H_2, O_2, N_2, F_2, Cl_2, Br_2, and I_2. Occasionally, the allotropic forms of some elements appear in these equations, for example, P_4, S_8, and O_3.

Electronic equations for the half-reactions can be written for synthesis and decomposition reactions.

Synthesis:
1. $2K + F_2 \rightarrow 2KF$

$$\text{Oxidation: } 2[K^0 \rightarrow K^+ + e^-]$$

$$\text{Reduction: } F_2^0 + 2e^- \rightarrow 2F^-$$

2. $2H_2 + O_2 \rightarrow 2H_2O$

$$\text{Oxidation: } 2[H_2^0 \rightarrow 2H^+ + 2e^-]$$
$$\text{Reduction: } O_2^0 + 4e^- \rightarrow 2O^{-2}$$

Decomposition:
1. $2NaCl \rightarrow 2Na + Cl_2$

$$\text{Oxidation: } 2Cl^- \rightarrow Cl_2^0 + 2e^-$$

$$\text{Reduction: } 2[Na^+ + e^- \rightarrow Na^0]$$

2. $2HgO \rightarrow 2Hg + O_2$

$$\text{Oxidation: } O^{-2} \rightarrow O^0 + 2e^-$$

$$\text{Reduction: } Hg^{+2} + 2e^- \rightarrow Hg^0$$

CAUTION: Mercury in chemical reactions is hazardous.

Single Replacement Reactions.
Single replacement reactions usually involve an uncombined metal reacting with a positive metal ion (cation) or an uncombined nonmetal reacting with a negative nonmetal ion (anion).

Single replacement reactions are oxidation-reduction reactions. For example, in the reaction of copper with silver nitrate, copper, the reducing agent, is oxidized, while silver (or silver nitrate), the oxidizing agent, is reduced. The nitrate ions are spectator ions.

$$Cu + 2AgNO_3 \rightarrow Cu(NO_3)_2 + 2Ag$$

$$\text{Oxidation: } Cu^0 \rightarrow Cu^{2+} + 2e^-$$

$$\text{Reduction: } 2[Ag^+ + e^- \rightarrow Ag^0]$$

Conservation of charge and conservation of atoms are maintained by the use of coefficients (in this case, 2).

The following equation shows a single replacement reaction involving nonmetals:

$$2KI + Cl_2 \rightarrow I_2 + 2KCl$$

The iodide ion is oxidized, while the chlorine ion is reduced.

$$\text{Oxidation: } 2I^- \rightarrow I_2 + 2e^-$$

$$\text{Reduction: } Cl_2 + 2e^- \rightarrow 2Cl^-$$

Chlorine is the oxidizing agent, the iodide ion (or potassium iodide) is the reducing agent, and K^+ ions are spectator ions.

Double Replacement Reactions.
These reactions involve two replacements, as in the generalized reaction

$$\begin{array}{cccccccc} +1 & -1 & & +1 & -1 & & +1 & -1 & & +1 & -1 \\ A & B & + & C & D & \rightarrow & A & D & + & C & B \end{array}$$

Double replacement reactions are essentially reactions between ions and thus do not involve oxidation-reduction. Note that there is no change in oxidation number.

QUESTIONS

1. In the reaction between metallic zinc and copper sulfate,

$$Zn^0 + CuSO_4 \rightarrow ZnSO_4 + Cu^0$$

one mole of cupric ions will (1) lose one mole of electrons (2) gain one mole of electrons (3) lose two moles of electrons (4) gain two moles of electrons
2. When the equation

$$Fe^{3+} + Sn^{2+} \rightarrow Fe^{2+} + Sn^{4+}$$

is balanced using the smallest whole numbers, the coefficient of Fe^{3+} is (1) 1 (2) 2 (3) 3 (4) 4
3. A mole of chlorine gas is reduced to chloride ions by (1) gaining one mole of electrons (2) losing one mole of electrons (3) gaining two moles of electrons (4) losing two moles of electrons
4. When the equation $NH_3 + O_2 \rightarrow N_2 + H_2O$ is balanced using the smallest whole numbers, the coefficient of the O_2 will be (1) 1 (2) 2 (3) 3 (4) 4
5. When the equation

$$Ca^0 + Al^{3+} \rightarrow Ca^{2+} + Al^0$$

is balanced with the smallest whole-number coefficients, the coefficient of Ca^0 is (1) 1 (2) 2 (3) 3 (4) 4
6. When the equation $Hg^0 + Ag^+ \rightarrow Ag^0 + Hg^{2+}$ is correctly balanced using smallest whole numbers, the coefficient of Ag^+ will be (1) 5 (2) 2 (3) 3 (4) 4
7. How many moles of electrons would be required to reduce completely 1.5 moles of Al^{3+} to Al? (1) 0.50 (2) 1.5 (3) 3.0 (4) 4.5
8. How many moles of electrons are needed to reduce one mole of Cu^{2+} to Cu^+? (1) 1 (2) 2 (3) 3 (4) 4
9. In the synthesis reaction $Cu^0 + Cl_2 \rightarrow CuCl_2$ (1) Cu^0 is reduced. (2) Cu^0 is oxidized. (3) Cl_2 is oxidized. (4) Cu^{2+} is oxidized.
10. In the decomposition reaction $2LiH \rightarrow 2Li + H_2$ (1) Li^+ is oxidized. (2) Li^0 is oxidized. (3) H_2^0 is reduced. (4) H^- is oxidized.
11. In the double replacement reaction

$$AgNO_3 + NaCl \rightarrow AgCl(s) + NaNO_3$$

(1) $AgNO_3$ is reduced. (2) $AgNO_3$ is oxidized. (3) NaCl is reduced. (4) $AgNO_3$ is neither reduced nor oxidized.

ELECTROCHEMISTRY

Half-Cells.

In the laboratory, redox reactions can be set up so that each half-reaction takes place separately. This can be done either in separate parts of the same vessel or in different vessels. Each half-reaction is referred to as a *half-cell reaction*, and the region where it takes place is referred to as a **half-cell**.

If the two half-reactions take place in separate vessels, the half-cells must be connected by an external conductor through which electrons can migrate, and by a porous partition, or **salt bridge**. The salt bridge permits the passage of ions, but does not allow the two solutions to mix.

The parts of the external conductor that extend into the solutions in the half-cells are called **electrodes**. The electrode at which reduction occurs is called the **cathode**, and the electrode at which oxidation occurs is called the **anode**.

✳ Standard Electrode Potentials.

The electrical potential of an electrochemical cell, given in volts, is a relative measure of the potential driving force of the redox reaction taking place within the cell. Some reactions occur spontaneously, releasing energy; others must have energy added in order to proceed. Measurements of the electrical potential of a redox reaction show how likely that reaction is to occur.

Electrical potentials are measured for the reduction half-reaction relative to a *standard reference electrode*, also called a *standard cell*. Hydrogen is the standard cell in Reference Table N (see page 110), and its reduction potential is defined as zero. The reduction potentials of more easily reduced particles have positive values, while less easily reduced particles have negative values. The reduction potentials of some common half-reactions are given in Reference Table N.

To use Reference Table N, remember that the half-reactions near the *top* of the table contain the most powerful *oxidizing* agents, and the half-reactions near the *bottom* contain the most powerful *reducing* agents. Thus, F_2 is the most powerful oxidizing agent because when it oxidizes a particle, it itself (the oxidizing agent) is reduced. Thus,

$$F_2(g) + 2e^- \rightarrow 2F^-$$

has the highest reduction potential ($+2.87$ v). Similarly, Li(s) is the most powerful reducing agent because when it reduces a particle, it itself (the reducing agent) is oxidized. Thus,

$$Li(s) \rightarrow Li^+ + e^-$$

has the highest oxidation potential ($+3.04$ v) or the lowest reduction potential (-3.04 v).

The more active nonmetals are nearer the top of the table, and the more active metals are nearer the bottom. Or, the closer to the top of the table, the more active is the nonmetal (the more pow-erful oxidizing agent). The closer to the bottom of the table, the more active is the metal (the more powerful reducing agent). Note that oxidizing agents appear on the *left* side of Table N and reducing agents on the *right* side.

✳ Equilibrium and Cell Potential.

As an electrochemical cell operates, its voltage decreases because the concentrations of reactants and products are changing. When equilibrium is reached, the net reaction stops, and the voltage drops to zero.

✳ Uses of Standard Electrode Potential.

The voltages for any two half-reactions in Reference Table N (see page 110) can be combined to give the net voltage (E^0) for the overall reaction. The voltage for an oxidation half-reaction is obtained by reversing the direction of the reduction half-reaction in Table N and by reversing the sign of the reduction potential. The voltages of both half-reactions are added together to give the overall potential. The overall potential is also referred to as the potential difference or net E^0.

For example, in the reaction

$$Al(s) + Cu^{2+} \rightarrow Al^{3+} + Cu(s)$$

$$\text{Oxidation: } Al^0 \rightarrow Al^{3+} + 3e^-$$

$$(E^0 = +1.66 \text{ v})$$

$$\text{Reduction: } Cu^{2+} + 2e^- \rightarrow Cu^0$$

$$(E^0 = +0.34 \text{ v})$$

To conserve electrons, the oxidation half-reaction becomes

$$2[Al^0 \rightarrow Al^{3+} + 3e^-]$$

and the reduction half-reaction becomes

$$3[Cu^{2+} + 2e^- \rightarrow Cu^0]$$

The net reaction is

$$2Al^0 + 3Cu^{2+} \rightarrow 2Al^{3+} + 2Cu^0$$

The net E^0 is

$$+1.66 \text{ v} + 0.34 \text{ v} = +2.00 \text{ v}$$

Note that E^0s are *not* multiplied by coefficients.

If the overall potential is positive, the reaction is spontaneous; if the overall potential is negative, the reaction requires an input of energy in order to proceed. If the overall potential is zero, the oxidation and reduction reactions are at equilibrium, and there will be no net oxidation or reduction.

✳ *Sample Problems*

1. What is the balanced equation for the reaction of metallic magnesium (Mg) with chlorine gas (Cl_2) to produce magnesium chloride ($MgCl_2$)? What is the net E^0 for the reaction? Is the reaction spontaneous?

Solution: Determine which substance is being oxidized and which one is being reduced. The general equation is:

$$Mg(s) + Cl_2(g) \rightarrow MgCl_2$$

The half-reactions are:

Oxidation:

$$Mg^0 \rightarrow Mg^{2+} + 2e^- \qquad E^0 = +2.37 \text{ v}$$

Reduction:

$$Cl_2{}^0 + 2e^- \rightarrow 2Cl^- \qquad \underline{E^0 = +1.36 \text{ v}}$$

Net:

$$Mg^0 + Cl_2 \rightarrow MgCl_2 \qquad E^0 = +3.73 \text{ v}$$

Since atoms and electrons are balanced, the overall equation is balanced. Magnesium is oxidized and chlorine is reduced. According to Reference Table N (see page 110), the E^0 for the reduction of Cl_2 to Cl^- is +1.36 volts; the E^0 for the reduction of Mg^{2+} to Mg^0 is -2.37 volts. Since in this reaction magnesium is being oxidized, not reduced, the sign of E^0 is reversed, making the value for magnesium +2.37 volts. Adding the two values makes the net $E^0 = +3.73$ volts. Since E^0 is positive, the reaction is spontaneous.

2. Does the following reaction proceed spontaneously?

$$Zn(s) + Pb^{2+} \rightarrow Zn^{2+} + Pb^0$$

Solution: Calculate E^0 for the net reaction:

Oxidation:

$$Zn \rightarrow Zn^{2+} + 2e^- \qquad E^0 = +0.76 \text{ v}$$

Reduction:

$$Pb^{2+} + 2e^- \rightarrow Pb \qquad \underline{E^0 = -0.13 \text{ v}}$$

Net:

$$Zn(s) + Pb^{2+} \rightarrow Zn^{2+} + Pb^0 \quad E^0 = +0.63 \text{ v}$$

Since the net E^0 is positive, the reaction is spontaneous. Zinc will replace lead ions.

3. Does the following reaction proceed spontaneously?

$$Br_2{}^0 + 2Cl^-(aq) \rightarrow Cl_2{}^0 + 2Br^-(aq)$$

Solution:

Oxidation:
$$2Cl^-(aq) \rightarrow Cl_2 + 2e^- \qquad E^0 = -1.36 \text{ v}$$
Reduction:
$$Br_2 + 2e^- \rightarrow 2Br^-(aq) \qquad \underline{E^0 = +1.09 \text{ v}}$$
Net:
$$Br_2{}^0 + 2Cl^-(aq) \rightarrow \qquad E^0 = -0.27 \text{ v}$$
$$Cl_2{}^0 + 2Br^-(aq)$$

Since the net E^0 is negative, the reaction is not spontaneous. Bromine will not replace chloride ions.

* QUESTIONS

In 1–19, refer to Reference Table N on page 110.

1. Given the reaction:

$$2Cr(s) + 3Cu^{2+}(aq) \rightarrow 2Cr^{3+}(aq) + 3Cu(s)$$

The potential difference (E^0) of the cell is (1) 0.40 v (2) 1.08 v (3) 1.25 v (4) 2.50 v

2. Given the reaction:

$$2Na(s) + Cl_2(g) \rightarrow 2Na^+ + 2Cl^-$$

What is the potential (E^0) for the overall reaction? (1) -1.35 v (2) $+1.35$ v (3) -4.07 v (4) $+4.07$ v

3. Given the reaction:

$$2Au^{3+}(aq) + 3Ni^0 \rightarrow 2Au^0 + 3Ni^{2+}(aq)$$

The cell potential (E^0) for the overall reaction is (1) 3.75 v (2) 2.25 v (3) 1.76 v (4) 1.25 v

4. What is the potential (E^0) for the reaction

$$Mg(s) + Br_2(\ell) \rightarrow Mg^{2+}(aq) + 2Br^-(aq)$$

(1) 1.06 v (2) 1.31 v (3) 2.37 v (4) 3.46 v

5. Which species can act either as an oxidizing agent or a reducing agent? (1) Na^0 (2) Fe^{2+} (3) Sn^0 (4) Zn^{2+}

6. Given the reaction:

$$Zn(s) + 2H^+(aq) + 2Cl^-(aq) \rightarrow$$
$$Zn^{2+}(aq) + 2Cl^-(aq) + H_2(g)$$

Which species is oxidized?
(1) $Zn(s)$ (2) H^+ (aq) (3) Cl^- (aq) (4) $H_2(g)$

7. Which pair will react spontaneously at 298 K? (1) $Cl_2 + F^-$ (2) $I_2 + Br^-$ (3) $F_2 + I^-$ (4) $Br_2 + Cl^-$

8. Which pair will react spontaneously at 298 K? (1) $Cu + H_2O$ (2) $Ag + H_2O$ (3) $Ca + H_2O$ (4) $Au + H_2O$

9. What is the standard reduction potential for the Cu^{2+}(aq)/Cu half-cell? (1) $+0.52$ v (2) $+0.34$ v (3) -0.52 v (4) -0.34 v

10. Which species can oxidize Sn^{2+} to Sn^{4+}? (1) Ag^+ (2) Fe^0 (3) Al^{3+} (4) H_2O

11. Which of the following Group 17 elements is the strongest oxidizing agent? (1) I_2 (2) Br_2 (3) Cl_2 (4) F_2

12. Which of the following alkaline earth elements is the strongest reducing agent? (1) Mg (2) Sr (3) Ca (4) Ba

13. Which species can be reduced by Zn? (1) Na^+ (2) H^+ (3) Ca^{2+} (4) Mg^{2+}

14. What is the E^0 for the chemical cell whose net reaction is

$$Sn(s) + 2Ag^+(aq) \rightarrow Sn^{2+}(aq) + 2Ag(s)$$

(1) 0.66 volt (2) 0.79 volt (3) 0.94 volt (4) 1.09 volt

15. Given the reaction:

$$\underline{\quad?\quad} + Ni^{2+}(aq) \rightarrow \underline{\quad?\quad} + Ni$$

If this reaction is spontaneous, the missing reactant could be (1) Zn^0 (2) Pb^0 (3) Cu^0 (4) Sn^0

16. Which of the following reacts spontaneously with $H^+(aq)$ to form $H_2(g)$ at 298 K? (1) $Fe^{2+}(aq)$ (2) $Au(s)$ (3) $Mg(s)$ (4) $MnO_4^-(aq)$

17. Which chemical reaction is *not* spontaneous?
(1) $AgNO_3 + NaCl \rightarrow AgCl + NaNO_3$
(2) $Cu + FeCl_2 \rightarrow CuCl_2 + Fe$
(3) $Zn + 2HCl \rightarrow ZnCl_2 + H_2$
(4) $2Al + 3Ni(NO_3)_2 \rightarrow 2Al(NO_3)_3 + 3Ni$

18. Given the reaction:

$$Zn(s) + 2Ag^+(aq) \rightarrow Zn^{2+}(aq) + 2Ag(s)$$

As the reaction takes place, which of the following is true? (1) The mass of $Zn(s)$ increases. (2) The mass of $Ag(s)$ decreases. (3) The concentration of $Zn^{2+}(aq)$ increases. (4) The concentration of $Ag^+(aq)$ increases.

19. The voltage of an electrochemical cell that has reached equilibrium is (1) greater than zero (2) less than zero (3) zero

Electrochemical Cells.

Oxidation-reduction reactions involve a flow of electrons, which is an electric current. In an **electrochemical cell**, a spontaneous redox reaction is used to generate an electric current. Such cells are also known as **galvanic** or **voltaic cells**. Batteries, such as those used in cars and flashlights, are electrochemical cells.

The Daniell Cell. A Daniell cell provides a simple illustration of the essential parts of an electrochemical cell (see Figure 8-1). A Daniell cell includes two standard half-cells. A zinc electrode and a copper electrode are connected by an external wire. The migration of ions between the solutions occurs through a salt bridge containing NH_4Cl. When the half-cells are connected and the switch is closed, a redox reaction occurs:

Oxidation: $Zn^0(s) \rightarrow Zn^{2+}(aq) + 2e^-$

Reduction: $Cu^{2+}(aq) + 2e^- \rightarrow Cu^0(s)$

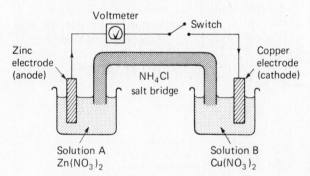

Figure 8-1. An electrochemical cell.

Electrons flow through the wire of the external circuit from the better reducing agent toward the poorer reducing agent. The relative effectiveness of metals as reducing agents is shown in Reference Table N (see page 110). In general, more active metals (those on the bottom of the table) are better reducing agents than less active metals.

Oxidation occurs at the zinc electrode, making it the anode. Since electrons are leaving the cell and entering the external circuit from this electrode, it is defined as the negative terminal in an electrochemical cell. Reduction occurs at the copper electrode, which is the cathode. Since electrons are flowing toward the copper, it is defined as the cathode, which is the positive terminal in an electrochemical cell.

The salt bridge prevents the solutions from becoming electrically charged. In the absence of a salt bridge, $Zn^{2+}(aq)$ ions, resulting from the oxidation of $Zn(s)$, would accumulate around the anode. The solution would then become positively charged and electrons could not flow to the copper half-cell. Similarly, $Cu^{2+}(aq)$ ions around the cathode would be discharged as $Cu(s)$, and the solution in the copper half-cell would become negatively charged. The salt bridge allows negative ions, $Cl^-(aq)$, to move to the zinc half-cell and positive ions, $NH_4^+(aq)$, to move to the zinc half-cell. This movement of ions maintains the electrical neutrality of the solution, and electrons can now flow from the zinc anode to the copper cathode.

Electrolytic Cells.

Redox reactions that do not occur spontaneously can be forced to proceed by the application of an electric current, a process known as **electrolysis**. Cells in which an electric current is applied to make a nonspontaneous reaction proceed are known as **electrolytic cells**. In electrolytic cells, an external source of electric current is connected so that the anode is the positive electrode, and the cathode is the negative electrode.

Electrolysis is used in electroplating, in the decomposition of fused compounds into their constituent elements, and in the decomposition of solutions of salts.

✱ Electroplating. In the electroplating process, a thin layer of metal is deposited on the surface of an electrical conductor. In an electroplating setup (see Figure 8-2, page 62), the object to be plated is connected to the cathode (−) of a direct current source. The metal to be plated on that object is connected to the anode (+). Both the object to be plated and the metal used in plating it are immersed in a solution containing ions of the metal to be plated. The anode of an electroplating apparatus is the bar of the metal that will form the plated surface. Oxidation occurs at this electrode. Reduction occurs at the cathode, which is the surface of the object to be plated. The reaction occurs when direct current is applied.

In the apparatus in Figure 8-2, copper, at the anode, is plated onto a metallic object, which acts as the cathode. The half-reactions are:

Cathode: $Cu^{2+} + 2e^- \rightarrow Cu^0(s)$

Anode: $Cu^0(s) \rightarrow Cu^{2+} + 2e^-$

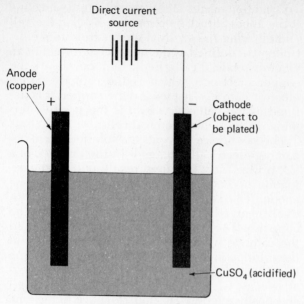

Direct current
source

Anode
(copper)

+

−

Cathode
(object to
be plated)

CuSO₄ (acidified)

Figure 8-2. Electroplating.

The mass of the anode decreases, while the mass of the cathode increases by the same amount.

✳ **Electrolysis of Fused Compounds.** Electrolysis of a fused (molten) compound can be carried out in an electrolytic cell, such as the **Downs cell**, shown in Figure 8-3. The cell is made of firebrick to maintain the high temperature required to melt sodium chloride. The half-reactions and net reaction are:

Cathode: $2[Na^+(\ell) + e^- \rightarrow Na^0(\ell)]$

Anode: $2Cl^-(\ell) \rightarrow Cl_2(g) + 2e^-$

Net reaction: $2NaCl(\ell) \rightarrow 2Na^0 + Cl_2(g)$

In electrolysis the negative pole is the cathode and the positive pole is the anode.

As with electroplating, a source of direct current is needed. Chloride ions from the melted sodium chloride are oxidized at the carbon anode to form chlorine gas, which is collected. Sodium ions are reduced at the iron cathode to form liquid sodium metal, which is drained from the cell.

✳ **Electrolysis of Salt Solutions.** Electrolysis of a water solution of a salt proceeds in a similar fashion. However, pure metals are not likely to be produced, since water is more easily reduced than are the ions of most metals. The electrolysis of sodium chloride solution is described in the following half-reactions and net reaction. Note that water rather than $Na^+(aq)$ is reduced.

Cathode: $2HOH + 2e^- \rightarrow H_2(g) + 2OH^-(aq)$

Anode: $2Cl^-(aq) \rightarrow Cl_2(g) + 2e^-$

Net reaction: $2NaCl(aq) + 2HOH \rightarrow 2NaOH(aq)$
$$+ H_2(g) + Cl_2(g)$$

The products are hydrogen gas, chlorine gas, and a solution of sodium hydroxide. $Na^+(aq)$ is a spectator ion.

✳ **Electrolysis of Water.** The apparatus shown in Figure 8-4 can be used for the electrolysis of water. Platinum electrodes are used in separate arms of the apparatus so that the hydrogen and oxygen gases do not mix and can be collected separately. A dilute solution of H_2SO_4 is generally used as the electrolyte. The half-reactions are:

Oxidation: $2H_2O \rightarrow O_2(g) + 4H^+ + 4e^-$

Reduction: $2[2H_2O + 2e^- \rightarrow H_2(g) + 2OH^-]$

Net Reaction:

$$6H_2O \rightarrow O_2(g) + 2H_2(g) + 4H^+ + 4OH^-$$

$$6H_2O \rightarrow O_2(g) + 2H_2(g) + 4H_2O$$

$$2H_2O(\ell) \rightarrow O_2(g) + 2H_2(g)$$

Notice that the volume of hydrogen produced is twice the volume of oxygen produced. Also, in the reaction, some water molecules are oxidized, while other water molecules are reduced.

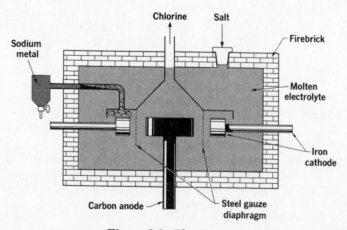

Figure 8-3. The Downs cell.

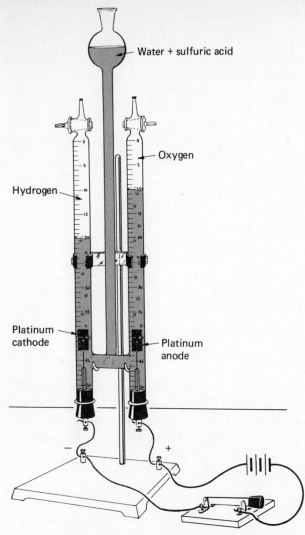

Figure 8-4. The electrolysis of water.

QUESTIONS

✱ 1.   What are the products of the electrolysis of one mole of water at STP? (1) one mole of hydrogen gas and one mole of oxygen gas (2) two moles of hydrogen gas and one mole of oxygen gas (3) one mole of hydrogen gas and one-half mole of oxygen gas (4) one-half mole of hydrogen gas and one-half mole of oxygen gas

✱ 2.   In electrolytic cells, negative ions are attracted to the (1) positive electrode, where they are oxidized (2) positive electrode, where they are reduced (3) negative electrode, where they are oxidized (4) negative electrode, where they are reduced

✱ 3.   Which atom forms an ion that is attracted to the anode in an electrolytic cell? (1) Cl (2) Li (3) Ca (4) Al

✱ 4.   In the electrolytic process used for copper plating, the object upon which the copper is to be plated is connected to a (1) positive cathode (2) negative cathode (3) positive anode (4) negative anode

✱ 5.   During the electrolysis of fused KBr, which reaction occurs at the positive electrode? (1) Br^- ions are reduced (2) Br^- ions are oxidized (3) K^+ ions are oxidized (4) K^+ ions are reduced

✱ 6.   Which reaction occurs at the cathode during the electrolysis of fused $MgCl_2$? (1) oxidation of Mg^{2+} ions (2) reduction of Mg^{2+} ions (3) oxidation of Cl^- ions (4) reduction of Cl^- ions

✱ 7.   Which half-reaction occurs at the negative electrode in an electrolytic cell in which an object is being plated with silver?
(1) $Ag^0 + e^- \rightarrow Ag^+$
(2) $Ag^+ + e^- \rightarrow Ag^0$
(3) $Ag^0 \rightarrow Ag^+ + e^-$
(4) $Ag^+ \rightarrow Ag^0 + e^-$

✱ 8.   During the electrolysis of fused $CaCl_2$, the half-reaction that occurs at the cathode is
(1) $Ca^{2+} + 2e^- \rightarrow Ca^0$
(2) $Ca^{2+} \rightarrow Ca^0 + 2e^-$
(3) $2Cl^- \rightarrow Cl_2 + 2e^-$
(4) $Cl_2 + 2e^- \rightarrow 2Cl^-$

✱ 9.   During the electrolysis of fused $BaCl_2$, which reaction occurs at the cathode? (1) Chloride ions are oxidized. (2) Chloride ions are reduced. (3) Barium ions are oxidized. (4) Barium ions are reduced.

✱ 10.   In an electrolytic cell, the reduction half-reaction occurs at a (1) positive anode (2) negative anode (3) positive cathode (4) negative cathode

Questions 11–13 apply to an electrochemical cell with the following half-reactions:

$$Al^{3+}(aq) + 3e^- \rightarrow Al(s) \qquad (E^0 = -1.66 \text{ volts})$$

$$Sn^{4+}(aq) + 2e^- \rightarrow Sn^{2+}(aq) \qquad (E^0 = +0.15 \text{ volt})$$

11.   Which species is the reducing agent? (1) Sn^{4+} (2) Sn^{2+} (3) Al^{3+} (4) Al

12.   What is the net E^0 for the reaction? (1) 1.51 volts (2) 1.81 volts (3) 2.87 volts (4) 3.77 volts

13.   In the balanced equation for the net reaction, what is the ratio of $Sn^{4+}(aq)$ to $Al^{3+}(aq)$? (1) 3:2 (2) 2:3 (3) 4:3 (4) 3:4

Base your answers to questions 14–17 on the following reaction between copper and concentrated nitric acid.

$$Cu + 4HNO_3 \rightarrow 2NO_2 + Cu(NO_3)_2 + 2H_2O$$

14.   The reducing agent in this reaction is (1) Cu (2) Cu^{2+} (3) H^+ (4) NO_2

15.   Which species is most likely to be present primarily in the gas phase? (1) HNO_3 (2) NO_2 (3) Cu (4) $Cu(NO_3)_2$

16.   During this reaction, the oxidation number of hydrogen (1) increases (2) decreases (3) remains the same

17.   If, after all the reactants are consumed, a strip of zinc is added to the solution, which of the following substances will form? (1) $H_2(g)$ (2) $N_2(g)$ (3) $HNO_3(aq)$ (4) Cu(s)

Base your answers to questions 18 and 19 on the following diagram, which represents a chemical cell at

Redox Reactions and Electrochemistry

298 K, and on Reference Table N (see page 110). The equation that accompanies the diagram represents the net cell reaction.

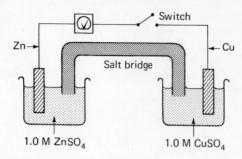

$$2Al^0(s) + 3Cu^{2+}(aq) \rightarrow 2Al^{3+}(aq) + 3Cu^0(s)$$

18. When the switch is closed, the maximum potential (E^0) for the cell will be   (1) +1.32 volts   (2) +2.00 volts   (3) −1.32 volts   (4) −2.00 volts

19. When the switch is closed, electrons in the external circuit will flow from   (1) Al to Al^{3+} (2) Al to Cu   (3) Cu to Al   (4) Cu to Cu^{2+}

Questions 20–22 refer to the following diagram of a chemical cell.

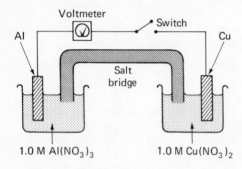

$$Zn^2 + 2e^- \rightarrow Zn(s) \quad (E^0 = -0.76 \text{ v})$$
$$Cu^{2+} + 2e^- \rightarrow Cu(s) \quad (E^0 = +0.34 \text{ v})$$

20. Which is the reduction half-reaction in this cell?
(1) $Cu \rightarrow Cu^{2+} + 2e^-$
(2) $Cu^{2+} + 2e^- \rightarrow Cu$
(3) $Zn^{2+} + 2e^- \rightarrow Zn$
(4) $Zn \rightarrow Zn^{2+} + 2e^-$

21. When the switch is closed, the standard potential (E^0) for the cell is   (1) 0.34 volt   (2) 0.42 volt   (3) 0.76 volt   (4) 1.10 volts

22. The salt bridge provides a path for the movement of   (1) ions   (2) electrons   (3) Cu atoms   (4) Zn atoms

✳ BALANCING COMPLEX REDOX EQUATIONS

Some redox equations are too complex to balance by inspection. Consider the equation:

$$H_2S + HNO_3 \rightarrow S + NO + H_2O$$

Hydrogen appears in more than one species on the left, and oxygen appears in more than one species on the right.

Two common approaches to balancing complex redox equations such as the preceding one are the electron-transfer method (also called the oxidation number method) and the ion-water method (also called the ion-electron method).

✳ Electron-Transfer Method.

The **electron-transfer method** of balancing redox equations is somewhat more cumbersome than the ion-water method. It includes all spectator ions as well as participating species. Unlike the ion-water method, however, its use is not restricted to water solutions.

The steps involved in the electron-transfer method will be illustrated by using the preceding equation.

1. Begin by assigning oxidation numbers to each element according to the rules in Table 8-1 on page 55.

$$\overset{[-2]}{\underset{[2(+1)]}{H_2S}} + \overset{[+5]}{\underset{[+1][3(-2)]}{HNO_3}} \rightarrow \overset{[0]}{S} + \overset{[+2]}{\underset{[-2]}{NO}} + \overset{[-2]}{\underset{[2(+1)]}{H_2O}}$$

2. Identify the elements that have undergone a change in oxidation number. These are the elements that have been oxidized and reduced. Write the electronic equations.

$$\text{Oxidation: } S^{-2} \rightarrow S^0 + 2e^-$$
$$\text{Reduction: } N^{+5} + 3e^- \rightarrow N^{+2}$$

3. Conserve electrons by multiplying each electronic equation by a coefficient that makes the electrons lost equal the electrons gained.

$$3[S^{-2} \rightarrow S^0 + 2e^-]$$
$$2[N^{+5} + 3e^- \rightarrow N^{+2}]$$

4. Add the two half-reactions.

$$3S^{-2} + 2N^{+5} \rightarrow 3S^0 + 2N^{+2}$$

5. Balance the given equation.

$$3H_2S + 2HNO_3 \rightarrow 3S + 2NO + 4H_2O$$

Notice that $4H_2O$ accounts for the H's (in $3H_2S$ and $2HNO_3$) and for the O's in HNO_3 that formed 2NO and $4H_2O$.

✳ *Sample Problem* _____

Balance the following equation by using the electron-transfer method:

$$I_2 + HNO_3 \rightarrow HIO_3 + NO_2 + H_2O$$

1. Assign oxidation numbers.

$$\overset{0}{I_2} + \overset{+1}{H}\overset{+5}{N}\overset{3(-2)}{O_3} \rightarrow \overset{+1}{H}\overset{+5}{I}\overset{3(-2)}{O_3} + \overset{+4}{N}\overset{2(-2)}{O_2}$$
$$+ \overset{2(+1)}{H_2}\overset{-2}{O}$$

2. Identify the elements that have undergone a change in oxidation number, and write the oxidation and reduction half-reactions.

Oxidation: $I_2 \rightarrow 2I^{+5} + 10e^-$

Reduction: $N^{+5} + e^- \rightarrow N^{+4}$

3. Conserve electrons by multiplying each half-reaction by a coefficient that makes the electrons lost equal the electrons gained.

$$I_2 \rightarrow 2I^{+5} + 10e^-$$

$$10[N^{+5} + e^- \rightarrow N^{+4}]$$

4. Add the two half-reactions.

$$I_2 + 10N^{+5} \rightarrow 2I^{+5} + 10N^{+4}$$

5. Balance the given equation.

$$I_2 + 10HNO_3 \rightarrow 2HIO_3 + 10NO_2 + 4H_2O$$

---

* Ion-Water Method.

The **ion-water method** of balancing complex redox equations is useful for reactions that take place in aqueous solution. The step-by-step approach used in this method will be illustrated by using the following partial equation:

$$Cr_2O_7{}^{2-} + N_2H_4{}^+ \rightarrow N_2{}^0 + Cr^{3+}$$

1. Write the half-reactions.

$$Cr_2O_7{}^{2-} \rightarrow Cr^{3+}$$

$$N_2H_4{}^+ \rightarrow N_2{}^0$$

2. Balance each half-reaction with respect to atoms other than H and O.

$$Cr_2O_7{}^{2-} \rightarrow 2Cr^{3+}$$

$$N_2H_4{}^+ \rightarrow N_2{}^0$$

3. Balance oxygen atoms by adding H_2O to the half-reactions where needed.

$$Cr_2O_7{}^{2-} \rightarrow 2Cr^{3+} + 7H_2O$$

$$N_2H_4{}^+ \rightarrow N_2{}^0$$

4. Add H^+ where needed to balance hydrogen. Do not forget to balance hydrogen introduced by the addition of water in Step 3.

$$14H^+ + Cr_2O_7{}^{2-} \rightarrow 2Cr^{3+} + 7H_2O$$

$$N_2H_4{}^+ \rightarrow N_2{}^0 + 4H^+$$

5. Add electrons to balance charges.

Reduction: $Cr_2O_7{}^{2-} + 14H^+ + 6e^- \rightarrow$

$$2Cr^{3+} + 2H_2O$$

Oxidation: $N_2H_4{}^+ \rightarrow N_2{}^0 + 4H^+ + 3e^-$

6. Choose multipliers for half-reactions so that the number of electrons lost equals the number of electrons gained.

$$1[Cr_2O_7{}^{2-} + 14H^+ + 6e^- \rightarrow 2Cr^{3+} + 7H_2O]$$

$$2[N_2H_4{}^+ \rightarrow N_2{}^0 + 4H^+ + 3e^-]$$

7. Combine the half-reactions to get the overall balanced equation.

$$14H^+ + Cr_2O_7{}^{2-} + 2N_2H_4{}^+ + 6e^- \rightarrow$$

$$2Cr^{3+} + 2N_2{}^0 + 7H_2O + 8H^+ + 6e^-$$

8. Combine like terms. If any species appear on both sides of the equation, subtract the one with the smaller coefficient from both sides. If the coefficients are equal, the terms will cancel out. The electrons always cancel out because the number gained must equal the number lost.

$$6H^+ + Cr_2O_7{}^{2-} + 2N_2H_4{}^+ \rightarrow$$

$$2Cr^{3+} + 2N_2 + 7H_2O$$

* Sample Problem

Use the ion-water method to balance the following equation:

$$BrO_3{}^- + I^- \rightarrow Br^- + I_2{}^0$$

1. Write the partial reactions.

$$BrO_3{}^- \rightarrow Br^-$$

$$I^- \rightarrow I_2{}^0$$

2. Balance each partial reaction with respect to atoms other than H and O.

$$BrO_3{}^- \rightarrow Br^-$$

$$2I^- \rightarrow I_2{}^0$$

3. Balance oxygen atoms by adding H_2O to the partial reactions where needed.

$$BrO_3{}^- \rightarrow Br^- + 3H_2O$$

$$2I^- \rightarrow I_2{}^0$$

4. Add H^+ where needed to balance hydrogen.

$$BrO_3{}^- + 6H^+ \rightarrow Br^- + 3H_2O$$

$$2I^- \rightarrow I_2{}^0$$

5. Add electrons to balance charges.

Reduction: $BrO_3{}^- + 6H^+ + 6e^- \rightarrow$

$$Br^- + 3H_2O$$

Oxidation: $2I^- \rightarrow I_2{}^0 + 2e^-$

6. Choose multipliers for half-reactions so that the number of electrons lost equals the number of electrons gained.

$$1[BrO_3{}^- + 6H^+ + 6e^- \rightarrow Br^- + 3H_2O]$$

$$3[2I^- \rightarrow I_2{}^0 + 2e^-]$$

7. Combine the half-reactions to get the overall balanced equation.

$$BrO_3{}^- + 6I^- + 6H^+ + 6e^- \rightarrow$$

$$Br^- + 3I_2{}^0 + 3H_2O + 6e^-$$

8. Combine like terms. If any species appear on both sides of the equation, subtract the one with the smaller coefficient from both sides. If the coefficients are equal, the terms will cancel out. The electrons always cancel out because the number lost must equal the number gained.

$$BrO_3^- + 6I^- + 6H^+ \rightarrow Br^- + 3I_2^0 + 3H_2O$$

✳ QUESTIONS

1. Given the reaction:

$$KMnO_4 + SnSO_4 + H_2SO_4 \rightarrow$$
$$Sn(SO_4)_2 + MnSO_4 + K_2SO_4 + H_2O$$

When the equation is completely balanced by using smallest whole numbers, the coefficient of H_2O is (1) 2 (2) 4 (3) 6 (4) 8

2. Given the equation:

$$Cr^0 + Sn^{2+} \rightarrow Cr^{3+} + Sn^0$$

What is the coefficient for Cr^{3+} when the equation is balanced by using smallest whole-number coefficients? (1) 1 (2) 2 (3) 3 (4) 6

3. Given the equation:

$$\_Fe^{3+} + \_Sn^{2+} \rightarrow \_Fe^{2+} + \_Sn^{4+}$$

When the equation is completely balanced by using smallest whole numbers, the coefficient of Fe^{3+} is (1) 1 (2) 2 (3) 3 (4) 4

4. Given the reaction:

$$\_K_2Cr_2O_7 + \_HCl \rightarrow$$
$$\_KCl + CrCl_3 + \_H_2O + \_Cl_2$$

When the equation is completely balanced by using smallest whole numbers, the coefficient of Cl_2 is (1) 1 (2) 2 (3) 3 (4) 4

5. Given the reaction:

$$\_KMnO_4 + \_HBr \rightarrow$$
$$\_KBr + \_MnBr_2 + \_H_2O + \_Br_2$$

When the equation is completely balanced by using smallest whole numbers, the coefficient of Br_2 is (1) 1 (2) 5 (3) 3 (4) 8

6. Given the reaction $\_KClO_3 \rightarrow \_KCl + \_O_2$. When the equation is completely balanced by using smallest whole numbers, the coefficient of O_2 is (1) 1 (2) 2 (3) 3 (4) 4

Organic Chemistry

The branch of chemistry that deals with the study of carbon compounds is called **organic chemistry**. Until the early 19th century, chemists believed that the compounds found in living things could not be produced in the laboratory. However, in 1828, the German chemist Friedrich Wöhler synthesized urea, $CO(NH_2)_2$, from ammonium chloride and silver cyanate. Wöhler's experiment marked the beginning of modern organic chemistry.

Although organic compounds can be synthesized from inorganic compounds, it is more efficient to begin with existing organic compounds. The raw materials from which organic compounds are produced include plant sources, such as petroleum, coal, and wood, and animal sources, such as fats and proteins.

The number of organic compounds that can be synthesized is infinitely large because of a unique characteristic of the carbon atom: it can form four covalent bonds with other carbon atoms and with many other kinds of atoms, especially hydrogen. Carbon atoms can bond together to form chainlike compounds of almost any length. Some of these chains of carbon atoms are open, while others form rings that are closed.

CHARACTERISTICS OF ORGANIC COMPOUNDS

Chemical Properties.

1. Organic compounds are generally nonpolar and tend to be soluble in nonpolar solvents and insoluble in water. Some organic compounds, however, including acetic acid, sugars, and alcohols, are somewhat polar and are soluble in water.

2. Organic compounds are generally nonelectrolytes. However, a few carbon compounds, including organic acids such as formic acid and oxalic acid, undergo ionization in water solution and are electrolytes.

3. Organic compounds generally have low melting and low boiling points. In nonpolar organic compounds, only weak attractive forces exist between molecules. The melting points of most of these compounds are below 300°C.

4. Reactions involving organic compounds that are nonionic are generally slower than those involving inorganic compounds. In organic compounds that are molecular, there is strong covalent bonding between atoms. Under these circumstances, the intermediate activated complexes, which are part of the reaction mechanism, have relatively high activation energies and do not form readily (see Unit 6, page 39). These factors account for the relatively slow rate of chemical change in reactions of organic compounds.

Bonding.
Covalent bonding between atoms is characteristic of carbon compounds. The carbon atom has four valence electrons, and it can form four covalent bonds. The four single bonds of the carbon atom are spatially directed toward the four corners of a regular tetrahedron (a four-faced pyramid).

Carbon atoms can form covalent bonds with other carbon atoms, producing compounds that are molecular in nature. Two adjacent carbon atoms can share one, two, or three pairs of electrons. Bonds involving one shared pair of electrons are called **single bonds**. Bonds involving two and three pairs of shared electrons are called **double bonds** and **triple bonds**, respectively.

Molecules that have only single bonds between carbon atoms are said to be **saturated**, while molecules that have one or more double or triple bonds between carbon atoms are said to be **unsaturated**. Unsaturated compounds tend to be more reactive than saturated compounds; the more multiple bonds a compound has, the more reactive it is likely to be.

Covalently bonded substances exhibit forces of attraction between molecules; these forces include van der Waals forces, dipole attraction, and hydrogen bonding. Where these forces are the weakest, the compounds are gases or liquids under ordinary temperatures and pressures. Stronger forces are associated with substances that are molecular solids under ordinary conditions.

Structural Formulas.
The geometry of molecules can be approximated in two dimensions by **structural formulas**. In structural formulas, a covalent bond is represented by a short line, or dash, between the chemical symbols representing atoms. Each dash represents a shared pair of electrons. A pair of atoms joined by two dashes represents a double bond; three dashes represent a triple bond.

Structural formulas show the number and kinds of atoms in a molecule. Since structural formulas are written in two dimensions, they do not fully represent the three-dimensional nature of the molecule. For example, molecules of methane, CH_4, have a tetrahedral arrangement in space. Different structural formulas for methane are shown in Figure 9-1 on page 68.

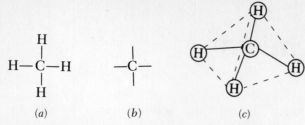

(a)   (b)   (c)

Figure 9-1. (*a*) Structural formula for methane showing all atoms. (*b*) Structural formula for methane in which symbols for hydrogen atoms are omitted. (*c*) Structural formula for methane showing its three-dimensional tetrahedral structure.

Isomers.

Compounds that have the same molecular formula but different structural formulas are called **isomers**. Compounds that are isomers have the same number and kind of atoms in their molecules, but the atoms are arranged in different sequences. In some instances, isomers may have different spatial arrangements of their atoms. As the number of atoms in molecules increases, the possibilities for different sequences and spatial arrangements also increases, along with the number of possible isomers. Figure 9-2 shows two pairs of isomers.

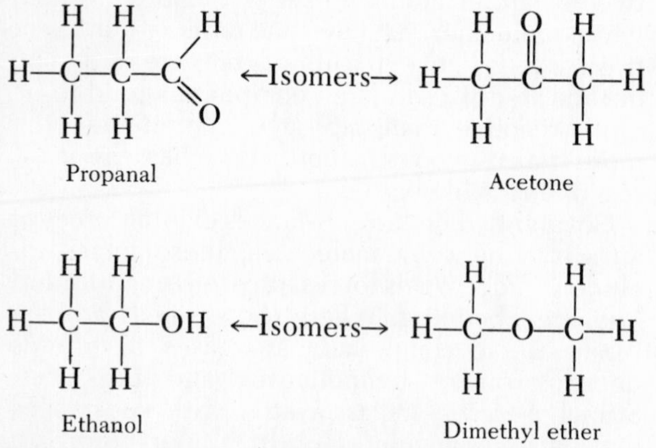

Propanal ←Isomers→ Acetone

Ethanol ←Isomers→ Dimethyl ether

Figure 9-2. Propanal and acetone (C_3H_6O) are isomers, as are ethanol and dimethyl ether (C_2H_6O).

QUESTIONS

1. Compared with inorganic compounds, organic compounds usually have (1) greater solubility in water (2) a tendency to form ions more rapidly (3) more rapid reaction rates (4) lower melting points

2. Which is characteristic of most organic compounds? (1) They have very strong intermolecular forces. (2) They are primarily ionic in character. (3) They have relatively low boiling points. (4) They have relatively low vapor pressures.

3. Organic compounds that are essentially nonpolar and exhibit weak intermolecular forces have (1) low melting points (2) low vapor pressure (3) high conductivity in solution (4) high boiling points

4. Which compound is an isomer of CH_3COOCH_3? (1) CH_3OCH_3 (2) CH_3CH_2COOH (3) CH_3COCH_3 (4) $CH_3CH_2CH_2OH$

5. Which compound below is an isomer of the following compound?

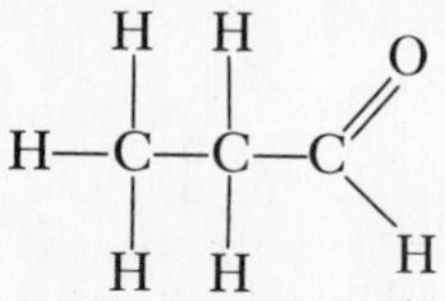

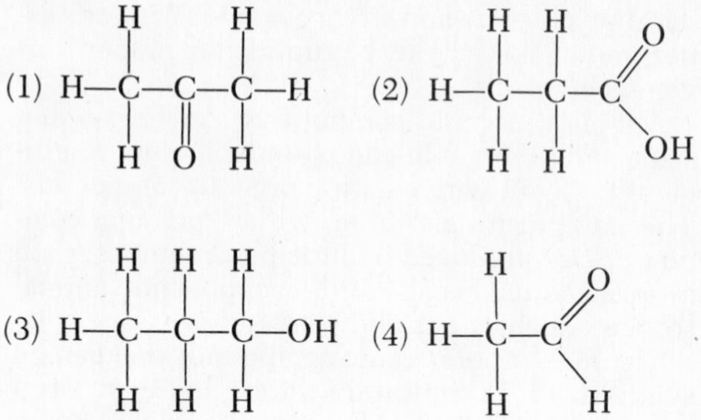

(1)   (2)

(3)   (4)

6. Which of the following has the greatest possible number of isomers? (1) C_4H_{10} (2) C_2H_6 (3) C_5H_{12} (4) C_3H_8

HYDROCARBONS

The most important kinds of organic compounds are the hydrocarbons, alcohols, organic acids, aldehydes, ketones, and ethers. Organic compounds are classified according to their composition, chemical structure, and properties.

Many organic compounds can be classified into groups that have related structures and properties. Such groups are called a **homologous series**. Each member of a homologous series differs from the preceding member by a common increment, usually —CH_2. Each member of a homologous series matches a common general formula. As the members of a homologous series increase in molecular size, the boiling points and freezing points of the compounds increase due to an increase in the strength of the van der Waals forces.

Compounds that contain only carbon and hydrogen are called **hydrocarbons**. Homologous series of hydrocarbons include the alkanes, alkenes, alkynes, and benzene series.

Alkanes.

Saturated, open-chain (also called straight-chain) hydrocarbons with the general formula C_nH_{2n+2} are called **alkanes**. The alkanes are also called the *methane series* or the *paraffin series*. Each alkane differs from the preceding member of the series by an increment of —CH_2. Isomerism is found among the alkanes beginning with the fourth member of the series, butane

Table 9-1. The Alkane Series

Name	Molecular Formula	Structural Formula	Some Isomers
Methane	CH_4		none
Ethane	C_2H_6 (CH_3CH_3)		none
Propane	C_3H_8 $(CH_3CH_2CH_3)$		none
Butane	C_4H_{10} $(CH_3CH_2CH_2CH_3)$	 butane	 2-methylpropane
Pentane	C_5H_{12} $(CH_3CH_2CH_2CH_2CH_3)$	 pentane	 2-methylbutane 2,2-dimethylpropane

(In the last column of the table, the numbers that precede the names of the alkanes identify the specific carbon atoms to which the methyl groups are attached.)

(C_4H_{10}). Table 9-1 shows the first five members of the alkane series and their isomers.

Alkenes.

The homologous series with the general formula C_nH_{2n} is known as the **alkene series**. Alkenes are unsaturated hydrocarbons with one carbon-carbon double bond. (Hydrocarbons that have two double bonds are not alkenes—they are called *dienes*.) Like the alkanes, each alkene differs from the preceding member of the series by an increment of —CH_2.

In this series, which is also known as the *ethylene series* or *olefin series*, the name of each member ends in "ene." The prefix of the name is determined by the number of carbon atoms in the compound and follows the same pattern as the alkane series. For example, the first member of the group has two carbon atoms and is named ethene. Table 9-2 on page 70 lists the first four members of this family and gives the molecular formula, the structural formula, and some isomers for each olefin.

Alkynes.

Hydrocarbons that have one triple bond are called **alkynes**. Members of this series have the general formula C_nH_{2n-2}. The names of all alkynes end in "yne," and each alkyne differs from the preceding member of the series by an increment of —CH_2. The prefixes for the names of these compounds are the same as those for the alkenes. The first member of the series is ethyne, C_2H_2. The common name of ethyne is **acetylene**, and the alkynes are also known as the *acetylene series*. The structural formula for acetylene is —$C\equiv C$—.

Benzene Series.

The series of closed-chain, or ring-shaped, hydrocarbons with the general formula C_nH_{2n-6} is called the **benzene series**. Members of this series are also known as the **aromatic hydrocarbons**. The name originally referred to their distinctive odors, but in modern use, it refers to the specific kind of bonding that is characteristic of the series. The first two mem-

Table 9-2. The Alkene Series

Name	Molecular Formula	Structural Formula	Straight and Branched Chain Isomers
Ethene (Ethylene)	C_2H_4	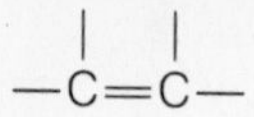 $-C=C-$	none
Propene	C_3H_6	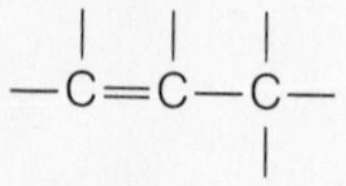 $-C=C-C-$	none
Butene	C_4H_8	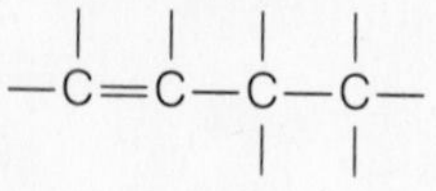 $-C=C-C-C-$ 1-butene	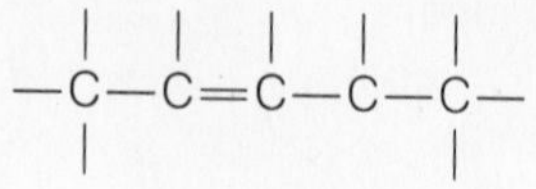 $-C-C=C-C-C-$ 2-butene
Pentene	C_5H_{10}	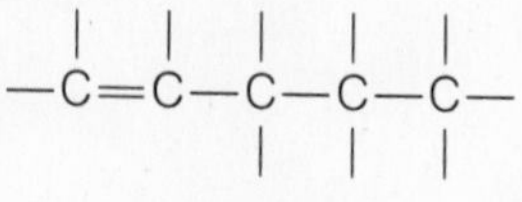 $-C=C-C-C-C-$ 1-pentene	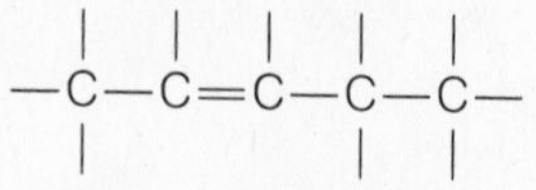 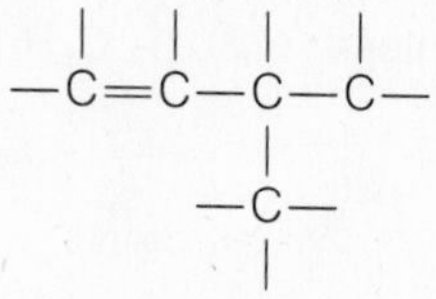 $-C-C=C-C-C-$ 2-pentene $-C=C-C-C-$ $-C-$ 3-methyl-1-butene

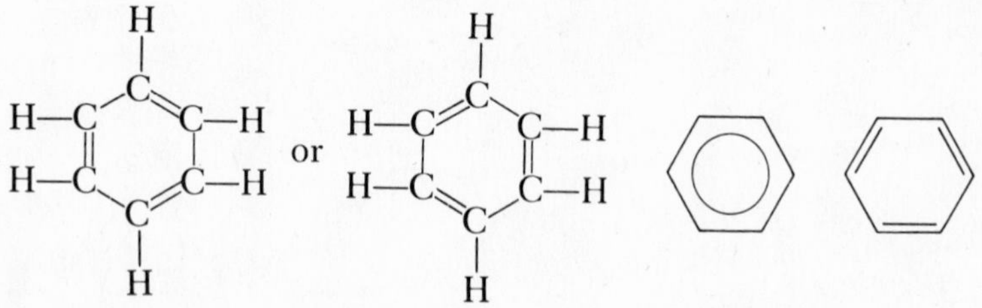

Figure 9-3. All of these structures represent the aromatic benzene ring.

bers of the series are benzene (C_6H_6) and toluene (C_7H_8).

In an aromatic ring, all of the carbon-carbon bonds are the same. Their structure and properties are intermediate between single bonds and double bonds because of the mobility of the electrons in the ring (see Figure 9-3a).

The structure of a benzene molecule can be simplified by using the structures shown in Figure 9-3b and c. The intermediate nature of the bonding makes benzene rather unreactive.

Toluene has a **methyl group** (—CH_3) substituted for a hydrogen atom on a benzene ring (see Figure 9-4).

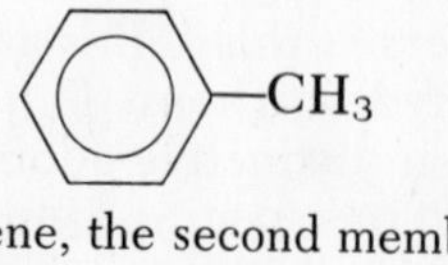

Figure 9-4. Toluene, the second member of the benzene series.

QUESTIONS

1. Which compound has a formula that corresponds to C_nH_{2n}? (1) ethylene (2) methane (3) propane (4) benzene
2. Which is a saturated hydrocarbon? (1) C_2H_6 (2) C_3H_6 (3) C_4H_8 (4) C_5H_{10}
3. How many carbon atoms are in a methyl group? (1) 1 (2) 2 (3) 3 (4) 4
4. Which compound is an isomer of butane?

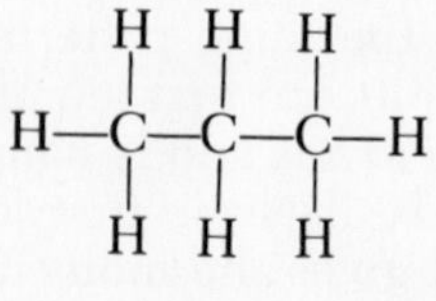

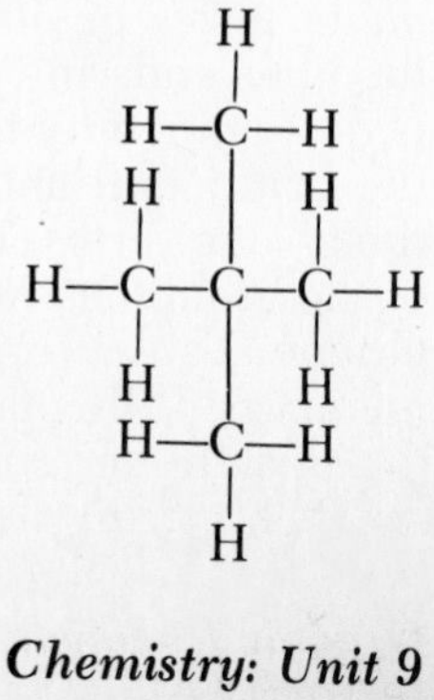

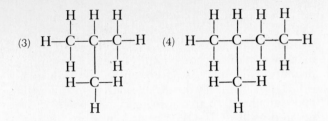

(3)   (4)

(3)   (4)

5. The compound $CH_3CH_2CH_2CH_3$ belongs to the series that has the general formula (1) C_nH_{2n-2} (2) C_nH_{2n+2} (3) C_nH_{n-6} (4) C_nH_{n+6}

6. Which molecule contains a triple covalent bond between adjacent carbon atoms? (1) C_2H_4 (2) C_2H_2 (3) C_3H_6 (4) C_3H_8

7. Each member of the alkane series differs from the preceding member by one additional carbon atom and (1) one hydrogen atom (2) two hydrogen atoms (3) three hydrogen atoms (4) four hydrogen atoms

8. A compound with the formula C_6H_6 is (1) benzene (2) toluene (3) butane (4) pentene

9. How many hydrogen atoms are in a molecule of ethyne? (1) 6 (2) 2 (3) 8 (4) 4

10. Which compound is unsaturated? (1) 1-chloropropane (2) 2-methylbutene (3) ethane (4) pentane

11. Which straight-chain alkene has the highest normal boiling point? (1) C_2H_4 (2) C_3H_6 (3) C_4H_8 (4) C_5H_{10}

12. Which structural formula represents toluene?

(1)   (2)

(3)   (4)

13. The total number of covalent bonds in a molecule of C_3H_8 is (1) 11 (2) 10 (3) 3 (4) 8

14. Molecules of 2-methylpropane and butane differ in their (1) structural formulas (2) molecular formulas (3) number of carbon atoms (4) number of covalent bonds

15. Which structural formula represents an unsaturated hydrocarbon?

(1)   (2)

16. Which is the correct molecular formula of pentene? (1) C_5H_8 (2) C_5H_{10} (3) C_5H_{12} (4) C_5H_{14}

17. The hydrocarbon C_7H_8 belongs to the same homologous series of hydrocarbons as (1) propene (2) pentene (3) butene (4) benzene

18. Which formula represents a hydrocarbon with a double covalent bond? (1) CH_3Cl (2) C_2H_4 (3) C_2H_6 (4) C_2H_3Cl

19. Which compound is a member of the alkyne series? (1) C_2H_2 (2) C_3H_6 (3) C_5H_{10} (4) C_6H_6

20. Which compound contains one double bond? (1) ethane (2) ethene (3) propane (4) propyne

21. Which compound is a member of the alkene series of hydrocarbons? (1) benzene (2) propene (3) toluene (4) butadiene

22. The members of the alkane series of hydrocarbons are similar in that each member has the same (1) empirical formula (2) general formula (3) structural formula (4) molecular formula

23. Which is the correct structural formula of propene?

(1)   (2)

(3)   (4)

24. Which compound has the lowest normal boiling point? (1) butane (2) ethane (3) methane (4) propane

25. The structures shown below may be used to represent (1) benzene (2) methane (3) ethyne (4) cyclopropane

or

26. Which compound contains a triple bond? (1) CH_4 (2) C_2H_2 (3) C_3H_6 (4) C_4H_{10}

ORGANIC ALCOHOLS AND ACIDS

In addition to hydrocarbons, there are other series of organic compounds in which one or more hydrogen atoms of a hydrocarbon have been replaced by other elements. The names of these compounds are usually related to the corresponding hydrocarbon. However, these derived compounds are not necessarily prepared directly from the hydrocarbon itself.

Most of these families of compounds contain functional groups. **A functional group** is a particular arrangement of a few atoms such as —OH in alcohols and —COOH in acids. The presence of a functional group accounts for the special properties in many organic compounds. Many organic compounds can be considered to be composed of a hydrocarbon chain or ring with one or more functional groups attached.

Alcohols.

Compounds in which one or more hydrogen atoms of a hydrocarbon have been replaced by an —OH group are **alcohols**. Ordinarily, no more than one —OH group can be attached to any one carbon atom in a hydrocarbon chain. Alcohols are classified according to the number of —OH groups in the molecule or according to the number of carbon chains attached to the carbon atom with the —OH group.

Alcohols are not bases. The —OH group of an alcohol does not form a hydroxide ion in aqueous solution.

Primary Alcohols. The most common alcohols are **primary alcohols**, compounds in which the —OH group is attached to a carbon atom on the end of a chain. Since the functional group can be at the end group of any hydrocarbon, a primary alcohol is frequently represented as R—OH, where "R" represents the rest of the molecule, usually a hydrocarbon chain. The end group of a primary alcohol is frequently written as —CH_2OH. This is the functional group of primary alcohols, so that a primary alcohol is designated as R—CH_2OH. Its structural formula is shown in Figure 9-5.

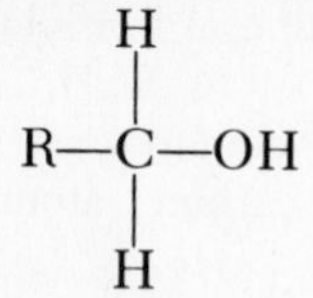

$$
\begin{array}{c}
H \\
| \\
R—C—OH \\
| \\
H
\end{array}
$$

Figure 9-5. The general structure of a primary alcohol.

Primary alcohols are named from the corresponding alkanes by replacing the final "e" with the ending "ol." Thus, the first member of the group is methanol, from methane, the second, ethanol, from ethane. The common names of the alcohols were formerly derived from the name of the corresponding alkane by changing the ending "ane" to "yl" and adding the name "alcohol." Thus, CH_3OH, methanol, was called methyl alcohol, and ethanol was called ethyl alcohol. The names and formulas of the five simplest primary alcohols are shown in Table 9-3. More complex alcohols are discussed on page 75.

Table 9-3. The First Five Primary Alcohols

Chemical Name	Common Name	Molecular Formula	Structural Formula
Methanol	Methyl alcohol	CH_3OH	—C—OH (methanol)
Ethanol	Ethyl alcohol	C_2H_5OH	—C—C—OH (ethanol)
Propanol	Propyl alcohol	C_3H_7OH	—C—C—C—OH (1-propanol)
Butanol	Butyl alcohol	C_4H_9OH	—C—C—C—C—OH (1-butanol)
Pentanol	Pentyl (amyl) alcohol	$C_5H_{11}OH$	—C—C—C—C—C—OH (1-pentanol)

Organic Acids.

Compounds that contain the functional group R—COOH are called **organic acids**, or **carboxylic acids**. The structural formula for the acid, or **carboxyl**, group is shown in Figure 9-6. Organic acids are named from the corresponding alkanes by replacing the final "e" with the ending "oic" and adding the word "acid." The first two members of this series are methanoic acid, HCOOH, and ethanoic acid, CH₃COOH. They are better known by their common names, formic acid and acetic acid (see Figure 9-7).

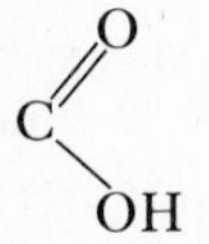

Figure 9-6. The general structure of an organic acid.

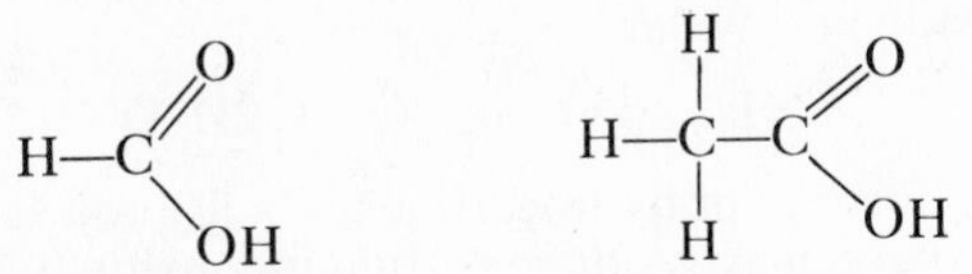

Formic acid
(methanoic acid)

Acetic acid
(ethanoic acid)

Figure 9-7. Structural formulas of formic acid and acetic acid.

An example of a long-chain organic acid is stearic acid, $C_{17}H_{35}COOH$, also called a **fatty acid**. Fatty acids are related to fats and are discussed on page 74.

QUESTIONS

1. Which is the formula for ethanol?

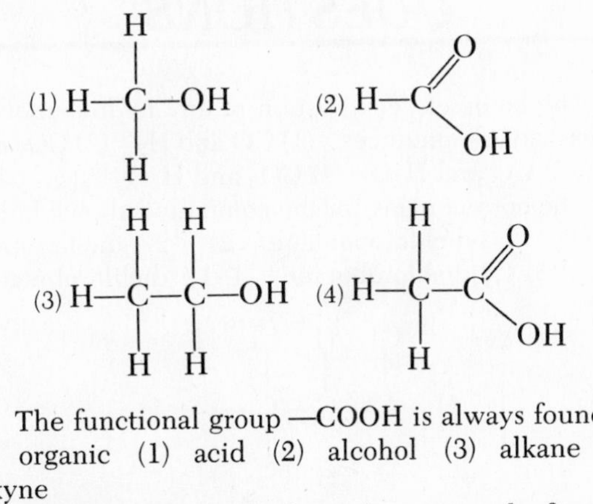

2. The functional group —COOH is always found in an organic (1) acid (2) alcohol (3) alkane (4) alkyne

3. Which compound has the general formula R—OH? (1) methanol (2) methane (3) methanoic acid (4) propene

4. What is the formula for pentanol? (1) C_5H_{12} (2) $C_5H_{11}OH$ (3) C_4H_{10} (4) C_4H_9OH

5. A particular arrangement of atoms that describes the properties of a series of compounds, such as organic acids or alcohols, is called a (1) carboxyl group (2) methyl group (3) functional group (4) hydroxyl group

6. The third member of the homologous series of primary alcohols is (1) ethanol (2) propanol (3) butanol (4) propane

7. Acetic acid, CH₃COOH, is the common name for (1) methanol (2) ethanoic acid (3) methanoic acid (4) ethanol

8. Compounds in which there is an —OH group attached to a carbon atom at the end of a hydrocarbon chain are called (1) organic acids (2) alkanes (3) aromatic compounds (4) primary alcohols

REACTIONS OF ORGANIC COMPOUNDS

Reactions of organic compounds generally occur more slowly than do reactions of inorganic compounds. Organic reactions often involve only the functional groups of the reacting species. This leaves the greater part of the reacting molecules relatively unchanged during the course of the reaction.

Substitution Reactions.

Reactions in which one kind of atom or group of atoms is replaced by another kind of atom or group of atoms are called **substitution reactions**. Except for combustion and thermal decomposition, reactions of saturated hydrocarbons are usually substitution reactions in which one or more hydrogen atoms are replaced.

When a halogen atom replaces a hydrogen atom in a saturated hydrocarbon, *halogen substitution* is said to have occurred. The products, called **halogen derivatives**, are named using a standard system. The suffix comes from the name of the straight-chain alkane with the same number of carbon atoms. The prefix shows which atoms or functional groups have been added and the carbon atom in the straight chain to which they are attached. A few examples of halogen derivatives are shown in Figure 9-8 on page 74. Note that structures (*b*) and (*c*) are isomers.

Addition Reactions.

The addition of one or more atoms, designated as X, to an unsaturated hydrocarbon molecule at a double or triple bond is called an **addition reaction**. As a result of addition reactions, the multiple bonds are broken and unsaturated molecules become saturated (see Figure 9-9, page 74).

Addition reactions have a high rate of reaction. Because addition reactions take place more easily than do substitution reactions, unsaturated compounds tend to be more reactive than are saturated compounds. For example, because alkynes are more unsaturated than alkenes, they are generally more reactive than alkenes.

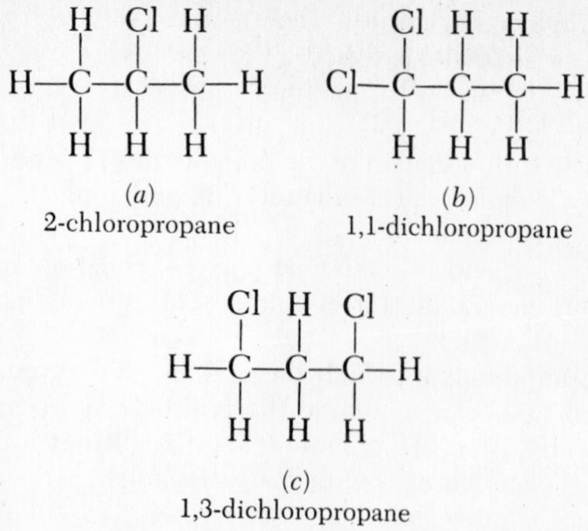

(a)
2-chloropropane

(b)
1,1-dichloropropane

(c)
1,3-dichloropropane

Figure 9-8. Structural formulas of three halogen derivatives. (The numbers in the names of the halogen derivatives identify the specific carbon atoms to which the halogen atoms are attached.)

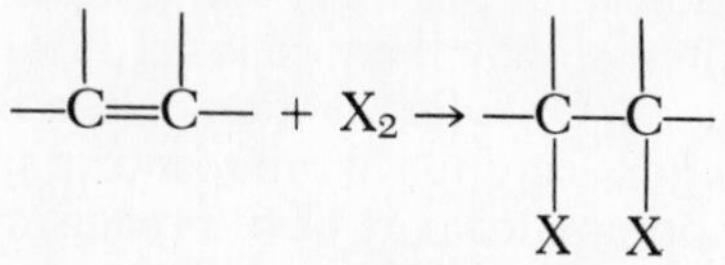

Figure 9-9. An addition reaction.

Addition of Halogens.
Halogen derivatives can be formed by the addition of halogens to unsaturated compounds, as well as by substitution reactions. The addition of chlorine and bromine takes place at appreciable rates, even at room temperature. Iodine is less reactive than chlorine and bromine in addition reactions.

Hydrogenation.
The addition of hydrogen to an unsaturated molecule is called **hydrogenation**. Hydrogenation reactions usually require the presence of a catalyst and elevated temperatures. The compounds formed are usually saturated hydrocarbons.

Fermentation.
The process in which enzymes from living organisms act as catalysts in the partial breakdown of an organic compound is called **fermentation**. Ethanol is a product of the fermentation of sugar (glucose) by yeast. The enzyme involved is called *zymase*.

$$C_6H_{12}O_6 \xrightarrow{\text{zymase}} 2C_2H_5OH + 2CO_2$$
sugar   ethanol   carbon dioxide

Esterification.
The reaction of an organic acid with an alcohol to form an ester and water is called **esterification**. Esters are covalent compounds with the general formula RCOOR'. The general equation for esterification is

$$RCOOH + R'OH \rightleftharpoons RCOOR' + H_2O$$
organic acid   alcohol   ester   water

Esterification proceeds slowly and is reversible. Sulfuric acid is often used in esterification reac-

tions to increase the yield of ester by acting as a dehydrating (water-removing) agent.

Many esters have pleasant aromas. The scents of many fruits, flowers, and perfumes are due to esters. Fats are esters produced by the reaction of glycerol, a trihydroxy alcohol (see page 76), and long-chain organic acids (see page 73).

Saponification.
The hydrolysis of fats by bases is called **saponification**. Soap, which is a salt of a long-chain organic acid, is produced when a fat (a glycerol stearate ester found in animal fat) is saponified by hot alkali (see page 76).

$$C_3H_5(C_{17}H_{35}COO)_3 + 3NaOH \rightarrow$$
fat   alkali

$$3C_{17}H_{35}COONa + C_3H_5(OH)_3$$
soap   glycerine

Oxidation.
In an excess of oxygen, saturated hydrocarbons burn completely to form carbon dioxide and water.

$$CH_4 + 2O_2 \rightarrow CO_2 + 2H_2O$$

The burning of hydrocarbons in a limited supply of oxygen may produce carbon monoxide (CO) or carbon (C).

$$2CH_4 + 3O_2 \rightarrow 2CO + 4H_2O$$

$$CH_4 + O_2 \rightarrow C + 2H_2O$$

Polymerization.
Large molecules can be formed from smaller molecules by **polymerization reactions**. The large molecules formed by polymerization consist of chains of repeating smaller subunits. Such large molecules are called *polymers*. Synthetic rubbers and plastics, such as polyethylene, are polymers. Naturally occurring polymers include proteins, starches, and many other chemicals produced by living organisms.

QUESTIONS

1. The complete combustion of any hydrocarbon in excess oxygen produces (1) CO and H_2 (2) CO_2 and H_2 (3) CO and H_2O (4) CO_2 and H_2O

2. The correct name for the compound shown below is (1) 1,3-dichloropentane (2) 2,4-dichloropentane (3) 1,3-dichlorobutane (4) 1,1-dichlorobutane

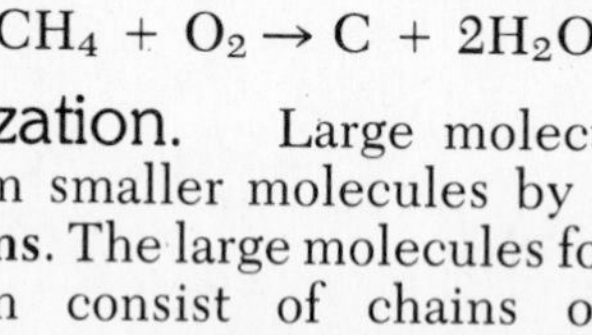

3. In the preparation of an ester, the yield of the ester is increased by the addition of (1) water (2) sodium chloride (3) sulfuric acid (4) sodium hydroxide

4. The reaction $C_3H_8 + Cl_2 \rightarrow C_3H_7Cl + HCl$ is an example of (1) substitution (2) addition (3) esterification (4) hydrogenation

74

5. Which equation represents an esterification reaction?

(1) $C_6H_{12}O_6 \rightarrow 2C_2H_5OH + 2CO_2$
(2) $C_5H_{10} + H_2 \rightarrow C_5H_{12}$
(3) $C_3H_8 + Cl_2 \rightarrow C_3H_7Cl + HCl$
(4) $HCOOH + CH_3OH \rightarrow HCOOCH_3 + HOH$

6. Which structural formula represents the product of the reaction between ethene and bromine (Br_2)?

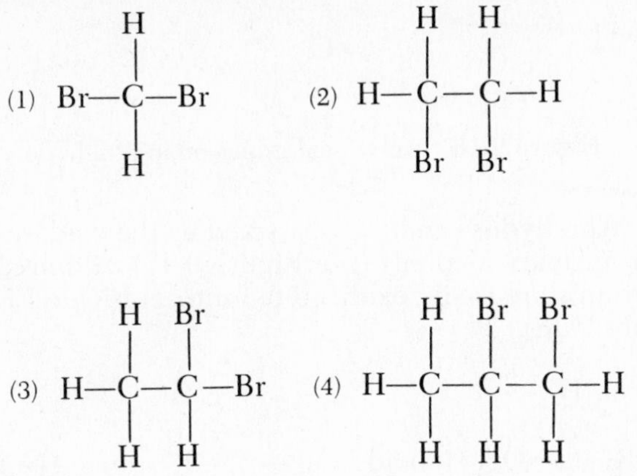

7. In an aqueous solution, which compound will be acidic? (1) CH_3COOH (2) CH_3CH_2OH (3) $C_3H_5(OH)_3$ (4) CH_3OH

8. The reaction $CH_4 + Br_2 \rightarrow CH_3Br + HBr$ is an example of (1) addition (2) hydrogenation (3) substitution (4) polymerization

9. A reaction between CH_3COOH and an alcohol produced the ester CH_3COOCH_3. The alcohol used in the reaction was (1) CH_3OH (2) C_2H_5OH (3) C_3H_7OH (4) C_4H_9OH

10. Which of the following structural formulas represents 2,2-dichloropropane?

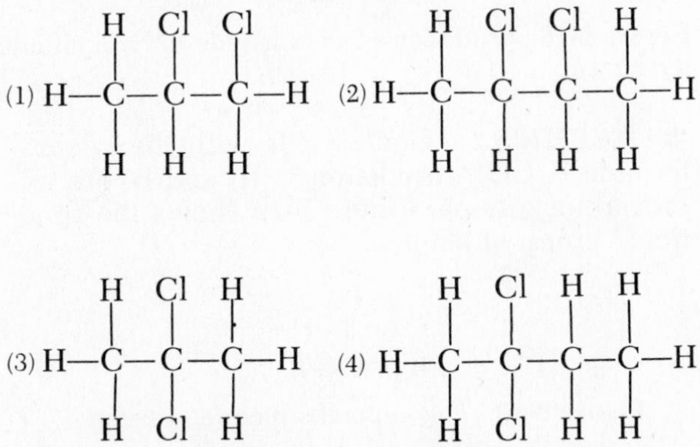

11. Which kind of reaction produces ethanol as one of the principal products? (1) esterification (2) saponification (3) neutralization (4) fermentation

12. Which compound will undergo a substitution reaction with chlorine? (1) CH_4 (2) C_2H_4 (3) C_3H_4 (4) C_4H_8

✳ CLASSES OF ALCOHOLS

Alcohols are classified according to the number of —OH groups they contain. Alcohols with one —OH group are monohydroxy alcohols, those with two —OH groups are dihydroxy alcohols, and those with three —OH groups are trihydroxy alcohols.

Alcohols are also classified according to the number of carbon chains attached to the carbon atom with the —OH groups.

✳ Monohydroxy Alcohols.
Alcohols that have one —OH group are **monohydroxy alcohols**.

✳ Primary Alcohols.
Primary monohydroxy alcohols were discussed on page 72. In **primary alcohols**, the —OH group is on the last carbon atom of the hydrocarbon chain. The general formula for a primary alcohol is R—CH_2OH.

✳ Secondary Alcohols.
Alcohols in which the carbon atom with the —OH group is bonded to two other carbon atoms are called **secondary alcohols**. In secondary alcohols, the —OH group is not located at the end of a hydrocarbon chain (see Figure 9-10). The general formula for secondary alcohols is R_1R_2CHOH, where R_1 and R_2 are hydrocarbon groups. An example of a secondary alcohol is 2-propanol, also called isopropyl alcohol (see Figure 9-11).

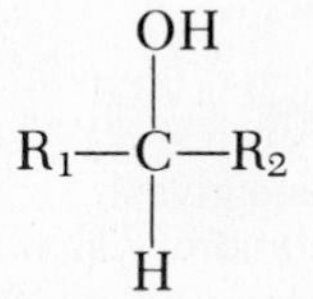

Figure 9-10. The general structure of secondary alcohols.

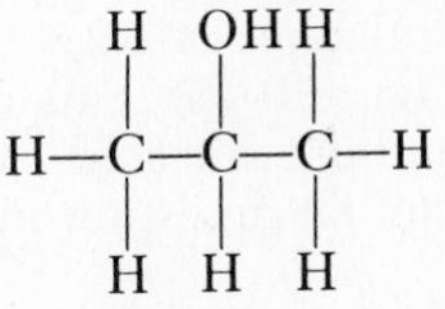

2-propanol

Figure 9-11. 2-propanol is a secondary alcohol. (Note that the OH group is on the second carbon.)

✳ Tertiary Alcohols.
Alcohols in which the carbon atom with the —OH group is bonded to three other carbon atoms are called **tertiary alcohols**. The general formula for a tertiary alcohol is $R_1R_2R_3COH$. The structural formula is shown in Figure 9-12. An example of a tertiary alcohol is 2-methyl-2-propanol, which is also known as tertiary butanol (see Figure 9-13, on page 76).

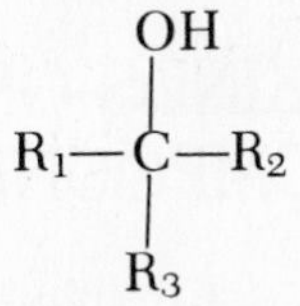

Figure 9-12. Structural formula of tertiary alcohols.

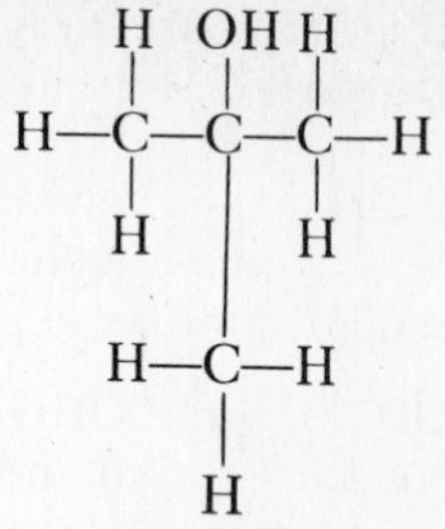

2-methyl-2-propanol

Figure 9-13. Tertiary butanol, or 2-methyl-2-propanol, is a tertiary alcohol.

✱ Dihydroxy Alcohols.

Compounds containing two —OH groups are known as **dihydroxy**, or **dihydric**, **alcohols**, or as **glycols**. The most important glycol is 1,2-ethanediol, commonly called **ethylene glycol** (see Figure 9-14). Ethylene glycol is used as a coolant and antifreeze in cars.

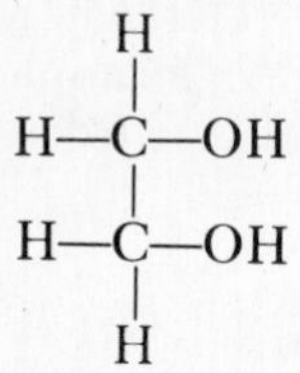

Ethylene glycol

Figure 9-14. Ethylene glycol, or 1,2-ethanediol, is the most widely used dihydroxy alcohol.

✱ Trihydroxy Alcohols.

Compounds containing three —OH groups are known as **trihydroxy**, or **trihydric**, **alcohols**. The most important trihydroxy alcohol is 1,2,3-propanetriol, or **glycerol** (see Figure 9-15). Fats are synthesized from glycerol and organic acids. Glycerol is also an end product of fat digestion in animals.

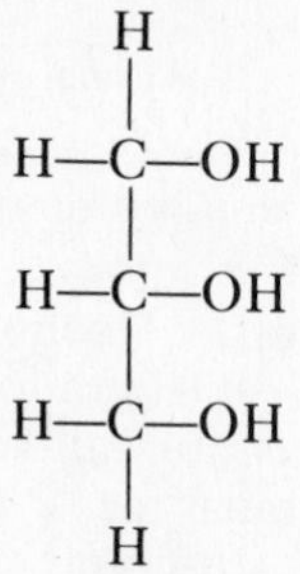

1,2,3-propanetriol
Glycerol

Figure 9-15. Glycerol, or 1,2,3-propanetriol, is the most important trihydroxy alcohol.

✱ OTHER KINDS OF ORGANIC COMPOUNDS

✱ Aldehydes.

Compounds with the general formula R—CHO are **aldehydes**. R can rep-

resent a hydrogen atom or any hydrocarbon group. The structural formula of the functional group of aldehydes is shown in Figure 9-16. Aldehydes are named from the corresponding alkanes by replacing the final "e" with "al." Thus, the first member of the group is methanal, HCHO, which is also known as **formaldehyde**.

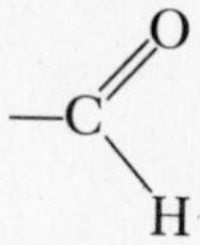

Figure 9-16. Functional group of an aldehyde.

Aldehydes can be synthesized by the oxidation of primary alcohols (see Figure 9-17). Aldehyde groups are easily oxidized to form acids (see Figure 9-18).

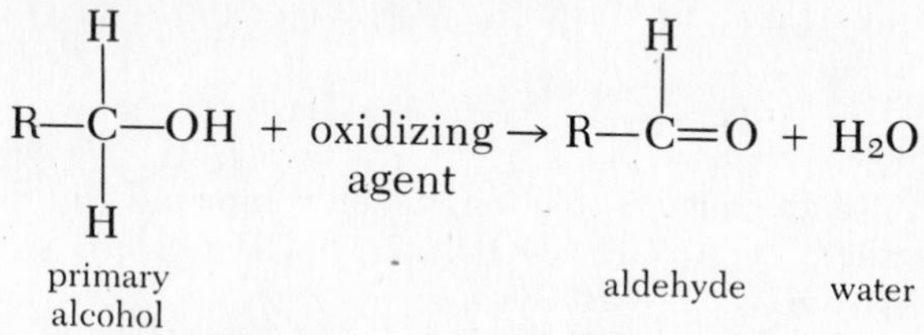

primary
alcohol
aldehyde   water

Figure 9-17. Synthesis of an aldehyde.

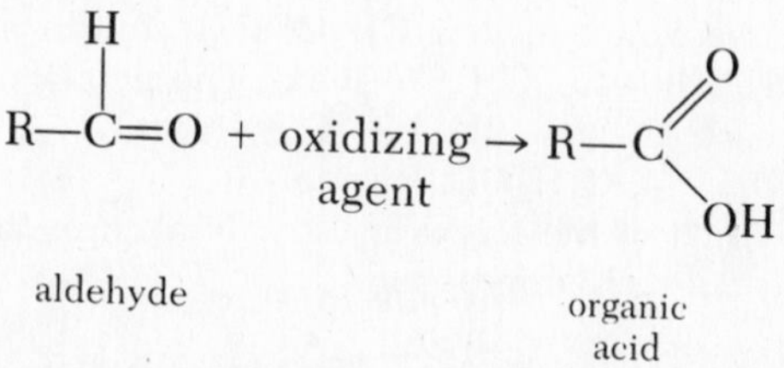

aldehyde
organic
acid

Figure 9-18. Oxidation of an aldehyde to form an organic acid.

✱ Ketones.

Compounds with the general formula R_1COR_2 are **ketones**. R_1 and R_2 are hydrocarbon groups. Figure 9-19 shows the functional group of ketones.

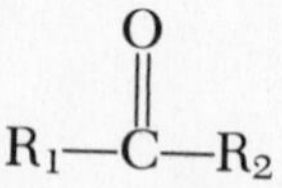

Figure 9-19. The general structure of ketones.

Propanone, which is commonly known as **acetone**, is the first and simplest member of this group (see Figure 9-20). Acetone is widely used as a solvent.

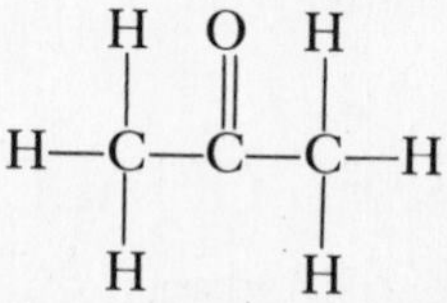

Acetone

Figure 9-20. Acetone, or propanone.

Ketones can be synthesized by the oxidation of secondary alcohols (see Figure 9-21).

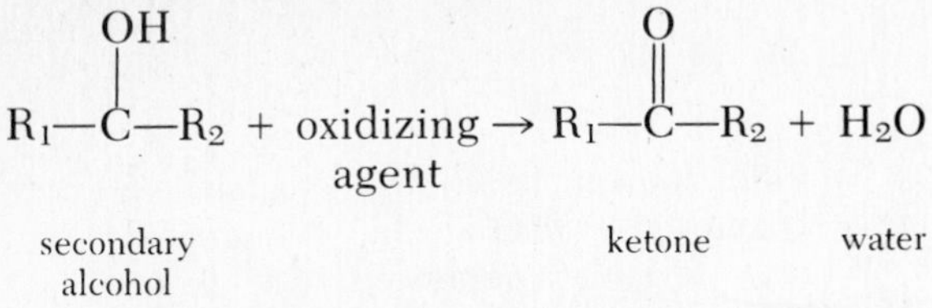

$$\underset{\substack{\text{secondary} \\ \text{alcohol}}}{R_1 - \overset{\overset{\displaystyle OH}{|}}{C} - R_2} + \underset{\text{agent}}{\text{oxidizing}} \rightarrow \underset{\text{ketone}}{R_1 - \overset{\overset{\displaystyle O}{\|}}{C} - R_2} + \underset{\text{water}}{H_2O}$$

Figure 9-21. Synthesis of a ketone by the oxidation of a secondary alcohol.

✳ Ethers.

Compounds with the general formula R_1OR_2 are **ethers**. The R_1 and R_2 represent any hydrocarbon groups. The best-known ether is **diethyl ether** ($C_2H_5OC_2H_5$), which has been used as an anesthetic.

Ethers can be synthesized by the dehydration of primary alcohols (see Figure 9-22).

$$\underset{\text{primary alcohols}}{R_1 - O\boxed{H} + R_2 - \boxed{OH}} \rightarrow \underset{\text{ether}}{R_1 - O - R_2} + \underset{\text{water}}{H_2O}$$

Figure 9-22. Dehydration of primary alcohols to produce ether.

✳ Polymers.

A **polymer** is a large molecule that is composed of many repeating smaller units called **monomers**. Naturally occurring polymers include starch, cellulose, proteins, and DNA. Synthetic polymers include nylon and polyethylene.

The process in which monomers are joined together to form polymers is called *polymerization*. Polymerization may involve condensation or addition.

✳ Condensation Reactions.

Polymerization that results from the bonding of monomers by a dehydration reaction is called **condensation polymerization** (see Figure 9-23). The condensation reaction may be repeated many times to produce long-chain polymers. For polymerization to occur, the monomers involved must have at least two functional groups. Materials formed by condensation polymerization include silicones, polyesters, polyamides, phenolic plastics, and nylons.

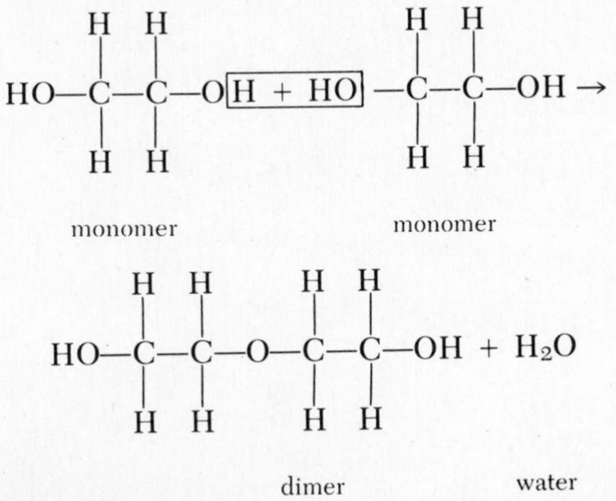

✳ Addition Reactions.

Polymerization that results from the joining of monomers of unsaturated compounds is called **addition polymerization**. The reaction occurs by the "opening" of double or triple bonds in the carbon chain (Figure 9-24). Vinyl plastics, such as polyethylene and polystyrene, are formed by addition polymerization.

$$nC_2H_4 \rightarrow (-C_2H_4-)_n$$

Figure 9-24. Some polymers are produced by addition polymerization.

✳ QUESTIONS

1. Which compound is a dihydroxy alcohol?
(1) $Al(OH)_3$ (2) $C_3H_5(OH)_3$
(3) $Ca(OH)_2$ (4) $C_2H_4(OH)_2$

2. Which compound is a trihydroxy alcohol? (1) glycerol (2) butanol (3) ethanol (4) methanol

3. Which structural formula below represents 1,2-ethanediol?

(1) 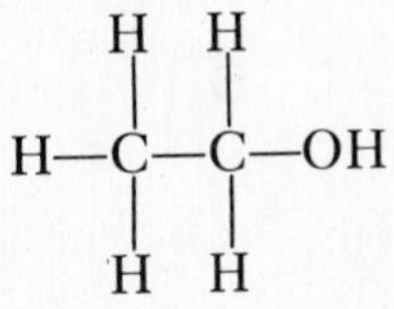 $H - \overset{\overset{\displaystyle H}{|}}{\underset{\underset{\displaystyle H}{|}}{C}} - \overset{\overset{\displaystyle H}{|}}{\underset{\underset{\displaystyle H}{|}}{C}} - OH$

(2) 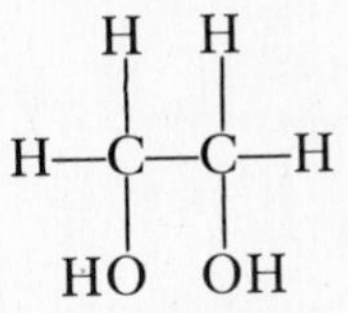 $H - \overset{\overset{\displaystyle H}{|}}{\underset{\underset{\displaystyle HO}{|}}{C}} - \overset{\overset{\displaystyle H}{|}}{\underset{\underset{\displaystyle OH}{|}}{C}} - H$

(3) 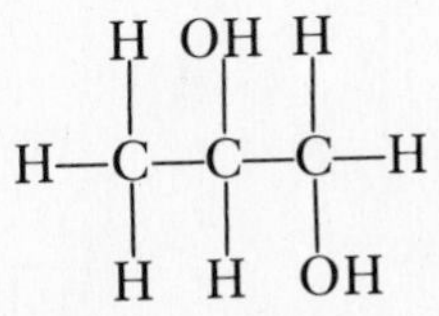 $H - \overset{\overset{\displaystyle H}{|}}{\underset{\underset{\displaystyle H}{|}}{C}} - \overset{\overset{\displaystyle OH}{|}}{\underset{\underset{\displaystyle H}{|}}{C}} - \overset{\overset{\displaystyle H}{|}}{\underset{\underset{\displaystyle OH}{|}}{C}} - H$

(4) 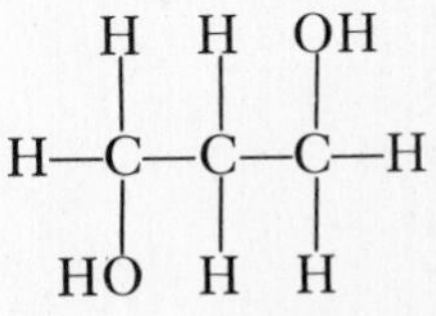 $H - \overset{\overset{\displaystyle H}{|}}{\underset{\underset{\displaystyle HO}{|}}{C}} - \overset{\overset{\displaystyle H}{|}}{\underset{\underset{\displaystyle H}{|}}{C}} - \overset{\overset{\displaystyle OH}{|}}{\underset{\underset{\displaystyle H}{|}}{C}} - H$

4. Which structural formula represents an aldehyde?

(1) 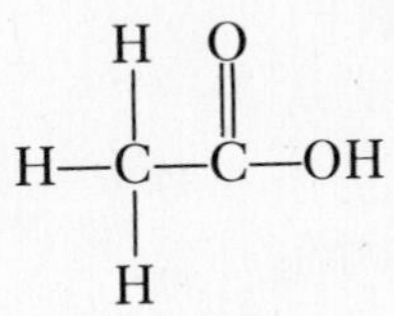 $H - \overset{\overset{\displaystyle H}{|}}{\underset{\underset{\displaystyle H}{|}}{C}} - \overset{\overset{\displaystyle O}{\|}}{C} - OH$

(2) 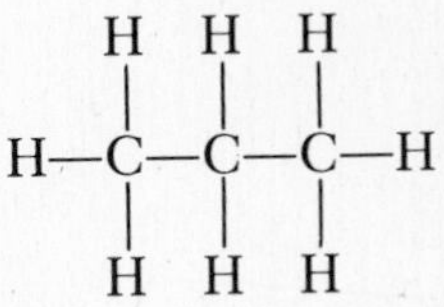 $H - \overset{\overset{\displaystyle H}{|}}{\underset{\underset{\displaystyle H}{|}}{C}} - \overset{\overset{\displaystyle H}{|}}{\underset{\underset{\displaystyle H}{|}}{C}} - \overset{\overset{\displaystyle H}{|}}{\underset{\underset{\displaystyle H}{|}}{C}} - H$

(3) 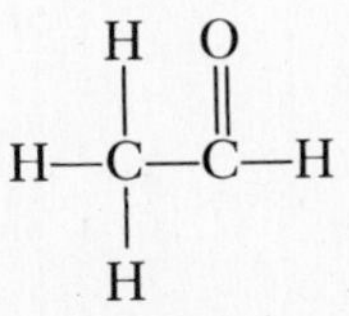 $H - \overset{\overset{\displaystyle H}{|}}{\underset{\underset{\displaystyle H}{|}}{C}} - \overset{\overset{\displaystyle O}{\|}}{C} - H$

(4) 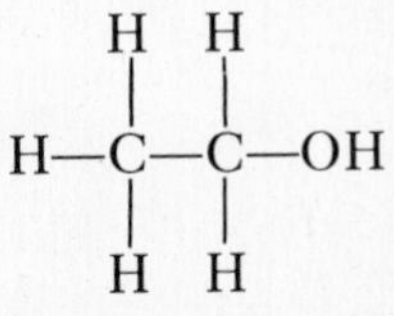 $H - \overset{\overset{\displaystyle H}{|}}{\underset{\underset{\displaystyle H}{|}}{C}} - \overset{\overset{\displaystyle H}{|}}{\underset{\underset{\displaystyle H}{|}}{C}} - OH$

$$\underset{\text{monomer}}{HO - \overset{\overset{\displaystyle H}{|}}{\underset{\underset{\displaystyle H}{|}}{C}} - \overset{\overset{\displaystyle H}{|}}{\underset{\underset{\displaystyle H}{|}}{C}} - O\boxed{H + HO}} \underset{\text{monomer}}{- \overset{\overset{\displaystyle H}{|}}{\underset{\underset{\displaystyle H}{|}}{C}} - \overset{\overset{\displaystyle H}{|}}{\underset{\underset{\displaystyle H}{|}}{C}} - OH} \rightarrow$$

$$\underset{\text{dimer}}{HO - \overset{\overset{\displaystyle H}{|}}{\underset{\underset{\displaystyle H}{|}}{C}} - \overset{\overset{\displaystyle H}{|}}{\underset{\underset{\displaystyle H}{|}}{C}} - O - \overset{\overset{\displaystyle H}{|}}{\underset{\underset{\displaystyle H}{|}}{C}} - \overset{\overset{\displaystyle H}{|}}{\underset{\underset{\displaystyle H}{|}}{C}} - OH} + \underset{\text{water}}{H_2O}$$

Figure 9-23. Monomers can be joined by condensation polymerization.

5. Which is the structural formula for glycerol?

(1)
```
    H
    |
H—C—OH
    |
H—C—OH
    |
    H
```

(2)
```
    H
    |
H—C—OH
    |
    H
```

(3)
```
   OH
    |
HO—C—OH
    |
    H
```

(4)
```
    H
    |
H—C—OH
    |
H—C—OH
    |
H—C—OH
    |
    H
```

6. Which is the general formula for an ether?

(1) R—OH

(2)
```
     O
     ‖
R—C
     |
     H
```

(3) R_1—O—R_2

(4)
```
     O
     ‖
R_1—C—R_2
```

7. Which is a tertiary alcohol?

(1)
```
   OH OH OH
    |  |  |
H—C—C—C—H
    |  |  |
    H  H  H
```

(2)
```
    H  H
    |  |
H—C—C—H
    |  |
   OH OH
```

(3)
```
  H OH H
  |  |  |
H—C—C—C—H
  |  |  |
  H  H  H
```

(4)
```
  H  H OH H
  |  |  |  |
H—C—C—C—C—H
  |  |  |  |
  H  H  H  H
```

8. An aldehyde can be oxidized to form (1) a ketone (2) an ester (3) an alcohol (4) an acid

9. Which formula represents a ketone? (1) CH_3COCH_3 (2) C_2H_5COOCH (3) C_2H_5COOH (4) CH_3CHO

10. The reaction represented by the equation below is (1) saponification (2) fermentation (3) esterification (4) polymerization

$$nC_2H_4 \rightarrow (-C_2H_4{}^-)_n$$

11. Which is the formula of methanal?

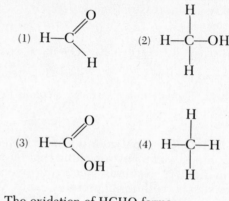

(1)
```
     O
     ‖
H—C
     |
     H
```

(2)
```
    H
    |
H—C—OH
    |
    H
```

(3)
```
     O
     ‖
H—C
     |
     OH
```

(4)
```
    H
    |
H—C—H
    |
    H
```

12. The oxidation of HCHO forms
(1) CH_3COOH
(2) CH_3OH
(3) HCOOH
(4) CH_3CHO

(Note: The contents of this unit are tested only in Part II of the Regents Examination.)

In chemistry, as in all sciences, a distinction is made between pure and applied research. Pure research is conducted to expand our knowledge of the natural world, without consideration of possible practical applications of that knowledge. Applied research also expands our knowledge, but it is conducted with a specific goal in mind, generally the production of a new product or process.

The goal of industrial processes is to obtain the maximum yield of the desired products with the maximum economic efficiency. Understanding and proper use of the chemical principles involved in an industrial process can increase the quality and yield of a product and decrease its cost.

EQUILIBRIUM AND REACTION RATES

Many industrial processes are based on the application of factors governing equilibrium and reaction rates. Without careful adjustment of these factors, including concentration, temperature, pressure, and catalysts, the processes would be too inefficient to be of practical importance.

The Haber Process.

During World War I, the German scientist Fritz Haber developed a technique for synthesizing ammonia from its component elements, nitrogen and hydrogen, discussed earlier on page 45. Nitrogen compounds are essential components of explosives and fertilizers. Haber's method, which is still widely used, involves adjustment of energy and reaction rate factors to make an otherwise slow reaction occur at a rate fast enough to make it economically feasible.

In the **Haber process**, molecular nitrogen obtained from air and molecular hydrogen obtained by the electrolysis of water combine according to the reaction

$$N_2(g) + 3H_2(g) \rightleftarrows 2NH_3(g) + heat$$

Increased pressure and decreased temperature cause the equilibrium point of the reaction to shift in the direction favoring the formation of ammonia. Since the reaction has a rather high activation energy, the rate of formation of ammonia is slow at low temperatures, and the temperature must be raised to increase the rate of formation.

On the other hand, the reaction is exothermic, and high temperatures decrease the yield of ammonia.

Haber's solution to these opposing requirements was to increase both temperature and pressure. At a temperature of about 400°C and pressures of 200 to 1,000 atmospheres, the reaction proceeds at an appreciable rate. Removal of the ammonia from the reaction vessel as it is formed (decreasing the concentration of product) also helps to increase the yield in accordance with Le Chatelier's principle. In modern industrial production of ammonia, a catalyst consisting of a mixture of iron, potassium oxide, and aluminum oxide is used.

The Contact Process.

Sulfuric acid, H_2SO_4, is the most widely used industrial chemical. It is used in the manufacture of explosives, drugs, detergents, dyes, fertilizers, and batteries, as well as in the refining of petroleum and in the preparation of metals for electroplating. Most sulfuric acid is produced by the contact process, a method that involves catalysts and the adjustment of reaction temperatures.

In the **contact process**, elemental sulfur or sulfide ores, such as iron pyrites, are burned to produce sulfur dioxide:

$$S + O_2 \rightleftarrows SO_2 + heat$$

or

$$2FeS_2 + 3O_2 \rightleftarrows 2FeO + 3SO_2$$

The sulfur dioxide is then further oxidized to sulfur trioxide, using finely divided platinum or vanadium pentoxide (V_2O_5) as a catalyst:

$$2SO_2 + O_2 \rightleftarrows 2SO_3 + heat$$

An increase in pressure and a decrease in temperature favor the formation of SO_3. Since the rate of formation of SO_3 is slow at low temperatures, the temperature must be raised to increase the rate of formation. However, since the reaction is exothermic, high temperatures decrease the yield of SO_3. In practice, reasonable yields of SO_3 are obtained when the temperature is kept between 400 and 600°C.

The sulfur trioxide is then absorbed by sulfuric acid to form fuming sulfuric acid:

$$SO_3 + H_2SO_4 \rightarrow H_2SO_4 \cdot SO_3 \text{ (or } H_2S_2O_7)$$

The fuming sulfuric acid is then diluted with water to yield sulfuric acid:

$$H_2S_2O_7 + H_2O \rightarrow 2H_2SO_4$$

QUESTIONS

1. Which reaction occurs during the contact process
(1) $2SO_2 + O_2 \rightarrow 2SO_3$
(2) $N_2 + 3H_2 \rightarrow 2NH_3$
(3) $2Al + Cr_2O_3 \rightarrow Al_2O_3 + 2Cr$
(4) $2NaCl \rightarrow 2Na + Cl_2$

2. The Haber process is used to produce (1) sulfur dioxide (2) ammonia (3) sulfuric acid (4) sodium chloride

3. Which compound is the final product of the contact process? (1) SO_2 (2) SO_3 (3) $H_2S_2O_7$ (4) H_2SO_4

4. Given the reaction at equilibrium:

$$N_2(g) + 3H_2(g) \rightleftarrows 2NH_3(g) + heat$$

Which change would shift the equilibrium to the right? (1) Increase the temperature. (2) Increase the pressure. (3) Decrease $[N_2]$. (4) Decrease $[H_2]$.

5. Which is *not* true of the Haber process? (1) The reaction is exothermic. (2) Heat is needed to increase the reaction rate. (3) Addition of ammonia to the reaction vessel increases the rate of the forward reaction. (4) Increased pressure increases the yield of ammonia.

6. Which of the following is part of the contact process? (1) H_2O_2 (2) SO_3 (3) H_2CO_3 (4) H_2S

7. In the contact process, the correct sequence of products is
(1) $H_2SO_4 \rightarrow H_2S_2O_7 \rightarrow SO_3 \rightarrow SO_2$
(2) $H_2S_2O_7 \rightarrow H_2SO_4 \rightarrow SO_2 \rightarrow SO_3$
(3) $SO_2 \rightarrow SO_3 \rightarrow H_2S_2O_7 \rightarrow H_2SO_4$
(4) $SO_3 \rightarrow SO_2 \rightarrow H_2S_2O_7 \rightarrow H_2SO_4$

8. Which of the following is *not* used as a catalyst in the industrial production of ammonia? (1) iron (2) potassium oxide (3) sulfur (4) aluminum oxide

9. Both the Haber process and the contact process (1) are endothermic (2) are exothermic (3) have low activation energies (4) do not require catalysts

10. The Haber process involves a type of chemical reaction called (1) hydrolysis (2) synthesis (3) analysis (4) electrolysis

REDOX REACTIONS

Many industrial processes involve redox reactions. The knowledge that different elements vary in their ability to attract electrons is applied to many metallurgical techniques, including refining and electroplating.

Reduction of Metals.
Metals, because they are generally active, are rarely found in nature in an uncombined state. Gold and silver are inactive metals and are notable exceptions. They are found free. Most metals occur as oxides (Fe_2O_3), sulfides (PbS or ZnS), or carbonates ($FeCO_3$ or $ZnCO_3$). The form in which a metal occurs is related to its chemical activity and to the stability of its compounds. In general, naturally occurring metal compounds have high stability and low solubility in water.

Most metals are found in an oxidized state in their ores. The ore must be reduced to obtain the pure metal. The method of reduction depends on the activity of the metal and the type of ore. The more reactive the metal, the more difficult is the task of reducing its ores. The Table of Standard Electrode Potentials (see Reference Table N, page 110) indicates the relative ease with which a metal ion can be reduced. Metal ions located near the top of the table are more easily reduced than those near the bottom.

The most active metals are obtained by electrolysis from their fused compounds. Group 1 and Group 2 metals are obtained by electrolysis of their fused salts.

$$2NaCl(fused) + electricity \rightarrow 2Na + Cl_2$$

Aluminum is extracted from its ore, bauxite, by electrolytic reduction (the Hall process) after aluminum oxide, Al_2O_3, has been separated from the rock.

$$2Al_2O_3 + electricity \rightarrow 4Al + 3O_2$$

Metals that form relatively stable compounds can be extracted from their compounds by stronger reducing agents. Because chromium is less active than aluminum, metallic aluminum will reduce chromium (III) oxide to metallic chromium:

$$2Al + Cr_2O_3 \rightarrow Al_2O_3 + 2Cr$$

Moderately active metals, such as zinc and iron, can be isolated by reduction of their oxides with carbon (coke) or carbon monoxide:

$$ZnO + C + heat \rightarrow Zn + CO$$

$$Fe_2O_3 + 3CO + heat \rightarrow 2Fe + 3CO_2$$

The reduction of Fe_2O_3 actually involves a series of oxidation-reduction reactions.

First, coke is oxidized to carbon dioxide:

$$C + O_2 \rightarrow CO_2$$

The carbon dioxide then reacts with some of the remaining coke, forming carbon monoxide:

$$CO_2 + C \rightarrow 2CO$$

The carbon monoxide reduces the iron oxide to metallic iron by the following series of reactions:

$$3Fe_2O_3 + CO \rightarrow 2Fe_3O_4 + CO_2$$

$$Fe_3O_4 + CO \rightarrow 3FeO + CO_2$$

$$FeO + CO \rightarrow Fe + CO_2$$

The carbon dioxide produced as a by-product of the reduction of iron is reduced again by the hot coke, forming carbon monoxide, and is reused.

If the ore of a metal is a sulfide or carbonate instead of an oxide, the metal must be converted to its oxide form before it can be isolated by reduction with carbon. Sulfide and carbonate ores are converted to oxides by *roasting*—heating the ore in air. The sulfur or carbon is driven off as CO_2 or SO_2, while the metal forms an oxide, which can then be reduced by carbon.

Corrosion.
Metals in their reduced state are usually vulnerable to oxidation. The undesirable oxidation of the surface of a metal is called **corrosion**. Corrosion can occur when a metal is exposed to moisture, molecular oxygen, carbon dioxide, hydrogen sulfide, or other compounds that can act as oxidizing agents. The tarnishing of silver and rusting of iron are familiar examples of corrosion. The more active the metal, the more susceptible it is to corrosion.

The corrosion of copper, zinc, and aluminum produces a protective film that adheres tightly to the surface of the metal and actually protects it from further corrosion. The rusting of iron, however, produces an oxide that does not adhere to the surface of the metal. It flakes off, exposing a fresh, unoxidized surface for further corrosion.

Iron and other metals that corrode easily can be protected in a variety of ways. They may be plated with self-protective metals, such as aluminum or zinc, or with corrosion-resistant metals, such as chromium or nickel. Iron may be covered with a more active metal, such as magnesium, which then corrodes preferentially, sparing the iron. Stainless steel, which is rust resistant, is an alloy (homogeneous mixture) of iron with corrosion-resistant metals, such as nickel and chromium. The coating of iron with paints, oils, or porcelain has also proved effective against corrosion.

Batteries.
Batteries are chemical cells in which spontaneous redox reactions are used to provide a source of electrical energy (see Unit 8, page 61).

1. In the **lead-acid**, or **lead storage**, **battery**, which is used in automobiles, electrical energy is produced by changes in the oxidation state of lead. When fully charged, the positive electrode (cathode) of this battery is PbO_2, while the negative electrode (anode) is Pb. These electrodes are immersed in a sulfuric acid solution, which is the electrolyte. Figure 10-1 shows a simplified version of a single lead storage cell.

At the anode, lead is oxidized to lead sulfate, $PbSO_4$. At the cathode, lead dioxide, in which lead has a +4 oxidation state, is reduced to lead sulfate, in which lead has a +2 oxidation state.

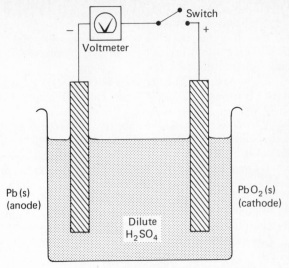

Figure 10-1. The lead storage cell.

The overall reaction in a lead-acid battery is:

$$Pb + PbO_2 + 2H_2SO_4 \underset{charge}{\overset{discharge}{\rightleftharpoons}}$$

$$2PbSO_4 + 2H_2O$$

Because the concentration of the electrolyte decreases with use, the voltage obtained from the cell also decreases with use. However, if electricity is supplied, the reverse reaction will occur, thus recharging the battery. In an automobile, the generator or alternator produces the electricity that keeps the battery charged.

2. Many rechargeable batteries are **nickel-cadmium cells**, in which electrical energy is produced by changes in the oxidation states of nickel and cadmium. In these cells, the positive electrode is nickel hydroxide, $Ni(OH)_3$, while the negative electrode is cadmium metal, Cd. The electrolyte in this battery is a solution of potassium hydroxide, KOH. The concentration of the electrolyte does not change during the following probable reaction.

$$2Ni(OH)_3 + Cd \underset{charge}{\overset{discharge}{\rightleftharpoons}} 2Ni(OH)_2 + Cd(OH)_2$$

QUESTIONS

1. Which of the following atmospheric gases is least likely to cause iron to corrode? (1) $O_2(g)$ (2) $CO_2(g)$ (3) $Ar(g)$ (4) $H_2O(g)$
2. Which metal must be combined with chromium to produce stainless steel? (1) radium (2) iron (3) copper (4) zinc
3. The self-protecting coating that forms on aluminum metal is (1) an oxide (2) a sulfide (3) an oxalate (4) a chloride
4. Which type of chemical reaction is the corrosion

of iron? (1) oxidation-reduction (2) substitution (3) polymerization (4) decomposition

5. Which of the following metals forms a self-protective coating when exposed to air and moisture? (1) zinc (2) calcium (3) iron (4) sodium

6. Which oxide will react with carbon (coke) to produce a free metal? (1) MgO (2) ZnO (3) Na_2O (4) Li_2O

7. Which represents the positive electrode of a nickel-cadmium battery? (1) $Ni(OH)_3$ (2) Cd (3) Ni (4) $Cd(OH)_2$

8. During discharge of a storage battery, the oxidation reaction that occurs is (1) Pb^0 to Pb^{+2} (2) Pb^0 to Pb^{+4} (3) Pb^{+4} to Pb^0 (4) Pb^{+2} to Pb^0

9. Which element is alloyed with iron to make it more resistant to corrosion? (1) sulfur (2) oxygen (3) nickel (4) lead

PETROLEUM

Petroleum is a natural, complex mixture of hydrocarbons. Gasoline and fuel oils are two products obtained from the refining of petroleum. Natural gas (mostly methane), which is a common fuel, is often found with petroleum. Bottled gases, such as propane and butane, are also obtained from petroleum. Petroleum is the starting material for plastics, synthetic textiles and rubber, and detergents.

Fractional Distillation. Different samples of petroleum contain different numbers and kinds of hydrocarbons. Components, or fractions, of the mixture can be separated by **fractional distillation**, a technique based on the fact that the different components of the mixture have different boiling points.

In fractional distillation, hot petroleum is pumped into a vertical, cylindrical tower called a *fractionation column*. The more volatile components vaporize at lower temperatures than do the less volatile ones. Thus, the various components are separated as the temperature of the mixture rises to the boiling points of the different fractions. The products of fractional distillation, in the order of decreasing volatility, include gasoline, kerosene, fuel oil, lubricating oils and greases, paraffin wax, and asphalt.

Cracking. Once the different components of petroleum have been separated by fractional distillation, the molecular structure of the less volatile fractions can be altered by a process called **cracking**. Cracking is used to increase the yield of the more volatile fractions. Through cracking, less volatile substances that are made up of large molecules, such as kerosene, can be broken down into more volatile substances that are made up of smaller molecules, such as gasoline. There are a number of different cracking techniques, but most involve increased temperature and the use of a catalyst, such as oxides of aluminum and silicon.

QUESTIONS

1. A process in which large molecules are broken down into smaller molecules, such as that used commercially to increase the yield of gasoline from petroleum, is called (1) polymerization (2) hydrogenation (3) esterification (4) cracking

2. The different components in crude petroleum can be separated according to their different boiling points by (1) the contact process (2) the Haber process (3) fractional distillation (4) cracking

3. Which equation represents a simple example of cracking?

(1) $N_2 + 3H_2 \xrightarrow{600°C} 2NH_3$
(2) $S + O_2 \rightarrow SO_2$
(3) $C_3H_8 + 5O_2 \rightarrow 3CO_2 + 4H_2O$
(4) $C_{14}H_{30} \xrightarrow{600°C} C_7H_{16} + C_7H_{14}$

4. A substance that is *not* obtained from petroleum is (1) gasoline (2) propane (3) kerosene (4) ammonia

5. Natural gas mostly consists of (1) propane (2) methane (3) butane (4) gasoline

6. Petroleum and natural gas are mixtures of (1) hydrocarbons (2) carbohydrates (3) alcohols (4) organic acids

7. Which of the following is *not* a direct product of fractional distillation? (1) paraffin wax (2) asphalt (3) fuel oil (4) synthetic rubber

8. During the fractional distillation of petroleum, the order of volatility of the products is (1) gasoline, fuel oil, kerosene (2) gasoline, kerosene, fuel oil (3) kerosene, fuel oil, gasoline (4) kerosene, gasoline, fuel oil

9. During cracking, the yield of gasoline (1) increases (2) decreases (3) remains the same

10. A metal that is usually obtained by electrolysis of its fused compound is (1) chromium (2) iron (3) lead (4) sodium

(*Note:* The contents of this unit are tested only in Part II of the Regents Examination.)

NATURAL TRANSMUTATION

In Unit 2, radioactivity was described as the spontaneous disintegration of the nucleus of certain atoms, accompanied by the emission of particles and/or radiant energy. As the nucleus disintegrates, or decays, the atoms of one element are transformed into atoms of another element. This transformation process occurs in nature and is described as **natural transmutation**. For example, the decay of uranium-238 produces thorium-234 and an alpha particle (the nucleus of a helium atom), as shown in the following nuclear equation:

$$^{238}_{92}U \rightarrow {}^{234}_{90}Th + {}^{4}_{2}He$$

For elements with atomic numbers greater than 83, the transmutation produces isotopes that are radioactive, and are called **radioisotopes**. Thus, $^{234}_{90}Th$ is a radioisotope that decays to form $^{234}_{91}Pa$ and an electron. The decay process continues in stages until nonradioactive Pb-206 is formed. Other examples of radioisotopes appear in Reference Table H (see page 107).

ARTIFICIAL TRANSMUTATION

Radioactive isotopes can also be made in the laboratory by the bombardment of atomic nuclei with high-energy particles such as protons, neutrons, and alpha particles. This process is called **artificial transmutation**. Bombardment of nuclei with accelerated particles can cause the nuclei to become unstable, and may result in the formation of new isotopes or even isotopes of different elements.

The particles used in artificial transmutation are accelerated by the application of electric and magnetic fields. **Particle accelerators** are machines that, initially, give charged particles sufficient kinetic energy to overcome the electrostatic forces of repulsion in the target nucleus and, then, penetrate it. For example, when beryllium is bombarded with protons, the following nuclear reaction occurs:

$$^{9}_{4}Be + {}^{1}_{1}H \rightarrow {}^{6}_{3}Li + {}^{4}_{2}He$$

The transmutation of aluminum as a result of bombardment with alpha particles is illustrated by the equation

$$^{27}_{13}Al + {}^{4}_{2}He \rightarrow {}^{30}_{15}P + {}^{1}_{0}n$$

Electric and magnetic fields can accelerate charged particles only. Neutrons cannot be accelerated in an ordinary particle accelerator.

NUCLEAR ENERGY

In nuclear reactions, mass is converted into energy. According to Einstein, the quantity of energy E that is formed equals the mass $m \times c^2$ (the velocity of light). The product of mc^2 is a very large number. Therefore the energies in nuclear reactions are much greater than those in ordinary chemical reactions, and, in some cases, a million or more times greater.

Fission Reactions.
The energy contained in the nucleus of an atom overcomes the forces of repulsion that arise from the positively charged protons present in the nucleus. This energy is called **binding energy**, and it also represents the energy required to break up a nucleus into its component parts.

Fission reactions involve the splitting of heavy nuclei to produce lighter nuclei. Fission occurs when neutrons are captured by a target nucleus, causing it to disintegrate. The result is the formation of fission fragments, the release of energy, and—most important—the release of two or more neutrons. For example, when uranium-235 (the target nucleus) is bombarded with neutrons, it undergoes a fission reaction that might be represented as

$$^{235}_{92}U + {}^{1}_{0}n \rightarrow {}^{90}_{38}Sr + {}^{143}_{54}Xe + 3{}^{1}_{0}n$$

Only atoms of elements with high atomic numbers, which are relatively unstable, can be used in fission reactions. When a heavy atom breaks up, new, more stable atoms are formed. The new atoms are more stable because of their higher nuclear binding energies.

Neutrons released during fission reactions can serve as starting points for further fission reactions. If the released neutrons are captured by other heavy nuclei, additional fissions will occur. These reactions will release energy and still more neutrons. Again, the neutrons that are released can cause still more fission reactions. This process is known as a **chain reaction**. Uncontrolled chain reactions result in the release of tremendous amounts of energy. Nuclear bombs use uncontrolled chain reactions.

Nuclear Reactors.

Chain reactions can be controlled, as well as uncontrolled. Under controlled conditions, nuclear energy can be channeled into useful forms. A **nuclear reactor** is a device designed to produce a controlled nuclear reaction, so that energy is released at a steady and predictable rate.

The two types of reactors presently in use are **fission reactors** and **breeder reactors**. Fission reactors produce energy from the fission of uranium-235. Breeder reactors use uranium-238, which is bombarded with neutrons to form the fissionable isotope, plutonium-239. However, the breeder reactor produces more fissionable fuel than it consumes. In this way, the breeder reactor is expected to meet the shortage of naturally occurring uranium that is forecast for the early part of the next century. Breeder reactors, however, are hazardous because they produce the very toxic plutonium-239, which has a half-life of almost 25,000 years. At the present time, the future of the breeder reactor is somewhat uncertain.

Fission reactors differ in design, but they all have certain components in common (see Figure 11-1).

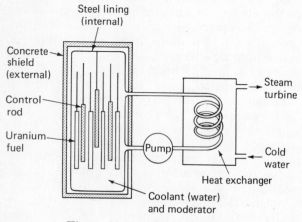

Figure 11-1. A fission reactor.

Fuels. Uranium-233, uranium-235, and plutonium-239 are the fissionable isotopes. The **fuels** of fission reactors include natural uranium (99.3 percent uranium-238 and 0.7 percent uranium-235) and enriched uranium (natural uranium enriched with 3 to 4 percent uranium-235).

Moderators. To control nuclear fission, it is necessary to decrease the speed of the neutrons released by the fission reactions. Substances that can quickly decrease the speed of neutrons without absorbing them are known as **moderators**. Neutrons are best slowed down by direct collisions with particles of similar mass. Hydrogen and its isotope deuterium are effective moderators. Water, **heavy water** (deuterium oxide), beryllium, and graphite are also commonly used as moderators.

Control Rods. The fission process within a re-

actor is prevented from becoming a runaway (uncontrolled) chain reaction by keeping the number of available neutrons steady. Since boron and cadmium are good absorbers of neutrons, **control rods** made of these metals are moved in and out of the reaction chamber to control the rate of reaction.

Coolants. Fission reactions generate enormous quantities of heat. To keep the temperatures within the reactor at reasonable levels, **coolants** are used. Materials commonly used as coolants include water, heavy water, air, helium, carbon dioxide, molten sodium, and molten lithium. Coolants carry the heat to heat exchangers and turbines. In some reactors, the coolant is also the moderator.

Shielding. The leakage of radiation into the environment is prevented by **shielding**. The internal shield, which is a steel lining, protects the walls of the reactor from radiation damage. The external shield, which is made of high-density concrete, protects the personnel who run the reactor from radiation poisoning.

Fusion Reactions.

Nuclear fusion is an energy-releasing process in which two light nuclei fuse to form a heavier nucleus. The energy released by a fusion reaction is much greater than that from a fission reaction.

Fusion reactions can occur only at extremely high temperatures and pressures. When the two lighter nuclei combine to form a heavier nucleus, a more stable atom with greater binding energy per nucleon is formed. However, the mass of the heavier nucleus is less than the sum of the masses of the two lighter nuclei. The "lost" mass (mass defect) is converted into energy according to the equation $E = mc^2$.

It is thought that the source of the sun's energy is a fusion reaction in which hydrogen atoms combine to form helium. The nuclear reaction in a hydrogen bomb is a fusion reaction; however, a fission reaction is used to trigger the fusion reaction.

Fuels. Deuterium ($_1^2$H) and tritium ($_1^3$H), isotopes of hydrogen, are used as fuels in fusion reactions. Heavy water is produced by concentrating the very small, or trace, amounts ordinarily present in water. Tritium is made by the nuclear transmutation

$$_3^6\text{Li} + _0^1\text{n} \rightarrow _1^3\text{H} + _2^4\text{He}$$

Energy Requirements. Since the nuclei involved in fusion reactions carry positive charges (from their protons), they naturally repel one another. As the nuclei are moved closer together, the force of repulsion increases. For the nuclei to interact, they must have enough kinetic energy to overcome the force of repulsion.

Since the force of repulsion increases as the

number of like charges increases, only nuclei with the lowest possible charge can be used. Fusion with hydrogen atoms (one proton per nucleus) proceeds very slowly. Fusion with deuterium atoms or with deuterium and tritium are useful because their greater masses more easily overcome the force of repulsion. The most rapid fusion reaction occurs between deuterium and tritium.

The technical problems with nuclear fusion are enormous. Nuclear scientists and engineers are attempting to develop techniques for dealing with the extremely high temperatures involved in fusion reactions and for containing these reactions. At this time, fusion reactions are not a practical source of energy.

Radioactive Wastes.

Fission reactions in nuclear reactors produce intensely radioactive wastes. Because these radioactive wastes may have long half-lives, they cannot be disposed of in any ordinary way. Solid and liquid radioactive wastes, such as strontium-90 and cesium-137, are usually encased in special containers and permanently stored underground in unpopulated areas. Some low-level radioactive wastes are diluted and released directly into the environment. Gaseous radioactive wastes, such as radon-222, krypton-85, and nitrogen-16, are stored until their radioactivity has decayed to safe levels, and then the gases are dispersed into the environment.

Uses of Radioisotopes.

In the Laboratory. Radioisotopes are chemically similar to stable isotopes of the same element. Thus, radioisotopes can be used as **tracers**, to follow the course of a chemical reaction without altering the reaction. For example, the paths of many organic reactions are studied by using the radioisotope carbon-14 as a tracer. Such experiments generally begin with one compound labeled, or tagged, with carbon-14. The labeled compound is then used in the reaction to be studied. By stopping the reaction at various points and determining which compounds now contain the carbon-14, the reaction sequence can be worked out.

In Medicine. Radioisotopes are also used in medical diagnosis and in therapy. Isotopes that have very short half-lives and are quickly eliminated from the body are used for diagnosis. For example, technetium-99 is used for locating brain tumors, and iodine-131 is used for diagnosing thyroid disorders. Radium-226 and cobalt-60 are used in cancer therapy.

In Industry. Radiation is used in manufacturing industries to measure the physical dimensions of products. It is also used in food preservation to kill bacteria, yeasts, molds, and insect eggs, allowing foods to be stored for longer periods of time.

In Geology and Archaeology. The decay of radioisotopes provides a consistently reliable method for dating rocks, fossils, and geologic events. For example, uranium-238, which decays to lead-206, has a half-life of 4.5 billion years. The ratio of uranium-238 to lead-206, present in a rock, can be used to determine the age of a rock.

Atmospheric nitrogen, largely $^{14}_{7}N$, in contact with cosmic radiation from outer space, is converted into $^{14}_{6}C$ as follows:

$$^{14}_{7}N + ^{1}_{0}n \text{ (from cosmic rays)} \rightarrow ^{14}_{6}C + ^{1}_{1}H$$

The C-14 radioisotope becomes part of the CO_2 (containing C-12) ingested by plants during photosynthesis (food-making). In this manner, C-14 enters the tissues of all living things. As it decays, $^{14}_{6}C$ is changed into $^{14}_{7}N$, which, in turn, re-forms the C-14 radioisotope. In time, the ratio C-14:C-12 becomes constant in all *living* matter. But when a living thing dies, it can no longer utilize CO_2. The supply of C-14 is cut off, and the C-14:C-12 ratio decreases until the amount of C-14 (half-life of 5,700 years) becomes fixed.

Thus, a piece of wood buried in the ground for centuries contains fewer C-14 radioisotopes than does a fresh piece of wood. By measuring the decay rates of each sample with very sensitive instruments, scientists can determine the approximate age of the buried wood. This procedure is called **carbon dating**.

QUESTIONS

1. In a nuclear reactor, the purpose of the moderator is to (1) absorb neutrons (2) split neutrons (3) produce neutrons (4) slow down neutrons
2. In a nuclear reactor, the radioisotope U-235 serves as a (1) shield (2) coolant (3) neutron absorber (4) fissionable material
3. Given the nuclear reaction:

$$^{235}_{92}U + ^{1}_{0}n \rightarrow ^{138}_{56}Ba + ^{95}_{36}Kr + 3^{1}_{0}n + \text{energy}$$

This equation can best be described as (1) fission (2) fusion (3) natural decay (4) endothermic
4. The most abundant isotope found in a naturally occurring uranium deposit is (1) $^{233}_{92}U$ (2) $^{235}_{92}U$ (3) $^{238}_{92}U$ (4) $^{239}_{92}U$
5. A fusion reaction differs from a fission reaction in that the fusion reaction to be initiated requires (1) extremely low temperatures (2) extremely high temperatures (3) heavy atomic nuclei as fuels (4) neutrons with low kinetic energy
6. The ratio of uranium-238 to lead-206 in a mineral is used to determine its (1) age (2) density (3) solubility (4) composition
7. The fuels that may be used in a fusion reaction are (1) $^{3}_{1}H$ and $^{235}_{92}U$ (2) $^{2}_{1}H$ and $^{239}_{94}Pu$ (3) $^{235}_{92}U$ and $^{239}_{94}Pu$ (4) $^{3}_{1}H$ and $^{2}_{1}H$
8. Which substance may be used as both the coolant

and moderator in a reactor? (1) boron (2) cadmium (3) heavy water (4) solid graphite

9. The equation $^2_1H + {}^2_1H \rightarrow {}^4_2He$ represents (1) alpha decay (2) beta decay (3) fission (4) fusion

10. Which particle cannot be accelerated by the electric or magnetic fields in a particle accelerator? (1) neutron (2) proton (3) alpha particle (4) beta particle

11. A nuclear reactor that produces fissionable material as well as energy is a (1) fission reactor (2) fusion reactor (3) breeder reactor (4) hydrogen reactor

12. The number of available neutrons in a fission reactor is limited by the (1) coolant (2) control rods (3) shielding (4) moderator

13. A radioactive gas that is a waste product of nuclear reactors is (1) carbon-12 (2) nitrogen-16 (3) oxygen-16 (4) nitrogen-14

14. Which of the following is true of plutonium-239? (1) It is produced in a fusion reactor. (2) It has a short half-life. (3) It is nontoxic. (4) It is a fissionable material.

15. The energy released by nuclear fusion is produced by (1) an ordinary chemical reaction (2) the conversion of mass into energy (3) the splitting of a heavy atom (4) the conversion of energy into mass

16. It is thought that the sun's energy is produced by (1) nuclear fission (2) ordinary exothermic chemical reactions (3) a breeder reaction (4) nuclear fusion

17. A technique for diagnosing disorders of the thyroid uses (1) iodine-131 (2) plutonium-239 (3) carbon-14 (4) uranium-238

18. Deuterium and tritium are (1) used in radioactive dating (2) isotopes of hydrogen (3) fuels in fission reactors (4) waste products of breeder reactors

19. In the reaction

$$X + {}^1_1H \rightarrow {}^6_3Li + {}^4_2He$$

the nucleus represented by X is (1) ^9_3Li (2) $^{10}_5B$ (3) ^9_4Be (4) $^{10}_6C$

20. Which equation represents artificial transmutation?

(1) $H_2O \rightarrow H^+ + OH^-$
(2) $UF_6 + 6Na \rightarrow 6NaF + U$
(3) $^{238}_{92}U \rightarrow {}^{234}_{90}Th + {}^4_2He$
(4) $^{27}_{13}Al + {}^4_2He \rightarrow {}^{30}_{15}P + {}^1_0n$

21. An example of a radioisotope used as a tracer is (1) C-12 (2) N-14 (3) C-14 (4) Th-234

22. The end product of the decay of U-238 is (1) Pa-234 (2) U-235 (3) Pb-206 (4) Pu-239

23. The number of known isotopes of hydrogen is (1) 1 (2) 2 (3) 3 (4) 4

24. When a living thing dies, the amount of C-14 (1) increases (2) decreases (3) remains the same

12 Laboratory Activities

(*Note:* The contents of this unit are tested only in Part II of the Regents Examination.)

MEASUREMENT

Measurement is an important part of laboratory work in science. In chemistry, whenever possible, observations are recorded as measurements. Volume, mass, temperature, and time are some commonly measured properties.

Most scientific measurements are made against given scales, which are used as standards of measurement. For example, a ruler, a balance, or a graduated cylinder represent such standards. Each scale is marked, or calibrated, with appropriate units. Consider the scale in Figure 12-1. An observer who was told not to estimate any readings might record this reading as 5.6 because the pointer is closest to the division indicating .6. If estimation is allowed, however, some observers might record this reading as 5.64, others as 5.65, 5.63, or 5.66. Because the last digit is an estimate, there is uncertainty in the observation.

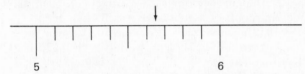

Figure 12-1. Units on a scale.

Significant Figures.
Counting is a common type of measurement, and a number expresses the result of the measurement. In such cases, the measurement is exact and can be expressed without error. In all other situations, however, measurement possesses some degree of error, or uncertainty.

In general, scientists agree that such measurements should contain only one estimated, or uncertain, digit. In ordinary scales, such as the one shown, measurements may be estimated to the nearest one-tenth of the smallest division on the scale. The certain digits plus the one estimated

digit are called **significant figures**. Thus, for the scale in Figure 12-1, a reading of 5.65 contains three significant, or meaningful, digits. A reading of 5.655 has two estimated digits, which would not be meaningful because it implies that the observer could choose between 5.654 and 5.656.

Zeros and Significant Figures. In a measurement, all digits *other than zeros* are significant. For example, a mass of 2.25 grams has 3 significant figures; a volume of 8.289 liters has 4 significant figures.

The position of a zero in a measurement helps to determine the number of significant figures that the measurement contains. A zero at the end of a number is called a **trailing zero**. When such a zero precedes the decimal point, it is a **left trailing zero**, and is always significant; when it follows, it is a **right trailing zero**, and is also always significant. A zero at the beginning of a number is a **leading zero**, and it may also be left or right of the decimal point. A zero that appears within a number is called an **embedded zero**.

Table 12-1 summarizes the uses of zeros in the interpretation of significant figures. For numbers *less than 1*, all zeros at the end of the number (trailing zeros) and all zeros between nonzero digits (embedded zeros) are significant. For example, 0.050 has two significant figures; 0.000208 has three significant figures.

Rounding Off.
The **precision** of a measurement indicates how closely the measurement can be reproduced. The precision of a measurement or a calculated result is indicated by the use of significant figures.

The calculated result of adding or subtracting should be rounded off so that it contains only one estimated digit. The precision of the calculated result must be the same as the precision of the *least* precise measurement in the values added

Table 12-1. Zeros in Significant Figures

Description	Location of Zero	Example	Significance	Purpose or Use
Trailing	left	570.	always significant	report observable value
Trailing	right	5.70	always significant	report observable value
Leading	left	0.75	not significant	locate decimal point
Leading	right	0.075	not significant	locate decimal point
Embedded	left	50.75	always significant	report observable value
Embedded	right	5.075	always significant	report observable value

or subtracted. Note the following examples:

Addition	Subtraction
32.6	531.46
431.33	− 86.3
6144.212	445.16 = 445.2
6608.142 = 6608.1	

In both examples, the precision of the least precise measurement is expressed in tenths. The results are therefore expressed in tenths.

In rounding off, when the digit to be dropped is more than 5, the preceding digit is increased by 1. For example, 2.4179 rounded off to three significant figures becomes 2.42.

When the digit to be dropped is less than 5, retain all the certain digits only. Thus, 15.64, rounded off to three significant figures, becomes 15.6. If the digit to be dropped is 5, the number preceding this digit becomes the next nearest *even* number. Thus, 22.15 becomes 22.2. Also, 22.45 becomes 22.4.

In multiplication and division, the calculated result should also be rounded off to the same number of significant figures as in the least precise number in the calculation. Note the following examples:

$$1.35 \times 4.2 = 5.67 = 5.7$$

The result is rounded off to two significant figures because 4.2 contains only two significant figures.

$$5.1 \div 2.13 = 2.39 = 2.4$$

The result is rounded off to two significant figures because 5.1 contains only two significant figures.

Percent Error.

The **accuracy** of a measurement refers to how close the measurement is to the accepted value.

The accuracy of experimental results is often expressed in terms of **percent error**.

percent error =

$$\frac{\text{observed value} - \text{accepted value}}{\text{accepted value}} \times 100\%$$

The **observed value** is the experimentally measured value or the value calculated from experimental results. The **accepted value** is the most probable value taken from generally accepted references. In some cases, the accepted value may be the average of many results from the same experiment. In such cases, the percent error may be referred to as the *percent difference* or *percent deviation*.

If the observed value is greater than the accepted value, the percent error will be positive. If the observed value is less than the accepted value, the percent error will be negative.

1. In an experiment, a student found that the percent of oxygen in a sample of $KClO_3$ was 41.3%. If the accepted value is 39.3%, the experimental percent error is

(1) $\dfrac{41.3 - 39.3}{39.3} \times 100\%$ (2) $\dfrac{39.3}{41.3} \times 100\%$

(3) $\dfrac{2}{41.3} \times 100\%$ (4) $\dfrac{2}{39.3} \times 100\%$

2. In the laboratory, a student determined the atomic mass of an element to be 28.02. The accepted value is 28.086. The difference between the student's observed value and the accepted value, expressed to the correct number of significant figures, is (1) 0.1 (2) 0.10 (3) 0.066 (4) 0.07

3. According to the rules for significant figures, the sum of 0.027 gram and 0.0023 gram should be expressed as (1) 0.029 gram (2) 0.0293 gram (3) 0.03 gram (4) 0.030 gram

4. In an experiment, the gram atomic mass of magnesium was determined to be 24.7. Compared to the accepted value of 24.3, the percent error for this determination was (1) 0.400 (2) 1.65 (3) 24.7 (4) 98.4

5. A student determined experimentally that the melting point of a substance was 55.2°C. If the accepted value of the melting point is 50.1°C, what is the percent error in the student's results? (1) 5.10% (2) 9.24% (3) 10.2% (4) 12.0%

6. The heat of vaporization of water is 540. calories per gram. In a laboratory experiment, a student determined the heat of vaporization of water to be 620. calories per gram. What is the percent error in the student's results? (1) 12.9% (2) 14.8% (3) 85.2% (4) 87.1%

7. Which measurement contains three significant figures? (1) 0.01 g (2) 0.010 g (3) 0.0100 g (4) 0.01000 g

8. According to the rules for significant figures, the total for the following addition problem should be stated as (1) 5,610 (2) 5,610.342 (3) 5,610.34 (4) 5,610.3

35.7
432.33
5142.312
5610.342

9. In an experiment, a student found that one mole of $KMnO_4$ had a mass of 149.91 grams. The accepted molar mass of this compound is 158.04 grams. What is the percent error in the student's results? (1) 1.05% (2) 5.14% (3) 5.42% (4) 8.13%

10. In determining the volume of a mole of gas at STP in the laboratory, a student's experimental value was 3.36 liters greater than the accepted value (22.4 liters).

The percent error contained in the student's value is closest to (1) 3.36 (2) 15.0 (3) 19.0 (4) 25.8

11. A cube has a volume of 8.0 cm³ and a mass of 21.6 grams. The density of the cube, in grams per cubic centimeter, is best expressed as (1) 2.7 (2) 2.70 (3) 0.37 (4) 0.370

LABORATORY SKILLS

During your introductory course in chemistry, you are expected to acquire all of the following basic laboratory skills.

Skill: Identifying Common Laboratory Equipment.

Figure 12-2 shows the basic equipment found in a chemistry laboratory. You should know the name and proper use of each type of apparatus shown.

Skill: Measuring With a Balance.

Triple-beam balances are commonly used in chemistry laboratories. Such balances have a single pan and three beams that carry sliding masses (see Figure 12-3, page 90). In general, these bal-

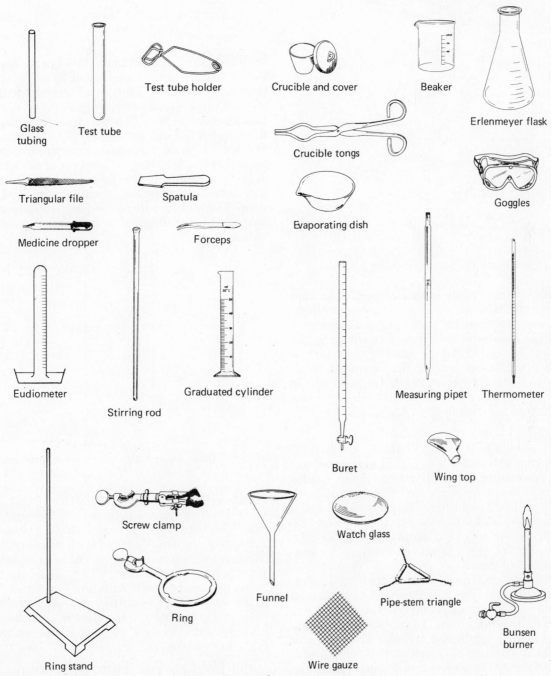

Figure 12-2. Laboratory equipment.

Laboratory Activities

ances are capable of measuring masses of up to 311 grams, and give measurements to one one-hundredth of a gram (0.01 gram). Before you use a balance, adjust the pointer so that it is at zero when the pan is empty. If the beams with the two heaviest masses are notched, make sure that the mass rests in the notch before making any measurements.

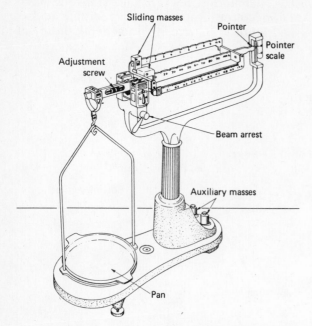

Figure 12-3. A triple-beam balance.

Before using a triple-beam balance, make sure that the pan is clean and dry. Never pour chemicals directly onto the pan. Instead, pour the chemical onto a piece of paper or into a watch glass (or beaker). Find the mass of the paper or watch glass before adding the chemical to be measured. Be sure to subtract the mass of the paper or watch glass from the total mass to obtain the mass of the chemical.

Skill: Using a Graduated Cylinder.
Graduated cylinders, also called **graduates**, are used to measure the volume of a liquid. Graduated cylinders commonly have volumes of 5, 10, 100, and 1,000 milliliters. When you choose a graduated cylinder to measure the volume of a liquid, choose one of appropriate size. For example, do not use a 1,000-mL graduate to measure 3 mL of liquid.

In narrow containers such as graduated cylinders and burets, the upper surface of contained water or other liquids is curved. The curved surface is called a **meniscus**. To measure the volume of liquid in a graduated cylinder or buret, you must keep your eye at a position that is level with the surface of the liquid (see Figure 12-4). The reading is then made from the bottom of the meniscus.

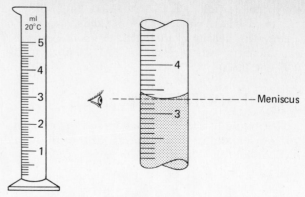

Figure 12-4. Reading the volume of a liquid.

Skill: Using Burets.
Most burets used in the laboratory have a capacity of 50 mL with calibrations for every 0.1 mL (see Figure 12-5). Such a buret can be read, with one estimated digit, to the nearest 0.01 mL. In actual practice, values to the nearest 0.1 mL are usually satisfactory. The volume of liquid dispensed from a buret is determined by observing and recording the starting volume, dispensing the desired quantity of liquid, then observing and recording the final volume. The volume dispensed is determined by subtracting the original volume from the final volume.

Figure 12-5. Calibrations on a buret.

Skill: Using Thermometers.
Most laboratory thermometers can be used to measure temperatures between $-10°C$ and $110°C$. These thermometers are usually filled with mercury. Such thermometers usually have a calibration marked for every degree (see Figure 12-6). Thus, the thermometer can be read, with one estimated digit, to the nearest 0.1°. Reporting with such precision is the usual practice in the laboratory. A temperature recorded as 21.4° implies an uncertainty of 0.1°, expressed as ±0.1°.

Skill: Using a Gas Burner Properly.
A common type of laboratory burner is a **Bunsen burner** (see Figure 12-7A). The flow of gas to a

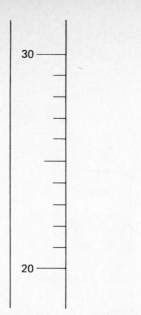

Figure 12-6. Calibrations on a thermometer.

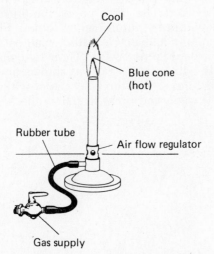

Figure 12-7A. A Bunsen burner.

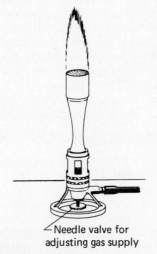

Figure 12-7B. Needle valve on a Meker burner.

Bunsen burner is regulated with the gas cock. In other types of laboratory burners, there is a needle valve on the base of the burner that can be used to adjust the gas flow (see Figure 12-7B). All laboratory burners have air flow regulators, or vents, that permit air to be premixed with the fuel gas. To operate the burner, open the gas cock and light the gas. Adjust the air flow until the flame shows a blue cone in the center. The blue cone is the hottest part of the flame.

Skill: Cutting, Bending, and Fire-Polishing Glass Tubing.
Tubing used in chemistry laboratories is usually made of low-melting soft glass, which can be easily scratched and broken. To cut glass tubing, lay it on a flat surface and hold it in place with one hand. With the other hand, use a triangular file to make a single scratch on the tubing. As shown in Figure 12-8, you then place your thumbs on either side of the scratch and snap the tubing. *CAUTION: If the tubing does not break easily, do not use force. Instead, make the scratch deeper.*

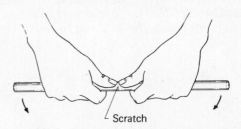

Figure 12-8. Breaking glass tubing.

The ends of freshly cut glass tubing are very sharp, and must be smoothed before the tubing can be used safely. To smooth freshly cut glass tubing, use a process called fire-polishing, which involves heating the glass to its melting point. To fire-polish a cut end of tubing, for example, hold it in the hottest part of the burner flame and rotate the glass (see Figure 12-9, page 92). When the flame turns bright yellow, turn off the burner, and place the glass on an insulated pad. The yellow flame shows that the glass was beginning to melt. *CAUTION: Hot glass tubing and cold glass tubing look alike. Always allow heated glass tubing to cool before you touch it.*

Many chemical experiments require glass tubing that is bent. Glass tubing bends easily when it is heated with a Bunsen burner. For this procedure, you must place a wing top (or fish tail) on your burner. The wing top spreads the flame and allows you to heat a wider surface of tubing. *CAUTION: Always make sure that your burner is turned off before you attempt to put on the wing top.*

Light your burner. Then hold the tubing (see Figure 12-10, page 92) and slowly rotate it in the flame. When the flame turns yellow, remove the

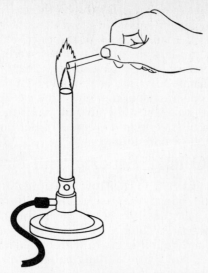

Figure 12-9. Fire-polishing glass tubing.

tubing from the flame. First, place it on an insulated pad and then gently bend it to the desired angle. *CAUTION: The heated part of the tubing will be very hot, so be sure not to touch it.*

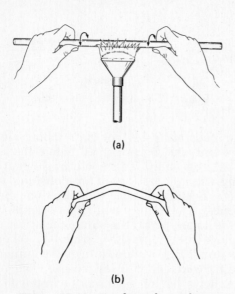

(a)

(b)

Figure 12-10. Bending glass tubing.

Skill: Using a Funnel and Filter Paper.

In chemistry experiments, it is often necessary to separate solids from liquids. If there is a large amount of liquid and the solid has collected at the bottom of the container, you can pour off, or decant, most of the liquid. As shown in Figure 12-11, allow the excess liquid to run along a stirring rod into a beaker. This will direct the flow of liquid into the beaker. Stop decanting before the solid begins to leave the container with the liquid. The solid can then be separated from the remaining liquid by filtration.

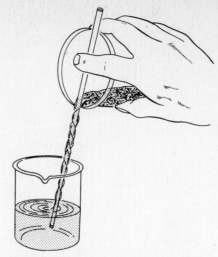

Figure 12-11. Decanting a liquid.

For filtration, you need a ring stand and ring, filter paper, a funnel, and a beaker. Place the funnel in the ring with its stem touching the inside of the beaker. The filter paper should fit completely within the funnel when folded. Fold the filter paper in half, and tear off a small part of one corner (see Figure 12-12). Then fold the filter paper in half again, open it as shown, and place it in the funnel. Wet the filter paper with a little distilled water and press it against the funnel.

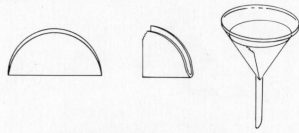

Figure 12-12. Preparing a filter.

Carefully pour the mixture along a glass stirring rod onto the filter paper. Pour the mixture slowly so that it does not overflow the filter paper. Retain the filtrate. When you have poured all of the mixture onto the filter paper, wash, using distilled water, any remaining solid from the original container onto the filter paper. Finally, rinse the solid residue on the filter with a small quantity of distilled water and combine the filtrates.

Skill: Removing Solid Chemicals From Containers.

Whenever possible, you should pour solid chemicals out of their containers directly into a beaker or onto a piece of weighing paper. (When you use a scoop or spoon to remove the chemicals from the container, you may introduce impurities.) To pour a solid from its bottle, tilt the bottle slightly, gently tap the side of the bottle, and rotate the bottle back and forth (see

Figure 12-13). The solid should pour out smoothly. (If not, loosen some of the solid with the scoop of a spoon.) If you want to transfer a solid from a beaker into a test tube, you should use a piece of creased paper as a funnel.

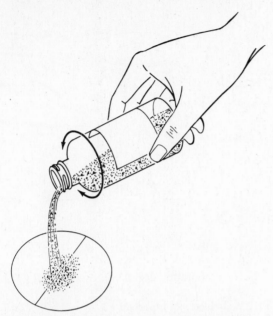

Figure 12-13. Pouring a solid chemical.

Skill: Pouring Liquids Safely.
To pour a liquid out of a stoppered reagent bottle, hold the stopper between your second and third fingers, as shown in Figure 12-14. Keeping the stopper between your fingers, remove it from the bottle. Pick up the bottle with the same hand, and pour the reagent into a clean container. When you have finished pouring, place the stopper back into the bottle. Never place a stopper from a re-

Figure 12-14. Pouring a liquid.

agent bottle on a work surface because the stopper might pick up other chemicals.

Skill: Diluting Acids Safely.
When you want to make an acid more dilute, always remember that you must add the *acid* to *water*. *CAUTION: Never pour water into an acid.* Follow the rules for the safe handling of liquids, and measure out the desired quantities of acid and water separately. Then slowly pour the acid along a glass stirring rod into the water, contained in a heat-resistant vessel.

Skill: Heating Materials Safely.
CAUTION: Whenever you use a burner in the laboratory, you should wear safety goggles. If the substance to be heated is in a test tube, you must make sure that the test tube is pointing away from you and from other, nearby students. (Boiling liquids sometimes spurt out of a test tube.)

QUESTIONS

1. The accompanying diagram represents a portion of a triple-beam balance. If the beams are in balance with the riders in the positions shown, what is the total mass in grams of the object being massed? (1) 460.62 grams (2) 466.20 grams (3) 466.62 grams (4) 460.20 grams

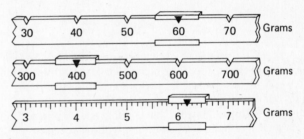

2. The accompanying diagram shows a portion of a buret. What is the correct reading? (1) 39.2 mL (2) 39.5 mL (3) 40.5 mL (4) 40.9 mL

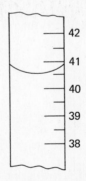

3. A small piece of copper metal is correctly placed on the pan of a triple-beam balance. The riders are all at the zero mark except for the rider on the 0–10 gram beam, which is located at the position shown. What is

the mass of the copper metal? (1) 0.455 g (2) 4.56 g (3) 0.55 g (4) 5.50 g

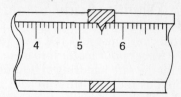

4. The process of filtration is performed in the laboratory to (1) form precipitates (2) remove water from solutions (3) separate dissolved particles from the solvent (4) separate undissolved substances from an aqueous mixture

5. Which diagram represents an Erlenmeyer flask?

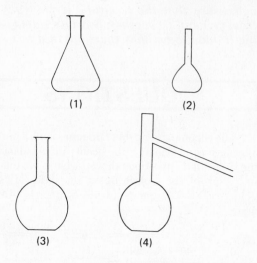

6. Which piece of laboratory equipment is most likely to be used to permit evaporation of a 1-milliliter sample of solution to dryness? (1) volumetric flask (2) buret (3) pipette (4) watch glass

7. A Bunsen burner that is not properly adjusted produces a flame that is orange-yellow in color and is sooty. The probable cause of this condition is that (1) no oxygen is mixing with the gas (2) no gas is mixing with the oxygen (3) insufficient oxygen is mixing with the gas (4) insufficient gas is mixing with the oxygen

8. Which diagram represents a pipette?

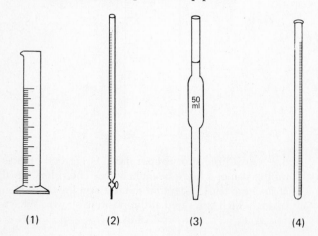

Questions 9–12 are based on the accompanying diagrams, which represent equipment from a chemistry laboratory.

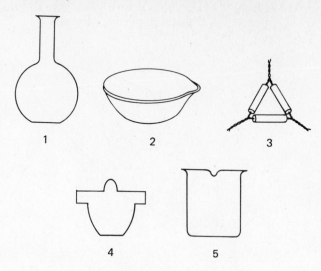

9. A crucible is represented by (1) 1 (2) 5 (3) 3 (4) 4

10. An evaporating dish is represented by (1) 5 (2) 2 (3) 3 (4) 4

11. A beaker is represented by (1) 1 (2) 2 (3) 5 (4) 4

12. A pipestem triangle is represented by (1) 5 (2) 2 (3) 3 (4) 4

LABORATORY ACTIVITIES

As part of your chemistry course, you should have performed a variety of laboratory activities. As a result of these activities, you should have developed the following skills.

Skill: Performing an Experiment Involving Phase Change; Interpreting a Simple Heating or Cooling Curve.

Heating or cooling curves show the temperature changes associated with phase changes from solid to liquid or from liquid to solid. Ice, paradichlorobenzene, or naphthalene are commonly used for determining heating or cooling curves. All three substances are solids at room temperature.

To obtain a cooling curve for paradichlorobenzene, for example, heat the substance to about 70°C and remove it from the heat source. Note the temperature. Stir the liquid gently with a thermometer and take a reading from the thermometer every 30 seconds. Continue to take readings until the substance becomes solid. A heating curve can be obtained by heating solid paradichlorobenzene and taking temperature readings until the entire solid has liquefied.

Figure 12-15 shows a typical heating curve. The flat portions of the curve show the phase changes.

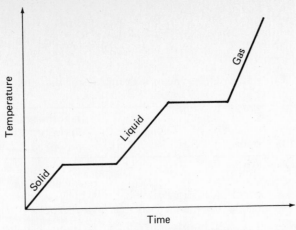

Figure 12-15. A heating curve.

Skill: Measuring Heats of Reactions.

You can use water as a calorimetric liquid to measure the heat of combustion of a candle.

This can be done with equipment such as a small (6–10 oz.) metal can and an ordinary candle. Attach the candle to a support such as the detached can lid. Crimp foil around the support to prevent loss of melting wax as shown in Figure 12-16.

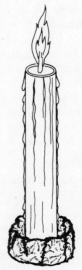

Figure 12-16. Assembly for measuring heat of combustion of a candle.

Weigh this candle assembly before lighting the candle. Weigh the clean empty can. Add about 150 mL of water to the can. Weigh the can with its contents. Observe and record the temperature of the water in the can. Light the candle and place it under the can. If possible, arrange a cardboard or plastic shield around the system to minimize heat loss. Heat the water until its temperature is about 20–30° higher than the original temperature. Extinguish the candle and record the high-

est temperature reached by the water. Weigh the candle.

Calculate the mass of the water.

$$mass_{water} =$$

(mass of can and water) − (mass of can)

Calculate the temperature change ΔT as follows:

$$\Delta T =$$

(final temperature) − (original temperature)

Calculate the mass of candle wax consumed as follows:

$$mass_{wax} = (\text{original mass}) - (\text{final mass})$$

Calculate the heat of combustion of candle wax ΔH in calories (or kilocalories) per gram of wax consumed.

$$\Delta H = \frac{grams_{H_2O}}{grams_{wax}} \times \frac{1 \text{ cal}}{\text{gram } C°} \times \Delta T$$

$$= calories/gram_{wax}$$

Sample Problem

Calculate the heat of combustion of candle wax by using the following data:

Data:

Mass of empty can	76.15 g
Mass of can with water	228.44 g
Original temperature of water	19.8°C
Original mass of candle assembly	24.92 g
Final mass of candle assembly	24.31 g
Final temperature of water	46.3°C

Calculations:

$$Mass_{water} = 228.44 \text{ g}_{H_2O} - 76.15 \text{ g}_{H_2O}$$

$$= 152.29 \text{ g}_{H_2O}$$

$$\Delta T = 46.3°C - 19.8°C$$

$$= 26.5°C$$

$$Mass_{wax} = 24.92 \text{ g}_{wax} - 24.31 \text{ g}_{wax}$$

$$= 0.61 \text{ g}_{wax}$$

For water: $\dfrac{1 \text{ cal}}{1 \text{ g}_{H_2O} \cdot °C}$

$$Heat = 152.29 \text{ g}_{H_2O} \times 26.5°C \times \frac{1 \text{ cal}}{1 \text{ g}_{H_2O} \cdot °C}$$

$$= 4.04 \times 10^3 \text{ cal}$$

$$\Delta H_{(comb.)} = \frac{4.04 \times 10^3 \text{ cal}}{0.61 \text{ g}_{wax}}$$

$$= \frac{6.6 \times 10^3 \text{ cal}}{1 \text{ g}_{wax}}$$

Skill: Identifying Endothermic and Exothermic Reactions.

You can measure temperature changes associated with an endothermic reaction by dissolving ammonium chloride in water. Temperature changes associated with an exothermic reaction can be measured by dissolving sodium hydroxide in water.

Place a known mass of water in a Styrofoam cup and record the temperature of the water. Add a known mass of ammonium chloride to the water and record the temperature of the water every 30 seconds until all of the solid has dissolved. The final water temperature will be lower than the initial water temperature because the reaction absorbs heat.

When sodium hydroxide is dissolved in water, the final water temperature will be higher than the initial water temperature because the reaction is exothermic.

Heat of solution is usually reported as calories or kilocalories per mole of solute. In order to determine this experimentally, a known mass of solute is dissolved in a known mass of water. The resulting temperature change is observed and recorded. The heat of solution, ΔH_{sol} can be calculated in the same manner that heat of combustion of candle wax was calculated on page 95.

Skill: Producing a Solubility Curve.

Sodium nitrate, potassium nitrate, and potassium chlorate are salts that show large increases in solubility with increasing temperature.

To develop a solubility curve, you must find the saturation temperatures of salt solutions of different concentrations. To find saturation temperature, place a known mass of solute in a test tube and add a known mass of water. Heat the mixture until all of the solute has dissolved. Put a thermometer into the test tube and allow the solution to cool. Record the temperature at which crystallization begins. This is the saturation temperature. Repeat the procedure using increasing masses of solute but using the same mass of water each time. Your data should include the mass of solute used, the mass of water used, and the temperature at which crystallization began.

To produce a solubility curve from your data, you must convert grams of salt per given mass of water to grams of salt per 100 grams of water. The data can then be plotted on a graph where the horizontal axis is temperature in degrees Celsius and the vertical axis is grams of salt per 100 g of water. (Solubility and solubility curves are discussed on pages 42–43.)

Skill: Distinguishing Between Inorganic and Organic Substances.

Sodium chloride and naphthalene (moth crystals) can be used to demonstrate differences in solubility, melting point, chemical reactivity, and electrical conductivity typical of inorganic and organic compounds. These differences are summarized in Table 12-2.

Table 12-2. Differences in Properties of Inorganic and Organic Substances

Property	Table Salt (NaCl)	Naphthalene Moth Crystals ($C_{10}H_8$)
Solubility in water in alcohol in acetone	very soluble slightly soluble nearly insoluble	nearly insoluble slightly soluble very soluble
Melting point °C	801	80.5
Chemical reactivity	does not readily decompose	vapor burns easily to form carbon and water
Electrical conductivity	conducts in the liquid phase (melted) and when dissolved in water	nonconductor

Skill: Identifying Metallic Ions by Flame Tests.

In a flame test, a loop of metal wire (platinum or nichrome) is dipped into a solution containing the metal ion to be tested. The loop is then placed in the flame of a Bunsen burner. The color of the flame changes, depending on which metal ion is present. Table 12-3 shows the flame test colors for various metal ions.

Before beginning any flame tests and between tests of different solutions, the metal loop should be cleaned by dipping it into hydrochloric acid and then inserting it into the flame of the burner.

Table 12-3. Flame Tests

Metallic Ion	Color
Potassium	violet
Sodium	yellow
Calcium	yellowish-red
Copper	green
Strontium	scarlet
Lithium	red

Skill: Determining the Percent by Mass of Water in a Hydrate.

Water of hydration is a definite mass of water that is part of a crystalline compound, such as $CuSO_4 \cdot 5H_2O$. Compounds containing water are called **hydrates**. Careful heating of the hydrate can drive off the water. The percentage of water in the hydrate can be calculated from the difference in mass of the compound before heating and after heating.

To find the percent by mass of water in a hydrate, place a known mass of the compound to be studied in a crucible. Then measure the mass of the compound and the crucible together. Heat the crucible gently for several minutes until the crystal turns to powder. Find the mass of the crucible with the remains of the crystal. Subtract your results from the initial mass of the crucible and crystal together. The difference is the mass of the water of hydration. Divide by the original mass of the hydrate and multiply by 100% to find the percent of water in the hydrate.

percent water =

$$\frac{\text{mass of water of hydration}}{\text{mass of hydrate}} \times 100\%$$

Skill: Determining the Volume of a Mole of Gas in a Reaction.

Hydrogen gas generated from the reaction of a known mass of magnesium with excess dilute HCl may be collected in a buret or in a eudiometer tube. The volume of the hydrogen may then be corrected to STP and related to the moles of magnesium used in the reaction.

Skill: Titrating.

The concentration of an unknown dilute acid (or base) is often found by titration against a base (or acid) of known concentration (the standard solution). For example, dilute solutions of sodium hydroxide or potassium hydroxide may be titrated against dilute solutions of hydrochloric or sulfuric acids. The end point of the titration can be determined by use of indicators, such as phenolphthalein, which are added to the unknown.

To determine the concentration, or molarity, of the unknown, you must know the volume of the unknown used in the titration, the molarity of the standard solution, and the volume of standard solution used in neutralizing the unknown. Write the balanced equation for the reaction. If the coefficients in the equation show that the mole ratio of the acid to the base is 1:1, the concentration of the unknown can be found by using the following formula:

$$\begin{array}{l}\text{volume} \\ \text{unknown}\end{array} \times \begin{array}{l}\text{concen-} \\ \text{tration} \\ \text{unknown}\end{array} = \begin{array}{l}\text{volume} \\ \text{standard} \\ \text{solution}\end{array} \times \begin{array}{l}\text{concen-} \\ \text{tration} \\ \text{standard} \\ \text{solution}\end{array}$$

(Titration is discussed in Unit 7, page 50.)

Skill: Writing Laboratory Reports.

A laboratory report is part of each laboratory activity. The report should be clearly and concisely written. Information and observations should be organized in a logical manner, often by using lists. Data should be reported in tables and graphs whenever appropriate. Conclusions should be based upon observations, and the reasons for each conclusion should be stated.

QUESTIONS

1. The data below were obtained by a student in an experiment to determine the percent of water in a hydrate:

mass of hydrate   5.0 g

mass of anhydrous compound   3.4 g

The percent of water in the hydrate is   (1) 68%   (2) 47%   (3) 32%   (4) 12%

2. As a result of dissolving a salt in water, a student found that the temperature of the water increased. From this observation alone, the student should conclude that the dissolving of the salt   (1) produced an acid solution   (2) produced a basic solution   (3) was endothermic   (4) was exothermic

3. During a titration, a student used 50.0 mL of 0.100-M acid. How many moles of acid, expressed with the proper number of significant figures, were used?   (1) 0.005   (2) 0.0050   (3) 0.00500   (4) 0.005000

4. The accompanying diagram shows a eudiometer tube in a water bath. The water levels inside and outside the tube are equal. If the atmospheric pressure is 750 torr, what is the pressure inside the tube?   (1) 740 torr   (2) 750 torr   (3) 760 torr   (4) 800 torr

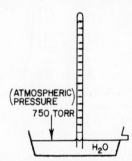

5. The volume of an acid required to neutralize exactly 15.00 milliliters of a base of nearly the same molarity could be measured most precisely if the acid were added to the solution of the base from a   (1) 100-mL graduate   (2) 125-mL Erlenmeyer flask   (3) 50-mL buret   (4) 50-mL beaker

Base your answers to questions 6 and 7 on the following table, which shows the data collected during the heating of a 5.0-gram sample of a hydrated salt.

Mass of Salt (g)	Heating Time (min)
5.0	0.0
4.1	5.0
3.1	10.
3.0	15.
3.0	30.
3.0	60.

6. After 60 minutes, how many grams of water appear to remain in the salt? (1) 0.00 (2) 2.0 (3) 1.9 (4) 0.90

7. What is the percent of water in the original sample? (1) 82% (2) 60% (3) 30% (4) 40%

8. Given the following titration data:

Volume of base (KOH) = 40.0 mL

Molarity of base = 0.20 M

Volume of acid (HCl) added = 20.0 mL

The concentration of HCl required for the acid to neutralize the base is (1) 1.0 M (2) 0.20 M (3) 0.10 M (4) 0.40 M

9. Which of the accompanying graphs could represent the uniform cooling of a substance, starting with the gaseous phase and ending with the solid phase?

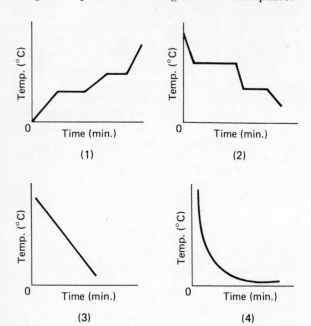

10. The following data were recorded while determining the solubility of a certain salt.

Temperature (°C)	Grams Solute/100. g H_2O
10	30
20	33
30	36
40	39
50	42

Which graph best represents the solubility of this salt?

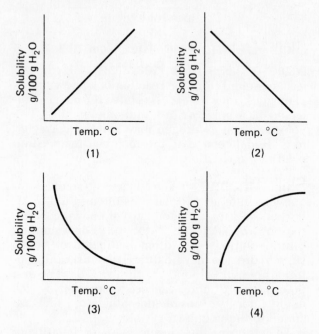

11. How many milliliters of 0.4 M HCl are required to neutralize completely 200 milliliters of 0.16 M potassium hydroxide? (1) 500 (2) 200 (3) 80 (4) 30

Reference Tables for Chemistry

The Reference Tables for Chemistry contain much useful information. You are rarely asked to memorize details of information in chemistry. Often you are instructed to refer to a particular table. At other times, you may have to decide whether or not to use the tables. Whenever you are unsure about the answer to a question, look through the tables for some information that may help.

Following are brief summaries of the kinds of information to be found in each of the Reference Tables and typical questions based upon these tables.

HOW TO USE THE REFERENCE TABLES FOR CHEMISTRY

A. Physical Constants and Conversion Factors.

Use Table A (see page 105) to change one unit of measure of a property to another unit of measure of the same property.

Units of length: Å and m

Units of energy: eV and J

Units of mass (of atoms): amu and g

Units of pressure: atm, kPa, mmHg, and torr

Units of energy (heat): kcal and J

Also use this table to find the numerical values for N_A, e, c, h, and R.

The physical constants for water given are molal freezing point depression, molal boiling point elevation, heat of fusion, and heat of vaporization.

1 A. The Angstrom unit is used to measure the same property as the (1) joule (2) torr (3) second (4) meter

2 A. One liter is equivalent in volume to (1) 1 cm^3 (2) 1 dm^3 (3) 1 C (4) 1 atm

3 A. Compared to the heat of fusion for water, the heat of vaporization is (1) greater (2) smaller (3) the same

4 A. Which fraction converts a pressure of 745 torr to kilopascals?

(1) $745 \times \dfrac{760}{101.3}$ (2) $745 + 101.3$

(3) $745 \times \dfrac{101.3}{760}$ (4) $745 - 101.3$

5 A. Which gives the heat of fusion of water in joules per gram?

(1) $\dfrac{4.18 \times 10^3}{79.72}$ (2) $\dfrac{79.72}{4.18 \times 10^3}$

(3) $4.18 \times 10^3 + 79.72$ (4) $4.18 \times 10^3 \times 79.72$

B. Standard Units.

Definitions of standard units (SI) and selected prefixes identifying the quantities to be used with those units are given in Table B (see page 105). Whenever you are uncertain about a prefix or unit, refer to this table to check your ideas.

1 B. Which is the standard unit used to measure a quantity of electricity? (1) kelvin (2) pascal (3) volt (4) coulomb

2 B. Which is the standard unit used to measure quantity of heat? (1) kelvin (2) liter (3) coulomb (4) joule

3 B. The symbol dL stands for (1) deciliter (2) demiliter (3) dynaliter (4) duraliter

4 B. Which represents the shortest length? (1) millimeter (2) kilometer (3) nanometer (4) centimeter

5 B. Which expression converts 100 meters to kilometers?

(1) $(100)^2 \times 10^{-3}$ (2) $(100)^2 \times 10^3$

(3) 100×10^{-3} (4) 100×10^3

C. Density and Boiling Points of Some Common Gases.

For Reference Table C, see page 106. Density is related to molecular mass. The theoretical density of a gas at STP can be determined from the formula:

$$D = \frac{\text{molecular mass}}{22.4 \text{ L}} \text{ at STP}$$

The molecular mass of a gas can be determined from the formula:

$$\text{molecular mass} = \text{density} \times 22.4$$

Note that the boiling points in the table are expressed in degrees Kelvin. As the boiling points of gases increase, the gases can be more easily liquefied. Thus, in the table, the gas that is most easily liquefied is sulfur dioxide; the most difficult, hydrogen.

The rates of diffusion of gases are inversely proportional to the square root of their molecular masses. Thus, hydrogen molecules diffuse four times as fast as do oxygen molecules.

1 C. Which compound has the *lowest* normal boiling point? (1) HCl (2) H_2S (3) NH_3 (4) CH_4

2 C. At STP, which gas has a greater density than air? (1) H_2 (2) NH_3 (3) Cl_2 (4) CH_4

3 C. At STP, which of the following gases will diffuse most rapidly? (1) Cl_2 (2) NH_3 (3) H_2 (4) N_2

4 C. As molecular mass increases, the density of gases (1) decreases (2) increases (3) remains the same

5 C. Which of the following gases has the greatest density at STP? (1) SO_2 (2) CO_2 (3) Cl_2 (4) N_2

D. Solubility Curves (grams solute/ 100 g H₂O).
Use the information in Table D (see page 106) to:

Determine solubility of a given substance at a given temperature.

Compare solubilities of several salts.

Estimate change in solubility as temperature changes.

Note that the solubilities of the three gases HCl, NH_3, and SO_2 decrease as temperature increases, while the solubility of the other substances, all solids, increases as temperature increases. Note also that solubilities are stated per 100 g H_2O.

1 D. When 100 grams of water saturated with KNO_3 at 70°C are cooled to 25°C, the total number of grams of KNO_3 that will precipitate is (1) 40 (2) 45 (3) 95 (4) 135

2 D. Which of the following substances is most soluble at 50°C? (1) $KClO_3$ (2) NH_3 (3) $NaCl$ (4) NH_4Cl

3 D. What is the maximum number of grams of NH_4Cl that will dissolve in 200 grams of water at 70°C? (1) 60 (2) 70 (3) 100 (4) 120

4 D. Which of the following substances is least soluble at 60°C? (1) NH_4Cl (2) KCl (3) $NaCl$ (4) NH_3

5 D. KCl and $NaCl$ have the same solubility at (1) 85°C (2) 75°C (3) 37°C (4) 20°C

E. Table of Solubilities in Water.
Table E (see page 106) gives the solubilities of 165 substances. It gives the name of each compound and its solubility in terms of five categories:

  i: nearly insoluble
 ss: slightly soluble
  s: soluble
  d: decomposes (reacts with water to form a new substance)
  n: not isolated (not yet produced in the laboratory)

Also use this table to predict formation of a precipitate when aqueous solutions containing these ions are mixed.

1 E. Which saturated salt solution is most concentrated? (1) $AgC_2H_3O_2(aq)$ (2) $Ag_2CO_3(aq)$ (3) $Ag_2S(aq)$ (4) $AgCl(aq)$

2 E. Which of the following compounds is most likely to have the *smallest* K_{sp}? (1) barium carbonate (2) calcium sulfate (3) magnesium nitrate (4) silver acetate

3 E. Which compound dissolves in water to form a saturated solution that is dilute? (1) aluminum sulfate (2) aluminum carbonate (3) aluminum acetate (4) aluminum chloride

4 E. Which sequence lists the three chlorides in order of increasing solubility?
(1) silver chloride, sodium chloride, lead chloride
(2) lead chloride, silver chloride, sodium chloride
(3) sodium chloride, lead chloride, silver chloride
(4) silver chloride, lead chloride, sodium chloride

5 E. Which substance has the smallest value for K_{sp}? (1) $CaCl_2$ (2) $CaBr_2$ (3) $CaSO_4$ (4) $Ca(NO_3)_2$

F. Selected Polyatomic Ions.
Table F (see page 107) lists 22 anions and 2 cations, giving the name, corresponding formula, and ionic charge for each one. Use this table to match names of salts with their correct formulas. For example, ammonium phosphate:

$$\text{ammonium} \quad \underbrace{NH_4{}^+ \quad PO_4{}^{3-}}_{(NH_4)_3PO_4} \quad \text{phosphate}$$
$$\text{ion} \qquad\qquad\qquad\qquad\qquad\qquad \text{ion}$$

Note that the subscript 3 on the ammonium ion is needed to maintain conservation of charge.

1 F. What is the correct formula for sodium thiosulfate? (1) $Na_2S_2O_4$ (2) Na_2SO_3 (3) Na_2SO_4 (4) $Na_2S_2O_3$

2 F. What is the correct formula for potassium hydride? (1) KH (2) KH_2 (3) KOH (4) $K(OH)_2$

3 F. What is the name of the calcium salt of sulfuric acid? (1) calcium thiosulfate (2) calcium sulfate (3) calcium sulfide (4) calcium sulfite

4 F. A binary compound of sodium is (1) sodium chlorate (2) sodium chlorite (3) sodium perchlorate (4) sodium chloride

5 F. Which is the formula for sodium perchlorate? (1) $NaClO$ (2) $NaClO_2$ (3) $NaClO_3$ (4) $NaClO_4$

G. Standard Energies of Formation of Compounds at 1 atm and 298 K.
Table G (see page 107) lists ΔH_f° and ΔG_f° for 22 substances at the specified conditions that are standard for thermodynamic properties. Use ΔH_f° to determine the amount of energy taken in or given off when a reaction for the formation of a compound from its elements occurs. Use ΔG_f° values to predict and compare stability of compounds. A negative value of ΔG_f° indicates that the compound forms spontaneously from its elements. Larger negative values for ΔG_f° indicate greater stability. Refer to the equations at the bottom of the table to see how heat and ΔH can be expressed.

1 G. Which compound forms spontaneously? (1) NO(g) (2) NO_2(g) (3) ICl(g) (4) HI(g)

2 G. Why does the reaction $K(s) + \frac{1}{2}Cl_2(g) \rightarrow KCl(s)$ occur spontaneously? (1) ΔS is positive. (2) ΔS is negative. (3) ΔG is positive. (4) ΔG is negative.

3 G. Which substance will form spontaneously from its elements in their standard states at 1 atmosphere and 298 K? (1) ethene (2) ethyne (3) hydrogen iodide (4) hydrogen fluoride

4 G. Which substance is formed from its elements in a reaction that is spontaneous and exothermic? (1) C_2H_2(g) (2) C_2H_4(g) (3) CO(g) (4) ICl(g)

5 G. Which substance is produced from its elements by an exothermic reaction with the greatest amount of energy produced per mole? (1) CO_2(g) (2) C_2H_2(g) (3) ICl(g) (4) NH_3(g)

H. Selected Radioisotopes.

Table H (see page 107) gives the symbol, mass number, half-life, and decay mode for 23 nuclides. Use the symbol to calculate the number of protons, neutrons, and electrons in the isotope. Use the half-life to determine the mass of a sample that remains after a stated period of decay. Also use the half-life to compare relative stabilities of isotopes. (Longer half-life indicates greater stability.) Use decay mode and information from Table J (names of particles) to determine the name of the nuclear emanation associated with a specific isotope.

1 H. How many grams of a 32-gram sample of ^{32}P will remain after 71.5 days? (1) 1 (2) 2 (3) 8 (4) 4

2 H. What is the number of hours required for potassium-42 to undergo 3 half-life periods? (1) 6.2 hours (2) 12.4 hours (3) 24.8 hours (4) 37.2 hours

3 H. After 62.0 hours, 1.0 gram remains unchanged from a sample of ^{42}K. How much ^{42}K was in the original sample? (1) 8.0 g (2) 16 g (3) 32 g (4) 64 g

4 H. Which radioisotope gives off beta particles as it decays? (1) ^{37}K (2) ^{32}P (3) ^{226}Ra (4) ^{238}U

5 H. Which radioisotope has the shortest half-life period? (1) ^{60}Co (2) ^{32}P (3) ^{90}Sr (4) ^{37}K

I. Heats of Reaction at 1 atm and 298 K.

Table I (see page 108) gives the chemical equation and ΔH for nine exothermic reactions and five endothermic reactions in kcal/mol. Six of the reactions involve combustion (burning in oxygen), seven are dissolving processes involving H_2O, and one involves acid-base neutralization. Use this information to match energy characteristics with a specific reaction.

1 I. The greatest amount of energy would be given up by the complete combustion of 1 mole of (1) CH_4(g) (2) C_3H_8(g) (3) $CH_3OH(\ell)$ (4) $C_6H_{12}O_6$(s)

2 I. Which salt dissolves in an exothermic reaction? (1) NH_4NO_3 (2) NaCl (3) $KClO_3$ (4) LiBr

3 I. How many kilocalories of heat are produced when a dilute water solution of a strong acid is neutralized by a dilute water solution of a strong base to produce 1 mole of water? (1) 13.8 (2) less than 13.8 (3) more than 13.8

4 I. Which is the heat of combustion (ΔH) for CH_4? (1) -212.8 kcal/mol (2) -212.8 kcal/gram (3) $+212.8$ kcal/mol (4) $+212.8$ kcal/gram

5 I. Which occurs when 1 mole of KNO_3 dissolves in water? (1) The temperature of the water increases as 8.3 kilocalories are absorbed. (2) The temperature of the water increases as 8.3 kilocalories are produced. (3) The temperature of the water decreases as 8.3 kilocalories are absorbed. (4) The temperature of the water decreases as 8.3 kilocalories are produced.

J. Symbols Used in Nuclear Chemistry.

In Table J (page 108), the names and symbols for eight particles are given. The symbols (often Greek letters) may be used in sentences, charts, and diagrams.

The other symbols, each with a subscript and superscript, are used in nuclear equations.

Note that the proton, deuteron, and triton are the nuclei of the three isotopes of hydrogen.

1 J. Which nuclear emission moving through an electric field would be deflected toward the positive electrode? (1) alpha particle (2) beta particle (3) gamma radiation (4) proton

2 J. Which is the symbol for the deuterium isotope of hydrogen? (1) ^1_1H (2) ^2_1H (3) ^3_1H (4) ^4_2H

3 J. Which two particles have approximately the same mass? (1) neutron and electron (2) neutron and deuteron (3) proton and neutron (4) proton and electron

4 J. The structure of an alpha particle is the same as that of a (1) lithium atom (2) neon atom (3) hydrogen nucleus (4) helium nucleus

5 J. In the reaction $^{27}_{13}Al + ^4_2He \rightarrow ^{30}_{15}P + X$, the particle represented by X is (1) a neutron (2) a beta particle (3) an electron (4) an alpha particle

K. Ionization Energies and Electronegativities.

First ionization energies are given in Table K (see page 108) for most members of groups 1, 2, and 13–18. Only the values for Fr and At are missing. At the time of the preparation of the table, there was insufficient information available on these elements. Electronegativities are given for the members of Groups 1, 2, and 13–17. (Electronegativities are not given for Group 18 elements since these elements are rarely involved in covalent bonding.)

First ionization energy is defined by the equation

$$M(g) + energy \rightarrow M^+(g) + e^-$$

where a gas phase atom is converted to a 1+ gas phase cation and a separated electron by the addition of energy.

1 K. Which 1-mole sample of atoms requires the *least* energy to form a mole of positive ions? (1) Ge (2) Ca (3) Ga (4) K

2 K. The element in Period 2 with the highest first ionization energy is (1) a noble gas (2) a halogen (3) an alkali metal (4) an alkaline earth metal

3 K. Which element in Period 3 has the *least* tendency to lose an electron? (1) argon (2) sodium (3) phosphorus (4) aluminum

4 K. An element that has a high ionization energy and tends to be chemically inactive would most likely be (1) an alkali metal (2) a transition element (3) a noble gas (4) a halogen

5 K. Which of the following compounds contains a bond with the greatest degree of ionic character? (1) CaO (2) $MgBr_2$ (3) PH_3 (4) CCl_4

L. Relative Strengths of Acids in Aqueous Solution at 1 atm and 298 K.

Table L (see page 109) gives 23 acid-base conjugate pairs. The value of K_a for most of these acids is given for their ionization in water solution. Use this information to compare acid strength. Also use this information to predict which proton donor/acceptor reactions can occur. Use the rule: An acid will donate its proton to any base below it in this table.

1 L. Which is an amphiprotic ion? (1) HSO_4^- (2) NH_4^+ (3) NO_3^- (4) Cl^-

2 L. According to the Brönsted-Lowry theory, which species could act only as an acid?

$$(1) \begin{bmatrix} H \\ \overset{..}{H:N:H} \\ \overset{..}{H} \end{bmatrix}^+ \quad (2)\ \overset{..}{H:N:H} \\ H$$

$$(3)\ \overset{..}{:\overset{..}{S}:}^{2-} \quad (4)\ H:\overset{..}{\underset{..}{O}}: \\ H$$

3 L. Which of the following acids ionizes to the *least* extent at 298 K? (1) HF (2) HNO_2 (3) H_2S (4) H_2O

4 L. According to Reference Table L, which of the following is the strongest Brönsted-Lowry acid? (1) HNO_2 (2) H_2S (3) CH_3COOH (4) H_3PO_4

5 L. In the reaction $HBr + H_2O \leftrightharpoons H_3O^+ + Br^-$, which is a conjugate acid-base pair? (1) HBr and Br^- (2) HBr and H_2O (3) H_3O^+ and Br^- (4) H_3O^+ and HBr

M. Constants for Various Equilibria at 1 atm and 298 K.

Table M (see page 109) includes values for K for nine reactions expressed as K_w, K_b, or K_{eq}. (Recall that K_a values were given in Table L.) Use these values to describe the extent to which a reaction occurs and to match K to a specific reaction.

This table also includes 12 values for K_{sp}. Use these values to compare solubilities of nearly insoluble salts. Salts of the form MX can be compared with each other. Similarly, salts for M_2X or MX_2 can also be compared to each other.

1 M. Which of the following compounds is *least* soluble in water at 298 K? (1) AgI (2) AgCl (3) $PbCO_3$ (4) $ZnCO_3$

2 M. Which compound is more soluble than $BaSO_4$ at 1 atmosphere and 298 K? (1) AgBr (2) $CaSO_4$ (3) AgI (4) $PbCrO_4$

3 M. A saturated solution of which salt would be most dilute? (1) AgCl (2) $BaSO_4$ (3) AgI (4) $PbCrO_4$

4 M. In a saturated solution of $BaSO_4$ at 1 atmosphere and 298 K, the product of $[Ba^{2+}] \times [SO_4^{2-}]$ is equal to (1) 1.1×10^{-10} (2) 1.1×10^{-5} (3) 1.1×10^5 (4) 1.1×10^{10}

5 M. Which substance will form a precipitate from a solution with the lowest concentration of Ag^+ (aq) when the concentration of the anion is 1.0 M? (1) AgBr (2) AgCl (3) AgI (4) $AgNO_3$

N. Standard Electrode Potentials.

Table N (see page 110) lists 37 reduction half-reactions and their corresponding E^0s. The E^0 of each half-reaction is given relative to the hydrogen half-reaction

$$2H^+ + 2e^- \rightarrow H_2(g)$$

that is defined as 0.00 volts.

The oxidizing agents are listed on the left side of the equations for the half-reactions. The reducing agents are listed on the right. Any oxidizing agent will react spontaneously with any reducing agent listed below it.

Use this table to determine the overall E^0 values for an electrochemical cell constructed by using any two standard half-cells. Use the reduction half-reactions and their E^0 values as written. Write the equation in reverse to show an oxidation half-reaction, and change the sign of its E^0 value. Choose multipliers to maintain equal gain and loss of electrons. Add the balanced half-reaction to get the overall reaction. Add their E^0 values to get the overall E^0 value.

1 N. Which metal can reduce Ni^{2+} ions? (1) Ag (2) Pb (3) Cu (4) Fe

2 N. Which of the following elements will replace Pb from $Pb(NO_3)_2$(aq)? (1) Mg(s) (2) Au(s) (3) Cu(s) (4) Ag(s)

3 N. Which molecule is most easily reduced? (1) Br_2 (2) Cl_2 (3) F_2 (4) I_2

4 N. Which half-reaction is used as the standard for determining the relative reducing tendencies of other Reference Table N half-reactions?
(1) $F_2(g) + 2e^- \rightarrow 2F^-$
(2) $Ag^+ + e^- \rightarrow Ag(s)$
(3) $Na^+ + e^- \rightarrow Na(s)$
(4) $2H^+ + 2e^- \rightarrow H_2(g)$

5 N. In the equation
$$Cu(s) + 2Ag^+(aq) \rightarrow Cu^{2+}(aq) + 2Ag(s)$$
the oxidizing agent is (1) Cu^0 (2) Ag^+ (3) Cu^{2+} (4) Ag^0

O. Vapor Pressure of Water.

Table O (page 110) gives values for the vapor pressure of water for various temperatures from 0°C to 110°C. Use these values to change the pressure according to the following formula, which is an application of Dalton's law:

$$P_{\text{wet gas}} = P_{\text{dry gas}} + P_{H_2O}$$

Also use these values to determine the boiling point of water at various listed pressures. For example, when the external pressure is 149.4 mm Hg, water will boil at 60°C.

1 O. What is the vapor pressure of water at 30°C?
(1) 31.8 torr   (2) (273 + 31.8) torr
(3) 760 torr   (4) $\dfrac{31.8}{760}$ torr

2 O. The vapor pressure of water at 75°C lies between (1) 4.6 and 233.7 torr (2) 233.7 and 295 torr (3) 233.7 and 355.1 torr (4) 355.1 and 760 torr

3 O. As water is heated from 0°C to 25°C, its vapor pressure increases by (1) 4.6 torr (2) 19.2 torr (3) 23.8 torr (4) 28.4 torr

4 O. What is the pressure of the carbon dioxide collected over water at 20°C as shown in the accompanying diagram? (1) 17.5 torr (2) 750 − 17.5 torr (3) 750 + 17.5 torr (4) $\dfrac{750}{17.5}$ torr

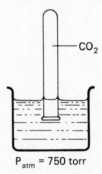

P_{atm} = 750 torr

5 O. When the external pressure is 200 torr, water will boil at about
(1) 67°C
(2) 67 K
(3) 200°C
(4) 200 K

P. Radii of Atoms.

Table P (see page 111) shows three versions of atomic radius arranged as a periodic table of the elements. Some elements have values for all three radii. Most have only one or two values. All are given in Angstrom units (Å): 1 Å = 10^{-10} m.

Covalent radius refers to half the distance between two atoms of the same element joined by a covalent bond. *Atomic radius* in metals refers to half the distance between two atoms as found in a metal-like crystal.

The *van der Waals radius* is based upon the apparent distance from the nucleus to the effective edge of the atom when the only forces of attraction present are the very weak van der Waals forces. It is also half the distance between the nuclei of two unbonded atoms.

1 P. Which of the following particles has the smallest radius? (1) Na^0 (2) K^0 (3) Na^+ (4) K^+
2 P. The element in Period 2 with the largest covalent atomic radius is (1) a halogen (2) a noble gas (3) an alkali metal (4) an alkaline earth metal
3 P. Proceeding from left to right in Period 2 of the Periodic Table, the covalent radius of the elements generally (1) decreases (2) increases (3) remains the same
4 P. The reactivity of the metals in Groups 1 and 2 generally increases with (1) increased ionization energy (2) increased atomic radius (3) decreased nuclear charge (4) decreased mass
5 P. As the elements in Group 1 are considered in order of increasing atomic number, the atomic radius of each successive element increases. This is primarily due to an increase in the number of (1) neutrons in the nucleus (2) electrons in the outermost shell (3) unpaired electrons (4) principal energy levels

Periodic Table.

The elements are shown arranged into 7 numbered periods and 18 numbered groups. The Periodic Table (see pages 112–113) shows pre-1984 group designations as Roman numerals. The elements are also arranged according to valence electron configuration into *s*-, *p*-, *d*-, and *f*-block sections. Transition elements and the lanthanoid and actinoid series are identified.

Specific information for each element is given in its location. See the key on top of the table. Note that weighted average atomic mass is given for most elements. The presence of a mass number in parentheses instead of an atomic mass indicates the mass number of the most stable or most common isotope.

For questions based on the Periodic Table, see Unit 4 of the text.

Reference Tables

PHYSICAL CONSTANTS AND CONVERSION FACTORS

Name	Symbol	Value(s)	Units
Angstrom unit	Å	1×10^{-10} m	meter
Avogadro number	N_A	6.02×10^{23} per mol	
Charge of electron	e	1.60×10^{-19} C	coulomb
Electron volt	eV	1.60×10^{-19} J	joule
Speed of light	c	3.00×10^8 m/s	meters/second
Planck's constant	h	6.63×10^{-34} J·s	joule-second
		1.58×10^{-37} kcal·s	kilocalorie-second
Universal gas constant	R	0.0821 L·atm/mol·K	liter-atmosphere/mole-kelvin
		1.98 cal/mol·K	calories/mole-kelvin
		8.31 J/mol·K	joules/mole-kelvin
Atomic mass unit	μ(amu)	1.66×10^{-24} g	gram
Volume standard, liter	L	1×10^3 cm^3 = 1 dm^3	cubic centimeters, cubic decimeter
Standard pressure, atmosphere	atm	101.3 kPa	kilopascals
		760 mmHg	millimeters of mercury
		760 torr	torr
Heat equivalent, kilocalorie	kcal	4.18×10^3 J	joules

Physical Constants for H₂O

Molal freezing point depression	1.86°C
Molal boiling point elevation	0.52°C
Heat of fusion	79.72 cal/g
Heat of vaporization	539.4 cal/g

STANDARD UNITS

Symbol	Name	Quantity	Selected Prefixes		
			Factor	Prefix	Symbol
m	meter	length	10^6	mega	M
kg	kilogram	mass	10^3	kilo	k
Pa	pascal	pressure	10^{-1}	deci	d
K	kelvin	thermodynamic temperature	10^{-2}	centi	c
mol	mole	amount of substance	10^{-3}	milli	m
J	joule	energy, work, quantity of heat	10^{-6}	micro	μ
s	second	time	10^{-9}	nano	n
C	coulomb	quantity of electricity			
V	volt	electric potential, potential difference			
L	liter	volume			

DENSITY AND BOILING POINTS OF SOME COMMON GASES

Name		Density grams/liter at STP*	Boiling Point (at 1 atm) K
Air	—	1.29	
Ammonia	NH_3	0.771	240
Carbon dioxide	CO_2	1.98	195
Carbon monoxide	CO	1.25	82
Chlorine	Cl_2	3.21	238
Hydrogen	H_2	0.0899	20
Hydrogen chloride	HCl	1.64	188
Hydrogen sulfide	H_2S	1.54	212
Methane	CH_4	0.716	109
Nitrogen	N_2	1.25	77
Nitrogen (II) oxide	NO	1.34	121
Oxygen	O_2	1.43	90
Sulfur dioxide	SO_2	2.92	263

*STP is defined as 273 K and 1 atm

SOLUBILITY CURVES

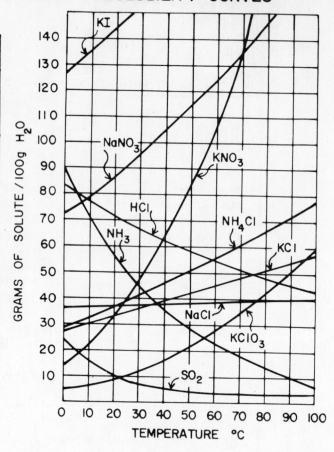

E

TABLE OF SOLUBILITIES IN WATER

i — nearly insoluble
ss — slightly soluble
s — soluble
d — decomposes
n — not isolated

	acetate	bromide	carbonate	chloride	chromate	hydroxide	iodide	nitrate	phosphate	sulfate	sulfide
Aluminum	ss	s	n	s	n	i	s	s	i	s	d
Ammonium	s	s	s	s	s	s	s	s	s	s	s
Barium	s	s	i	s	i	s	s	s	i	i	d
Calcium	s	s	i	s	s	ss	s	s	i	ss	d
Copper II	s	s	i	s	i	i	n	s	i	s	i
Iron II	s	s	i	s	n	i	s	s	i	s	i
Iron III	s	s	n	s	i	i	n	s	i	ss	d
Lead	s	ss	i	ss	i	i	ss	s	i	i	i
Magnesium	s	s	i	s	s	i	s	s	i	s	d
Mercury I	ss	i	i	i	ss	n	i	s	i	ss	i
Mercury II	s	ss	i	s	ss	i	i	s	i	d	i
Potassium	s	s	s	s	s	s	s	s	s	s	s
Silver	ss	i	i	i	ss	n	i	s	i	ss	i
Sodium	s	s	s	s	s	s	s	s	s	s	s
Zinc	s	s	i	s	s	i	s	s	i	s	i

SELECTED POLYATOMIC IONS

Hg_2^{2+}	dimercury (I)	CrO_4^{2-}	chromate
NH_4^+	ammonium	$Cr_2O_7^{2-}$	dichromate
$C_2H_3O_2^-$	acetate	MnO_4^-	permanganate
CH_3COO^-		MnO_4^{2-}	manganate
CN^-	cyanide	NO_2^-	nitrite
CO_3^{2-}	carbonate	NO_3^-	nitrate
HCO_3^-	hydrogen carbonate	OH^-	hydroxide
		PO_4^{3-}	phosphate
$C_2O_4^{2-}$	oxalate	SCN^-	thiocyanate
ClO^-	hypochlorite	SO_3^{2-}	sulfite
ClO_2^-	chlorite	SO_4^{2-}	sulfate
ClO_3^-	chlorate	HSO_4^-	hydrogen sulfate
ClO_4^-	perchlorate	$S_2O_3^{2-}$	thiosulfate

STANDARD ENERGIES OF FORMATION OF COMPOUNDS AT 1 atm AND 298 K

Compound	Heat (Enthalpy) of Formation* kcal/mol ($\triangle H_f^\circ$)	Free Energy of Formation kcal/mol ($\triangle G_f^\circ$)
Aluminum oxide $Al_2O_3(s)$	−400.5	−378.2
Ammonia $NH_3(g)$	−11.0	−3.9
Barium sulfate $BaSO_4(s)$	−352.1	−325.6
Calcium hydroxide $Ca(OH)_2(s)$	−235.7	−214.8
Carbon dioxide $CO_2(g)$	−94.1	−94.3
Carbon monoxide $CO(g)$	−26.4	−32.8
Copper (II) sulfate $CuSO_4(s)$	−184.4	−158.2
Ethane $C_2H_6(g)$	−20.2	−7.9
Ethene (ethylene) $C_2H_4(g)$	12.5	16.3
Ethyne (acetylene) $C_2H_2(g)$	54.2	50.0
Hydrogen fluoride $HF(g)$	−64.8	−65.3
Hydrogen iodide $HI(g)$	6.3	0.4
Iodine chloride $ICl(g)$	4.3	−1.3
Lead (II) oxide $PbO(s)$	−51.5	−45.0
Magnesium oxide $MgO(s)$	−143.8	−136.1
Nitrogen (II) oxide $NO(g)$	21.6	20.7
Nitrogen (IV) oxide $NO_2(g)$	7.9	12.3
Potassium chloride $KCl(s)$	−104.4	−97.8
Sodium chloride $NaCl(s)$	−98.3	−91.8
Sulfur dioxide $SO_2(g)$	−70.9	−71.7
Water $H_2O(g)$	−57.8	−54.6
Water $H_2O(\ell)$	−68.3	−56.7

* Minus sign indicates an exothermic reaction.

Sample equations:

$$2Al(s) + \frac{3}{2} O_2(g) \rightarrow Al_2O_3(s) + 400.5 \text{ kcal}$$

$$2Al(s) + \frac{3}{2} O_2(g) \rightarrow Al_2O_3(s) \quad \triangle H = -400.5 \text{ kcal/mol}$$

SELECTED RADIOISOTOPES

Nuclide	Half-Life	Decay Mode
^{198}Au	2.69 d	β^-
^{14}C	5730 y	β^-
^{60}Co	5.26 y	β^-
^{137}Cs	30.23 y	β^-
^{220}Fr	27.5 s	α
^3H	12.26 y	β^-
^{131}I	8.07 d	β^-
^{37}K	1.23 s	β^+
^{42}K	12.4 h	β^-
^{85}Kr	10.76 y	β^-
$^{85m}Kr*$	4.39 h	γ
^{16}N	7.2 s	β^-
^{32}P	14.3 d	β^-
^{239}Pu	2.44×10^4 y	α
^{226}Ra	1600 y	α
^{222}Rn	3.82 d	α
^{90}Sr	28.1 y	β^-
^{99}Tc	2.13×10^5 y	β^-
$^{99m}Tc*$	6.01 h	γ
^{232}Th	1.4×10^{10} y	α
^{233}U	1.62×10^5 y	α
^{235}U	7.1×10^8 y	α
^{238}U	4.51×10^9 y	α

y = years; d = days; h = hours; s = seconds

*m = meta stable or excited state of the same nucleus. Gamma decay from such a state is called an isomeric transition (IT).

Nuclear isomers are different energy states of the same nucleus, each having a different measurable lifetime.

HEATS OF REACTION AT 1 atm and 298 K	
Reaction	$\triangle H$ (kcal)
$CH_4(g) + 2O_2(g) \rightarrow CO_2(g) + 2H_2O(\ell)$	−212.8
$C_3H_8(g) + 5O_2(g) \rightarrow 3CO_2(g) + 4H_2O(\ell)$	−530.6
$CH_3OH(\ell) + \frac{3}{2}O_2(g) \rightarrow CO_2(g) + 2H_2O(\ell)$	−173.6
$C_6H_{12}O_6(s) + 6O_2(g) \rightarrow 6CO_2(g) + 6H_2O(\ell)$	−669.9
$CO(g) + \frac{1}{2}O_2(g) \rightarrow CO_2(g)$	−67.7
$C_8H_{18}(\ell) + \frac{25}{2}O_2(g) \rightarrow 8CO_2(g) + 9H_2O(\ell)$	−1302.7
$KNO_3(s) \xrightarrow{H_2O} K^+(aq) + NO_3^-(aq)$	+8.3
$NaOH(s) \xrightarrow{H_2O} Na^+(aq) + OH^-(aq)$	−10.6
$NH_4Cl(s) \xrightarrow{H_2O} NH_4^+(aq) + Cl^-(aq)$	+3.5
$NH_4NO_3(s) \xrightarrow{H_2O} NH_4^+(aq) + NO_3^-(aq)$	+6.1
$NaCl(s) \xrightarrow{H_2O} Na^+(aq) + Cl^-(aq)$	+0.9
$KClO_3(s) \xrightarrow{H_2O} K^+(aq) + ClO_3^-(aq)$	+9.9
$LiBr(s) \xrightarrow{H_2O} Li^+(aq) + Br^-(aq)$	−11.7
$H^+(aq) + OH^-(aq) \rightarrow H_2O(\ell)$	−13.8

SYMBOLS USED IN NUCLEAR CHEMISTRY		
alpha particle	^4_2He	α
beta particle (electron)	$^0_{-1}e$	β^-
gamma radiation		γ
neutron	^1_0n	n
proton	^1_1H	p
deuteron	^2_1H	
triton	^3_1H	
positron	$^0_{+1}e$	β^+

IONIZATION ENERGIES AND ELECTRONEGATIVITIES

313 ← First Ionization Energy (kcal/mol of atoms)
H
2.2 ← Electronegativity*

1	2	13	14	15	16	17	18
H 313 / 2.2							He 567
Li 125 / 1.0	Be 215 / 1.5	B 191 / 2.0	C 260 / 2.6	N 336 / 3.1	O 314 / 3.5	F 402 / 4.0	Ne 497
Na 119 / 0.9	Mg 176 / 1.2	Al 138 / 1.5	Si 188 / 1.9	P 242 / 2.2	S 239 / 2.6	Cl 300 / 3.2	Ar 363
K 100 / 0.8	Ca 141 / 1.0	Ga 138 / 1.6	Ge 182 / 1.9	As 226 / 2.0	Se 225 / 2.5	Br 273 / 2.9	Kr 323
Rb 96 / 0.8	Sr 131 / 1.0	In 133 / 1.7	Sn 169 / 1.8	Sb 199 / 2.1	Te 208 / 2.3	I 241 / 2.7	Xe 280
Cs 90 / 0.7	Ba 120 / 0.9	Tl 141 / 1.8	Pb 171 / 1.8	Bi 168 / 1.9	Po 194 / 2.0	At — / 2.2	Rn 248
Fr — / 0.7	Ra 122 / 0.9						

* Arbitrary scale based on fluorine = 4.0

RELATIVE STRENGTHS OF ACIDS IN AQUEOUS SOLUTION AT 1 atm AND 298 K

Conjugate Pairs	
ACID BASE	K_a
$HI = H^+ + I^-$	very large
$HBr = H^+ + Br^-$	very large
$HCl = H^+ + Cl^-$	very large
$HNO_3 = H^+ + NO_3^-$	very large
$H_2SO_4 = H^+ + HSO_4^-$	large
$H_2O + SO_2 = H^+ + HSO_3^-$	1.5×10^{-2}
$HSO_4^- = H^+ + SO_4^{2-}$	1.2×10^{-2}
$H_3PO_4 = H^+ + H_2PO_4^-$	7.5×10^{-3}
$Fe(H_2O)_6^{3+} = H^+ + Fe(H_2O)_5(OH)^{2+}$	8.9×10^{-4}
$HNO_2 = H^+ + NO_2^-$	4.6×10^{-4}
$HF = H^+ + F^-$	3.5×10^{-4}
$Cr(H_2O)_6^{3+} = H^+ + Cr(H_2O)_5(OH)^{2+}$	1.0×10^{-4}
$CH_3COOH = H^+ + CH_3COO^-$	1.8×10^{-5}
$Al(H_2O)_6^{3+} = H^+ + Al(H_2O)_5(OH)^{2+}$	1.1×10^{-5}
$H_2O + CO_2 = H^+ + HCO_3^-$	4.3×10^{-7}
$HSO_3^- = H^+ + SO_3^{2-}$	1.1×10^{-7}
$H_2S = H^+ + HS^-$	9.5×10^{-8}
$H_2PO_4^- = H^+ + HPO_4^{2-}$	6.2×10^{-8}
$NH_4^+ = H^+ + NH_3$	5.7×10^{-10}
$HCO_3^- = H^+ + CO_3^{2-}$	5.6×10^{-11}
$HPO_4^{2-} = H^+ + PO_4^{3-}$	2.2×10^{-13}
$HS^- = H^+ + S^{2-}$	1.3×10^{-14}
$H_2O = H^+ + OH^-$	1.0×10^{-14}
$OH^- = H^+ + O^{2-}$	$< 10^{-36}$
$NH_3 = H^+ + NH_2^-$	very small

Note: $H^+(aq) = H_3O^+$

Sample equation: $HI + H_2O = H_3O^+ + I^-$

CONSTANTS FOR VARIOUS EQUILIBRIA AT 1 atm AND 298 K

$H_2O(\ell) = H^+(aq) + OH^-(aq)$	$K_w = 1.0 \times 10^{-14}$
$H_2O(\ell) + H_2O(\ell) = H_3O^+(aq) + OH^-(aq)$	$K_w = 1.0 \times 10^{-14}$
$CH_3COO^-(aq) + H_2O(\ell) = CH_3COOH(aq) + OH^-(aq)$	$K_b = 5.6 \times 10^{-10}$
$Na^+F^-(aq) + H_2O(\ell) = Na^+(OH)^- + HF(aq)$	$K_b = 1.5 \times 10^{-11}$
$NH_3(aq) + H_2O(\ell) = NH_4^+(aq) + OH^-(aq)$	$K_b = 1.8 \times 10^{-5}$
$CO_3^{2-}(aq) + H_2O(\ell) = HCO_3^-(aq) + OH^-(aq)$	$K_b = 1.8 \times 10^{-4}$
$Ag(NH_3)_2^+(aq) = Ag^+(aq) + 2NH_3(aq)$	$K_{eq} = 8.9 \times 10^{-8}$
$N_2(g) + 3H_2(g) = 2NH_3(g)$	$K_{eq} = 6.7 \times 10^5$
$H_2(g) + I_2(g) = 2HI(g)$	$K_{eq} = 3.5 \times 10^{-1}$

Compound	K_{sp}	Compound	K_{sp}
AgBr	5.0×10^{-13}	Li_2CO_3	2.5×10^{-2}
AgCl	1.8×10^{-10}	$PbCl_2$	1.6×10^{-5}
Ag_2CrO_4	1.1×10^{-12}	$PbCO_3$	7.4×10^{-14}
AgI	8.3×10^{-17}	$PbCrO_4$	2.8×10^{-13}
$BaSO_4$	1.1×10^{-10}	PbI_2	7.1×10^{-9}
$CaSO_4$	9.1×10^{-6}	$ZnCO_3$	1.4×10^{-11}

STANDARD ELECTRODE POTENTIALS

Ionic Concentrations 1 M Water At 298 K, 1 atm

Half-Reaction	E^0 (volts)
$F_2(g) + 2e^- \rightarrow 2F^-$	+2.87
$8H^+ + MnO_4^- + 5e^- \rightarrow Mn^{2+} + 4H_2O$	+1.51
$Au^{3+} + 3e^- \rightarrow Au(s)$	+1.50
$Cl_2(g) + 2e^- \rightarrow 2Cl^-$	+1.36
$14H^+ + Cr_2O_7^{2-} + 6e^- \rightarrow 2Cr^{3+} + 7H_2O$	+1.23
$4H^+ + O_2(g) + 4e^- \rightarrow 2H_2O$	+1.23
$4H^+ + MnO_2(s) + 2e^- \rightarrow Mn^{2+} + 2H_2O$	+1.22
$Br_2(\ell) + 2e^- \rightarrow 2Br^-$	+1.09
$Hg^{2+} + 2e^- \rightarrow Hg(\ell)$	+0.85
$Ag^+ + e^- \rightarrow Ag(s)$	+0.80
$Hg_2^{2+} + 2e^- \rightarrow 2Hg(\ell)$	+0.80
$Fe^{3+} + e^- \rightarrow Fe^{2+}$	+0.77
$I_2(s) + 2e^- \rightarrow 2I^-$	+0.54
$Cu^+ + e^- \rightarrow Cu(s)$	+0.52
$Cu^{2+} + 2e^- \rightarrow Cu(s)$	+0.34
$4H^+ + SO_4^{2-} + 2e^- \rightarrow SO_2(aq) + 2H_2O$	+0.17
$Sn^{4+} + 2e^- \rightarrow Sn^{2+}$	+0.15
$2H^+ + 2e^- \rightarrow H_2(g)$	0.00
$Pb^{2+} + 2e^- \rightarrow Pb(s)$	−0.13
$Sn^{2+} + 2e^- \rightarrow Sn(s)$	−0.14
$Ni^{2+} + 2e^- \rightarrow Ni(s)$	−0.26
$Co^{2+} + 2e^- \rightarrow Co(s)$	−0.28
$Fe^{2+} + 2e^- \rightarrow Fe(s)$	−0.45
$Cr^{3+} + 3e^- \rightarrow Cr(s)$	−0.74
$Zn^{2+} + 2e^- \rightarrow Zn(s)$	−0.76
$2H_2O + 2e^- \rightarrow 2OH^- + H_2(g)$	−0.83
$Mn^{2+} + 2e^- \rightarrow Mn(s)$	−1.19
$Al^{3+} + 3e^- \rightarrow Al(s)$	−1.66
$Mg^{2+} + 2e^- \rightarrow Mg(s)$	−2.37
$Na^+ + e^- \rightarrow Na(s)$	−2.71
$Ca^{2+} + 2e^- \rightarrow Ca(s)$	−2.87
$Sr^{2+} + 2e^- \rightarrow Sr(s)$	−2.89
$Ba^{2+} + 2e^- \rightarrow Ba(s)$	−2.91
$Cs^+ + e^- \rightarrow Cs(s)$	−2.92
$K^+ + e^- \rightarrow K(s)$	−2.93
$Rb^+ + e^- \rightarrow Rb(s)$	−2.98
$Li^+ + e^- \rightarrow Li(s)$	−3.04

VAPOR PRESSURE OF WATER

°C	torr (mmHg)	°C	torr (mmHg)
0	4.6	26	25.2
5	6.5	27	26.7
10	9.2	28	28.3
15	12.8	29	30.0
16	13.6	30	31.8
17	14.5	40	55.3
18	15.5	50	92.5
19	16.5	60	149.4
20	17.5	70	233.7
21	18.7	80	355.1
22	19.8	90	525.8
23	21.1	100	760.0
24	22.4	105	906.1
25	23.8	110	1074.6

Radii of atoms

KEY

Symbol → **F**
Covalent Radius, Å → 0.64
Atomic Radius in Metals, Å → (−)
Van der Waals Radius, Å → 1.35

A dash (−) indicates data are not available.

Each cell lists: Symbol / Covalent Radius / Atomic Radius in Metals / Van der Waals Radius (Å)

1	2	3	4	5	6	7	8	9	10	11	12	13	14	15	16	17	18
H 0.37 / (−) / 1.2																	**He** (−) / (−) / 1.22
Li 1.23 / 1.52 / (−)	**Be** 0.89 / 1.13 / (−)											**B** 0.88 / (−) / 2.08	**C** 0.77 / (−) / 1.85	**N** 0.70 / (−) / 1.54	**O** 0.66 / (−) / 1.40	**F** 0.64 / (−) / 1.35	**Ne** (−) / (−) / 1.60
Na 1.57 / 1.54 / 2.31	**Mg** 1.36 / 1.60 / (−)											**Al** 1.25 / 1.43 / (−)	**Si** 1.17 / (−) / 2.0	**P** 1.10 / (−) / 1.90	**S** 1.04 / (−) / 1.85	**Cl** 0.99 / (−) / 1.81	**Ar** (−) / (−) / 1.91
K 2.03 / 2.27 / 2.31	**Ca** 1.74 / 1.97 / (−)	**Sc** 1.44 / 1.61 / (−)	**Ti** 1.32 / 1.45 / (−)	**V** 1.22 / 1.32 / (−)	**Cr** 1.17 / 1.25 / (−)	**Mn** 1.17 / 1.24 / (−)	**Fe** 1.17 / 1.24 / (−)	**Co** 1.16 / 1.25 / (−)	**Ni** 1.15 / 1.25 / (−)	**Cu** 1.17 / 1.28 / (−)	**Zn** 1.25 / 1.33 / (−)	**Ga** 1.25 / 1.22 / (−)	**Ge** 1.22 / 1.23 / (−)	**As** 1.21 / (−) / 2.0	**Se** 1.17 / (−) / 2.0	**Br** 1.14 / (−) / 1.95	**Kr** 1.89 / (−) / 1.98
Rb 2.16 / 2.48 / 2.44	**Sr** 1.92 / 2.15 / (−)	**Y** 1.62 / 1.81 / (−)	**Zr** 1.45 / 1.60 / (−)	**Nb** 1.34 / 1.43 / (−)	**Mo** 1.29 / 1.36 / (−)	**Tc** (−) / 1.36 / (−)	**Ru** 1.24 / 1.33 / (−)	**Rh** 1.25 / 1.35 / (−)	**Pd** 1.28 / 1.38 / (−)	**Ag** 1.34 / 1.44 / (−)	**Cd** 1.41 / 1.49 / (−)	**In** 1.50 / 1.63 / (−)	**Sn** 1.40 / 1.41 / (−)	**Sb** 1.41 / (−) / 2.2	**Te** 1.37 / (−) / 2.20	**I** 1.33 / (−) / 2.15	**Xe** 2.09 / (−) / (−)
Cs 2.35 / 2.65 / 2.62	**Ba** 1.98 / 2.17 / (−)	**La-Lu**	**Hf** 1.44 / 1.56 / (−)	**Ta** 1.34 / 1.43 / (−)	**W** 1.30 / 1.37 / (−)	**Re** 1.28 / 1.37 / (−)	**Os** 1.26 / 1.34 / (−)	**Ir** 1.26 / 1.36 / (−)	**Pt** 1.29 / 1.38 / (−)	**Au** 1.34 / 1.44 / (−)	**Hg** 1.44 / 1.60 / (−)	**Tl** 1.55 / 1.70 / (−)	**Pb** 1.54 / 1.75 / (−)	**Bi** 1.52 / 1.55 / (−)	**Po** 1.53 / 1.67 / (−)	**At** (−) / (−) / (−)	**Rn** 2.14 / (−) / (−)
Fr (−) / 2.7 / (−)	**Ra** (−) / 2.20 / (−)	**Ac-Lr**															

La	Ce	Pr	Nd	Pm	Sm	Eu	Gd	Tb	Dy	Ho	Er	Tm	Yb	Lu
1.69	1.65	1.65	1.64	(−)	1.66	1.85	1.61	1.59	1.59	1.58	1.57	1.56	1.70	1.56
1.88	1.83	1.83	1.82	1.81	1.80	2.04	1.80	1.78	1.77	1.77	1.76	1.75	1.94	1.73
(−)	(−)	(−)	(−)	(−)	(−)	(−)	(−)	(−)	(−)	(−)	(−)	(−)	(−)	(−)

Ac	Th	Pa	U	Np	Pu	Am	Cm	Bk	Cf	Es	Fm	Md	No	Lr
(−)	(−)	(−)	(−)	(−)	(−)	(−)	(−)	(−)	(−)	(−)	(−)	(−)	(−)	(−)
1.88	1.80	1.61	1.39	1.31	1.51	1.84	(−)	(−)	(−)	(−)	(−)	(−)	(−)	(−)
(−)	(−)	(−)	(−)	(−)	(−)	(−)	(−)	(−)	(−)	(−)	(−)	(−)	(−)	(−)

Periodic Table of the Elements

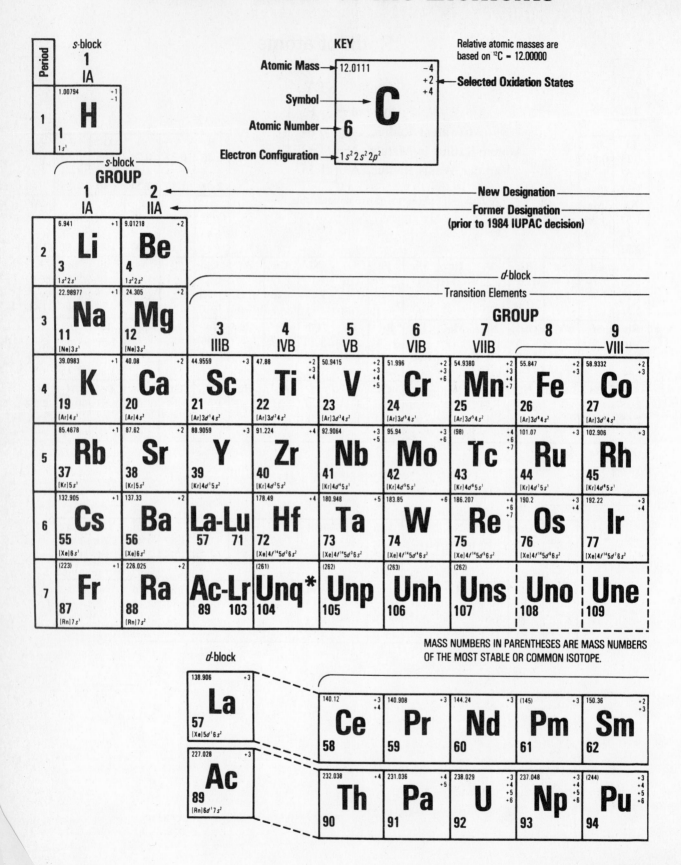

KEY

Relative atomic masses are based on $^{12}C = 12.00000$

Atomic Mass — 12.0111
Selected Oxidation States — −4, +2, +4
Symbol — C
Atomic Number — 6
Electron Configuration — $1s^2 2s^2 2p^2$

MASS NUMBERS IN PARENTHESES ARE MASS NUMBERS OF THE MOST STABLE OR COMMON ISOTOPE.

Periodic Table (partial) — p-block, s-block, f-block

Group 18 / 0

4.00260 · 0
He
2 · $1s^2$

p-block — GROUP

13 IIIA	14 IVA	15 VA	16 VIA	17 VIIA	18 / 0
10.81 +3 **B** 5 $1s^2 2s^2 2p^1$	12.0111 −4 +2 +4 **C** 6 $1s^2 2s^2 2p^2$	14.0067 −3 −2 −1 +1 +2 +3 +4 +5 **N** 7 $1s^2 2s^2 2p^3$	15.9994 −2 **O** 8 $1s^2 2s^2 2p^4$	18.998403 −1 **F** 9 $1s^2 2s^2 2p^5$	20.179 0 **Ne** 10 $1s^2 2s^2 2p^6$
26.98154 +3 **Al** 13 $[Ne]3s^2 3p^1$	28.0855 −4 +2 +4 **Si** 14 $[Ne]3s^2 3p^2$	30.97376 −3 +3 +5 **P** 15 $[Ne]3s^2 3p^3$	32.06 −2 +4 +6 **S** 16 $[Ne]3s^2 3p^4$	35.453 −1 +1 +3 +5 +7 **Cl** 17 $[Ne]3s^2 3p^5$	39.948 0 **Ar** 18 $[Ne]3s^2 3p^6$

10	11 IB	12 IIB	13	14	15	16	17	18
58.69 +2 +3 **Ni** 28 $[Ar]3d^8 4s^2$	63.546 +1 +2 **Cu** 29 $[Ar]3d^{10} 4s^1$	65.39 +2 **Zn** 30 $[Ar]3d^{10} 4s^2$	69.72 +3 **Ga** 31 $[Ar]3d^{10} 4s^2 4p^1$	72.59 −4 +2 +4 **Ge** 32 $[Ar]3d^{10} 4s^2 4p^2$	74.9216 −3 +3 +5 **As** 33 $[Ar]3d^{10} 4s^2 4p^3$	78.96 −2 +4 +6 **Se** 34 $[Ar]3d^{10} 4s^2 4p^4$	79.904 −1 +1 +5 **Br** 35 $[Ar]3d^{10} 4s^2 4p^5$	83.80 0 +2 **Kr** 36 $[Ar]3d^{10} 4s^2 4p^6$
106.42 +2 +4 **Pd** 46 $[Kr]4d^{10} 5s^0$	107.868 +1 **Ag** 47 $[Kr]4d^{10} 5s^1$	112.41 +2 **Cd** 48 $[Kr]4d^{10} 5s^2$	114.82 +3 **In** 49 $[Kr]4d^{10} 5s^2 5p^1$	118.71 +2 +4 **Sn** 50 $[Kr]4d^{10} 5s^2 5p^2$	121.75 −3 +3 +5 **Sb** 51 $[Kr]4d^{10} 5s^2 5p^3$	127.60 −2 +4 +6 **Te** 52 $[Kr]4d^{10} 5s^2 5p^4$	126.905 −1 +5 +7 **I** 53 $[Kr]4d^{10} 5s^2 5p^5$	131.29 0 +2 +4 +6 **Xe** 54 $[Kr]4d^{10} 5s^2 5p^6$
195.08 +2 +4 **Pt** 78 $[Xe]4f^{14} 5d^9 6s^1$	196.967 +1 +3 **Au** 79 $[Xe]4f^{14} 5d^{10} 6s^1$	200.59 +1 +2 **Hg** 80 $[Xe]4f^{14} 5d^{10} 6s^2$	204.383 +1 +3 **Tl** 81 $[Xe]4f^{14} 5d^{10} 6s^2 6p^1$	207.2 +2 +4 **Pb** 82 $[Xe]4f^{14} 5d^{10} 6s^2 6p^2$	208.980 +3 +5 **Bi** 83 $[Xe]4f^{14} 5d^{10} 6s^2 6p^3$	(209) +2 +4 **Po** 84 $[Xe]4f^{14} 5d^{10} 6s^2 6p^4$	(210) **At** 85 $[Xe]4f^{14} 5d^{10} 6s^2 6p^5$	(222) 0 **Rn** 86 $[Xe]4f^{14} 5d^{10} 6s^2 6p^6$

* The systematic names and symbols for elements of atomic numbers greater than 103 will be used until the approval of trivial names by IUPAC.

f-block

Lanthanoid Series

151.96 +2 +3 **Eu** 63	157.25 +3 **Gd** 64	158.925 +3 **Tb** 65	162.50 +3 **Dy** 66	164.930 +3 **Ho** 67	167.26 +3 **Er** 68	168.934 +3 **Tm** 69	173.04 +2 +3 **Yb** 70	174.967 +3 **Lu** 71

Actinoid Series

(243) +3 +4 +5 +6 **Am** 95	(247) +3 **Cm** 96	(247) +3 +4 **Bk** 97	(251) +3 **Cf** 98	(252) **Es** 99	(257) **Fm** 100	(258) **Md** 101	(259) **No** 102	(260) **Lr** 103

Ozone Defense: UV Breaks Through!

The title above may sound like the headline on the sports pages of your local newspaper. The Ozones could be your state's championship basketball team. And UV might stand for a challenger from another region.

Well, ozone isn't a basketball team. But it does possess a defense against invaders from another region. The region is outer space. And UV is the ultraviolet radiation that streams through it from the sun.

As you probably know, UV radiation can be deadly to living things. It can pass easily into cells and scramble DNA tucked away in their nuclei. This scrambled DNA loses its ability to direct the cell's normal functions.

The cell may simply die, or it may go on living as some kind of mutant, such as a cancer cell. As a matter of fact, UV light is the primary cause of most skin cancers. And the frequency of these cancers is on the increase. But what has this to do with ozone?

Ozone is a form of oxygen that is concentrated in Earth's stratosphere, a layer of the atmosphere that begins 8 to 18 km above Earth's surface and stretches upward to about 50 km. However, unlike molecules of oxygen nearer Earth's surface which consist of two atoms of oxygen, ozone is made up of three oxygen atoms. These oxygen triplets have a unique atmospheric property. They absorb large amounts of UV radiation: this is the "ozone defense."

The reference to "UV breaks through" indicates that in some parts of the atmosphere the concentration of ozone has dropped so drastically as to let increased amounts of UV radiation zip through to the Earth's surface.

At first, the greatest drops in ozone concentration were recorded over the Antarctic. These drops were so great that the areas stripped of ozone became known as "ozone holes."

These holes were created by a chemical reaction involving chlorofluorocarbons, or *CFCs*, which are commonly used as refrigerants in air conditioners and refrigerators, and in aerosol sprays and foams. As they are used, CFCs escape into the air and rise upward.

Eventually, when CFCs reach the stratosphere, sunlight breaks them down to produce, among other things, free chlorine. This highly reactive substance takes an oxygen chunk out of an ozone molecule to form chlorine monoxide (ClO). What's more, ClO is itself a highly reactive compound that can further nibble away at ozone molecules. What remains of the ozone molecule is ordinary O_2, which does not block the sun's UV radiation.

If the thinning of the ozone layer were occurring only over the virtually unpopulated Antarctic continent, almost all of Earth's inhabitants would have little to be concerned about. But in January of 1992 alarming data were collected from a high-flying NASA ER-2 research airplane. The data prompted ozone researcher James G. Anderson to exclaim, "We don't like what we see. This isn't good news."

What Anderson and other scientists "saw" were tremendous amounts of ClO molecules over northern New England and Canada. The concentration was a record-breaking 1.5 parts per billion (ppb). Levels of ClO this high are capable of chewing up ozone molecules at a rate of 1–2 percent a day! Was this really happening?

Earth-monitoring satellites were put on the case. Satellites measured ozone concentrations over the whole Northern Hemisphere. The results confirmed the fears of scientists. Average ozone levels over the Northern Hemisphere had dropped 10–15 percent below normal. These concentrations were the lowest ever recorded for this region of Earth.

Fortunately, in 1990, 93 industrialized countries agreed to ban the use of CFCs by the year 2000. But can we afford to wait that long to shore up our defenses against UV radiation? What do you think?

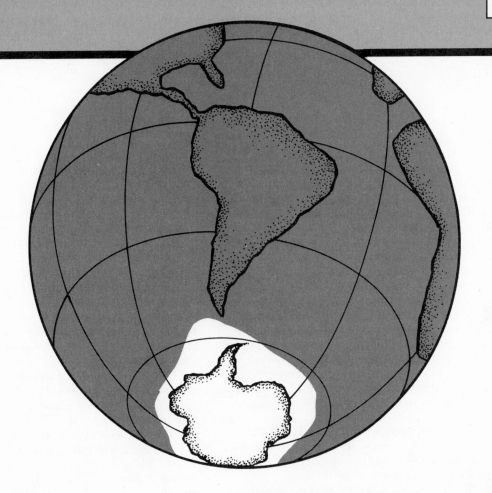

Questions

1. The formula for ozone is
   a. O.
   b. O_2.
   c. O_3.
   d. ClO.

2. The part of a CFC that destroys ozone is
   a. chlorine.
   b. fluorine.
   c. carbon.
   d. oxygen.

3. Which of the following chemical equations best represents the destruction of ozone due to CFCs?
   a. $Fl_2 + O_3 \rightarrow Fl_2O + O_2$
   b. $C_2 + O_3 \rightarrow 2CO + O_2$
   c. $2Cl_2 + 2O_3 \rightarrow 4ClO + O_2$
   d. $Cl + O_3 \rightarrow ClO + O_2$

4. To what was James G. Anderson referring when he said: "We don't like what we see"?

5. On a separate sheet of paper, propose a plan for preserving the ozone layer. Consider and discuss the impact of your proposal on the environment, commerce, the economy, and on individual consumers.

Radon: Basement Beast?

The scene is a graveyard. Wisps of mist snake through the gray tombstones. A young woman walks across the damp soil. Suddenly, the ground cracks open. An icy hand reaches up from the broken soil and clamps tightly on the woman's ankle.

Many people in the movie theater scream. Others giggle nervously. They are comforted by the knowledge that what they are viewing isn't real.

Yet there is something in the ground below the theater, below your home, and below your feet that is real. And according to some scientists, it is as dangerous to you as the movie monster was to the young woman. The danger is radon, which, as you know, is not the name of a Hollywood monster but a chemical element.

In a real sense, radon *is* like the Hollywood monster you just read about. It does lurk in the ground. But it doesn't reach out to clutch your ankle. Instead, its target is your lungs.

One form of radon, Rn-222, is the sixth generation descendant of the decay of U-238. And U-238 is stored in rock in the ground. What's more, Rn-222 is a gas. So if there are cracks in the ground or, more importantly, cracks in your basement's floor, Rn-222 can seep into your house.

That in itself might not be of concern, except that the U-238 decay chain does not end with Rn-222. Radon-222 is itself radioactive. It also decays and does so by emitting an alpha particle.

When you inhale Rn-222, or its sister isotope Rn-220 (which is part of another decay chain) or some of the decay products of Rn-222 and Rn-220, alpha particles zip through cells in your lungs. Every once in a while some of these particles knife through a chromosome in a cell's nucleus. The chromosome is damaged and, if conditions are right, the cell may multiply abnormally. Instead of producing specialized lung cells, it gives rise to unspecialized cancer cells. The result? Lung cancer!

Although there is plenty of evidence that this sequence of events can take place, what divides scientists is the level of radiation that sets the process in motion.

The Environmental Protection Agency (EPA) recommends that action be taken if basement radon levels reach 4 picocuries per liter of air. A picocurie (pCi) is a unit of radiation equal to one trillionth of a curie. (One curie is the quantity of a radioisotope that decays at a rate of 3.7×10^{10} disintegrations per second.) A National Research Council (NRC) study, however, reported that there was a great deal of "uncertainty" associated with defining at what levels serious risks to people begin. Besides, if EPA standards were adopted, the "action" many home owners would have to take could cost up to $10,000. Those actions would include sealing the basement and/or building special venting systems to reduce radon levels to those found in outside air.

What actions, if any, should be taken to clean radon out of basements? Under what conditions? What do you think?

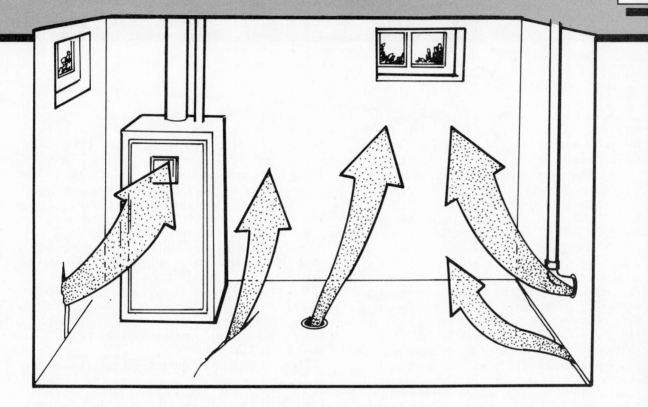

Questions

1. Rn-222 is an isotope of
   a. uranium.
   b. thorium.
   c. lead.
   d. radon.

2. Rn-222 emits
   a. Rn-220.
   b. alpha particles.
   c. U-238.
   d. beta particles.

3. The EPA recommends that action be taken if basement levels of radiation reach
   a. 1 pCi/L of air.   c. 3 pCi/L of air.
   b. 2 pCi/L of air.   d. 4 pCi/L of air.

4. What is the sequence of events by which Rn-222 or Rn-220 can cause lung cancer?

5. The EPA and NRC appear to differ on what constitutes a radon risk level. On a separate sheet of paper, suggest a survey or experiment that would help to resolve this controversy.

Food Additives: Adding Up to Trouble?

How would you like to eat a piece of moldy bread? Would a gray hunk of steak entice you? And how would you respond to a strip of rancid bacon, a brown maraschino cherry, or a scoop of diet ice cream no sweeter than a cup of water?

Your answers would undoubtedly be "negative, negative" and, very definitely, "negative." Now, no food manufacturer wants you to respond negatively to its products. Yet that's exactly what you might do if all the foods mentioned above were delivered to you in their natural state. So to satisfy you, the consumer, and to compete with other food manufacturers for your dollar, food producers add a wide variety of substances to the products you eat.

There's no question that these substances improve how food looks, tastes, and lasts. But some people are concerned about whether some of these substances are good for you. Let's take a look at one family of food additives, what they do to food, and whether concern about their use is justified.

Since most people love sweet-tasting foods but hate calories, and since most naturally sweet foods are loaded with calories, people usually have difficulty getting one without the other. This dilemma confronted people until the invention of artificial, no-calorie sweeteners like saccharin, aspartame, and acesulfame-K. Was this a sweet-lover's dream come true?

According to some critics, the answer is yes if you focus only on eliminating calories. But if your focus is on eating only healthy foods, the critics weigh in with a hefty "no," or at least an admonition to be careful.

Although each of these artificial sweeteners has been approved for human use by the U.S. Food and Drug Administration (FDA), critics point to facts that might sour you on products containing these sweeteners. For example, some studies revealed that saccharin can cause bladder cancer in rats. This led the FDA to ban saccharin in 1977. But people wanted it so badly that Congress later reversed the ban.

Well, there's always aspartame, you might say. This sweetener consists of two amino acids, phenylalanine (PHE) and aspartic acid. Now, what could be better, you might think. These are two of the 23 amino acids you need to build proteins. They couldn't be more natural.

True, but they are not delivered along with their 21 other family members, as they would be in, say, a bite of steak. And this unbalanced amino acid delivery may make problems for your brain. How?

PHE, as well as all the other natural amino acids, gets through the protective blood-brain barrier by hitching rides on substances called transport molecules. However, these transport molecules can carry only so many amino acids. If PHE takes up a disproportionate number of "seats" in the transport molecule's "passenger car," other amino acids won't get to the brain. Result? Essential brain chemicals called neurotransmitters might not be properly constructed. This could lead to symptoms such as headaches, mood changes, and even seizures.

"Might" and "could" are not very convincing terms, counter supporters of the use of aspartame. Hold on, respond the critics. How about the more than 6,000 aspartame users who complained of side effects to the FDA by mid-1988? Most of the side effects were neurological, such as headaches, changes in mood and, in some rare cases, seizures.

O.K., you come back, I'll switch to acesulfame-K. Critics say that's fine if you're willing to risk getting cancer, since that's what this sweetener has reportedly produced in lab animals. But animal studies, say the manufacturers of ace-sulfame-K, saccharin, and many other food additives, can't always be taken seriously. How come? The animals are fed amounts of the additive in proportions that no human being would ever eat.

Who should you listen to in the battle of food additives? What do you think?

Recipe
1 Cup flour
2 Eggs
1 Tbs Aspartame

Questions

1. Some lab studies found that saccharin causes
   a. headaches.
   b. bladder cancer in people.
   c. bladder cancer in rats.
   d. seizures.

2. Saccharin was
   a. approved by the FDA and Congress.
   b. banned by the FDA but approved by Congress.
   c. banned by the FDA and Congress.
   d. approved by the FDA and banned by Congress.

3. Aspartame consists of
   a. one amino acid.   c. 23 amino acids.
   b. two amino acids.   d. no amino acids.

4. What argument did the manufacturers of saccharin use to counter evidence that suggests this sweetener may cause cancer in people?

5. On a separate sheet of paper, discuss the pros and cons of using food additives. Support your discussion with library research and cite references.

Fluoridation: Cracks in the Cavity Cure?

"There is no controversy. Fluoridation is a proven preventative of tooth decay," declared Phil Weintraub of the American Dental Association.

Fluoridation improves the dental health of children of "all races and all socioeconomic classes," seconded Ernest Newbrun, a University of California dental researcher.

"Very preliminary data from recent health studies . . . indicate that fluoride may be a carcinogen," stated a memo from the office of Michael Cook, the top drinking water scientist at the Environmental Protection Agency (EPA).

"You would have to have rocks in your head . . . to allow your child [to drink] much more than two parts per million [fluoride]," warned a member of a panel brought together by the United States Surgeon General in 1983.

"No other procedure in the history of medicine has been praised so highly nor at the same time condemned so thoroughly," summed up Dr. George L. Walgbott in his book *Fluoridation: The Great Dilemma.*

So what is this great dilemma? What's the fuss all about?

More than 120 million people in the United States drink water to which fluorides have been deliberately added. In most cases, the concentration of fluorides in this water does not exceed one part per million (1 ppm), although the EPA considers 4 ppm to be the upper limit of safety.

Fluorides were first added to drinking water in the United States in 1945. At that time, scientists had obtained evidence that fluorides could reduce the incidence of dental *caries*, or cavities, in children. Ten- to fifteen-year tests were carried out in two U.S. cities—Grand Rapids, Michigan, and Newburgh, New York.

The results from Grand Rapids were encouraging. The rate of cavities in children between the ages of 12 and 14 dropped by 53–60 percent. Soon many other communities began adding fluorides to their drinking water. As of 1990, the people of 41 of the 50 largest cities in the United States were drinking fluoridated water.

Then some perplexing data began to emerge. In 1987, a study of 40,000 school-age children performed by the National Institute of Dental Research (NIDR) revealed only an 18% reduction in cavities among kids who drank fluoridated water against kids who did not drink fluoridated water. What's more, some researchers suggested the difference might be due to better health habits and the use of fluoridated toothpastes and mouth rinses, rather than to the drinking of fluoridated water.

Some alarming data came from a study of rats performed by the National Toxicology Program, which had been ordered by Congress to find out whether fluorides caused cancer. The results of the study were reported in 1990. No rats drinking water with 0-11 ppm fluoride developed cancer. But one rat on 45 ppm fluoride developed a rare form of bone cancer, as did three rats on a dose of 79 ppm.

The results were labeled "equivocal," that is, suspicious but uncertain. As David Rall, Director of the National Institute of Environmental Health Sciences, put it: "It's like there's a little flashing yellow light on the instrument panel . . . [that] says you better look at this more carefully." What do you think?

2. In 1990, of the 50 largest cities in the United States, how many were serving up artificially fluoridated water to their citizens?
a. 4　　　　　　　c. 41
b. 21　　　　　　d. 50

3. Early data revealed that fluorides administered regularly to children reduced dental caries by 53–60%. More recent data indicate that this figure was closer to
a. 10%　　　　　c. 60%
b. 18%　　　　　d. 100%

4. Why might you consider the National Toxicology Program's rat study to be "equivocal"?

5. On a separate sheet of paper, write a report on the pros and cons of continuing the practice of fluoridating drinking water. Do additional library research to support each position.

Questions

1. The number of people who drink artificially fluoridated water in the United States is approximately
a. 1.2 million.　　　c. 120 million.
b. 12 million.　　　d. 220 million.

Water: Does It Deserve a (Plum)Bum Rap?

The last thing you might expect to come out of your faucet is lead. Yet according to a recent *Consumer Reports* survey, more than 50 percent of the water samples of some United States' communities contain lead.

Should the people in these communities be concerned? That may depend on how much lead the water holds. The Environmental Protection Agency (EPA) set standards in 1991 that identifies 15 ppb (parts per billion) lead in drinking water as an *action level*, that is, a concentration requiring a remedy.

The *Consumer Reports* test revealed that this limit was exceeded in 4 percent of the water samples analyzed. What's more, in certain communities the percentage was about 2 to 4.5 times greater—although it varied depending on whether the water testing procedure was first draw or purged line. These procedures are very significant because they can pinpoint the cause of the lead pollution.

A *first draw sample* is taken from a faucet that has not been opened for a number of hours. A *purged line sample* is taken after water has been allowed to run out of the faucet for a period of time—one minute in the *Consumer Reports* tests.

"Let's say the first draw sample is shown to hold 15 ppb lead, but the purged line sample holds less than 2 ppb lead. You can conclude that the lead leached into the water in the home. That's because it takes about a minute to empty standing water in a home's pipes. After one minute, the water being tested is freshly flowing from outside pipes. If the purged line water also shows a high lead content, the problem is likely to be outside of the home.

In the home, lead leaches into the water from copper pipes whose joints are bonded by lead solder. Although the use of lead solder for this purpose was outlawed in 1988, buildings and homes constructed before that date may have water pipes soldered with lead. In addition, brass and bronze faucets are allowed to contain up to 8 percent lead, some of which can leach into water.

The main source of lead from outside the home is a water utility's service lines, some of which may be made of lead. But this is only part of the story. The chemistry of the water plays a key role in determining how much lead leaches into the water from such pipes.

As the *Consumer Reports* article put it, ". . . lead is more likely to dissolve in water that is acidic, has a low mineral content [soft water], and . . . [is] hot." In contrast, water that has a high mineral content, or hard water, inhibits the leaching of lead into the water. This happens because, over time, the minerals in hard water tend to coat the insides of pipes, providing a barrier between the lead in the pipe and the water.

But why worry about lead in drinking water in the first place? Among other things, lead attacks a person's nervous system. In the brain, lead interferes with the work of enzymes that are responsible for brain development. Many studies have shown that lead poisoning can cause mild to serious mental retardation, especially when consumed by young children. Researchers have found that even small amounts of lead can reduce a child's IQ a few points. So what can be done if your water contains lead?

If the source of lead is piping or faucets in your home you can do a number of things. The simplest thing to do is run your water for a few minutes before you use it for drinking or cooking. You could, of course, switch to bottled spring water.

If the lead is coming from outside your home, you can install a variety of water treatment devices, all of which cost money. Should your local utility company absorb some of these costs? Should it be forced to correct the problem? Should your water bills go up if the company fixes the problem? What do you think?

Questions

1. The "action level" of lead in drinking water is
   a. 2 ppb.   c. 10 ppb.
   b. 5 ppb.   d. 15 ppb.

2. A first draw lead concentration of 20 ppb followed by a purged line reading of 0 ppb indicates the source of lead pollution is
   a. only in utility service pipes.
   b. both in utility service pipes and in home plumbing.
   c. only in home plumbing.
   d. neither in home plumbing nor in utility service pipes.

3. Leaching of lead from utility service pipes increases when water is
   a. hard and alkaline.
   b. hard and acidic.
   c. soft and alkaline.
   d. soft and acidic.

4. Describe the most common sources of lead in drinking water.

5. On a separate sheet of paper, discuss your views concerning how utility companies should or should not be regulated with regard to lead pollution of drinking water. If possible, obtain a copy of Proposition 65, a California law related to this topic, and compare it to your views.

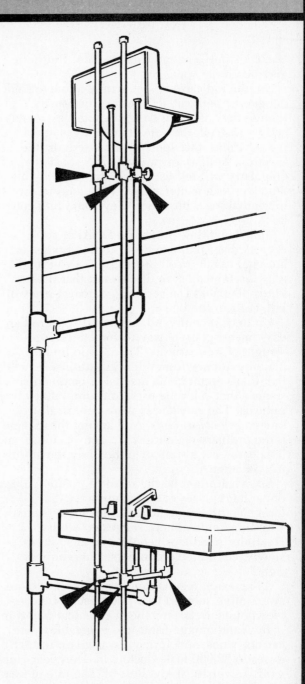

Antioxidants: A Radical Solution?

Look out! The radicals are free! But help may be on the way.

No, the radicals we are writing about are not dangerous political activists on the loose . . . although they are both dangerous and extremely active. Instead, they are atoms, or groups of linked atoms, that sport an unpaired, or free, electron. And, as anyone who has studied chemistry will tell you, such atoms are highly reactive. As a matter of fact, they tend to *oxidize* anything with which they come into contact.

That "anything" might be DNA, or substances that hold together cell membranes or are vital to other cell processes. As you might guess, scientists have discovered that these kinds of attacks can seriously damage, or even kill, cells in the body.

Up until recently, no one had discovered an easy or inexpensive way to combat the onslaught of free radicals. Then, little by little, bits of evidence from scientific studies revealed that there might be an arsenal of common substances that could be used to counterattack free radicals. The substances were generically known as *antioxidants*. And among these were three ordinary chemicals, vitamins C and E and beta carotene, a substance the body transforms into vitamin A.

So, what might be the result if people gulped down large doses of these substances in pill form? Nothing beneficial, said some scientists. Unwanted side effects, suggested others. Healthier people or people who aged more slowly, countered still others. But who was right?

As research results came pouring in, the answers often seemed to support each of these viewpoints. Beta carotene, a chemical found in yellow and orange fruits and vegetables, like carrots, yams, and apricots, was given in high doses to 22,000 male doctors in a ten-year Harvard University study. Result? The rate of heart attacks and strokes in these subjects was only half that of the untreated subjects in the study. And there were no side effects. Yet, a study conducted in Finland on 29,000 male smokers seemed to indicate that those taking a daily beta carotene supplement were more likely to develop lung cancers than those who did not take the pills.

Vitamin E, found in vegetable oil, nuts, margarine, wheat germ, and green leafy vegetables may provide a number of benefits when taken in large doses. Results from two major studies showed a much lower rate of heart disease among men and women taking a daily dose of vitamin E. Says Dr. Daniel Menzel in the April 6, 1992 issue of *Time*: "We have fed animals in our labs vitamin E and have found that they have fewer lung lesions and live longer" when exposed to air pollutants than do animals not given the vitamin. How about side effects? When given to people, high doses of vitamin E may sometimes cause diarrhea and headaches. Or worse—results from the Finnish study showed a slightly higher rate of strokes among those men taking the vitamin E supplements.

Vitamin C, which is found in foods like citrus fruits, berries, and tomatoes, appears to protect people against cataracts, a vision-threatening eye disease that affects one in seven people in the United States over the age of 65. What's more, vitamin C along with vitamin E and beta carotene appears to protect many people against various cancers. Side effects? In large doses, vitamin C may cause diarrhea.

So, should we all gobble up large doses of these three substances to ward off the attack of free radicals?

"We get all the vitamins we need in our diets," argues Dr. Victor Herbert of New York City's Mount Sinai Medical School. By giving large doses of vitamins "we're going to be able to get people to live a lot longer," counters Dr. Bruce Ames of the University of California at Berkeley. And, straddling the scientific fence, Dr. Walter Willett of the Harvard School of Public Health simply says: "At this time I say don't take megadoses, but I'm not ruling out that in two or three years we might change our mind." What do you think?

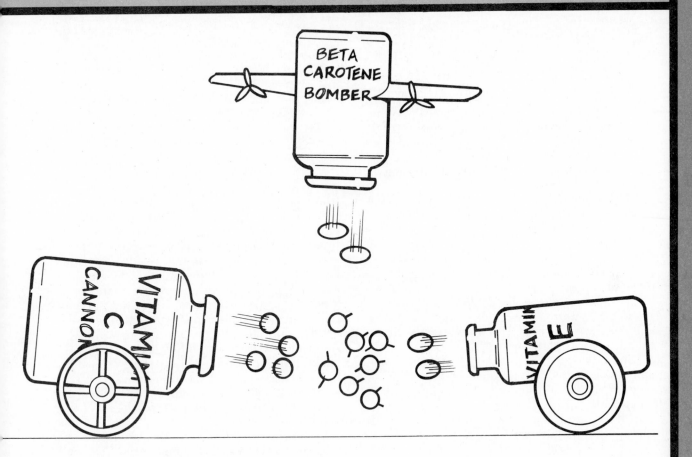

Questions

1. A free radical
   a. possesses only paired electrons.
   b. possesses an unpaired electron.
   c. is a neutral atom.
   d. is a vitamin.

2. Beta carotene is a chemical found in
   a. nuts.   c. yams.
   b. tomatoes.   d. margarine.

3. The substance that protects against cataracts
   is
   a. vitamin C.   c. beta carotene.
   b. vitamin E.   d. a free radical.

4. What evidence supports the contention that beta carotene protects against heart attacks?

5. On a separate sheet of paper, state your position on the following question: Should people take large doses of vitamins C and E and beta carotene? Discuss the reasoning underlying your response.

Acid Rain: Is It Giving Ms. Liberty Hives?

Some people get hives or a rash when they touch something to which they are allergic. And, in a sense, that's what scientists have found is happening to the Statue of Liberty. Ms. Liberty, however, isn't alive. So how come she's coming down with a skin problem?

As you might guess, Ms. Liberty's blemishes aren't really human. Nevertheless, they are real. Certain parts of the statue are sprouting dark splotches. Why?

To start our search for the answer, let's take a close look at Ms. Liberty and the cosmetics that cover her surface. When this symbol of welcome was "born" her skin glistened like the surface of a newly minted penny. That's because, like the penny, Ms. Liberty's skin was made of copper.

As the lady "beside the golden door" aged she began to turn a delightful shade of green. She developed what is called a *patina*, a thin chemical coating. In Ms. Liberty's case, the coating consisted of a mixture of chemical compounds of copper, all of which are green or blue-green. These compounds, which include brochantite ($Cu_4 (OH)_6 SO_4$) and antlerite ($Cu_3 (OH)_4 SO_4$), form when copper reacts with gases in the air and water.

Now, you might think that if Ms. Liberty could speak, she would complain bitterly about turning green with age. In truth, however, she would glory in her greenness. You see, a patina protects the underlying metal from corrosion, so Ms. Liberty's skin would be preserved under her cosmetic coating.

It appeared that Ms. Liberty's dark blotches meant something was wrong with her patina. These blotches seemed to be caused by bald spots in the coating. But what was causing the bald spots?

Robert Baboian, an expert in the corrosion of metals, suggested that acid rain was the culprit. Acid rain forms when factory gases, like sulfur dioxide and oxides of nitrogen, enter the atmosphere and become dissolved in raindrops.

This produces weak concentrations of sulfuric and nitric acids—but not too weak to do damage to trees, marine life, and statues.

Dr. Baboian pointed out that acid rain has two effects: it breaks down brochantite and promotes the deposition of antlerite. In other words, it reduces the presence of one component in patina while increasing the other.

You might think that this kind of a trade-off would result in a neutral effect. This would be true if it were not for the fact that antlerite is more soluble in water than brochantite. Put another way, acid rain inhibits the production of brochantite while fog, mist, snow, and rain wash away antlerite. The net result is a thinner layer of patina, which eventually leads to the exposure of patches of underlying copper.

No way! says geochemist Richard A. Livingston. "It's not possible for the acid rain to have an effect on the statue at all," he said in the August 17, 1991, issue of *Science News*. To back up his contention, Livingston showed that the concentration of acids in rain falling on the statue was not great enough to form antlerite. So what was causing the dark patches on Ms. Liberty?

Livingston analyzed the dark patches and discovered that they contained a mineral of copper chloride. He knew where the copper came from: Ms. Liberty's skin. But where did the chloride come from? Sea spray, said Livingston. The water surrounding the statue is full of chloride salts, not the least of which is NaCl.

Now it was Baboian's turn to cry, No way! Among other things, Baboian pointed out that as acid rain evaporates it becomes more concentrated—concentrated enough to spark the formation of antlerite.

Who's right? What do you think? (By the way, it seems Ms. Liberty's blotches don't wear any faster than her patina. Her complexion may be tarnished but her skin is as healthy as ever.)

Questions

1. The Statue of Liberty's skin is made of
   a. salt.
   b. copper.
   c. iron.
   d. sulfur dioxide.

2. Brochantite and antlerite are both
   a. oxides.
   b. sulfides.
   c. sulfites.
   d. sulfates.

3. Acid rain is the product of water and
   a. sulfur dioxide and oxides of nitrogen.
   b. chlorides and sulfur dioxide.
   c. chlorides and oxides of nitrogen.
   d. oxides and chlorides.

4. How do Drs. Baboian and Livingston differ concerning the blotching of the Statue of Liberty?

5. On a separate sheet of paper, describe an experiment designed to test the hypotheses of Drs. Baboian and Livingston.

Tomorrow's Cars: Fill 'em Up or Plug 'em In?

"California wants only ZEVs" might sound like some sort of new kind of discrimination. But after some digging, you would discover that the end result of an all-ZEV society is beneficial for us all.

A ZEV, it turns out, is a *zero emission vehicle*, that is, one out of whose tailpipe comes nothing. As a matter of fact, ZEVs don't have tailpipes at all. That's because a true zero emission vehicle doesn't burn gasoline or any other fuel. It runs on battery electricity, and under normal conditions batteries don't emit fumes.

According to California law, ZEVs are to be gradually integrated into the state's car population. In California, that translates into 2 percent of new cars sold in 1998 and 10 percent by 2003. The problem is finding battery technology to make such cars convenient and affordable. Many critics, like *Motor Trend* magazine's Jeff Karr, say that the law is moving faster than the technology. As Karr puts it in the February 1993 issue of the magazine, ". . . legislation is pushing the technology much too fast."

To get an idea of the state of the technology as of early 1993, take a look at the table below.

It shows the performance of seven kinds of batteries tested in the same vehicle. The source of the table is the Electric Power Research Institute, an organization that includes 660 U.S. power companies and which has earmarked $262 million for research into batteries that could power ZEVs.

Let's clarify the table a little bit. *Range* means the distance the vehicle will travel before its batteries must be recharged by plugging them into an external source of electric current. *Acceleration* refers to the number of seconds it takes for the vehicle to go from a dead stop to 100 kilometers per hour (about 62 miles per hour). *Lifespan* refers to the number of kilometers the vehicle will travel before its battery pack will have to be entirely replaced, a costly bit of maintenance.

Based on the data in the table, none of the batteries would be convenient to use for very long trips, since the most efficient would have to be recharged every 450 km, or 280 miles. But this would not be a drawback for cars used to commute to work or for average daily use.

With the exception of cars powered by the

Performance of Different Car Battery Packs

Type of battery	Range (km)	Acceleration 0-100 kph (sec)	Lifespan (km)	Year available (estimated)
Lead acid (advanced)	90	47	27,000	1993
Lead acid (woven)	150	7	68,000	1995
NiH	240	14	120,000	1995
NaS	250	19	38,000	1996
NiCad	170	18	68,000	1996
Li-polymer	450	14	158,000	2001
AFS flywheel	450	4	450,000	1995

AFS flywheel battery, getting from zero to 60 mph would be a very leisurely process—too leisurely, no doubt, for many people. And as of the early 1990s, the cost of buying these cars would be greater than comparable gas-driven vehicles. But on the plus side, you get a society no longer dependent on importing foreign oil for transportation and one whose air is a great deal cleaner than it now is.

Are we moving too fast toward the age of ZEVs? Is California asking too much of us and auto manufacturers? What do you think?

Questions

1. According to California law, by 1998
    a. 1% of new cars sold must be ZEVs.
    b. 2% of new cars sold must be ZEVs.
    c. 10% of new cars sold must be ZEVs.
    d. 100% of new cars sold must be ZEVs.

2. The shortest lived battery now under consideration for ZEVs is the
    a. advanced lead acid.
    b. woven lead acid.
    c. NiCad.
    d. AFS flywheel.

3. Which of the following batteries has to be recharged the least often?
    a. NiH.
    b. NaS.
    c. NiCad.
    d. Li-polymer.

4. What is writer Jeff Karr's view of California's ZEV legislation?

5. On a separate sheet of paper, explain the impact of California's zero emission vehicle legislation on consumers, auto manufacturers, and the population at large.

UNIT 8

129

Cleaning Up Chemical Wastes: Who Pays?

On any hot summer day in the early part of the twentieth century, people swarmed out of the city of Syracuse in central New York State to seek relief in the cool waters of nearby Onondaga Lake. But by the 1940s, the citizens of Syracuse could no longer use the lake to escape the heat, for in that decade swimming in the once-clear water was banned. Within a few years, fishing in the lake was also declared unsafe and was prohibited.

What turned the lake into off-limits territory? And who is going to pay to restore it to a place where people can once again splash happily and safely?

As with the more than 34,000 chemically polluted sites in the United States, the answer to the first question is easy. But the answer to the second is both complex and controversial. In the case of Onondaga Lake, its waters became the dumping grounds for chemicals from two factories, one of which has been abandoned. To add to the problem, the lake became—and up until 1993 still was—the recipient of raw and processed sewage from surrounding communities.

In the early 1990s, the people of Onondaga County demanded that the lake be cleaned up. This led to a plan developed by County Executive Nicholas Pirro to clean up the lake. The plan included a number of actions. One would involve improved treatment of sewage headed for the lake and the diverting of some of the sewage to a nearby river. Another involved getting rid of the industrial chemical wastes that over the years had accumulated in the lake.

County Executive Pirro's plan called for a 20-year cleanup that would cost $834 million. But from where would the money come? Not from the federal government, said Richard Cahill of the United States Environmental Protection Agency (EPA). Why not? Under federal law, Lake Onondaga must get on line for federal funds behind bodies of water used for drinking water.

The law, enacted by Congress in 1980, is officially called the Comprehensive Environmental Response, Compensation and Liability Act, also known as the Superfund law. Among other things, this law defines who should help pay for cleaning up polluted areas.

For example, the law states that companies that contributed to the pollution should help clean it up. Since the county's sewage system as well as industrial companies contributed to the pollution, both appear to be responsible for the cleanup. But the county simply doesn't have enough money to handle its end of the job.

One of the companies, Bristol-Myers Squibb Company, agreed to contribute $30 million for the building of a waste-water treatment plant. But that would still leave the county short by $804 million. That's too much, said Pirro, who declared that the plan could not go into effect unless 75 percent of the money for the cleanup came from funds other than those of the county.

According to United States Senator Daniel Patrick Moynihan, the federal government is not a likely source of such funds, especially when federal officials, including the president, have pledged to cut the federal deficit.

As Senator Moynihan put it in an article that appeared in *The New York Times* on May 6, 1993: ". . .there's a leakage of reality in Onondaga County. . . . I will do what I can, but the county will have to pay for the cleanup principally on its own. The time of grants is gone."

Do you agree with Senator Moynihan? If not, what would you propose? Should the federal government pump out millions of dollars to clean up the lake? Should someone else? What do you think?

Questions

1. What was the source of Lake Onondaga's pollution?
   a. only industrial chemicals
   b. only sewage
   c. both industrial chemicals and sewage
   d. neither industrial chemicals nor sewage

2. The number of chemically polluted sites in the United States is about
   a. 340
   b. 3,400
   c. 34,000
   d. 340,000

3. When referring to Onondaga County's request for federal funds to clean its lake, who said "The time of grants is gone."
   a. Nicholas Pirro
   b. Richard Cahill
   c. Bill Clinton
   d. Daniel Patrick Moynihan

4. What does one of the provisions of the Superfund law define?

5. On a separate sheet of paper, discuss your views of the Onondaga Lake issue. Among other things, compare and evaluate the positions of Nicholas Pirro, Richard Cahill, and Daniel Patrick Moynihan.

Ethanol: Fuel of the Future?

Are these the billboard ads of the future? They could be if backers of ethanol as a transportation fuel have their way.

Ethanol, as you may know, is the second simplest organic alcohol. Methanol is the simplest. Like methanol, ethanol consists of nothing but carbon, hydrogen, and oxygen atoms. When it burns—and it does burn—it produces nothing more frightening than water and carbon dioxide.

Compare this to the products of petroleum and gasoline combustion—all sorts of nitrogen and sulfur gases, ozone, and a host of hydrocarbon byproducts—and you appreciate the case made for replacing gasoline with ethanol as a transportation fuel. What's more, say supporters of ethanol as a fuel, its use would decrease our dependence on foreign oil, tip the balance of world trade in our favor, and help slow world climate changes due to increased levels of carbon dioxide pumped into the air by internal combustion engines.

Hold on, you might say, didn't I just read that the combustion of ethanol *produces* carbon dioxide? Right! But the plan is to obtain ethanol from the fermentation of cellulose, that is, from plant products such as grass, wood, and corn.

The growth processes of these plants removes carbon dioxide from the atmosphere through photosynthesis. As a matter of fact, according to an article written by a group of scientists headed by Lee R. Lynd of Dartmouth College, and published in the March 15, 1991, issue of *Science*, the amount of carbon dioxide added to the atmosphere by the manufacture and combustion of ethanol ". . . is precisely that which was previously removed from the atmospheric pool by photosynthesis." The net result? No additional carbon dioxide in the air and, thus, no carbon dioxide induced change in the world's climate.

All this sounds promising except for at least one important problem. As Lynd puts it, ". . . approximately 1.25 gallons of ethanol are needed to travel the same distance as that obtained from 1 gallon of gasoline." That would make transportation by car, bus, and truck at least 25 percent more expensive. And "at least" means just that since it's more costly to produce ethanol than gasoline, which would further increase the cost of travel.

The cost of producing ethanol from cellulose has, however, come down over the past ten years or so. And some researchers predict that it will be equal to that of gasoline by the year 2000. But what should we do till then? Keep pumping gasoline into our tanks and pollutants into our air? Begin the switch to ethanol but pay the price of higher transportation costs? Or do something else? But what?

One tactic, which was being used in 1990, was to lop six cents a gallon from the federal tax on gasoline that contained at least some ethanol. But this, of course, would tend to increase the federal deficit, something everyone is trying to decrease. Another approach undertaken in the 1980s was to give federal tax breaks and loan guarantees to companies that built ethanol factories. Such companies also got free supplies of surplus corn from which ethanol was made. But is this special treatment fair? And don't average taxpayers have to foot the bill for these handouts?

How should we contribute to the switch to ethanol? Should we do it at all? What do you think?

Questions

1. Pure ethanol consists of
   a. carbon, hydrogen, oxygen, nitrogen, and sulfur.
   b. carbon, hydrogen, oxygen, and nitrogen.
   c. carbon, hydrogen, and oxygen.
   d. carbon and hydrogen.

2. The combustion of ethanol produces
   a. nitrogen and sulfur gases
   b. carbon dioxide and water
   c. carbon dioxide and sulfur gases
   d. water and nitrogen gases.

3. The distance a car will travel on a gallon of gasoline is
   a. 0.25 that traveled on a gallon of ethanol.
   b. 0.75 that traveled on a gallon of ethanol.
   c. 1.00 that traveled on a gallon of ethanol.
   d. 1.25 that traveled on a gallon of ethanol.

4. What do proponents of ethanol as a transportation fuel suggest would be the major benefits of switching from gasoline to this alcohol?

5. On a separate sheet of paper, give your views on whether we should switch from gasoline to ethanol as a transportation fuel and, if so, under what conditions.

Irradiated Food: Short on Safety?

Look out! The radura may be coming.

A radura looks innocent. Any flower would. But this is no ordinary flower. It's a symbol that you may spot on a package of fresh strawberries, or on a jar of spice. And in the future, the radura may bloom on labels of foods from chickens to clams.

A label that bears a radura informs a shopper that a food product has been irradiated. The food has most probably spent a short time on a conveyor belt that rode by a source of gamma radiation, such as cesium-137 or cobalt-60.

During that journey on the conveyer belt, the food was zapped with up to 3,000,000 rads. A *rad* is a unit of absorbed radiation dosage. To get an idea of the wallop 3,000,000 rads packs, consider that an ordinary chest X ray delivers about 20 millirads, or 20 thousandths of a rad. So 3,000,000 rads is equivalent to the radiation of 150,000,000 chest X rays!

Why expose food to such enormous doses of radiation? To preserve them and make them healthier for people to eat, say proponents of irradiating foods. These advocates of food irradiation point out that food decay is caused by microorganisms like bacteria. What's more, they say, certain serious diseases that strike human beings are caused by bacteria and other food contaminants, like salmonella bacteria in chicken and other poultry, trichina worms in pork, and hepatitis-causing viruses in shellfish.

Radiation deals death blows to both food-spoiling and disease-causing organisms. It also increases the shelf life of foods, which saves consumers money. The foods they buy simply last longer. As food irradiation supporter William McGivney puts it, ". . . irradiation offers a means to decontaminate, disinfect and retard the spoilage of the food supply." This can't be anything but a benefit to consumers, right?

Maybe not, says critic Donald B. Louria, chairman of the preventive medicine department at the New Jersey Medical School in Newark, New Jersey. In an article published in the September 1990 issue of *The Bulletin of the Atomic Scientists*, Louria states: "At dispute . . . are the quality of the FDA [Food and Drug Administration] safety assessment, the loss of nutritional value that irradiated foods undergo, the risk of environmental contamination posed by irradiation facilities, and the possible cancer-causing nature of irradiated foods."

Louria accuses the FDA of considering only five of 441 studies done to determine the safety of irradiated foods. Three of the studies "do not document the safety of food irradiation . . ." Louria insists. On the contrary, Louria reports that these studies implicated irradiated foods in the weight loss and miscarriage of test animals. Louria also pointed to studies done in India and China that, although not conclusive, hinted at a possible link between irradiated foods and the production of abnormal chromosomes in people who ate those foods.

Aside from the question of safety, there is the issue of the effect of irradiation on the nutrient content of foods. Evidence exists that implicates irradiation in the destruction of vitamins E, A, C, and some B complex vitamins. Supporters of irradiation suggest this problem can easily be overcome by adding vitamins to such foods, or having people take vitamin supplements.

Critics suggest another potential hazard. Although irradiation does not make foods radioactive, it does break up some substances that occur naturally in them. Experiments show that some of these substances may cause cells to mutate. Might such mutations lead to cancers? No one seems to know the answer.

Finally, the building of many factories to irradiate foods would require the shipment of large quantities of radioactive materials across the country. Accidents might allow such materials to pollute the environment and threaten lives.

There seems to be a lot of mights, maybes, and unknowns mixed in with hard facts in this issue. Based on your knowledge of the mix, what do you think should be done?

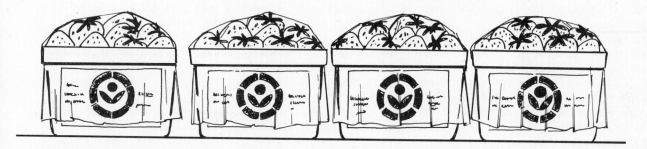

Questions

1. Foods are irradiated with
   a. alpha particles.
   b. beta particles.
   c. gamma rays.
   d. X rays.

2. Poultry products would be irradiated to rid them of
   a. hepatitis-causing viruses.
   b. salmonella bacteria.
   c. trichina worms.
   d. mold.

3. Evidence exists that irradiation of food destroys
   a. vitamin A only.
   b. B complex vitamins only.
   c. vitamin C only.
   d. vitamins A, E, C, and some B complex.

4. Describe four criticisms of the irradiation of food.

5. On a separate sheet of paper, discuss your views concerning the irradiation of foods. Include in your discussion your reaction to the various arguments in favor of and against food irradiation.

Glossary

Absolute zero: The lowest temperature possible (never reached), 0 K.

Accuracy: A term that describes how close a measurement is to its true or accepted value.

Acetone: Propanone, the first and simplest member of the ketone group.

Acetylene: Ethyne, C_2H_2, the first member of the alkyne series.

Acid: Any species (molecule or ion) that can donate a proton to another species.

Activated complex: An unstable intermediate product of a chemical reaction.

Activation energy: The energy required to form the activated complex and initiate a chemical reaction.

Addition polymerization: The result of joining monomers of unsaturated compounds, usually hydrocarbons, by "opening" double or triple bonds in the carbon chain.

Addition reaction: A reaction that occurs when one or more atoms are added to an unsaturated hydrocarbon molecule at a double or triple bond.

Alcohol: A hydrocarbon in which one or more hydrogen atoms have been replaced by an —OH group.

Aldehydes: A group of organic compounds represented by the general formula R—CHO, where R represents one hydrogen atom or any hydrocarbon group.

Alkadiene: A hydrocarbon that has two double bonds and the general formula C_nH_{2n-2}.

Alkali metals: The elements of Group 1 of the Periodic Table (the first vertical column).

Alkaline earth metals: The elements of Group 2 of the Periodic Table (the second vertical column).

Alkane (methane) series: A group of saturated hydrocarbons with the general formula C_nH_{2n+2}.

Alkene (olefin) series: A group of unsaturated hydrocarbons with one carbon-carbon double bond and the general formula C_nH_{2n}.

Alkyne series: A group of unsaturated hydrocarbons with one triple bond and the general formula C_nH_{2n-2}.

Alpha decay: The emission of alpha particles, the nuclei of helium atoms, from the nuclei of naturally occurring radioactive isotopes.

Alpha particle: A radioactive emanation that has the same composition as the nucleus of a helium atom, two protons and two neutrons.

Amphoteric (or **amphiprotic**): A substance that can act either as an acid or as a base. In the Brönsted-Lowry system, amphoteric substances are listed as both acids and bases.

Anion: A negatively charged ion.

node: In any electrochemical cell, the electrode at which oxidation occurs.

atic hydrocarbon: Another name for members of benzene series.

Artificial transmutation: The bombardment of the nucleus of an atom with high-energy particles such as protons, neutrons, and alpha particles in order to make that nucleus artificially radioactive.

Atom: The smallest unit of all matter.

Atomic mass unit (amu): The mass of an atom as given in amu; the atomic mass of carbon-12 is defined as 12 amu.

Atomic number: The number of protons in the nucleus of an atom.

Average kinetic energy: The temperature of a body.

Avogadro's hypothesis: Equal volumes of all gases, measured at the same temperature and pressure, contain the same number of particles.

Avogadro's number: The number of atoms in 1 gram atomic mass of any element (approximately 6.02×10^{23}) or the number of molecules in 1 gram molecular mass (1 mole) of any compound.

Base: Any species (molecule or ion) that can combine with (accept) a proton.

Benzene series: A group of hydrocarbons with the general formula C_nH_{2n-6}.

Beta decay: The emission of beta particles, or high-speed electrons, from the nucleus of naturally occurring radioactive isotopes, increasing the atomic number by 1.

Beta particle: A high-speed electron emitted in many radioactive processes.

Binary compound: A compound containing two elements and whose name usually ends in *-ide*.

Boiling point: The temperature at which a liquid boils. At the boiling point, the vapor pressure of the liquid is equal to the atmospheric pressure.

Boiling point elevation: The elevation of the boiling point of a solvent due to the presence of a nonvolatile solute and proportional to the concentration of dissolved solute particles.

Boyle's law: At constant temperature, the volume of a given mass of gas varies inversely with the pressure exerted on it.

Breeder reactor: A type of nuclear reactor that produces both energy and plutonium-239, a nuclear fuel. The reactor produces more fuel than it consumes.

Brönsted-Lowry acid (or **base**): A proton donor (or acceptor).

Calorie: The quantity of energy required to raise the temperature of 1 gram of water 1C°.

Calorimeter: A device that measures heat absorbed or released in a chemical reaction.

Carbon dating: A procedure in which radioactive isotopes are used to determine the age of ancient objects.

Carboxylic acid: An organic acid with the general formula R—COOH.

Catalyst: A substance that increases the rate of reaction without itself being chemically altered.

Cathode: In any electrochemical cell, the electrode at which reduction occurs.

Cation: A positively charged ion.

Celsius scale: A temperature scale with 100 degrees between the melting point of ice, defined as 0°, and the boiling point of water, defined as 100°.

Chain reaction: A fission reaction in which the products (neutrons) continue to sustain the reaction.

Charles' law: At constant pressure, the volume of a given mass of gas varies directly with the Kelvin (absolute) temperature.

Chemical bond: The force of attraction that holds atoms together.

Chemical cell: See **electrochemical cell**.

Chemical change: A change in which new materials or substances are formed.

Chemical equation: A statement employing chemical symbols that describes the qualitative and quantitative relationships in a chemical reaction.

Chemical kinetics: The branch of chemistry concerned with the rates at which chemical reactions occur and the physical mechanisms, or pathways, along which they proceed.

Chemistry: The study of the nature of matter and the changes that matter undergoes.

Colligative properties: Properties that vary with the concentration of solute particles.

Colloid: A homogeneous mixture containing particles large enough to reflect a beam of light.

Common ion effect: The decrease in ionization of a weak electrolyte by the addition of a salt with an ion common to the solution of the electrolyte.

Compound: A substance that can be decomposed by chemical action into simpler substances.

Concentrated solution: A solution with a relatively large amount of solute compared to the amount of solvent.

Conceptual definition: A definition based on interpretation of observation and empirical evidence. (See also **operational definition**.)

Condensation: An exothermic change from gas to liquid.

Condensation polymerization: The result of the bonding of monomers by a dehydration reaction.

Conjugate pair: In the Brönsted-Lowry theory, an acid and its corresponding base; they differ only by the presence or absence of a transferable proton.

Contact process: A process for making concentrated sulfuric acid.

Control rods: Rods made of boron or cadmium that can be moved in and out of a nuclear reactor to control the rate of a fission reaction.

Coordinate covalent bond: A bond in which both electrons of a shared pair in a covalent bond are donated by the same atom.

Corrosion: A redox reaction between a metal and substances in its surroundings that destroys the metal.

Covalent atomic radius: One-half of the distance between the nuclei of atoms joined by a covalent bond.

Covalent bond: A bond formed by the sharing of electrons.

Cracking: A process in which large molecules of hydrocarbons are broken down into smaller molecules.

Crystal: A structure in which the particles of a substance are arranged in a regular geometric pattern.

Dalton's law: The total pressure of a gas mixture is equal to the sum of the individual pressures of the gases comprising the mixture.

Daniell cell: An electrochemical cell using copper and zinc half-cells.

Decomposition: A chemical reaction in which a substance is broken down into simpler substances.

Dehydrating agent: A substance that removes water.

ΔH: See **heat of reaction**.

Density: Mass per unit of volume.

Deuterium: An isotope of hydrogen, ^{2}H.

Dilute solution: A solution with very little solute compared to the amount of solvent.

Dipole: An asymmetrical molecule whose centers of positive and negative charge are located at different parts of the molecule.

Dipole-dipole attraction: The force of attraction between dipoles.

Dissociation: The separation of an ionic or covalent compound into simpler species.

Double bond: A bond involving two shared pairs of electrons.

Double replacement: A chemical reaction in which two binary (or ternary) compounds react to form new compounds.

Ductile substance: A solid material or substance that can be drawn out to form a thin wire.

E^0: Standard electrode potential that describes the spontaneity of a redox reaction.

Effectiveness of collisions: The likelihood that a chemical change will occur following a collision of reacting particles.

Electrochemical cell: An arrangement of half-cells producing a flow of electrons (electric current).

Electrode: A metallic conductor in any electrochemical cell.

Electrolysis: The decomposition of an electrolyte by an electric current.

Electrolyte: A substance whose aqueous solution conducts electric current.

Electron: The fundamental unit of negative charge.

Electron cloud: The space around the nucleus of an atom where its electrons are found; an orbital.

Electronegativity: A measure of the ability of a nucleus to attract the electrons in a covalent bond.

Electroplating: The process of coating a metal in an electrolytic cell.

Element: A substance that cannot be decomposed by ordinary chemical means into simpler substances.

Empirical formula: The simplest whole-number ratio in which atoms combine to form a compound.

Endothermic reaction: A reaction that has a positive ΔH in which energy is absorbed and the potential energy of the products is greater than the potential energy of the reactants.

End point: The point at which neutralization occurs in an acid-base titration.

Energy: The capacity to do work.

Energy level: The energy of an electron associated with its location in the charge cloud and its distance from the nucleus of the atom.

Enthalpy: A measure of the potential energy in chemical bonds.

Enthalpy change: ΔH; commonly known as *heat of reaction*.

Entropy: A measure of the disorder, randomness, or lack of organization in a system.

Enzyme: An organic catalyst.

Equilibrium: A state of balance between two opposing reactions (physical or chemical) occurring at the same rate.

Equilibrium constant (K_{eq}): The numerical value of the ratio between the concentrations of the products and the concentrations of the reactants in a system at equilibrium.

Ester: An organic compound formed when an alcohol reacts with a carboxylic acid; represented by the general formula R—COO—R'.

Esterification: The reaction of an organic acid with an alcohol to give an ester and water.

Ether: A hydrocarbon derivative represented by the formula R—O—R'.

Evaporation: A spontaneous change from liquid to gas.

Excited state: The condition of an atom that exists from absorption of energy, characterized by the movement of one or more electrons to higher energy levels.

Exothermic reaction: A reaction that has a negative ΔH in which energy is released and the potential energy of the products is less than the potential energy of the reactants.

Family: See **group**.

Fermentation: A process in which enzymes act as catalysts to produce alcohol from carbohydrates.

Fission reaction: See **nuclear fission**.

Fission reactor: A type of nuclear reactor presently in use that produces energy from the fission of uranium.

Fractional distillation: A technique used to separate components of a mixture, based on the differences in their boiling points.

Free energy change (ΔG): The difference between energy change (ΔH) and entropy change (ΔS) according to the formula $\Delta G = \Delta H - T\Delta S$; ($\Delta G$) must be negative for a change to be spontaneous.

Freezing point: The temperature at which a liquid and its solid form can coexist in equilibrium.

Freezing point depression: The depression of the freezing point of the solvent due to the presence of a solute and proportional to the concentration of dissolved solute particles.

Fuel (nuclear): Fissionable isotopes used in nuclear reactors.

Function group: A particular arrangement of atoms associated with certain chemical and physical properties that are characteristic of a series of organic compounds.

Fused: Term for a molten substance that is a solid at room temperature.

Fusion reaction: See **nuclear fusion**.

Galvanic cell: See **electrochemical cell**.

Gamma radiation: Short-wave-length radiation similar to high-energy X-rays.

Gas: A phase of matter that takes the shape and volume of its container.

Glycerol: A trihydroxy alcohol.

Glycol: A dihydroxy alcohol containing two —OH groups, such as ethylene glycol.

Graham's law: Under the same conditions of temperature and pressure, gases diffuse at a rate inversely proportional to the square root of their molecular masses.

Gram atomic mass (gram-atom): The atomic mass of an element expressed in grams; also known as *one mole of an element*.

Gram formula mass: The sum of the masses of all atoms in a formula, expressed in grams.

Gram molecular mass: The sum of the atomic masses of all atoms in a molecular formula, expressed in grams.

Ground state: The normal state of an atom with all of its electrons in their lowest available energy levels.

Group: A family of elements represented by a column in the Periodic Table.

Haber process: A commercial process for the production of ammonia from nitrogen and hydrogen.

Half-cell: A strip of metal in contact with its ions.

Half-life: The time required for one-half of the nuclei of a given sample of a radioactive element to undergo decay.

Half-reaction: One-half of a redox reaction, representing either a loss of electrons (oxidation) or a gain of electrons (reduction).

Halogen: An element that is a member of Group 17 of the Periodic Table.

Halogen derivative: An organic compound that is the product of halogen substitution or addition.

Halogen substitution: A reaction in which one or more hydrogen atoms of a saturated hydrocarbon are replaced by a corresponding number of halogen atoms.

Heat: The form of energy most often associated with chemical change.

Heat of fusion: The amount of energy required to convert one gram of a substance from solid to liquid at its melting point.

Heat of reaction (ΔH): The difference in heat content between the products and reactants of a reaction; also known as *enthalpy change*.

Heat of vaporization: The amount of energy required to convert one gram of a substance from liquid to vapor at its boiling point.

Heavy water: deuterium oxide, D_2O.

Heterogeneous substance: A sample of a substance

that is not uniform throughout in its properties, composition, or phase.

Homogeneous substance: A sample of a substance that is uniform throughout in its properties, composition, or phase.

Homologous series: A group of organic compounds with the same general formula and similar structures and properties.

Hydrated salt: A solid compound containing a definite number of water molecules bonded directly to the solid crystal.

Hydration: The addition of water to a compound or an ion.

Hydrocarbon: A compound that contains atoms of hydrogen and carbon only.

Hydrogen bonding: The intermolecular attraction between the hydrogen on one molecule and an element of small atomic radius and high electronegativity on another molecule.

Hydrogenation: The addition of hydrogen to an unsaturated hydrocarbon or hydrocarbon derivative.

Hydrolysis: The reaction of a salt with water to form a slightly acidic or basic solution.

Ideal gas: An imaginary gas that obeys the gas laws perfectly.

Immiscible: Term for two liquids that will not mix to form a solution.

Increment: The number and kind of atoms by which each member of a homologous series differs from the preceding member.

Indicators: Organic substances that change color at definite pH values.

Inert (rare or noble) gases: Group 18 elements in the Periodic Table.

Insoluble: Term for a solid or gaseous substance that does not dissolve in a liquid.

Ionic bond: A bond between oppositely charged particles formed when electrons are transferred between atoms.

Ionic radius: An arbitrary designation that describes the size of an ion, or the size of the electron cloud associated with an ion.

Ionic solids: Crystalline solids containing ions.

Ionization: The process of forming ions, often by the reaction between solvent and solute molecules.

Ionization constant (K_i): The numerical value of the equilibrium ratio of dissociated ions to undissociated compound.

Ionization energy: The amount of energy required to remove the most loosely bound electron from an atom in the gas phase.

Isomers: Compounds that have the same molecular formula but different structural formulas.

Isotopes: Atoms with the same atomic number but different atomic masses.

K_a: The ionization constant of a weak acid.

K_{sp}: The solubility product constant.

K_w: The ion product of water.

Kelvin scale: A temperature scale with 100 degrees between the melting point of ice and the boiling point of water, with 0° representing absolute zero, or the point of zero kinetic energy.

Kernel: Term used to refer to all parts of the atom except the valence electrons.

Ketones: A group of organic compounds having the general formula R—CO—R′.

Kilocalorie: One thousand calories.

Kinetic energy: The energy of a body in motion.

Kinetic theory of gases: A theory that explains the behavior of gases by assuming that they consist of individual molecules in random motion.

Law: A statement or mathematical formula that summarizes certain experimental observations.

Lead storage battery: A cell in which the change in oxidation states of lead is used to produce electricity.

Le Chatelier's principle: When a system at equilibrium is subjected to a stress, the system will shift so as to relieve the stress and move to a new equilibrium.

Liquid: A phase of matter that takes the shape but not necessarily the volume of its container.

Malleable: Term for the ability of a metal to be hammered or rolled into thin sheets.

Mass number: The numerical sum of the protons and neutrons in an atomic nucleus.

Matter: Anything that occupies space and has mass.

Melting point: The temperature at which a solid and its liquid form can coexist in equilibrium.

Meniscus: The curved shape that the surface of a liquid takes in a glass container.

Metal: An element that contains atoms that lose electrons to form positive ions in chemical reactions. Metals exhibit certain characteristics such as conductivity, luster, and malleability.

Metalloid: An element with some of the properties of metals and some of the properties of nonmetals.

Miscible: Term for two liquids that can mix to form a solution.

Mixture: A combination of two or more substances of variable composition not chemically combined.

Moderator: A substance that can slow down neutrons, used in nuclear reactors to control fission reactions.

Molal boiling point constant: A constant that can be multiplied by the molality of the solution to determine the boiling point elevation.

Molal freezing point constant: A constant that can be multiplied by the molality of the solution to determine the freezing point depression.

Molality (m): The concentration of a solution expressed in moles of solute per kilogram of solvent.

Molar volume: The volume of one mole of a gas, usually expressed as 22.4 L at STP.

Molarity (M): The concentration of a solution, expressed in moles of solute per liter of solution.

Mole of an element: A fixed quantity containing Avogadro's number (6.02×10^{23}) of atoms and equal to the gram atomic mass of the element.

Mole of a compound: A fixed quantity containing Avogadro's number of molecules and equal to the gram formula mass of the compound.

Molecular formula: A statement of the exact number of each kind of atom in a molecule or compound.

Molecular solids: Solids formed by molecules of covalently bonded atoms.

Molecule: The smallest subdivision of a substance that has all the properties of the substance.

Monohydroxy alcohols: Hydrocarbon derivatives containing one —OH group per molecule.

Monomer: A small molecule that joins with other identical molecules to form a polymer (large molecule).

Network solid: Covalently bonded atoms linked in a network that extends throughout a large sample.

Neutralization: A reaction in which one mole of H^+ from an acid combines with one mole of OH^- from a base to form water.

Neutron: A nuclear particle that does not have an electrical charge.

Nonelectrolyte: A substance whose aqueous solution does not conduct electric current.

Nonmetal: An element that tends to form negative ions.

Nonpolar: Term for a bond or a molecule with uniform distribution of charge.

Nonpolar bond: A covalent bond in which the electron pair that forms the bond is shared equally by two atoms.

Nonvolatile: Term for a liquid with negligible vapor pressure.

Normal boiling point: The temperature at which the vapor pressure of a liquid equals 1 atmosphere.

Normal freezing point: The temperature at which a liquid will change to a solid at 1 atmosphere.

Nuclear emanation: The release of alpha, beta, or gamma particles from the nucleus of a naturally occurring radioactive isotope.

Nuclear fission: A reaction in which heavy nuclei are split into light nuclei.

Nuclear fusion: The process of combining two light nuclei to form a heavier nucleus and releasing an even greater amount of energy than in a fission reaction.

Nuclear reactor: A device designed to produce controlled nuclear reactions so that energy is released at a steady and predictable rate.

Nucleons: The particles that compose the nucleus of an atom, generally protons and neutrons.

Operational definition: A definition based on observed characteristics, without interpretation of empirical evidence. (See also **conceptual definition**.)

Orbital: The average region of most probable electron location.

Organic acid: A hydrocarbon derivative that has the general formula R—COOH.

Organic chemistry: The branch of chemistry dealing with the compounds of carbon.

Oxidation number (oxidation state): The charge that an atom has, or appears to have, when certain rules for assigning charge are used.

Oxidation-reduction (redox) reaction: A chemical reaction in which electrons are removed from some species and transferred to others.

Oxidizing agent: An electron acceptor; by accepting one or more electrons, an oxidizing agent causes another species to become oxidized and is itself reduced.

Particle accelerator: A device using magnetic and electric fields to accelerate charged particles in order to penetrate a target nucleus.

Percent error: A method of describing the accuracy of a numerical result in an experiment.

% error =

$$\frac{(\text{observed value} - \text{expected value})}{\text{expected value}} \times 100$$

Periodic law: The properties of the elements are periodic functions of their atomic numbers.

pH: The negative logarithm (base 10) of the hydrogen ion concentration in a water solution (pH = $-\log[H^+]$). pH = 7 for a neutral solution; acidic solutions have pH values less than 7; basic solutions have pH values greater than 7.

Phase: Term for any one of the three possible physical states of matter: solid, liquid, or gas.

Phase equilibrium: The equilibrium established between two different phases of a substance, such as ice and water, when a phase change is reversible.

Physical change: A change of state or physical property in which no new materials or substances are formed.

Polarity: Term used to describe a molecule in which one end has a slightly positive charge and the other end has a slightly negative charge because of asymmetrical arrangement of polar bonds.

Polar covalent bond: A covalent bond in which the electron pair is not shared equally by the two atoms; generally, a covalent bond in which the electron pair is shared by atoms of different elements.

Polyatomic ion: A bonded group of atoms that behaves as a unit and carries a charge.

Polymer: A large molecule composed of many repeating smaller units called *monomers*.

Polymerization: A process whereby large molecules are formed from smaller molecules. The manufacture of synthetic rubber is an example.

Potential energy: Chemical energy, the energy stored in chemical bonds.

Precision: The degree of reproducibility of a measurement.

Primary alcohol: A monohydroxy alcohol in which one —OH group is attached to an end carbon of a hydrocarbon chain.

Proton: The fundamental unit of positive electrical charge.

Quantum (plural quanta): A discrete amount of energy absorbed or radiated.

Quantum number: A number used to describe the energy of an electron.

Radioactivity: The spontaneous breakdown of an atomic nucleus, yielding particles and radiant energy.

Radioisotope: An isotope with an unstable nucleus that undergoes radioactive decay.

Reaction rate: The rate at which reactants are consumed or products formed in a chemical reaction.

Redox: See **oxidation-reduction**.

Reducing agent: An electron donor; by donating one or more electrons, a reducing agent causes another species to become reduced and is itself oxidized.

Reduction potential: An indicator of how easily a substance can be reduced, compared to a standard. More easily reduced substances have positive reduction potentials, while less easily reduced substances have negative reduction potentials.

Roasting: Heating an ore in air, a process used to convert sulfate and carbonate ores into oxides.

Rule of Eight (octet rule): The atoms in a molecule and their electrons are arranged so that each atom achieves the electron configuration of an inert gas atom, that is, eight electrons.

Salt: An ionic compound that dissociates to form cations other than H^+ and anions other than OH^-.

Salt bridge: A U-shaped tube containing a solution of an electrolyte that permits the passage of ions between solutions in the two half-cells of an electrochemical cell while preventing the solutions from mixing.

Saponification: The hydrolysis of a fat to produce a soap and glycerine.

Saturated hydrocarbon: A hydrocarbon that contains single carbon-carbon bonds.

Saturated solution: A solution that contains all the solute it can hold at a given temperature.

Secondary alcohol: An alcohol in which the —OH group is bonded to a carbon atom that, in turn, is bonded to two other carbon atoms.

Shell: See **energy level**.

Shielding effect: Weakening of the force between the nucleus and the outermost valence electrons because of the presence of electrons at inner energy levels that act as barriers.

Significant figures: In a measurement, the digits that are certain plus one uncertain digit.

Single covalent bond: A bond formed by the sharing of one pair of electrons by two atoms.

Single replacement: A chemical reaction in which an element reacts with a binary (or ternary) compound to form a new element and a new binary (or ternary) compound.

Solid: A phase of matter that has a definite shape and volume.

Solubility product constant (K_{sp}): The equilibrium constant for a dissociated salt in equilibrium with its undissociated form present as excess solid phase.

Soluble: Term for a solid or gaseous substance that can be dissolved in a liquid.

Solute: The substance or substances that are present in lesser proportions in a solution and are dissolved.

Solution: A homogeneous mixture of two or more substances.

Solvent: The substance that is present in greater proportion in a solution and does the dissolving.

Spectator ion: An ion that does not undergo any change in a chemical reaction.

Spectral lines: Characteristic lines produced by radiant energy of a specific frequency emitted when electrons in an atom in the excited state return to lower energy levels.

Spontaneous reaction: A reaction that can occur in nature under a given set of conditions; ΔG is negative for a spontaneous reaction.

Stable: Term for a compound or system at a relatively low energy level and thus less likely to undergo chemical change.

Standard conditions (STP): The standard conditions of temperature and pressure of the measurement of gases, 0°C and 1 atmosphere of pressure.

Standard electrode potential (E^0 value): The electrical potential of an electrochemical cell measured relative to a standard hydrogen electrode defined as zero.

Standard solution: A solution of known concentration used to determine the unknown concentration of another solution.

Stock system: A system used to name compounds of metals that have more than one possible ionic charge; a Roman numeral indicating the charge immediately follows the name of the metal, for example, chromium (III) chloride.

Stoichiometry: The study of the quantitative relationships in chemical formulas and equations.

Structural formula: A formula showing the arrangement of atoms in a molecule in a two-dimensional format using dashes to represent covalent bonds.

Sublevels (subshells): Subdivisions of the principal energy levels in an atom.

Sublimation: A change from the solid phase directly to the gas phase without passing through any apparent liquid phase. Solids that sublime have high vapor pressures and low intermolecular attractions.

Substance: Any variety of matter for which all samples have identical composition and properties.

Substitution reaction: A reaction in which one kind of atom or group of atoms is replaced by another kind of atom or group of atoms.

Supersaturated solution: A solution that contains more solute than its ordinary capacity at a given temperature.

Synthesis: A chemical reaction in which atoms of elements combine to form compounds.

Temperature: A measure of the average kinetic energy of a body.

Ternary compound: A compound consisting of three elements.

Tertiary alcohol: An alcohol in which the —OH group is bonded to a carbon atom that, in turn, is bonded to three additional carbon atoms.

Tetrahedron: A central atom joined to four other atoms, all the covalent bonds having equal angles of 109.5° between each pair of bonds.

Theory (model): A statement or picture that tries to account for certain experimental observations.

Thermometer: A device used to measure temperature,

with calibrations based on the fixed freezing point and boiling point of water.

Titration: A technique used to find the concentration of an acid or base or any other kind of solution through the mixing of measured volumes.

Tracer: A radioisotope used to follow the course of a chemical reaction without altering the reaction.

Transition elements: Elements found in Groups 3 through 12 of the Periodic Table in which electrons from the two outermost sublevels may be involved in a chemical reaction; these elements generally exhibit multiple positive ionic charges and oxidation states.

Transmutation: The change of one element into another due to changes in the nucleus caused by radioactive decay or bombardment by subatomic particles.

Trihydroxy alcohols: Hydrocarbon compounds containing three —OH groups, such as glycerine.

Triple covalent bond: A bond formed by three shared pairs of electrons between two atoms.

Tritium: An isotope of hydrogen with the formula ^3H.

Unsaturated hydrocarbon: A hydrocarbon that contains at least one carbon-carbon double or triple bond.

Unsaturated solution: A solution that contains less solute than its ordinary capacity at a given temperature.

Valence electrons: Those electrons found in the outermost energy level; most chemical properties of an atom are related to the valence electrons.

Van der Waals forces: Weak forces of attraction that exist between all molecules, especially nonpolar molecules.

Vapor: Term frequently used to refer to the gas phase of a substance that is ordinarily a liquid or solid at room temperature.

Vapor pressure: The pressure exerted by a saturated vapor in a closed system; vapor pressure increases as the temperature of the liquid increases.

Volatile: Term used to describe a liquid or solid that has a high vapor pressure and thus is easily converted to the gas phase.

Voltaic cell: See **electrochemical cell.**

Weak acid: An acid, such as acetic acid, that is only very slightly ionized in water solution; K_a values for weak acids are much less than 1.

Weak base: A base, such as ammonium hydroxide, that is only very slightly ionized in water solution; K_b values for weak bases are much less than 1.

Index

Sample Examinations

CHEMISTRY
JUNE 1993

Part I

Answer all 56 questions in this part.   [65]

Directions (1–56): For *each* statement or question, select the word or expression that, of those given, best completes the statement or answers the question. Record your answer on the separate answer sheet in accordance with the directions on the front page of this booklet.

1 If two systems at different temperatures have contact with each other, heat will flow from the system at
(1) 20.°C to a system at 303 K
(2) 30.°C to a system at 313 K
(3) 40.°C to a system at 293 K
(4) 50.°C to a system at 333 K

2 The graph below represents the uniform heating of a solid, starting below its melting point.

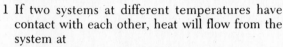

Which portion of the graph shows the solid and liquid phases of the substance existing in equilibrium?
(1) *AB*   (3) *CD*
(2) *BC*   (4) *DE*

3 What occurs when the temperature of 10.0 grams of water is changed from 15.5°C to 14.5°C?
1 The water absorbs 10.0 calories.
2 The water releases 10.0 calories.
3 The water absorbs 155 calories.
4 The water releases 145 calories.

4 Under the same conditions of temperature and pressure, a liquid differs from a gas because the particles of the liquid
1 are in constant straight-line motion
2 take the shape of the container they occupy
3 have no regular arrangement
4 have stronger forces of attraction between them

5 Compared to the mass of an SO_2 molecule, the mass of an O_2 molecule is
1 one-fourth as great   3 the same
2 one-half as great   4 twice as great

6 Under which conditions does a real gas behave most nearly like an ideal gas?
1 high pressure and low temperature
2 high pressure and high temperature
3 low pressure and low temperature
4 low pressure and high temperature

7 Which statement best describes an electron?
1 It has a smaller mass than a proton and a negative charge.
2 It has a smaller mass than a proton and a positive charge.
3 It has a greater mass than a proton and a negative charge.
4 It has a greater mass than a proton and a positive charge.

8 Which principal energy level has no *f* sublevel?
(1) 5   (3) 3
(2) 6   (4) 4

9 What is the mass number of an atom which contains 28 protons, 28 electrons, and 34 neutrons?
(1) 28   (3) 62
(2) 56   (4) 90

10 In an experiment, alpha particles were used to bombard gold foil. As a result of this experiment, the conclusion was made that the nucleus of an atom is
1 smaller than the atom and positively charged
2 smaller than the atom and negatively charged
3 larger than the atom and positively charged
4 larger than the atom and negatively charged

11 Given the reaction: $^{131}_{53}I \rightarrow \,^{131}_{54}Xe + X$
Which particle is represented by *X*?
1 alpha   3 neutron
2 beta   4 proton

12 Which orbital notation represents an atom in the ground state with 6 valence electrons?

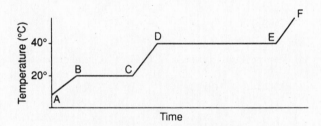
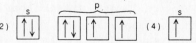
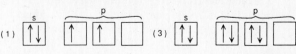

13 A white crystalline salt conducts electricity when it is melted and when it is dissolved in water. Which type of bond does this salt contain?

1 ionic
2 metallic
3 covalent
4 network

14 Which diagram best represents the structure of a water molecule?

(1)

(2)

(3) $O—H—O$

(4) $H—H—O$

15 What is the total number of moles of oxygen atoms present in 1 mole of $Mg(ClO_3)_2$?

(1) 5
(2) 2
(3) 3
(4) 6

16 Which bond has the greatest ionic character?

(1) $H—Cl$
(2) $H—F$
(3) $H—O$
(4) $H—N$

17 Which type of bonding accounts for the unusually high boiling point of water?

1 ionic bonding
2 covalent bonding
3 hydrogen bonding
4 network bonding

18 Which is the correct formula for carbon (II) oxide?

(1) CO
(2) CO_2
(3) C_2O
(4) C_2O_3

19 Based on Reference Table G, which of the following compounds is *least* stable?

(1) $CO(g)$
(2) $CO_2(g)$
(3) $HF(g)$
(4) $HI(g)$

20 Which electronegativity is possible for an alkali metal?

(1) 1.0
(2) 2.0
(3) 3.0
(4) 4.0

21 When metals form ions, they tend to do so by

1 losing electrons and forming positive ions
2 losing electrons and forming negative ions
3 gaining electrons and forming positive ions
4 gaining electrons and forming negative ions

22 Boron and arsenic are similar in that they both

1 have the same ionization energy
2 have the same covalent radius
3 are in the same family of elements
4 are metalloids (semimetals)

23 Group 18 (0) elements Kr and Xe have selected oxidation states of other than zero. These oxidation states are an indication that these elements have

1 no chemical reactivity
2 some chemical reactivity
3 stable nuclei
4 unstable nuclei

24 The color of Na_2CrO_4 is due to the presence of

1 a noble gas
2 a halogen
3 a transition element
4 an alkali metal

25 Given the reaction:

$$Ca + 2H_2O \rightarrow Ca(OH)_2 + H_2$$

What is the total number of moles of Ca needed to react completely with 4.0 moles of H_2O?

(1) 1.0
(2) 2.0
(3) 0.50
(4) 4.0

26 The percent by mass of Ca in $CaCl_2$ is equal to

(1) $\frac{40}{111} \times 100$
(2) $\frac{111}{40} \times 100$
(3) $\frac{3}{1} \times 100$
(4) $\frac{1}{3} \times 100$

27 What is the total mass of 3.01×10^{23} atoms of helium gas?

(1) 8.00 g
(2) 2.00 g
(3) 3.50 g
(4) 4.00 g

28 Given the reaction:

$$2C_2H_6(g) + 7O_2(g) \rightarrow 4CO_2(g) + 6H_2O(g)$$

What is the total number of liters of carbon dioxide formed by the complete combustion of 28.0 liters of $C_2H_6(g)$?

(1) 14.0 L
(2) 28.0 L
(3) 56.0 L
(4) 112 L

29 When sodium chloride is dissolved in water, the resulting solution is classified as a

1 heterogeneous compound
2 homogeneous compound
3 heterogeneous mixture
4 homogeneous mixture

30 According to Reference Table D, a temperature change from 60°C to 90°C has the *least* effect on the solubility of

(1) SO_2
(2) NH_3
(3) KCl
(4) $KClO_3$

31 Which series of physical changes represents an entropy increase during each change?
1 gas → liquid → solid
2 liquid → gas → solid
3 solid → gas → solid
4 solid → liquid → gas

32 Given the reaction at equilibrium:

$$2H_2(g) + O_2(g) \rightleftharpoons 2H_2O(g) + heat$$

Which concentration changes occur when the temperature of the system is increased?
1 The $[H_2]$ decreases and the $[O_2]$ decreases.
2 The $[H_2]$ decreases and the $[O_2]$ increases.
3 The $[H_2]$ increases and the $[O_2]$ decreases.
4 The $[H_2]$ increases and the $[O_2]$ increases.

33 The change of reactants into products will always be spontaneous if the products, compared to the reactants, have
1 lower enthalpy and lower entropy
2 lower enthalpy and higher entropy
3 higher enthalpy and lower entropy
4 higher enthalpy and higher entropy

Base your answers to questions 34 and 35 on the potential energy diagram of a chemical reaction shown below.

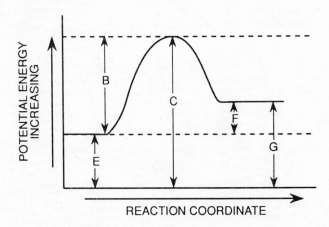

34 Which interval represents the heat of reaction ($\triangle H$)?
(1) E   (3) C
(2) F   (4) G

35 Interval B represents the
1 potential energy of the products
2 potential energy of the reactants
3 activation energy
4 activated complex

36 Based on Reference Table L, which solution best conducts electricity?
(1) 0.1 M HCl   (3) 0.1 M H_2S
(2) 0.1 M CH_3COOH (4) 0.1 M H_3PO_4

37 Based on Reference Table E, a 1-gram quantity of which salt, when placed in 250 milliliters of water and stirred, will produce a solution with the greatest electrical conductivity?
(1) AgI   (3) $AgNO_3$
(2) AgCl   (4) Ag_2CO_3

38 According to the Brönsted-Lowry theory, an acid is
1 a proton donor, only
2 a proton acceptor, only
3 a proton donor and a proton acceptor
4 neither a proton donor nor a proton acceptor

39 Which salt is formed when hydrochloric acid is neutralized by a potassium hydroxide solution?
1 potassium chloride
2 potassium chlorate
3 potassium chlorite
4 potassium perchlorate

40 Given the equation:

$$H_2O + HF \rightleftharpoons H_3O^+ + F^-$$

Which pair represents Brönsted-Lowry acids?
(1) HF and F^- (3) H_2O and F^-
(2) HF and H_3O^+ (4) H_2O and H_3O^+

41 What is the pH of a solution that has an OH^- ion concentration of 1×10^{-5} mole per liter ($K_w = 1 \times 10^{-14}$)?
(1) 1   (3) 7
(2) 5   (4) 9

42 Which half-reaction correctly represents reduction?
(1) $Fe^{2+} + 2e^- \rightarrow Fe$
(2) $Fe^{2+} + e^- \rightarrow Fe^{3+}$
(3) $Fe + 2e^- \rightarrow Fe^{2+}$
(4) $Fe + e^- \rightarrow Fe^{3+}$

43 In which compound does hydrogen have an oxidation number of –1?
(1) NH_3 (3) HCl
(2) KH   (4) H_2O

44 In the reaction $2H_2(g) + O_2(g) \rightarrow 2H_2O(g)$, the oxidizing agent is
(1) H_2 (3) H^+
(2) O_2 (4) O^{2-}

45 Which reaction occurs when a strip of magnesium metal is placed in a solution of $CuCl_2$?
1 The chloride ion is oxidized.
2 The chloride ion is reduced.
3 The magnesium metal is oxidized.
4 The magnesium metal is reduced.

46 Given the reaction:

$$Zn(s) + Cu^{2+}(aq) \rightarrow Zn^{2+}(aq) + Cu(s)$$

Which particles must be transferred from one reactant to the other reactant?

1 ions   3 protons
2 neutrons   4 electrons

47 Which redox equation is correctly balanced?

(1) $Cr^{3+} + Mg \rightarrow Cr + Mg^{2+}$
(2) $Al^{3+} + K \rightarrow Al + K^{+}$
(3) $Sn^{4+} + H_2 \rightarrow Sn + 2H^{+}$
(4) $Br_2 + Hg \rightarrow Hg^{2+} + 2Br^{-}$

48 Organic chemistry is the chemistry of compounds containing the element

1 carbon   3 nitrogen
2 hydrogen   4 oxygen

49 The isomers CH_3OCH_3 and CH_3CH_2OH differ in

1 molecular formula
2 molecular structure
3 number of atoms
4 formula mass

50 Given the molecule:

$$H-\overset{\overset{\displaystyle H}{|}}{\underset{\underset{\displaystyle H}{|}}{C}}-H$$

Replacing a hydrogen atom on this molecule with the functional group —OH will change the original properties of the molecule to those of an

1 ester   3 acid
2 ether   4 alcohol

51 Which structural formula represents a member of the series of hydrocarbons having the general formula C_nH_{2n-2}?

(1) structure of ethane

(2) structure of ethene

(3) $H-C \equiv C-H$

(4) structure of propene

52 What is the total number of valence electrons in a carbon atom in the ground state?

(1) 6   (3) 12
(2) 2   (4) 4

Note that questions 53 through 56 have only three choices.

53 As the elements of Group 17 (VIIA) are considered in order of increasing atomic number, the nonmetallic character of each successive element

1 decreases
2 increases
3 remains the same

54 As the atoms of the metals of Group 1 (IA) in the ground state are considered in order from top to bottom, the number of occupied principal energy levels

1 decreases
2 increases
3 remains the same

55 As the mass number of the isotopes of hydrogen increases, the number of protons

1 decreases
2 increases
3 remains the same

56 As $Cu(NO_3)_2$ is dissolved in pure water, the pH of the resulting solution

1 decreases
2 increases
3 remains the same

Part II

This part consists of twelve groups, each containing five questions. Each group tests a major area of the course. Choose seven of these twelve groups. Be sure that you answer all five questions in each group chosen. Record the answers to these questions on the separate answer sheet in accordance with the directions on the front page of this booklet. [35]

Group 1 — Matter and Energy

If you choose this group, be sure to answer questions 57–61.

57 Which phase change represents sublimation?

1 solid → gas   3 gas → solid
2 solid → liquid   4 gas → liquid

58 Which property of a sample of mercury is different at 320 K than at 300 K?

1 atomic mass
2 atomic radius
3 vapor pressure
4 melting point

59 Which statement describes a chemical property of the element iodine?
1 Its crystals are a metallic gray.
2 It dissolves in alcohol.
3 It forms a violet-colored gas.
4 It reacts with hydrogen to form a gas.

60 The characteristic which distinguishes a true solid from other phases of matter at STP is that in a true solid, the particles are
1 vibrating and changing their relative positions
2 vibrating without changing their relative positions
3 motionless but changing their relative positions
4 motionless without changing their relative positions

61 The volume of a given mass of an ideal gas at constant pressure is
1 directly proportional to the Kelvin temperature
2 directly proportional to the Celsius temperature
3 inversely proportional to the Kelvin temperature
4 inversely proportional to the Celsius temperature

Group 2 — Atomic Structure

If you choose this group, be sure to answer questions 62–66.

62 Neutral atoms of ^{35}Cl and ^{37}Cl differ with respect to their number of
1 electrons
2 protons
3 neutrons
4 positrons

63 What is the total number of electrons present in an atom of $^{59}_{27}Co$?
(1) 27
(2) 32
(3) 59
(4) 86

64 Which of the following atoms has the greatest nuclear charge?
(1) Al
(2) Ar
(3) Si
(4) Na

65 An element has an atomic number of 18. What is the principal quantum number (n) of its outermost electrons?
(1) 1
(2) 2
(3) 3
(4) 4

66 What is the total mass of ^{222}Rn remaining in an original 160-milligram sample of ^{222}Rn after 19.1 days?
(1) 2.5 mg
(2) 5.0 mg
(3) 10. mg
(4) 20. mg

Group 3 — Bonding

If you choose this group, be sure to answer questions 67–71.

67 In a nonpolar covalent bond, electrons are
1 located in a mobile "sea" shared by many ions
2 transferred from one atom to another
3 shared equally by two atoms
4 shared unequally by two atoms

68 Which compound has the same empirical and molecular formula?
1 acetylene
2 ethene
3 ethane
4 methane

69 When the equation
$$\_C_8H_{16} + \_O_2 \rightarrow \_CO_2 + \_H_2O$$ is correctly balanced using the smallest whole number coefficients, the coefficient of O_2 is
(1) 1
(2) 8
(3) 12
(4) 16

70 Which species can form a coordinate covalent bond with an H^+ ion?
(1) H·
(2) H:$^-$
(3) H^+
(4) H:H

71 In which chemical system are molecule-ion attractions present?
(1) KCl(g)
(2) KCl(ℓ)
(3) KCl(s)
(4) KCl(aq)

Group 4 — Periodic Table

If you choose this group, be sure to answer questions 72–76.

72 Which atom has a radius larger than the radius of its ion?
(1) Cl
(2) Ca
(3) S
(4) Se

73 The chemical properties of the elements are periodic functions of their atomic
1 masses
2 weights
3 numbers
4 radii

74 Which of the following substances is the best conductor of electricity?
(1) NaCl(s)
(2) Cu(s)
(3) $H_2O(\ell)$
(4) $Br_2(\ell)$

75 Which halogen is a solid at STP?
1 fluorine
2 chlorine
3 bromine
4 iodine

76 Atoms of nonmetals generally react with atoms of metals by
1 gaining electrons to form ionic compounds
2 gaining electrons to form covalent compounds
3 sharing electrons to form ionic compounds
4 sharing electrons to form covalent compounds

Group 5 — Mathematics of Chemistry

If you choose this group, be sure to answer questions 77–81.

77 What is the empirical formula of a compound composed of 2.8% by mass of boron and 97% by mass of iodine?

(1) BI_2 (3) BI_3

(2) B_2I (4) B_3I

78 A gas has a volume of 2 liters at 323 K and 3 atmospheres. When its temperature is changed to 273 K and the pressure is changed to 1 atmosphere, the new volume of the gas would be equal to

(1) $2 \text{ L} \times \dfrac{273 \text{ K}}{323 \text{ K}} \times \dfrac{1 \text{ atm}}{3 \text{ atm}}$

(2) $2 \text{ L} \times \dfrac{323 \text{ K}}{273 \text{ K}} \times \dfrac{1 \text{ atm}}{3 \text{ atm}}$

(3) $2 \text{ L} \times \dfrac{273 \text{ K}}{323 \text{ K}} \times \dfrac{3 \text{ atm}}{1 \text{ atm}}$

(4) $2 \text{ L} \times \dfrac{323 \text{ K}}{273 \text{ K}} \times \dfrac{3 \text{ atm}}{1 \text{ atm}}$

79 Which gas could have a density of 2.05 grams per liter at STP?

(1) N_2O_3 (3) HF

(2) NO_2 (4) HBr

80 What is the total number of calories of heat energy absorbed when 10.0 grams of water is vaporized at its normal boiling point?

(1) 7.97   (3) 5390

(2) 53.9   (4) 7970

81 How many moles of a nonvolatile, nonelectrolyte solute are required to lower the freezing point of 1,000 grams of water by 5.58 C°?

(1) 1   (3) 3

(2) 2   (4) 4

Group 6 — Kinetics and Equilibrium

If you choose this group, be sure to answer questions 82–86.

82 Based on Reference Table G, which compound forms spontaneously even though the $\triangle H$ for its formation is positive?

(1) $C_2H_4(g)$ (3) $ICl(g)$

(2) $C_2H_2(g)$ (4) $HI(g)$

83 Given the reaction at equilibrium:

$$AgCl(s) \rightleftharpoons Ag^+(aq) + Cl^-(aq)$$

The addition of Cl^- ions will cause the concentration of $Ag^+(aq)$ to

1 decrease as the amount of AgCl(s) decreases
2 decrease as the amount of AgCl(s) increases
3 increase as the amount of AgCl(s) decreases
4 increase as the amount of AgCl(s) increases

84 The expression $\triangle H - T\triangle S$ is equal to the change in

1 binding energy   3 free energy
2 ionization energy   4 activation energy

85 At room temperature, which reaction would be expected to have the fastest reaction rate?

(1) $Pb^{2+}(aq) + S^{2-}(aq) \rightarrow PbS(s)$
(2) $2H_2(g) + O_2(g) \rightarrow 2H_2O(\ell)$
(3) $N_2(g) + 2O_2(g) \rightarrow 2NO_2(g)$
(4) $2KClO_3(s) \rightarrow 2KCl(s) + 3O_2(g)$

86 Which statement is true for a saturated solution?

1 It must be a concentrated solution.
2 It must be a dilute solution.
3 Neither dissolving nor crystallizing is occurring.
4 The rate of dissolving equals the rate of crystallizing.

Group 7 — Acids and Bases

If you choose this group, be sure to answer questions 87–91.

87 When an Arrhenius base is placed in H_2O, the only negative ion present in the solution is

(1) OH^- (3) H^-

(2) H_3O^- (4) O^{2-}

88 Which solution will change red litmus to blue?

(1) $HCl(aq)$ (3) $CH_3OH(aq)$

(2) $NaCl(aq)$ (4) $NaOH(aq)$

89 A chloride ion, $[:\overset{..}{\underset{..}{Cl}}:]^-$, acts as a Brönsted base when it combines with

1 an OH^- ion   3 an H^- ion
2 a K^+ ion   4 an H^+ ion

90 Which equation illustrates amphoterism?

(1) $NaCl \rightarrow Na^+ + Cl^-$
(2) $NaOH \rightarrow Na^+ + OH^-$
(3) $H_2O + H_2O \rightarrow H_3O^+ + OH^-$
(4) $HCl + H_2O \rightarrow H_3O^+ + Cl^-$

91 In a titration, the endpoint of a neutralization reaction was reached when 37.6 milliliters of an HCl solution was added to 17.3 milliliters of a 0.250 M NaOH solution. What was the molarity of the HCl solution?

(1) 0.115 M   (3) 0.250 M
(2) 0.203 M   (4) 0.543 M

Group 8 — Redox and Electrochemistry

If you choose this group, be sure to answer questions 92–96.

Base your answers to questions 92 and 93 on the diagram below which represents an electrochemical cell.

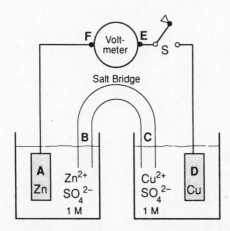

92 Which statement correctly describes the direction of flow for the ions in this cell when the switch is closed?

1 Ions move through the salt bridge from B to C, only.
2 Ions move through the salt bridge from C to B, only.
3 Ions move through the salt bridge in both directions.
4 Ions do not move through the salt bridge in either direction.

93 When the switch is closed, which group of letters correctly represents the direction of electron flow?

(1) $A \rightarrow B \rightarrow C \rightarrow D$ (3) $D \rightarrow C \rightarrow B \rightarrow A$
(2) $A \rightarrow F \rightarrow E \rightarrow D$ (4) $D \rightarrow E \rightarrow F \rightarrow A$

94 Based on Reference Table N, which metal will react with H^+ ions to produce $H_2(g)$?

(1) Au   (3) Cu
(2) Ag   (4) Mg

95 What is the standard electrode potential (E^0) assigned to the half-reaction $Cu^{2+} + 2e^- \rightarrow Cu(s)$ when compared to the standard hydrogen half-reaction?

(1) +0.34 V   (3) +0.52 V
(2) −0.34 V   (4) −0.52 V

96 Which species acts as the anode when the reaction $Zn(s) + Pb^{2+}(aq) \rightarrow Zn^{2+}(aq) + Pb(s)$ occurs in an electrochemical cell?

(1) $Zn(s)$ (3) $Pb^{2+}(aq)$
(2) $Zn^{2+}(aq)$ (4) $Pb(s)$

Group 9 — Organic Chemistry

If you choose this group, be sure to answer questions 97–101.

97 The products of condensation polymerization are a polymer and

1 carbon dioxide   3 ethanol
2 water   4 glycerol

98 Given the equation:

$$C_6H_{12}O_6 \rightarrow 2C_2H_5OH + 2CO_2$$

The chemical process illustrated by this equation is

1 fermentation   3 esterification
2 saponification   4 polymerization

99 Which two compounds are monohydroxy alcohols?

1 ethylene glycol and ethanol
2 ethylene glycol and glycerol
3 methanol and ethanol
4 methanol and glycerol

100 Which type of compound is represented by the structural formula shown below?

$$H-\underset{\underset{H}{|}}{\overset{\overset{H}{|}}{C}}-\underset{\underset{H}{|}}{\overset{\overset{H}{|}}{C}}-O-\underset{\underset{H}{|}}{\overset{\overset{H}{|}}{C}}-\underset{\underset{H}{|}}{\overset{\overset{H}{|}}{C}}-H$$

1 a ketone   3 an ester
2 an aldehyde   4 an ether

101 Which is the structural formula for 2-chlorobutane?

(1) H—C—C—C—C—H (with H H H Cl above and H H H Cl below)

(2) H—C—C—C—C—H (with H H H Cl above and H H H H below)

(3) H—C—C—C—C—H (with H Cl H H above and H H H H below)

(4) H—C—C—C—C—H (with H H Cl H above and H H Cl H below)

Group 10 — Applications of Chemical Principles

If you choose this group, be sure to answer questions 102–106.

102 Given the lead-acid battery reaction:

$$Pb + PbO_2 + 2H_2SO_4 \underset{charge}{\overset{discharge}{\rightleftharpoons}} 2PbSO_4 + 2H_2O$$

When the reaction produces electricity, which element changes oxidation states?
(1) Pb   (3) H
(2) O   (4) S

103 During fractional distillation of petroleum, which of the following fractions has the *lowest* boiling point?
(1) C_8H_{18} (3) $C_{15}H_{32}$
(2) $C_{12}H_{26}$ (4) $C_{18}H_{38}$

104 What is the original source of many textiles and most plastics?
1 coal   3 petroleum
2 wood   4 mineral ores

105 Given a reaction that occurs in the contact process:

$$2SO_2(g) + O_2(g) \rightleftharpoons 2SO_3(g) + heat$$

Adding a catalyst to this system causes the
1 activation energy to decrease
2 activation energy to increase
3 heat of reaction to decrease
4 heat of reaction to increase

106 Given the reaction:

$$2Al + Cr_2O_3 \rightarrow Al_2O_3 + 2Cr$$

When this reaction is used to produce chromium, the aluminum is acting as
1 a catalyst   3 an oxidizing agent
2 an alloy   4 a reducing agent

Group 11 — Nuclear Chemistry

If you choose this group, be sure to answer questions 107–111.

107 The diagram below shows a nuclear reaction in which a neutron is captured by a heavy nucleus.

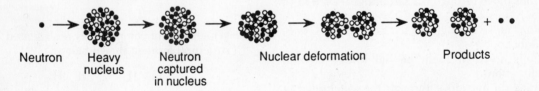

Neutron   Heavy nucleus   Neutron captured in nucleus   Nuclear deformation   Products

Which type of reaction is illustrated by the diagram?
1 an endothermic fission reaction
2 an exothermic fission reaction
3 an endothermic fusion reaction
4 an exothermic fusion reaction

108 Heavy water and graphite are two examples of materials that can be used in a nuclear reactor to slow down neutrons. These materials are called
1 fuels   3 coolants
2 shields   4 moderators

110 Which radioisotope is used to diagnose thyroid disorders?
1 cobalt-60   3 technetium-99
2 iodine-131   4 uranium-238

111 Given the transmutation:

$$^1_0n + ^{235}_{92}U \rightarrow ^{141}_{56}Ba + X + 3^1_0n$$

The element X has an atomic number of
(1) 36   (3) 92
(2) 89   (4) 93

Which particle can *not* be accelerated in a magnetic field?
ha particle   3 neutron
particle   4 proton

Group 12 — Laboratory Activities

If you choose this group, be sure to answer questions 112–116.

112 Which diagram represents a test tube holder (clamp)?

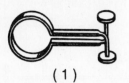

(1)

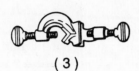

(3)

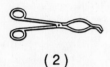

(2)

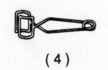

(4)

113 In a laboratory exercise to determine the volume of a mole of a gas at STP, a student determines the volume to be 2.25 liters greater than the accepted value of 22.4 liters. The percent error in the student's value is
(1) 2.25 %
(3) 20.2 %
(2) 10.0 %
(4) 24.7 %

114 To determine the density of an irregularly shaped object, a student immersed the object in 21.2 milliliters of H_2O in a graduated cylinder, causing the level of the H_2O to rise to 27.8 milliliters. If the object had a mass of 22.4 grams, what was the density of the object?
(1) 27.8 g/mL
(3) 3.0 g/mL
(2) 6.6 g/mL
(4) 3.4 g/mL

115 A material will be used to fill an empty beaker to level A, as shown in the diagram below.

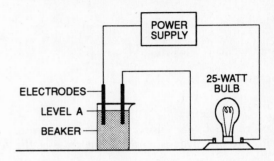

Which material, when used to fill the beaker to level A, would cause the bulb to glow brightly?
(1) $C_6H_{12}O_6(s)$
(3) KCl(s)
(2) $C_6H_{12}O_6(aq)$
(4) KCl(aq)

116 A solid is dissolved in a beaker of water. Which observation suggests that the process is endothermic?
1 The solution gives off a gas.
2 The solution changes color.
3 The temperature of the solution decreases.
4 The temperature of the solution increases.

CHEMISTRY
JUNE 1993

ANSWER SHEET

Pupil..

Teacher..

School..

Record all of your answers on this answer sheet in accordance with the instructions on the front page of the test booklet.

Part I (65 credits)

1	1 2 3 4	21	1 2 3 4	41	1 2 3 4
2	1 2 3 4	22	1 2 3 4	42	1 2 3 4
3	1 2 3 4	23	1 2 3 4	43	1 2 3 4
4	1 2 3 4	24	1 2 3 4	44	1 2 3 4
5	1 2 3 4	25	1 2 3 4	45	1 2 3 4
6	1 2 3 4	26	1 2 3 4	46	1 2 3 4
7	1 2 3 4	27	1 2 3 4	47	1 2 3 4
8	1 2 3 4	28	1 2 3 4	48	1 2 3 4
9	1 2 3 4	29	1 2 3 4	49	1 2 3 4
10	1 2 3 4	30	1 2 3 4	50	1 2 3 4
11	1 2 3 4	31	1 2 3 4	51	1 2 3 4
12	1 2 3 4	32	1 2 3 4	52	1 2 3 4
13	1 2 3 4	33	1 2 3 4	53	1 2 3
14	1 2 3 4	34	1 2 3 4	54	1 2 3
15	1 2 3 4	35	1 2 3 4	55	1 2 3
16	1 2 3 4	36	1 2 3 4	56	1 2 3
17	1 2 3 4	37	1 2 3 4		
18	1 2 3 4	38	1 2 3 4		
19	1 2 3 4	39	1 2 3 4		
20	1 2 3 4	40	1 2 3 4		

Part II (35 credits)

Answer the questions in only seven of the twelve groups in this part. Be sure to mark the answers to the groups of questions you choose in accordance with the instructions on the front cover of the test booklet. Leave blank the five groups of questions you do not choose to answer.

Group 1 Matter and Energy				
57	1	2	3	4
58	1	2	3	4
59	1	2	3	4
60	1	2	3	4
61	1	2	3	4

Group 2 Atomic Structure				
62	1	2	3	4
63	1	2	3	4
64	1	2	3	4
65	1	2	3	4
66	1	2	3	4

Group 3 Bonding				
67	1	2	3	4
68	1	2	3	4
69	1	2	3	4
70	1	2	3	4
71	1	2	3	4

Group 4 Periodic Table				
72	1	2	3	4
73	1	2	3	4
74	1	2	3	4
75	1	2	3	4
76	1	2	3	4

Group 5 Mathematics of Chemistry				
77	1	2	3	4
78	1	2	3	4
79	1	2	3	4
80	1	2	3	4
81	1	2	3	4

Group 6 Kinetics and Equilibrium				
82	1	2	3	4
83	1	2	3	4
84	1	2	3	4
85	1	2	3	4
86	1	2	3	4

Group 7 Acids and Bases				
87	1	2	3	4
88	1	2	3	4
89	1	2	3	4
90	1	2	3	4
91	1	2	3	4

Group 8 Redox and Electrochemistry				
92	1	2	3	4
93	1	2	3	4
94	1	2	3	4
95	1	2	3	4
96	1	2	3	4

Group 9 Organic Chemistry				
97	1	2	3	4
98	1	2	3	4
99	1	2	3	4
100	1	2	3	4
101	1	2	3	4

Group 10 Applications of Chemical Principles				
102	1	2	3	4
103	1	2	3	4
104	1	2	3	4
105	1	2	3	4
106	1	2	3	4

Group 11 Nuclear Chemistry				
107	1	2	3	4
108	1	2	3	4
109	1	2	3	4
110	1	2	3	4
111	1	2	3	4

Group 12 Laboratory Activities				
112	1	2	3	4
113	1	2	3	4
114	1	2	3	4
115	1	2	3	4
116	1	2	3	4

CHEMISTRY
JUNE 1994

Part I

Answer all 56 questions in this part. [65]

Directions (1–56): For *each* statement or question, select the word or expression that, of those given, best completes the statement or answers the question. Record your answer on the separate answer sheet in accordance with the directions on the front page of this booklet.

1 The amount of energy needed to change a given mass of ice to water at constant temperature is called the heat of
1 condensation   3 fusion
2 crystallization   4 formation

2 Which equation represents the phase change called sublimation?
(1) $CO_2(s) \rightarrow CO_2(g)$
(2) $H_2O(s) \rightarrow H_2O(\ell)$
(3) $H_2O(\ell) \rightarrow H_2O(g)$
(4) $NaCl(\ell) \rightarrow NaCl(s)$

3 Which substance can *not* be decomposed into simpler substances?
1 ammonia   3 methane
2 aluminum   4 methanol

4 In which sample are the particles arranged in a regular geometric pattern?
(1) $HCl(\ell)$ (3) $N_2(g)$
(2) $NaCl(aq)$ (4) $I_2(s)$

5 How many calories are equivalent to 35 kilocalories?
(1) 0.035 calorie   (3) 3,500 calories
(2) 0.35 calorie   (4) 35,000 calories

6 How does the ground state electron configuration of the hydrogen atom differ from that of a ground state helium atom?
1 Hydrogen has one electron in a higher energy level.
2 Hydrogen has two electrons in a lower energy level.
3 Hydrogen contains a half-filled orbital.
4 Hydrogen contains a completely filled orbital.

7 Which type of radiation would be attracted to the positive electrode in an electric field?
(1) $_{-1}^{0}e$ (3) $_{2}^{3}He$
(2) $_{1}^{1}H$ (4) $_{0}^{1}n$

8 Which electron configuration represents an atom in an excited state?
(1) $1s^2 2s^2$ (3) $1s^2 2s^2 2p^6$
(2) $1s^2 2s^2 3s^1$ (4) $1s^2 2s^2 2p^6 3s^1$

9 Which electron transition represents the release of energy?
(1) $1s$ to $3p$ (3) $3p$ to $1s$
(2) $2s$ to $2p$ (4) $2p$ to $3s$

10 The atomic number of any atom is equal to the number of
1 neutrons in the atom, only
2 protons in the atom, only
3 neutrons plus protons in the atom
4 protons plus electrons in the atom

11 The mass of an electron is approximately $\frac{1}{1836}$ times the mass of
(1) $_{1}^{1}H$ (3) $_{1}^{3}H$
(2) $_{1}^{2}H$ (4) $_{2}^{4}He$

12 Which nuclear reaction is classified as alpha decay?
(1) $_{6}^{14}C \rightarrow _{7}^{14}N + _{-1}^{0}e$
(2) $_{19}^{42}K \rightarrow _{20}^{42}Ca + _{-1}^{0}e$
(3) $_{88}^{226}Ra \rightarrow _{86}^{222}Rn + _{2}^{4}He$
(4) $_{1}^{3}H \rightarrow _{-1}^{0}e + _{2}^{3}He$

13 Which diagram correctly shows the relationship between electronegativity and atomic number for the elements of Period 3?

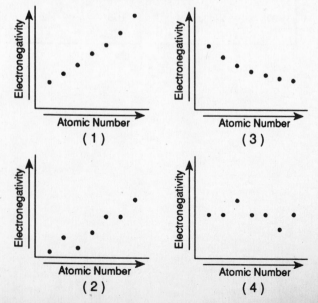

14 Which statement is true concerning the reaction $N(g) + N(g) \rightarrow N_2(g)$ + energy?

1 A bond is broken and energy is absorbed.
2 A bond is broken and energy is released.
3 A bond is formed and energy is absorbed.
4 A bond is formed and energy is released.

15 Hydrogen bonding is strongest between molecules of

(1) H_2S (3) H_2Se
(2) H_2O (4) H_2Te

16 A chemical formula is an expression used to represent

1 mixtures, only
2 elements, only
3 compounds, only
4 compounds and elements

17 When calcium chloride is dissolved in water, to which end of the adjacent water molecules will a calcium ion be attracted?

1 the oxygen end, which is the negative pole
2 the oxygen end, which is the positive pole
3 the hydrogen end, which is the negative pole
4 the hydrogen end, which is the positive pole

18 How do the chemical properties of the Na atom and the Na^+ ion compare?

1 They are the same because each has the same atomic number.
2 They are the same because each has the same electron configuration.
3 They are different because each has a different atomic number.
4 They are different because each has a different electron configuration.

19 Which element in Group 16 (VIA) has *no* stable isotopes?

1 sulfur   3 tellurium
2 selenium   4 polonium

20 Which element is a member of the halogen family?

(1) K   (3) I
(2) B   (4) S

21 Most nonmetals have the properties of

1 high ionization energy and poor electrical conductivity
2 high ionization energy and good electrical conductivity
3 low ionization energy and poor electrical conductivity
4 low ionization energy and good electrical conductivity

22 The metalloids that are included in Group 15 (VA) are antimony (Sb) and

(1) N   (3) As
(2) P   (4) Bi

23 Which of the following atoms has the largest atomic radius?

(1) Na   (3) Mg
(2) K   (4) Ca

24 In which group does each element have a total of four electrons in the outermost principal energy level?

(1) 1 (IA)   (3) 16 (VIA)
(2) 18 (0)   (4) 14 (IVA)

25 Which properties are characteristic of the Group 1 (IA) metals?

1 high reactivity and the formation of stable compounds
2 high reactivity and the formation of unstable compounds
3 low reactivity and the formation of stable compounds
4 low reactivity and the formation of unstable compounds

26 Which quantity is equivalent to 39 grams of LiF?

(1) 1.0 mole   (3) 0.50 mole
(2) 2.0 moles   (4) 1.5 moles

27 Which quantity represents 0.500 mole at STP?

(1) 22.4 liters of nitrogen
(2) 11.2 liters of oxygen
(3) 32.0 grams of oxygen
(4) 28.0 grams of nitrogen

28 When 0.50 liter of a 12 M solution is diluted to 1.0 liter, the molarity of the new solution is

(1) 6.0 M   (3) 12 M
(2) 2.4 M   (4) 24 M

29 What is the percent by mass of oxygen in Fe_2O_3 (formula mass = 160)?

(1) 16%   (3) 56%
(2) 30.%   (4) 70.%

30 Given the equation:

$$6CO_2(g) + 6H_2O(\ell) \rightarrow C_6H_{12}O_6(s) + 6O_2(g)$$

What is the *minimum* number of liters of $CO_2(g)$, measured at STP, needed to produce 32.0 grams of oxygen?

(1) 264 L   (3) 32.0 L
(2) 192 L   (4) 22.4 L

31 Given the reaction:

$$Mg(s) + 2HCl(aq) \rightarrow MgCl_2(aq) + H_2(g)$$

The reaction occurs more rapidly when a 10-gram sample of Mg is powdered, rather than in one piece, because powdered Mg has

1 less surface area
2 more surface area
3 a lower potential energy
4 a higher potential energy

32 According to Reference Table *I*, in which reaction do the products have a higher energy content than the reactants?

(1) $CH_4(g) + 2O_2(g) \rightarrow CO_2(g) + 2H_2O(\ell)$

(2) $CH_3OH(\ell) + \frac{3}{2}O_2(g) \rightarrow CO_2(g) + 2H_2O(\ell)$

(3) $NH_4Cl(s) \xrightarrow{H_2O} NH_4^+(aq) + Cl^-(aq)$

(4) $NaOH(s) \xrightarrow{H_2O} Na^+(aq) + OH^-(aq)$

33 Which equation correctly represents the free energy change in a chemical reaction?
(1) $\Delta G = \Delta H + T\Delta S$
(2) $\Delta G = \Delta H - T\Delta S$
(3) $\Delta G = \Delta T - \Delta H\Delta S$
(4) $\Delta G = \Delta S - T\Delta H$

34 Adding a catalyst to a chemical reaction will
1 lower the activation energy needed
2 lower the potential energy of the reactants
3 increase the activation energy needed
4 increase the potential energy of the reactants

35 Under which conditions are gases most soluble in water?
1 high pressure and high temperature
2 high pressure and low temperature
3 low pressure and high temperature
4 low pressure and low temperature

36 A solution of a base differs from a solution of an acid in that the solution of a base
1 is able to conduct electricity
2 is able to cause an indicator color change
3 has a greater $[H_3O^+]$
4 has a greater $[OH^-]$

37 Given the reaction:

$HCl(g) + H_2O(\ell) \rightarrow H_3O^+(aq) + Cl^-(aq)$

Which reactant acted as a Brönsted-Lowry acid?
(1) HCl(g), because it reacted with chloride ions
(2) $H_2O(\ell)$, because it produced hydronium ions
(3) HCl(g), because it donated protons
(4) $H_2O(\ell)$, because it accepted protons

38 Which of the following aqueous solutions is the *poorest* conductor of electricity? [Refer to Reference Table L]
(1) 0.1 M H_2S
(2) 0.1 M HF
(3) 0.1 M HNO_2
(4) 0.1 M HNO_3

39 According to the Arrhenius theory, the acidic property of an aqueous solution is due to an excess of
(1) H_2
(2) H^+
(3) H_2O
(4) OH^-

40 Which pH value indicates the most basic solution?
(1) 7
(2) 8
(3) 3
(4) 11

41 A 3.0-milliliter sample of HNO_3 solution is exactly neutralized by 6.0 milliliters of 0.50 M KOH. What is the molarity of the HNO_3 sample?
(1) 1.0 M
(2) 0.50 M
(3) 3.0 M
(4) 1.5 M

42 As 100 milliliters of 0.10 molar KOH is added to 100 milliliters of 0.10 molar HCl at 298 K, the pH of the resulting solution will
1 decrease to 3
2 decrease to 14
3 increase to 7
4 increase to 13

43 What is the oxidation number of oxygen in HSO_4^-?
(1) +1
(2) –2
(3) +6
(4) –4

44 Which half-reaction correctly represents a reduction reaction?
(1) $Sn^0 + 2e^- \rightarrow Sn^{2+}$
(2) $Na^0 + e^- \rightarrow Na^+$
(3) $Li^0 + e^- \rightarrow Li^+$
(4) $Br_2^0 + 2e^- \rightarrow 2Br^-$

45 Given the reaction:
$2Na + 2H_2O \rightarrow 2Na^+ + 2OH^- + H_2$
Which substance is oxidized?
(1) H_2
(2) H^+
(3) Na
(4) Na^+

46 Which change occurs when an Sn^{2+} ion is oxidized?
1 Two electrons are lost.
2 Two electrons are gained.
3 Two protons are lost.
4 Two protons are gained.

47 Based on Reference Table *N*, which of the following elements is the strongest reducing agent?
(1) Fe
(2) Sr
(3) Cu
(4) Cr

48 An electrochemical cell that generates electricity contains half-cells that produce
1 oxidation half-reactions, only
2 reduction half-reactions, only
3 spontaneous redox reactions
4 nonspontaneous redox reactions

49 Which structural formula represents a molecule of butane?

(1)
$$H-\underset{H}{\overset{H}{C}}=\underset{H}{\overset{H}{C}}-\underset{}{\overset{H}{C}}=\underset{}{\overset{H}{C}}-H$$

(2)
$$H-\underset{H}{\overset{H}{C}}-\underset{}{\overset{H}{C}}=\underset{}{\overset{H}{C}}-\underset{H}{\overset{H}{C}}-H$$

(3)
$$H-\underset{H}{\overset{H}{C}}-\underset{H}{\overset{H}{C}}-\underset{H}{\overset{H}{C}}-\underset{H}{\overset{H}{C}}-H$$

(4)
$$H-C\equiv C-\underset{H}{\overset{H}{C}}-\underset{H}{\overset{H}{C}}-H$$

50 If a hydrocarbon molecule contains a triple bond, its IUPAC name ends in

1 "ane"   3 "one"
2 "ene"   4 "yne"

51 Which compound is an organic acid?

(1) CH_3OH (3) CH_3COOH
(2) CH_3OCH_3 (4) CH_3COOCH_3

52 Which structural formula represents the product formed from the reaction of Cl_2 and C_2H_4?

(1)
$$H-\underset{Cl}{\overset{H}{C}}-\underset{Cl}{\overset{H}{C}}-H$$

(2)
$$H-\underset{}{\overset{Cl}{C}}=\underset{}{\overset{Cl}{C}}-H$$

(3) $H-C\equiv C-Cl$

(4)
$$H-\underset{H}{\overset{H}{C}}-\underset{H}{\overset{H}{C}}-Cl$$

53 Which homologous series contains the compound toluene?

1 alkene   3 alkyne
2 benzene   4 alkane

Note that questions 54 through 56 have only three choices.

54 As the elements in Group 17 (VIIA) are considered in order from top to bottom, the strength of the van der Waals forces between the atoms of each successive element is

1 less   3 the same
2 greater

55 As the number of effective collisions between the reactant particles in a chemical reaction decreases, the rate of the reaction

1 decreases   3 remains the same
2 increases

56 A sealed container of nitrogen gas contains 6×10^{23} molecules at STP. As the temperature increases, the mass of the nitrogen will

1 decrease
2 increase
3 remain the same

Part II

This part consists of twelve groups, each containing five questions. Each group tests a major area of the course. Choose seven of these twelve groups. Be sure that you answer all five questions in each group chosen. Record the answers to these questions on the separate answer sheet in accordance with the directions on the front page of this booklet.   [35]

Group 1 — Matter and Energy

If you choose this group, be sure to answer questions 57–61.

57 Which pair must represent atoms of the same element?

(1) $^{14}_{6}X$ and $^{14}_{7}X$ (3) $^{2}_{1}X$ and $^{4}_{2}X$
(2) $^{12}_{6}X$ and $^{13}_{6}X$ (4) $^{13}_{6}X$ and $^{14}_{7}X$

58 Which graph best represents a change of phase from a gas to a solid?

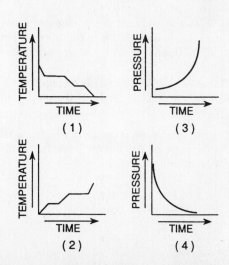

59 At 1 atmosphere and 20°C, all samples of $H_2O(\ell)$ must have the same

1 mass   3 volume
2 density   4 weight

60 The total quantity of molecules contained in 5.6 liters of a gas at STP is

(1) 1.0 mole   (3) 0.50 mole
(2) 0.75 mole   (4) 0.25 mole

61 A sample of gas has a volume of 2.0 liters at a pressure of 1.0 atmosphere. When the volume increases to 4.0 liters, at constant temperature, the pressure will be

(1) 1.0 atm   (3) 0.50 atm
(2) 2.0 atm   (4) 0.25 atm

Group 2 — Atomic Structure

If you choose this group, be sure to answer questions 62–66.

62 Which radioactive sample would contain the greatest remaining mass of the radioactive isotope after 10 years?

(1) 2.0 grams of ^{198}Au (3) 4.0 grams of ^{32}P
(2) 2.0 grams of ^{42}K (4) 4.0 grams of ^{60}Co

63 Neutral atoms of the same element can differ in their number of

1 neutrons   3 protons
2 positrons   4 electrons

64 In which reaction is the first ionization energy greatest?

(1) $Na + energy \rightarrow Na^+ + e^-$
(2) $K + energy \rightarrow K^+ + e^-$
(3) $Mg + energy \rightarrow Mg^+ + e^-$
(4) $Al + energy \rightarrow Al^+ + e^-$

65 If 75.0% of the isotopes of an element have a mass of 35.0 amu and 25.0% of the isotopes have a mass of 37.0 amu, what is the atomic mass of the element?

(1) 35.0 amu   (3) 36.0 amu
(2) 35.5 amu   (4) 37.0 amu

66 What is the maximum number of electrons that may be present in the fourth principal energy level of an atom?

(1) 8   (3) 18
(2) 2   (4) 32

Group 3 — Bonding

If you choose this group, be sure to answer questions 67–71.

67 Which compound contains ionic bonds?

(1) N_2O (3) CO
(2) Na_2O (4) CO_2

68 What is the total number of moles of atoms in one mole of $(NH_4)_2SO_4$?

(1) 10   (3) 14
(2) 11   (4) 15

69 A substance was found to be a soft, nonconducting solid at room temperature. The substance is most likely

1 a molecular solid   3 a metallic solid
2 a network solid   4 an ionic solid

70 Two atoms with an electronegativity difference of 0.4 form a bond that is

1 ionic, because electrons are shared
2 ionic, because electrons are transferred
3 covalent, because electrons are shared
4 covalent, because electrons are transferred

71 Which species contains a coordinate covalent bond?

(1) $Cl \cdot Cl$ (3) $Na^+ [Cl]^-$

(2) $H \cdot Cl$ (4) $\left[H \cdot N \cdot H \right]^+$ with H above and below N

Group 4 — Periodic Table

If you choose this group, be sure to answer questions 72–76.

72 As the elements Li to F in Period 2 of the Periodic Table are considered in succession, how do the relative electronegativity and the covalent radius of each successive element compare?

1 The relative electronegativity decreases, and the covalent radius decreases.
2 The relative electronegativity decreases, and the covalent radius increases.
3 The relative electronegativity increases, and the covalent radius decreases.
4 The relative electronegativity increases, and the covalent radius increases.

73 A characteristic of most nonmetallic solids is that they are

1 brittle
2 ductile
3 malleable
4 conductors of electricity

74 In which category of elements in the Periodic Table do all of the atoms have valence electrons in the second principal energy level?
1 Group 2 (IIA)
2 Period 2
3 the alkaline earth family
4 the alkali metals family

75 Which element can form a chloride with a general formula of MCl_2 or MCl_3?

(1) Fe   (3) Mg
(2) Al   (4) Zn

76 Which ion has the same electron configuration as an H^- ion?

(1) Cl^- (3) K^+
(2) F^- (4) Li^+

Group 5 — Mathematics of Chemistry

If you choose this group, be sure to answer questions 77–81.

77 What is the molecular formula of a compound with the empirical formula P_2O_5 and a gram-molecular mass of 284 grams?

(1) P_2O_5 (3) $P_{10}O_4$
(2) P_5O_2 (4) P_4O_{10}

78 How many molecules are in 0.25 mole of CO?

(1) 1.5×10^{23} (3) 3.0×10^{23}
(2) 6.0×10^{23} (4) 9.0×10^{23}

79 If the pressure and Kelvin temperature of 2.00 moles of an ideal gas at STP are doubled, the resulting volume will be

(1) 5.60 L   (3) 22.4 L
(2) 11.2 L   (4) 44.8 L

80 The freezing point of a 1.00-molal solution of $C_2H_4(OH)_2$ is closest to

(1) $+1.86°C$ (3) $-3.72°C$
(2) $-1.86°C$ (4) $+3.72°C$

81 The molarity (M) of a solution is equal to the

(1) $\dfrac{\text{number of grams of solute}}{\text{liter of solvent}}$

(2) $\dfrac{\text{number of grams of solute}}{\text{liter of solution}}$

(3) $\dfrac{\text{number of moles of solute}}{\text{liter of solvent}}$

(4) $\dfrac{\text{number of moles of solute}}{\text{liter of solution}}$

Group 6 — Kinetics and Equilibrium

If you choose this group, be sure to answer questions 82–86.

82 Given the reaction at equilibrium:

$$Mg(OH)_2(s) \rightleftharpoons Mg^{2+}(aq) + 2OH^-(aq)$$

The solubility product constant for this reaction is correctly written as

(1) $K_{sp} = [Mg^{2+}][2OH^-]$

(2) $K_{sp} = [Mg^{2+}] + [2OH^-]$

(3) $K_{sp} = [Mg^{2+}][OH^-]^2$

(4) $K_{sp} = [Mg^{2+}] + [OH^-]^2$

83 Based on Reference Table D, which salt solution could contain 42 grams of solute per 100 grams of water at 40°C?
1 a saturated solution of $KClO_3$
2 a saturated solution of KCl
3 an unsaturated solution of NaCl
4 an unsaturated solution of NH_4Cl

84 The value of the equilibrium constant of a chemical reaction will change when there is an increase in the
1 temperature
2 pressure
3 concentration of the reactants
4 concentration of the products

85 Given a saturated solution of silver chloride at constant temperature:

$$AgCl(s) \rightleftharpoons Ag^+(aq) + Cl^-(aq)$$

As NaCl(s) is dissolved in the solution, the concentration of the Ag^+ ions in the solution
1 decreases, and the concentration of Cl^- ions increases
2 decreases, and the concentration of Cl^- ions remains the same
3 increases, and the concentration of Cl^- ions increases
4 increases, and the concentration of Cl^- ions remains the same

86 In which reaction will the point of equilibrium shift to the left when the pressure on the system is increased?

(1) $C(s) + O_2(g) \rightleftharpoons CO_2(g)$
(2) $CaCO_3(s) \rightleftharpoons CaO(s) + CO_2(g)$
(3) $2Mg(s) + O_2(g) \rightleftharpoons 2MgO(s)$
(4) $2H_2(g) + O_2(g) \rightleftharpoons 2H_2O(g)$

Group 7 — Acids and Bases

If you choose this group, be sure to answer questions 87–91.

87 If an aqueous solution turns blue litmus red, which relationship exists between the hydronium ion and hydroxide ion concentrations?

(1) $[H_3O^+] > [OH^-]$
(2) $[H_3O^+] < [OH^-]$
(3) $[H_3O^+] = [OH^-] = 10^{-7}$
(4) $[H_3O^+] = [OH^-] = 10^{-14}$

88 Which metal will react with hydrochloric acid and produce $H_2(g)$?

(1) Au   (3) Mg
(2) Cu   (4) Hg

89 The concentration of hydrogen ions in a solution is 1.0×10^{-5} M at 298 K. What is the concentration of hydroxide ions in the same solution?

(1) 1.0×10^{-14} M   (3) 1.0×10^{-7} M
(2) 1.0×10^{-9} M   (4) 1.0×10^{-5} M

90 Given the reactions X and Y below:

$$X: H_2O + NH_3 \rightarrow NH_4^+ + OH^-$$
$$Y: H_2O + HSO_4^- \rightarrow H_3O^+ + SO_4^{2-}$$

Which statement describes the behavior of the H_2O in these reactions?

1 Water acts as an acid in both reactions.
2 Water acts as a base in both reactions.
3 Water acts as an acid in reaction X and as a base in reaction Y.
4 Water acts as a base in reaction X and as an acid in reaction Y.

91 In the reaction
$H_2PO_4^- + H_2O \rightleftharpoons H_3PO_4 + OH^-$, which pair represents an acid and its conjugate base?

(1) H_2O and $H_2PO_4^-$
(2) H_2O and H_3PO_4
(3) H_3PO_4 and OH^-
(4) H_3PO_4 and $H_2PO_4^-$

Group 8 — Redox and Electrochemistry

If you choose this group, be sure to answer questions 92–96.

92 Based on Reference Table N, which half-cell has a lower reduction potential than the standard hydrogen half-cell?

(1) $Cu^{2+} + 2e^- \rightarrow Cu(s)$
(2) $Fe^{2+} + 2e^- \rightarrow Fe(s)$
(3) $I_2(s) + 2e^- \rightarrow 2I^-$
(4) $Cl_2(g) + 2e^- \rightarrow 2Cl^-$

93 Which equation represents a redox reaction?

(1) $2Na^+ + S^{2-} \rightarrow Na_2S$
(2) $H^+ + C_2H_3O_2^- \rightarrow HC_2H_3O_2$
(3) $NH_3 + H^+ + Cl^- \rightarrow NH_4^+ + Cl^-$
(4) $Cu + 2Ag^+ + 2NO_3^- \rightarrow$
      $2Ag + Cu^{2+} + 2NO_3^-$

94 Which half-reaction shows both the conservation of mass and the conservation of charge?

(1) $Cl_2 + 2e^- \rightarrow 2Cl^-$
(2) $Cl_2 \rightarrow Cl^- + 2e^-$
(3) $2Br^- + 2e^- \rightarrow Br_2$
(4) $Br^- \rightarrow Br_2 + 2e^-$

95 In an electrolytic cell, to which electrode will a positive ion migrate and undergo reduction?

1 the anode, which is negatively charged
2 the anode, which is positively charged
3 the cathode, which is negatively charged
4 the cathode, which is positively charged

96 Given the equation:

$$\_KMnO_4 + \_HCl \rightarrow$$
$$\_KCl + \_MnCl_2 + \_Cl_2 + \_H_2O$$

What is the coefficient of H_2O when the equation is correctly balanced?

(1) 8   (3) 16
(2) 2   (4) 4

Group 9 — Organic Chemistry

If you choose this group, be sure to answer questions 97–101.

97 Which is a product of a condensation reaction?

(1) O_2 (3) H_2
(2) CO_2 (4) H_2O

98 A molecule of ethane and a molecule of ethene both have the same

1 empirical formula
2 molecular formula
3 number of carbon atoms
4 number of hydrogen atoms

99 Which is an example of a monohydroxy alcohol?

1 methanal   3 glycol
2 methanol   4 glycerol

100 Which property is generally characteristic of an organic compound?

1 low melting point
2 high melting point
3 soluble in polar solvents
4 insoluble in nonpolar solvents

101 Which is the structural formula of an aldehyde?

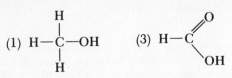

Group 10 — Applications of Chemical Principles

If you choose this group, be sure to answer questions 102–106.

102 Given the reaction for the nickel-cadmium battery:

$$2NiOOH + Cd + 2H_2O \rightarrow$$
$$2Ni(OH)_2 + Cd(OH)_2$$

Which species is oxidized during the discharge of the battery?

(1) Ni^{3+} (3) Cd
(2) Ni^{2+} (4) Cd^{2+}

103 Petroleum is a natural source of

1 alcohols   3 esters
2 hydrocarbons   4 ketones

104 Which acid is formed during the contact process?

(1) HNO_2 (3) H_2SO_4
(2) HNO_3 (4) H_2S

105 Group 1 and Group 2 metals are obtained commercially from their fused compounds by

1 reduction with CO
2 reduction by heat
3 reduction with Al
4 electrolytic reduction

106 Which balanced equation represents a cracking reaction?

(1) $C_4H_{10} \rightarrow C_2H_6 + C_2H_4$
(2) $C_4H_8 + 6O_2 \rightarrow 4CO_2 + 4H_2O$
(3) $C_4H_{10} + Br_2 \rightarrow C_4H_9Br + HBr$
(4) $C_4H_8 + Br_2 \rightarrow C_4H_8Br_2$

Group 11 — Nuclear Chemistry

If you choose this group, be sure to answer questions 107–111.

107 Bombarding a nucleus with high-energy particles that change it from one element into another is called

1 a half-reaction
2 a breeder reaction
3 artificial transmutation
4 natural transmutation

108 Given the nuclear reaction:

$$^{14}_{7}N + ^{4}_{2}He \rightarrow ^{1}_{1}H + X$$

Which isotope is represented by the X when the equation is correctly balanced?

(1) $^{17}_{8}O$ (3) $^{17}_{9}F$
(2) $^{18}_{8}O$ (4) $^{18}_{9}F$

109 Which conditions are required to form $^{4}_{2}He$ during the fusion reaction in the Sun?

1 high temperature and low pressure
2 high temperature and high pressure
3 low temperature and low pressure
4 low temperature and high pressure

110 The temperature levels in a nuclear reactor are maintained primarily by the use of

1 shielding   3 moderators
2 coolants   4 control rods

111 In an experiment, radioactive $Pb^*(NO_3)_2$ [* indicates radioactive Pb^{2+} ions] was added to the following equilibrium system:

$$PbCl_2(s) \rightleftharpoons Pb^{2+}(aq) + 2Cl^-(aq)$$

When equilibrium was reestablished, some of the $PbCl_2(s)$ was recovered from the system and dried. Testing showed the $PbCl_2(s)$ was radioactive. Which statement is best supported by this result?

1 At equilibrium, the rates of chemical change are equal.
2 At equilibrium, the rates of chemical change are unequal.
3 The process of dynamic equilibrium is demonstrated.
4 The process of dynamic equilibrium is not demonstrated.

Group 12 — Laboratory Activities

If you choose this group, be sure to answer questions 112–116.

112 Which diagram represents an Erlenmeyer flask?

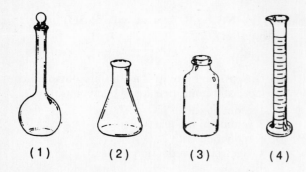

(1)   (2)   (3)   (4)

113 Salt *A* and salt *B* were dissolved separately in 100-milliliter beakers of water. The water temperatures were measured and recorded as shown in the table below.

	Salt A	Salt B
Initial water temperature:	25.1°C	25.1°C
Final water temperature:	30.2°C	20.0°C

Which statement is a correct interpretation of these data?

1 The dissolving of only salt *A* was endothermic.
2 The dissolving of only salt *B* was exothermic.
3 The dissolving of both salt *A* and salt *B* was endothermic.
4 The dissolving of salt *A* was exothermic and the dissolving of salt *B* was endothermic.

114 Which measurement has the greatest number of significant figures?
(1) 6.060 mg
(2) 60.6 mg
(3) 606 mg
(4) 60600 mg

115 The graph below was constructed by a student to show the relationship between temperature and time as heat was uniformly added to a solid below its melting point.

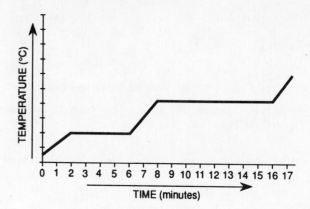

What is the total length of time that the solid phase was in equilibrium with the liquid phase?
(1) 6 min
(2) 10 min
(3) 8 min
(4) 4 min

116 The following data were collected at the endpoint of a titration performed to find the molarity of an HCl solution.

Volume of acid (HCl) used = 14.4 mL
Volume of base (NaOH) used = 22.4 mL
Molarity of standard base (NaOH) = 0.20 M

What is the molarity of the acid solution?
(1) 1.6 M
(2) 0.64 M
(3) 0.31 M
(4) 0.13 M

CHEMISTRY
JUNE 1994

ANSWER SHEET

Pupil ....

Teacher...

School...

Record all of your answers on this answer sheet in accordance with the instructions on the front page of the test booklet.

Part I (65 credits)

1	1	2	3	4	**21**	1	2	3	4	**41**	1	2	3	4
2	1	2	3	4	**22**	1	2	3	4	**42**	1	2	3	4
3	1	2	3	4	**23**	1	2	3	4	**43**	1	2	3	4
4	1	2	3	4	**24**	1	2	3	4	**44**	1	2	3	4
5	1	2	3	4	**25**	1	2	3	4	**45**	1	2	3	4
6	1	2	3	4	**26**	1	2	3	4	**46**	1	2	3	4
7	1	2	3	4	**27**	1	2	3	4	**47**	1	2	3	4
8	1	2	3	4	**28**	1	2	3	4	**48**	1	2	3	4
9	1	2	3	4	**29**	1	2	3	4	**49**	1	2	3	4
10	1	2	3	4	**30**	1	2	3	4	**50**	1	2	3	4
11	1	2	3	4	**31**	1	2	3	4	**51**	1	2	3	4
12	1	2	3	4	**32**	1	2	3	4	**52**	1	2	3	4
13	1	2	3	4	**33**	1	2	3	4	**53**	1	2	3	4
14	1	2	3	4	**34**	1	2	3	4	**54**	1	2	3	
15	1	2	3	4	**35**	1	2	3	4	**55**	1	2	3	
16	1	2	3	4	**36**	1	2	3	4	**56**	1	2	3	
17	1	2	3	4	**37**	1	2	3	4					
18	1	2	3	4	**38**	1	2	3	4					
19	1	2	3	4	**39**	1	2	3	4					
20	1	2	3	4	**40**	1	2	3	4					

FOR TEACHER USE ONLY

Credits

Part I ....
(Use table below)

Part II ....

Total ....

Rater's Initials ....

Part I Credits

Directions to Teacher.
In the table below, draw a circle around the number of right answers and the adjacent number of credits. Then write the number of credits (not the number right) in the space provided above.

No. Right	Credits	No. Right	Credits
56	65	28	41
55	64	27	40
54	63	26	39
53	62	25	39
52	62	24	38
51	61	23	37
50	60	22	36
49	59	21	35
48	58	20	34
47	57	19	33
46	56	18	33
45	56	17	32
44	55	16	31
43	54	15	30
42	53	14	29
41	52	13	27
40	51	12	25
39	51	11	23
38	50	10	21
37	49	9	19
36	48	8	17
35	47	7	14
34	46	6	12
33	45	5	10
32	45	4	8
31	44	3	6
30	43	2	4
29	42	1	2
		0	0

No. right...............

Part II (35 credits)

Answer the questions in only seven of the twelve groups in this part. Be sure to mark the answers to the groups of questions you choose in accordance with the instructions on the front cover of the test booklet. Leave blank the five groups of questions you do not choose to answer.

Group 1 Matter and Energy	Group 2 Atomic Structure	Group 3 Bonding	Group 4 Periodic Table
57 1 2 3 4	62 1 2 3 4	67 1 2 3 4	72 1 2 3 4
58 1 2 3 4	63 1 2 3 4	68 1 2 3 4	73 1 2 3 4
59 1 2 3 4	64 1 2 3 4	69 1 2 3 4	74 1 2 3 4
60 1 2 3 4	65 1 2 3 4	70 1 2 3 4	75 1 2 3 4
61 1 2 3 4	66 1 2 3 4	71 1 2 3 4	76 1 2 3 4

Group 5 Mathematics of Chemistry	Group 6 Kinetics and Equilibrium	Group 7 Acids and Bases	Group 8 Redox and Electrochemistry
77 1 2 3 4	82 1 2 3 4	87 1 2 3 4	92 1 2 3 4
78 1 2 3 4	83 1 2 3 4	88 1 2 3 4	93 1 2 3 4
79 1 2 3 4	84 1 2 3 4	89 1 2 3 4	94 1 2 3 4
80 1 2 3 4	85 1 2 3 4	90 1 2 3 4	95 1 2 3 4
81 1 2 3 4	86 1 2 3 4	91 1 2 3 4	96 1 2 3 4

Group 9 Organic Chemistry	Group 10 Applications of Chemical Principles	Group 11 Nuclear Chemistry	Group 12 Laboratory Activities
97 1 2 3 4	102 1 2 3 4	107 1 2 3 4	112 1 2 3 4
98 1 2 3 4	103 1 2 3 4	108 1 2 3 4	113 1 2 3 4
99 1 2 3 4	104 1 2 3 4	109 1 2 3 4	114 1 2 3 4
100 1 2 3 4	105 1 2 3 4	110 1 2 3 4	115 1 2 3 4
101 1 2 3 4	106 1 2 3 4	111 1 2 3 4	116 1 2 3 4

CHEMISTRY
JUNE 1995

Part I

Answer all 56 questions in this part. [65]

Directions (1–56): For *each* statement or question, select the word or expression that, of those given, best completes the statement or answers the question. Record your answer on the separate answer sheet in accordance with the directions on the front page of this booklet.

1 Which statement best describes the production of a chlorine molecule according to the reaction $Cl + Cl \rightarrow Cl_2 + 58$ kcal?

  1 A bond is broken, and the reaction is exothermic.

  2 A bond is broken, and the reaction is endothermic.

  3 A bond is formed, and the reaction is exothermic.

  4 A bond is formed, and the reaction is endothermic.

2 Which set of properties does a substance such as $CO_2(g)$ have?

  1 definite shape and definite volume

  2 definite shape but no definite volume

  3 no definite shape but definite volume

  4 no definite shape and no definite volume

3 Which quantity of heat does a kilocalorie represent?

  (1) 100 calories

  (2) 1000 calories

  (3) $\frac{1}{100}$ of a calorie

  (4) $\frac{1}{1000}$ of a calorie

4 Which substance can *not* be decomposed by a chemical change?

  1 ammonia   3 methane

  2 carbon   4 water

5 When sugar is dissolved in water, the resulting solution is classified as a

  1 homogeneous mixture

  2 heterogeneous mixture

  3 homogeneous compound

  4 heterogeneous compound

6 Which is the electron configuration of an atom in the excited state?

  (1) $1s^2 2s^2 2p^2$ (3) $1s^2 2s^2 2p^5 3s^2$

  (2) $1s^2 2s^2 2p^1$ (4) $1s^2 2s^2 2p^6 3s^1$

7 Which is the correct orbital notation of a lithium atom in the ground state?

8 A particle of matter contains 6 protons, 7 neutrons, and 6 electrons. This particle must be a

  1 neutral carbon atom

  2 neutral nitrogen atom

  3 positively charged carbon ion

  4 positively charged nitrogen ion

9 Which kind of particle, when passed through an electric field, would be attracted to the negative electrode?

  1 an alpha particle   3 a neutron

  2 a beta particle   4 an electron

10 What is the approximate mass of an electron?

  (1) 1 atomic mass unit   (3) $\frac{1}{1836}$ of a proton

  (2) $\frac{1}{12}$ of a C–12 atom   (4) $\frac{1835}{1836}$ of a proton

11 The mass number of an atom is always equal to the total number of its

  1 electrons, only

  2 protons, only

  3 electrons plus protons

  4 protons plus neutrons

12 Which substance is a conductor of electricity?
  (1) NaCl(s)
  (2) NaCl(ℓ)
  (3) $C_6H_{12}O_6$(s)
  (4) $C_6H_{12}O_6$(ℓ)

13 Which formula is an empirical formula?
  (1) K_2O
  (2) H_2O_2
  (3) C_2H_6
  (4) C_6H_6

14 Molecule-ion attractions are found in
  (1) K(s)
  (2) Kr(g)
  (3) KCl(ℓ)
  (4) KCl(aq)

15 Which formula is correctly paired with its name?
  (1) $MgCl_2$ — magnesium chlorine
  (2) K_2O — phosphorus dioxide
  (3) $CuCl_2$ — copper (II) chloride
  (4) FeO — iron (III) oxide

16 How many moles of hydrogen atoms are present in one mole of $C_2H_4(OH)_2$?
  (1) 6
  (2) 2
  (3) 8
  (4) 4

17 In the diagram of an ammonium ion below, why is bond A considered to be coordinate covalent?

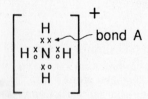

  1 Hydrogen provides a pair of electrons to be shared with nitrogen.
  2 Nitrogen provides a pair of electrons to be shared with hydrogen.
  3 Hydrogen transfers a pair of electrons to nitrogen.
  4 Nitrogen transfers a pair of electrons to hydrogen.

18 Which structural formula represents a polar molecule?

  (1) N≡N
  (3) H—C—H (with H above and below)
  (2) S=C=S
  (4) H—N—H (with H below)

 element is classified as a semimetal d)?
  (3) Pb
  (4) P

20 Which element in Group 15 would most likely have luster and good electrical conductivity?
  (1) N
  (2) P
  (3) Bi
  (4) As

21 Which is the electron configuration of an atom of a Period 3 element?
  (1) $1s^2 2s^1$
  (2) $1s^2 2s^2 2p^1$
  (3) $1s^2 2s^2 2p^3$
  (4) $1s^2 2s^2 2p^6 3s^1$

22 Which of the following elements has the largest covalent radius?
  1 beryllium
  2 magnesium
  3 calcium
  4 strontium

23 When a metal reacts with a nonmetal, the metal will
  1 lose electrons and form a positive ion
  2 lose protons and form a positive ion
  3 gain electrons and form a negative ion
  4 gain protons and form a negative ion

24 Which statement best describes the alkaline earth elements?
  1 They have one valence electron, and they form ions with a 1+ charge.
  2 They have one valence electron, and they form ions with a 1– charge.
  3 They have two valence electrons, and they form ions with a 2+ charge.
  4 They have two valence electrons, and they form ions with a 2– charge.

25 Which compound has the *least* ionic character?
  (1) KCl
  (2) $CaCl_2$
  (3) $AlCl_3$
  (4) CCl_4

26 Which statement best explains why Na is *not* found in nature?
  1 Na is very reactive, and it forms stable compounds.
  2 Na is very reactive, and it forms unstable compounds.
  3 Na is very unreactive, and it forms stable compounds.
  4 Na is very unreactive, and it forms unstable compounds.

27 What is the gram molecular mass of calcium nitrate, $Ca(NO_3)_2$?
  (1) 164 g
  (2) 150. g
  (3) 102 g
  (4) 70.0 g

28 What is the molarity of a KF(aq) solution containing 116 grams of KF in 1.00 liter of solution?
  (1) 1.00 M
  (2) 2.00 M
  (3) 3.00 M
  (4) 4.00 M

29 What is the total number of atoms in 1 mole of calcium?

(1) 1   (3) 6×10^{23}

(2) 20   (4) $20(6 \times 10^{23})$

30 What is the percent by mass of water in the hydrate $Na_2CO_3 \cdot 10H_2O$ (formula mass = 286)?

(1) 6.89%   (3) 26.1%

(2) 14.5%   (4) 62.9%

31 At STP, 32.0 liters of O_2 contains the same number of molecules as

(1) 22.4 liters of Ar   (3) 32.0 liters of H_2

(2) 28.0 liters of N_2 (4) 44.8 liters of He

32 According to Reference Table *D*, which compound's solubility decreases most rapidly as the temperature changes from 10°C to 70°C?

(1) NH_4Cl (3) HCl

(2) NH_3 (4) KCl

33 Under which conditions will the rate of a chemical reaction always decrease?

1 The concentration of the reactants decreases, and the temperature decreases.

2 The concentration of the reactants decreases, and the temperature increases.

3 The concentration of the reactants increases, and the temperature decreases.

4 The concentration of the reactants increases, and the temperature increases.

34 Which is a property of a reaction that has reached equilibrium?

1 The amount of products is greater than the amount of reactants.

2 The amount of products is equal to the amount of reactants.

3 The rate of the forward reaction is greater than the rate of the reverse reaction.

4 The rate of the forward reaction is equal to the rate of the reverse reaction.

35 Based on Reference Table *G*, which reaction occurs spontaneously?

(1) $2C(s) + 3H_2(g) \rightarrow C_2H_6(g)$

(2) $2C(s) + 2H_2(g) \rightarrow C_2H_4(g)$

(3) $N_2(g) + 2O_2(g) \rightarrow 2NO_2(g)$

(4) $N_2(g) + O_2(g) \rightarrow 2NO(g)$

36 Which procedure will increase the solubility of KCl in water?

1 stirring the solute and solvent mixture

2 increasing the surface area of the solute

3 raising the temperature of the solvent

4 increasing the pressure on the surface of the solvent

37 According to the Arrhenius theory, a substance that is classified as an acid will always yield

(1) $H^+(aq)$ (3) $OH^-(aq)$

(2) $NH_4^+(aq)$ (4) $CO_3^{2-}(aq)$

38 What is the net ionic equation for a neutralization reaction?

(1) $H^+ + H_2O \rightarrow H_3O^+$

(2) $H^+ + NH_3 \rightarrow NH_4^+$

(3) $2H^+ + 2O^{2-} \rightarrow 2OH^-$

(4) $H^+ + OH^- \rightarrow H_2O$

39 Given the reaction:

$$HNO_2(aq) \rightleftharpoons H^+(aq) + NO_2^-(aq)$$

The ionization constant, K_a, is equal to

(1) $\dfrac{[HNO_2]}{[H^+][NO_2^-]}$ (3) $\dfrac{[NO_2^-]}{[H^+][HNO_2]}$

(2) $\dfrac{[H^+][NO_2^-]}{[HNO_2]}$ (4) $\dfrac{[H^+][HNO_2]}{[NO_2^-]}$

40 Based on Reference Table *L*, which of the following 0.1 M aqueous solutions is the best conductor of electricity?

(1) HF   (3) HNO_2

(2) H_2S (4) CH_3COOH

41 How many milliliters of 4.00 M NaOH are required to exactly neutralize 50.0 milliliters of a 2.00 M solution of HNO_3?

(1) 25.0 mL   (3) 100. mL

(2) 50.0 mL   (4) 200. mL

42 Which reaction best illustrates amphoterism?

(1) $H_2O + HCl \rightarrow H_3O^+ + Cl^-$

(2) $NH_3 + H_2O \rightarrow NH_4^+ + OH^-$

(3) $H_2O + H_2SO_4 \rightarrow H_3O^+ + HSO_4^-$

(4) $H_2O + H_2O \rightarrow H_3O^+ + OH^-$

43 Given the oxidation-reduction reaction:

$$Hg^{2+} + 2I^- \rightarrow Hg(\ell) + I_2(s)$$

Which equation correctly represents the half-reaction for the reduction that occurs?

(1) $Hg^{2+} \rightarrow Hg(\ell) + 2e^-$

(2) $Hg^{2+} + 2e^- \rightarrow Hg(\ell)$

(3) $2I^- \rightarrow I_2(s) + 2e^-$

(4) $2I^- + 2e^- \rightarrow I_2(s)$

44 In any oxidation-reduction reaction, the total number of electrons gained is
1 less than the total number of electrons lost
2 greater than the total number of electrons lost
3 equal to the total number of electrons lost
4 unrelated to the total number of electrons lost

45 The oxidation number of nitrogen in N_2O is
(1) +1
(2) +2
(3) –1
(4) –2

46 When 1 mole of Sn^{4+} ions is reduced to 1 mole of Sn^{2+} ions, 2 moles of electrons are
1 lost by Sn^{4+}
2 lost by Sn^{2+}
3 gained by Sn^{4+}
4 gained by Sn^{2+}

47 The purpose of the salt bridge in an electro-chemical cell is to
1 prevent the migration of ions
2 permit the migration of ions
3 provide a direct path for electron flow
4 prevent electron flow

48 Given the reaction:

$$2KCl(\ell) \rightarrow 2K(s) + Cl_2(g)$$

In this reaction, the K^+ ions are
1 reduced by losing electrons
2 reduced by gaining electrons
3 oxidized by losing electrons
4 oxidized by gaining electrons

49 What is the maximum number of covalent bonds that an atom of carbon can form?
(1) 1
(2) 2
(3) 3
(4) 4

50 Which class of organic compounds can be represented as $R-OH$?
1 acids
2 alcohols
3 esters
4 ethers

51 What is the geometric shape of a methane molecule?
1 triangular
2 rectangular
3 octahedral
4 tetrahedral

52 Which molecule contains a total of three carbon atoms?
(1) 2-methylpropane
(2) 2-methylbutane
(3) propane
(4) butane

53 Which is the general formula for an alkyne?
(1) C_nH_{2n-2}
(2) C_nH_{2n+2}
(3) C_nH_{2n}
(4) C_nH_{2n-6}

Note that questions 54 through 56 have only three choices.

54 As the temperature of a given sample of a gas is increased at constant pressure, the volume of the gas will
1 decrease
2 increase
3 remain the same

55 As HCl(aq) is added to a basic solution, the pH of the solution will
1 decrease
2 increase
3 remain the same

56 Given the reaction: $A(g) + B(g) \rightarrow C(g)$

As the concentration of $A(g)$ increases, the frequency of collisions of $A(g)$ with $B(g)$
1 decreases
2 increases
3 remains the same

Part II

This part consists of twelve groups, each containing five questions. Each group tests a major area of the course. Choose seven of these twelve groups. Be sure that you answer all five questions in each group chosen. Record the answers to these questions on the separate answer sheet in accordance with the directions on the front page of this booklet. [35]

Group 1 — Matter and Energy

If you choose this group, be sure to answer questions 57–61.

57 Which statement describes a characteristic of all compounds?
1 Compounds contain one element, only.
2 Compounds contain two elements, only.
3 Compounds can be decomposed by chemical means.
4 Compounds can be decomposed by physical means.

58 The pressure on 30. milliliters of an ideal gas increases from 760 torr to 1520 torr at constant temperature. The new volume is

(1) $30. \text{ mL} \times \dfrac{760 \text{ torr}}{1520 \text{ torr}}$

(2) $30. \text{ mL} \times \dfrac{1520 \text{ torr}}{760 \text{ torr}}$

(3) $\dfrac{760 \text{ torr}}{30. \text{ mL}} \times 1520 \text{ torr}$

(4) $\dfrac{1520 \text{ torr}}{30. \text{ mL}} \times 760 \text{ torr}$

59 Which phase change results in a release of energy?

(1) $Br_2(\ell) \rightarrow Br_2(s)$ (3) $H_2O(s) \rightarrow H_2O(\ell)$
(2) $I_2(s) \rightarrow I_2(g)$ (4) $NH_3(\ell) \rightarrow NH_3(g)$

60 The *minimum* number of fixed points required to establish the Celsius temperature scale for a thermometer is
(1) 1   (3) 3
(2) 2   (4) 4

61 Which substance is a binary compound?
1 oxygen   3 glycerol
2 chlorine   4 ammonia

Group 2 — Atomic Structure

If you choose this group, be sure to answer questions 62–66.

62 Which atom in the ground state contains one completely filled *p*-orbital?
(1) N   (3) He
(2) O   (4) Be

63 A gamma ray is best described as having
1 no electric charge and no mass
2 a negative charge and no mass
3 a positive charge and a mass number of 2
4 a positive charge and a mass number of 4

64 If one-eighth of the mass of the original sample of a radioisotope remains unchanged after 4,800 years, the isotope could be
(1) ^3H (3) ^{90}Sr
(2) ^{42}K (4) ^{226}Ra

65 An atom of an element has the electron configuration $1s^2 2s^2 2p^2$. What is the total number of valence electrons in this atom?
(1) 6   (3) 5
(2) 2   (4) 4

66 What is the total number of electrons in a Mg^{2+} ion?
(1) 10   (3) 12
(2) 2   (4) 24

Group 3 – Bonding

If you choose this group, be sure to answer questions 67–71.

67 Given the unbalanced equation:

$$\_Ag(s) + \_H_2S(g) \rightarrow \_Ag_2S(s) + \_H_2(g)$$

What is the sum of the coefficients when the equation is completely balanced using the smallest whole-number coefficients?

(1) 5   (3) 10
(2) 8   (4) 4

68 Which ion has the electron configuration of a noble gas?

(1) Cu^{2+} (3) Ca^{2+}
(2) Fe^{2+} (4) Hg^{2+}

69 Which is a molecular substance?

(1) CO_2 (3) KCl
(2) CaO   (4) $KClO_3$

70 Given the phase change: $H_2(g) \rightarrow H_2(\ell)$

Which kind of force acts between molecules of H_2 during this phase change?

1 hydrogen bond   3 molecule-ion
2 ionic bond   4 van der Waals

71 Given the electron dot formula: $H : \ddot{X} :$
                                    H

The attraction for the bonding electrons would be greatest when X represents an atom of

(1) S   (3) Se
(2) O   (4) Te

Group 4 – Periodic Table

If you choose this group, be sure to answer questions 72–76.

72 A nonmetal could have an electronegativity of
(1) 1.0   (3) 1.6
(2) 2.0   (4) 2.6

Which group below contains elements with the greatest variation in chemical properties?

1) Li, Be, B   (3) B, Al, Ga
) Li, Na, K   (4) Be, Mg, Ca

74 A property of most nonmetals in the solid state is that they are
1 good conductors of heat
2 good conductors of electricity
3 brittle
4 malleable

75 A transition element in the ground state could have an electron configuration of
(1) $1s^2 2s^2 2p^6 3s^2 3p^6 4s^2$
(2) $1s^2 2s^2 2p^6 3s^2 3p^6 3d^5 4s^2$
(3) $1s^2 2s^2 2p^6 3s^2 3p^6 3d^{10} 4s^2 4p^5$
(4) $1s^2 2s^2 2p^6 3s^2 3p^6 3d^{10} 4s^2 4p^6$

76 An atom of which of the following elements has the *smallest* covalent radius?
(1) Li   (3) C
(2) Be   (4) F

Group 5 – Mathematics of Chemistry

If you choose this group, be sure to answer questions 77–81.

77 Given the reaction: $2PbO \rightarrow 2Pb + O_2$

What is the total volume of O_2, measured at STP, produced when 1.00 mole of PbO decomposes?
(1) 5.60 L   (3) 22.4 L
(2) 11.2 L   (4) 44.8 L

78 What is the mass in grams of 3.0×10^{23} molecules of CO_2?
(1) 22 g   (3) 66 g
(2) 44 g   (4) 88 g

79 Why is salt (NaCl) put on icy roads and sidewalks in the winter?
1 It is ionic and lowers the freezing point of water.
2 It is ionic and raises the freezing point of water.
3 It is covalent and lowers the freezing point of water.
4 It is covalent and raises the freezing point of water.

80 Which gas diffuses most rapidly at STP?
(1) Ar   (3) N_2
(2) Kr   (4) O_2

81 How many calories of heat are absorbed when 70.00 grams of water is completely vaporized at its boiling point?
(1) 7,706   (3) 3,776
(2) 77.06   (4) 37,760

Group 6 — Kinetics and Equilibrium

If you choose this group, be sure to answer questions 82–86.

82 Which reaction system tends to become *less* random as reactants form products?

(1) $C(s) + O_2(g) \rightarrow CO_2(g)$
(2) $S(s) + O_2(g) \rightarrow SO_2(g)$
(3) $I_2(s) + Cl_2(g) \rightarrow 2ICl(g)$
(4) $2Mg(s) + O_2(g) \rightarrow 2MgO(s)$

83 Given the equilibrium system at 25°C:

$$NH_4Cl(s) \rightleftharpoons NH_4^+(aq) + Cl^-(aq)$$
$$(\Delta H = +3.5 \text{ kcal/mole})$$

Which change will shift the equilibrium to the right?

1 decreasing the temperature to 15°C
2 increasing the temperature to 35°C
3 dissolving NaCl crystals in the equilibrium mixture
4 dissolving NH_4NO_3 crystals in the equilibrium mixture

84 What is the correct equilibrium expression (K_{sp}) for the reaction below?

$$Ca_3(PO_4)_2(s) \rightleftharpoons 3Ca^{2+}(aq) + 2PO_4^{3-}(aq)$$

(1) $K_{sp} = [3Ca^{2+}][2PO_4^{3-}]$
(2) $K_{sp} = [3Ca^{2+}] + [2PO_4^{3-}]$
(3) $K_{sp} = [Ca^{2+}]^3 [PO_4^{3-}]^2$
(4) $K_{sp} = [Ca^{2+}]^3 + [PO_4^{3-}]^2$

85 What is the value of ΔG for any chemical reaction at equilibrium?

1 one
2 zero
3 greater than one
4 less than one but not zero

86 Based on Reference Table *M*, which of the following salts is the most soluble in water?

(1) $PbCrO_4$ (3) $BaSO_4$
(2) $AgBr$ (4) $ZnCO_3$

Group 7 — Acids and Bases

If you choose this group, be sure to answer questions 87–91.

87 Which formulas represent a conjugate acid-base pair?

(1) CH_3COOH and CH_3COO^-
(2) H_3O^+ and OH^-
(3) H_2SO_4 and SO_4^{2-}
(4) H_3PO_4 and PO_4^{3-}

88 Which substance, when dissolved in water, is a Brönsted-Lowry acid?

(1) CH_3OH (3) C_2H_5COOH
(2) $NaOH$ (4) CH_3COO^-

89 Which of the following compounds is the strongest electrolyte?

(1) NH_3 (3) H_3PO_4
(2) H_2O (4) H_2SO_4

90 Red litmus will turn blue when placed in an aqueous solution of

(1) HCl (3) CH_3OH
(2) CH_3COOH (4) $NaOH$

91 Given the reaction at equilibrium:

$$HSO_4^- + H_2O \rightleftharpoons H_3O^+ + SO_4^{2-}$$

The two Brönsted bases are

(1) H_2O and H_3O^+
(2) H_2O and SO_4^{2-}
(3) H_3O^+ and HSO_4^-
(4) H_3O^+ and SO_4^{2-}

Group 8 — Redox and Electrochemistry

If you choose this group, be sure to answer questions 92–96.

Base your answers to questions 92 and 93 on Reference Table *N* and the diagram below.

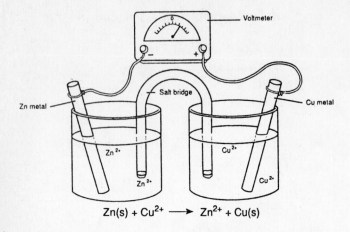

$$Zn(s) + Cu^{2+} \longrightarrow Zn^{2+} + Cu(s)$$

92 When this cell operates, the electrons flow from the
1 copper half-cell to the zinc half-cell through the wire
2 copper half-cell to the zinc half-cell through the salt bridge
3 zinc half-cell to the copper half-cell through the wire
4 zinc half-cell to the copper half-cell through the salt bridge

93 What is the potential (E^0) of this cell?
(1) +1.10 V   (3) –1.10 V
(2) +0.42 V   (4) –0.42 V

94 Based on Reference Table *N*, which ion will reduce Ag^+ to Ag?
(1) F^- (3) Br^-
(2) I^- (4) Cl^-

95 Given the equation for the electrolysis of a fused salt:

$$2LiCl(\ell) + \text{electricity} \longrightarrow 2Li(\ell) + Cl_2(g)$$

Which reaction occurs at the cathode?
(1) $2Cl^- \longrightarrow Cl_2(g) + 2e^-$
(2) $2Cl^- + 2e^- \longrightarrow Cl_2(g)$
(3) $Li^+ + e^- \longrightarrow Li(\ell)$
(4) $Li^+ \longrightarrow Li(\ell) + e^-$

96 Given the reaction:

$$Zn + 2HCl \longrightarrow ZnCl_2 + H_2$$

Which statement best describes what happens to the zinc?
1 The oxidation number changes from +2 to 0, and the zinc is reduced.
2 The oxidation number changes from 0 to +2, and the zinc is reduced.
3 The oxidation number changes from +2 to 0, and the zinc is oxidized.
4 The oxidation number changes from 0 to +2, and the zinc is oxidized.

Group 9 — Organic Chemistry

If you choose this group, be sure to answer questions 97–101.

97 Given the structural formulas for three alcohols:

All are classified as
1 monohydroxy alcohols
2 secondary alcohols
3 tertiary alcohols
4 primary alcohols

98 Which structural formula correctly represents 2-butene?

99 Which compounds are isomers?

(1) CH_3Br and CH_2Br_2

(2) CH_3OH and CH_3CH_2OH

(3) CH_3OH and CH_3CHO

(4) CH_3OCH_3 and CH_3CH_2OH

100 Condensation polymerization is best described as

1 a dehydration reaction

2 a cracking reaction

3 a reduction reaction

4 an oxidation reaction

101 Which type of reaction do ethane molecules and ethene molecules undergo when they react with chlorine?

1 Ethane and ethene both react by addition.

2 Ethane and ethene both react by substitution.

3 Ethane reacts by substitution and ethene reacts by addition.

4 Ethane reacts by addition and ethene reacts by substitution.

Group 10 — Applications of Chemical Principles

If you choose this group, be sure to answer questions 102–106.

102 Which type of chemical reaction generates the electrical energy produced by a battery?

1 oxidation-reduction   3 neutralization

2 substitution   4 addition

103 Given the reaction at equilibrium:

$$2SO_2(g) + O_2(g) \rightleftharpoons 2SO_3(g) + heat$$

Which change will shift the equilibrium to the right?

1 adding a catalyst

2 adding more $O_2(g)$

3 decreasing the pressure

4 increasing the temperature

104 Which commercial products are derived primarily from petroleum?

1 mineral acids and plastics

2 fertilizers and rubber

3 plastics and textiles

4 textiles and fertilizers

105 Petroleum is classified chemically as

1 a substance   3 an element

2 a compound   4 a mixture

106 Which metal forms a self-protective coating against corrosion?

(1) Fe   (3) Zn

(2) Cu   (4) Mg

Group 11 — Nuclear Chemistry

If you choose this group, be sure to answer questions 107–111.

107 Given the nuclear equation:

$$^9_4Be + X \rightarrow \, ^6_3Li + \, ^4_2He$$

What is the identity of particle X in this equation?

(1) ^1_1H (3) $^0_{-1}e$

(2) ^2_1H (4) ^1_0n

108 Which fields are used in accelerators to speed up charged particles?

1 magnetic fields, only

2 electric fields, only

3 magnetic and electric fields

4 magnetic and gravitational fields

109 Which nuclear equation represents artificial transmutation?

(1) $^{238}_{92}U \rightarrow \, ^{234}_{90}Th + \, ^4_2He$

(2) $^{27}_{13}Al + \, ^4_2He \rightarrow \, ^{30}_{15}P + \, ^1_0n$

(3) $^{226}_{88}Ra \rightarrow \, ^4_2He + \, ^{222}_{86}Rn$

(4) $^{14}_6C \rightarrow \, ^{14}_7N + \, ^0_{-1}e$

110 The number of neutrons available in a fission reactor is adjusted by the

1 moderator   3 shielding

2 control rods   4 coolant

111 Which substance is sometimes used to slow down the neutrons in a nuclear reactor?

(1) U–233   (3) sulfur

(2) Pu–236   (4) heavy water

Group 12 — Laboratory Activities

If you choose this group, be sure to answer questions 112–116.

112 Solubility data for salt X is shown in the table below.

Temperature (°C)	Solubility $\left(\dfrac{\text{g salt } X}{100 \text{ g H}_2\text{O}}\right)$
10	5
20	10
30	15
40	20
50	30
60	35

Which graph most closely represents the data shown in the table?

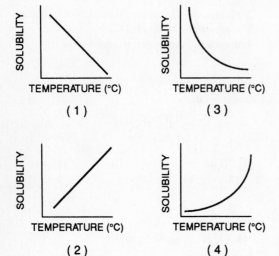

113 A student calculated the percent by mass of water in a hydrate to be 37.2%. If the accepted value is 36.0%, the percent error in the student's calculation is equal to

(1) $\dfrac{1.2}{37.2} \times 100$ (3) $\dfrac{37.2}{36.0} \times 100$

(2) $\dfrac{1.2}{36.0} \times 100$ (4) $\dfrac{36.0}{37.2} \times 100$

114 The graph below represents the cooling curve of a substance starting at a temperature below the boiling point of the substance.

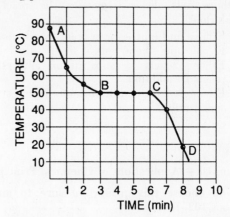

During which interval was the substance completely in the solid phase?

(1) A to B (3) B to C
(2) A to C (4) C to D

115 What is the sum of
  6.6412 g + 12.85 g + 0.046 g + 3.48 g,
expressed to the correct number of significant figures?

(1) 23 g   (3) 23.017 g
(2) 23.0 g   (4) 23.02 g

116 What occurs as potassium nitrate is dissolved in a beaker of water, indicating that the process is endothermic?

1 The temperature of the solution decreases.
2 The temperature of the solution increases.
3 The solution changes color.
4 The solution gives off a gas.

CHEMISTRY
JUNE 1995

ANSWER SHEET

Pupil ....

Teacher..

School..

Record all of your answers on this answer sheet in accordance with the instructions on the front page of the test booklet.

Part I (65 credits)

1	1 2 3 4	21	1 2 3 4	41	1 2 3 4
2	1 2 3 4	22	1 2 3 4	42	1 2 3 4
3	1 2 3 4	23	1 2 3 4	43	1 2 3 4
4	1 2 3 4	24	1 2 3 4	44	1 2 3 4
5	1 2 3 4	25	1 2 3 4	45	1 2 3 4
6	1 2 3 4	26	1 2 3 4	46	1 2 3 4
7	1 2 3 4	27	1 2 3 4	47	1 2 3 4
8	1 2 3 4	28	1 2 3 4	48	1 2 3 4
9	1 2 3 4	29	1 2 3 4	49	1 2 3 4
10	1 2 3 4	30	1 2 3 4	50	1 2 3 4
11	1 2 3 4	31	1 2 3 4	51	1 2 3 4
12	1 2 3 4	32	1 2 3 4	52	1 2 3 4
13	1 2 3 4	33	1 2 3 4	53	1 2 3 4
14	1 2 3 4	34	1 2 3 4	54	1 2 3
15	1 2 3 4	35	1 2 3 4	55	1 2 3
16	1 2 3 4	36	1 2 3 4	56	1 2 3
17	1 2 3 4	37	1 2 3 4		
18	1 2 3 4	38	1 2 3 4		
19	1 2 3 4	39	1 2 3 4		
20	1 2 3 4	40	1 2 3 4		

Part II (35 credits)

Answer the questions in only seven of the twelve groups in this part. Be sure to mark the answers to the groups of questions you choose in accordance with the instructions on the front cover of the test booklet. Leave blank the five groups of questions you do not choose to answer.

Group 1 — Matter and Energy	Group 2 — Atomic Structure	Group 3 — Bonding	Group 4 — Periodic Table
57 1 2 3 4	62 1 2 3 4	67 1 2 3 4	72 1 2 3 4
58 1 2 3 4	63 1 2 3 4	68 1 2 3 4	73 1 2 3 4
59 1 2 3 4	64 1 2 3 4	69 1 2 3 4	74 1 2 3 4
60 1 2 3 4	65 1 2 3 4	70 1 2 3 4	75 1 2 3 4
61 1 2 3 4	66 1 2 3 4	71 1 2 3 4	76 1 2 3 4

Group 5 — Mathematics of Chemistry	Group 6 — Kinetics and Equilibrium	Group 7 — Acids and Bases	Group 8 — Redox and Electrochemistry
77 1 2 3 4	82 1 2 3 4	87 1 2 3 4	92 1 2 3 4
78 1 2 3 4	83 1 2 3 4	88 1 2 3 4	93 1 2 3 4
79 1 2 3 4	84 1 2 3 4	89 1 2 3 4	94 1 2 3 4
80 1 2 3 4	85 1 2 3 4	90 1 2 3 4	95 1 2 3 4
81 1 2 3 4	86 1 2 3 4	91 1 2 3 4	96 1 2 3 4

Group 9 — Organic Chemistry	Group 10 — Applications of Chemical Principles	Group 11 — Nuclear Chemistry	Group 12 — Laboratory Activities
97 1 2 3 4	102 1 2 3 4	107 1 2 3 4	112 1 2 3 4
98 1 2 3 4	103 1 2 3 4	108 1 2 3 4	113 1 2 3 4
99 1 2 3 4	104 1 2 3 4	109 1 2 3 4	114 1 2 3 4
100 1 2 3 4	105 1 2 3 4	110 1 2 3 4	115 1 2 3 4
101 1 2 3 4	106 1 2 3 4	111 1 2 3 4	116 1 2 3 4

CHEMISTRY
JUNE 1996

Part I

Answer all 56 questions in this part. [65]

Directions (1–56): For *each* statement or question, select the word or expression that, of those given, best completes the statement or answers the question. Record your answer on the separate answer sheet in accordance with the directions on the front page of this booklet.

1 What is the vapor pressure of a liquid at its normal boiling temperature?

(1) 1 atm   (3) 273 atm
(2) 2 atm   (4) 760 atm

2 A sealed container has 1 mole of helium and 2 moles of nitrogen at 30°C. When the total pressure of the mixture is 600 torr, what is the partial pressure of the nitrogen?

(1) 100 torr   (3) 400 torr
(2) 200 torr   (4) 600 torr

3 Solid X is placed in contact with solid Y. Heat will flow spontaneously from X to Y when

(1) X is 20°C and Y is 20°C
(2) X is 10°C and Y is 5°C
(3) X is –25°C and Y is –10°C
(4) X is 25°C and Y is 30°C

4 Which graph represents the relationship between volume and Kelvin temperature for an ideal gas at constant pressure?

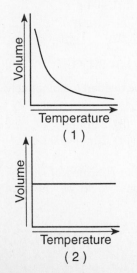

(1)

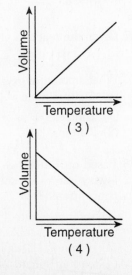

(3)

(2)

(4)

5 An example of a binary compound is

(1) potassium chloride
(2) ammonium chloride
(3) potassium chlorate
(4) ammonium chlorate

6 Which kind of radiation will travel through an electric field on a pathway that remains unaffected by the field?

(1) a proton   (3) an electron
(2) a gamma ray   (4) an alpha particle

7 The major portion of an atom's mass consists of

(1) electrons and protons
(2) electrons and neutrons
(3) neutrons and positrons
(4) neutrons and protons

8 Which atom contains exactly 15 protons?

(1) phosphorus-32   (3) oxygen-15
(2) sulfur-32   (4) nitrogen-15

9 Element X has two isotopes. If 72.0% of the element has an isotopic mass of 84.9 atomic mass units, and 28.0% of the element has an isotopic mass of 87.0 atomic mass units, the average atomic mass of element X is numerically equal to

(1) $(72.0 + 84.9) \times (28.0 + 87.0)$

(2) $(72.0 - 84.9) \times (28.0 + 87.0)$

(3) $\dfrac{(72.0 \times 84.9)}{100} + \dfrac{(28.0 \times 87.0)}{100}$

(4) $(72.0 \times 84.9) + (28.0 \times 87.0)$

10 Given the equation: $^{14}_{6}C \rightarrow {}^{14}_{7}N + X$

Which particle is represented by the letter X?

(1) an alpha particle   (3) a neutron
(2) a beta particle   (4) a proton

11 The atom of which element in the ground state has 2 unpaired electrons in the $2p$ sublevel?

(1) fluorine   (3) beryllium
(2) nitrogen   (4) carbon

12 Which atoms contain the same number of neutrons?

(1) ^1_1H and ^3_2He (3) ^3_1H and ^3_2He
(2) ^2_1H and ^4_2He (4) ^3_1H and ^4_2He

13 Which hydrocarbon formula is also an empirical formula?

(1) CH_4 (3) C_3H_6
(2) C_2H_4 (4) C_4H_8

14 The potential energy possessed by a molecule is dependent upon

(1) its composition, only
(2) its structure, only
(3) both its composition and its structure
(4) neither its composition nor its structure

15 Which is a correctly balanced equation for a reaction between hydrogen gas and oxygen gas?

(1) $H_2(g) + O_2(g) \rightarrow H_2O(\ell) + heat$
(2) $H_2(g) + O_2(g) \rightarrow 2H_2O(\ell) + heat$
(3) $2H_2(g) + 2O_2(g) \rightarrow H_2O(\ell) + heat$
(4) $2H_2(g) + O_2(g) \rightarrow 2H_2O(\ell) + heat$

16 The atom of which element has an ionic radius smaller than its atomic radius?

(1) N   (3) Br
(2) S   (4) Rb

17 Which molecule contains a polar covalent bond?

(1) $\overset{\times\times}{\underset{\times\times}{\times}}I\overset{\cdot\cdot}{\underset{\cdot\cdot}{\times}}I\overset{\cdot\cdot}{\cdot\cdot}$ (3) $H \overset{\cdot}{\underset{\times}{\times}}N\overset{\cdot}{\underset{\cdot}{\times}} H$ over H

(2) $H \overset{\cdot}{\times} H$ (4) $:N\overset{\times}{\underset{\times}{\times}}N\overset{\times}{\times}$

18 Which is the correct formula for nitrogen (I) oxide?

(1) NO   (3) NO_2
(2) N_2O (4) N_2O_3

19 Which element in Group 15 has the strongest metallic character?

(1) Bi   (3) P
(2) As   (4) N

20 Which halogens are gases at STP?

(1) chlorine and fluorine
(2) chlorine and bromine
(3) iodine and fluorine
(4) iodine and bromine

21 What is the total number of atoms represented in the formula $CuSO_4 \cdot 5H_2O$?

(1) 8   (3) 21
(2) 13   (4) 27

22 When combining with nonmetallic atoms, metallic atoms generally will

(1) lose electrons and form negative ions
(2) lose electrons and form positive ions
(3) gain electrons and form negative ions
(4) gain electrons and form positive ions

23 Which set of elements contains a metalloid?

(1) K, Mn, As, Ar   (3) Ba, Ag, Sn, Xe
(2) Li, Mg, Ca, Kr   (4) Fr, F, O, Rn

24 Atoms of elements in a group on the Periodic Table have similar chemical properties. This similarity is most closely related to the atoms'

(1) number of principal energy levels
(2) number of valence electrons
(3) atomic numbers
(4) atomic masses

25 Which element in Period 2 of the Periodic Table is the most reactive nonmetal?

(1) carbon   (3) oxygen
(2) nitrogen   (4) fluorine

26 What is the gram formula mass of $(NH_4)_3PO_4$?

(1) 113 g   (3) 149 g
(2) 121 g   (4) 404 g

27 Given the reaction:

$$CH_4 + 2O_2 \rightarrow CO_2 + 2H_2O$$

What amount of oxygen is needed to completely react with 1 mole of CH_4?

(1) 2 moles   (3) 2 grams
(2) 2 atoms   (4) 2 molecules

28 Based on Reference Table E, which of the following saturated solutions would be the *least* concentrated?

(1) sodium sulfate
(2) potassium sulfate
(3) copper (II) sulfate
(4) barium sulfate

29 What is the total number of moles of H_2SO_4 needed to prepare 5.0 liters of a 2.0 M solution of H_2SO_4?

(1) 2.5   (3) 10.
(2) 5.0   (4) 20.

30 Given the reaction:

$$Ca(s) + 2H_2O(\ell) \rightarrow Ca(OH)_2(aq) + H_2(g)$$

When 40.1 grams of Ca(s) reacts completely with the water, what is the total volume, at STP, of $H_2(g)$ produced?

(1) 1.00 L   (3) 22.4 L
(2) 2.00 L   (4) 44.8 L

31 Which is the correct equilibrium expression for the reaction below?

$$4NH_3(g) + 7O_2(g) \rightleftarrows 4NO_2(g) + 6H_2O(g)$$

(1) $K = \dfrac{[NO_2][H_2O]}{[NH_3][O_2]}$ (3) $K = \dfrac{[NH_3][O_2]}{[NO_2][H_2O]}$

(2) $K = \dfrac{[NO_2]^4[H_2O]^6}{[NH_3]^4[O_2]^7}$ (4) $K = \dfrac{[NH_3]^4[O_2]^7}{[NO_2]^4[H_2O]^6}$

32 The potential energy diagram below shows the reaction $X + Y \rightleftarrows Z$.

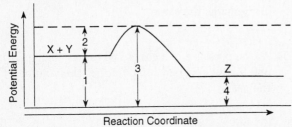

When a catalyst is added to the reaction, it will change the value of

(1) 1 and 2   (3) 2 and 3
(2) 1 and 3   (4) 3 and 4

33 Which conditions will increase the rate of a chemical reaction?

(1) decreased temperature and decreased concentration of reactants
(2) decreased temperature and increased concentration of reactants
(3) increased temperature and decreased concentration of reactants
(4) increased temperature and increased concentration of reactants

34 A solution exhibiting equilibrium between the dissolved and undissolved solute must be

(1) saturated   (3) dilute
(2) unsaturated   (4) concentrated

35 Which 0.1 M solution has a pH greater than 7?

(1) $C_6H_{12}O_6$ (3) KCl
(2) CH_3COOH (4) KOH

36 What color is phenolphthalein in a basic solution?

(1) blue   (3) yellow
(2) pink   (4) colorless

37 According to Reference Table L, which of the following is the strongest Brönsted-Lowry acid?

(1) HS^- (3) HNO_2
(2) H_2S (4) HNO_3

38 When HCl(aq) is exactly neutralized by NaOH(aq), the hydrogen ion concentration in the resulting mixture is

(1) always less than the concentration of the hydroxide ions
(2) always greater than the concentration of the hydroxide ions
(3) always equal to the concentration of the hydroxide ions
(4) sometimes greater and sometimes less than the concentration of the hydroxide ions

39 If 20. milliliters of 4.0 M NaOH is exactly neutralized by 20. milliliters of HCl, the molarity of the HCl is

(1) 1.0 M   (3) 5.0 M
(2) 2.0 M   (4) 4.0 M

40 The value of the ionization constant of water, K_w, will change when there is a change in

(1) temperature
(2) pressure
(3) hydrogen ion concentration
(4) hydroxide ion concentration

41 Based on Reference Table L, which species is amphoteric?

(1) NH_2^- (3) I^-
(2) NH_3 (4) HI

42 A redox reaction is a reaction in which

(1) only reduction occurs
(2) only oxidation occurs
(3) reduction and oxidation occur at the same time
(4) reduction occurs first and then oxidation occurs

43 Given the reaction:

$$\_\_Mg + \_\_Cr^{3+} \rightarrow \_\_Mg^{2+} + \_\_Cr$$

When the equation is correctly balanced using smallest whole numbers, the sum of the coefficients will be

(1) 10 (3) 5
(2) 7 (4) 4

44 Oxygen has an oxidation number of –2 in

(1) O_2 (3) Na_2O_2
(2) NO_2 (4) OF_2

45 Given the statements:

A The salt bridge prevents electrical contact between solutions of half-cells.
B The salt bridge prevents direct mixing of one half-cell solution with the other.
C The salt bridge allows electrons to migrate from one half-cell to the other.
D The salt bridge allows ions to migrate from one half-cell to the other.

Which two statements explain the purpose of a salt bridge used as part of a chemical cell?

(1) A and C (3) C and D
(2) A and D (4) B and D

46 When a substance is oxidized, it

(1) loses protons
(2) gains protons
(3) acts as an oxidizing agent
(4) acts as a reducing agent

47 In the reaction $Cu + 2Ag^+ \rightarrow Cu^{2+} + 2Ag$, the oxidizing agent is

(1) Cu (3) Ag^+
(2) Cu^{2+} (4) Ag

48 A compound that is classified as organic must contain the element

(1) carbon (3) oxygen
(2) nitrogen (4) hydrogen

49 Which substance is a product of a fermentation reaction?

(1) glucose (3) ethanol
(2) zymase (4) water

50 Which of the following hydrocarbons has the *lowest* normal boiling point?

(1) ethane (3) butane
(2) propane (4) pentane

51 What type of reaction is

$$CH_3CH_3 + Cl_2 \rightarrow CH_3CH_2Cl + HCl?$$

(1) an addition reaction
(2) a substitution reaction
(3) a saponification reaction
(4) an esterification reaction

52 Which compound is a saturated hydrocarbon?

(1) ethane (3) ethyne
(2) ethene (4) ethanol

Note that questions 53 through 56 have only three choices.

53 As atoms of elements in Group 16 are considered in order from top to bottom, the electronegativity of each successive element

(1) decreases
(2) increases
(3) remains the same

54 As the pressure of a gas at 760 torr is changed to 380 torr at constant temperature, the volume of the gas

(1) decreases
(2) increases
(3) remains the same

55 Given the change of phase: $CO_2(g) \rightarrow CO_2(s)$
As $CO_2(g)$ changes to $CO_2(s)$, the entropy of the system

(1) decreases
(2) increases
(3) remains the same

56 In heterogeneous reactions, as the surface area of the reactants increases, the rate of the reaction

(1) decreases
(2) increases
(3) remains the same

Part II

This part consists of twelve groups, each containing five questions. Each group tests a major area of the course. Choose seven of these twelve groups. Be sure that you answer all five questions in each group chosen. Record the answers to these questions on the separate answer sheet in accordance with the directions on the front page of this booklet. [35]

Group 1 — Matter and Energy

If you choose this group, be sure to answer questions 57–61.

57 What is the total number of calories of heat energy absorbed by 15 grams of water when it is heated from 30.°C to 40.°C?

(1) 10.   (3) 25
(2) 15   (4) 150

58 The graph below represents the uniform cooling of a sample of a substance, starting with the substance as a gas above its boiling point.

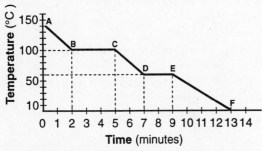

Which segment of the curve represents a time when both the liquid and the solid phases are present?

(1) EF   (3) CD
(2) BC   (4) DE

59 Which change of phase is exothermic?

(1) $NaCl(s) \rightarrow NaCl(\ell)$
(2) $CO_2(s) \rightarrow CO_2(g)$
(3) $H_2O(\ell) \rightarrow H_2O(s)$
(4) $H_2O(\ell) \rightarrow H_2O(g)$

60 According to the kinetic theory of gases, which assumption is correct?

(1) Gas particles strongly attract each other.
(2) Gas particles travel in curved paths.
(3) The volume of gas particles prevents random motion.
(4) Energy may be transferred between colliding particles.

61 A compound differs from a mixture in that a compound always has a

(1) homogeneous composition
(2) maximum of two components
(3) minimum of three components
(4) heterogeneous composition

Group 2 — Atomic Structure

If you choose this group, be sure to answer questions 62–66.

62 An ion with 5 protons, 6 neutrons, and a charge of 3+ has an atomic number of

(1) 5   (3) 8
(2) 6   (4) 11

63 Electron X can change to a higher energy level or a lower energy level. Which statement is true of electron X?

(1) Electron X emits energy when it changes to a higher energy level.
(2) Electron X absorbs energy when it changes to a higher energy level.
(3) Electron X absorbs energy when it changes to a lower energy level.
(4) Electron X neither emits nor absorbs energy when it changes energy level.

64 What is the highest principal quantum number assigned to an electron in an atom of zinc in the ground state?

(1) 1   (3) 5
(2) 2   (4) 4

65 The first ionization energy of an element is 176 kilocalories per mole of atoms. An atom of this element in the ground state has a total of how many valence electrons?

(1) 1   (3) 3
(2) 2   (4) 4

66 What is the total number of occupied s orbitals in an atom of nickel in the ground state?

(1) 1   (3) 3
(2) 2   (4) 4

Group 3 — Bonding

If you choose this group, be sure to answer questions 67–71.

67 What is the chemical formula for nickel (II) hypochlorite?

(1) $NiCl_2$ (3) $NiClO_2$
(2) $Ni(ClO)_2$ (4) $Ni(ClO)_3$

68 Based on Reference Table G, which of the following compounds is most stable?

(1) $CO(g)$ (3) $NO(g)$
(2) $CO_2(g)$ (4) $NO_2(g)$

69 The attractions that allow molecules of krypton to exist in the solid phase are due to

(1) ionic bonds
(2) covalent bonds
(3) molecule-ion forces
(4) van der Waals forces

70 Oxygen, nitrogen, and fluorine bond with hydrogen to form molecules. These molecules are attracted to each other by

(1) ionic bonds
(2) hydrogen bonds
(3) electrovalent bonds
(4) coordinate covalent bonds

71 An atom of which of the following elements has the greatest ability to attract electrons?

(1) silicon   (3) nitrogen
(2) sulfur   (4) bromine

Group 4 — Periodic Table

If you choose this group, be sure to answer questions 72–76.

72 Which electron configuration represents the atom with the largest covalent radius?

(1) $1s^1$ (3) $1s^2 2s^2$
(2) $1s^2 2s^1$ (4) $1s^2 2s^2 2p^1$

73 A solution of $Cu(NO_3)_2$ is colored because of the presence of the ion

(1) Cu^{2+} (3) O^{2-}
(2) N^{5+} (4) NO_3^{1-}

74 Which element is more reactive than strontium?

(1) potassium   (3) iron
(2) calcium   (4) copper

75 At STP, which substance is the best conductor of electricity?

(1) nitrogen   (3) sulfur
(2) neon   (4) silver

76 The oxide of metal X has the formula XO. Which group in the Periodic Table contains metal X?

(1) Group 1   (3) Group 13
(2) Group 2   (4) Group 17

Group 5 — Mathematics of Chemistry

If you choose this group, be sure to answer questions 77–81.

77 Given the same conditions of temperature and pressure, which noble gas will diffuse most rapidly?

(1) He   (3) Ar
(2) Ne   (4) Kr

78 What is the total number of molecules of hydrogen in 0.25 mole of hydrogen?

(1) 6.0×10^{23} (3) 3.0×10^{23}
(2) 4.5×10^{23} (4) 1.5×10^{23}

79 The volume of a 1.00-mole sample of an ideal gas will decrease when the

(1) pressure decreases and the temperature decreases
(2) pressure decreases and the temperature increases
(3) pressure increases and the temperature decreases
(4) pressure increases and the temperature increases

80 A 0.100-molal aqueous solution of which compound has the *lowest* freezing point?

(1) $C_6H_{12}O_6$ (3) $C_{12}H_{22}O_{11}$
(2) CH_3OH (4) $NaOH$

81 What is the empirical formula of a compound that contains 85% Ag and 15% F by mass?

(1) AgF (3) AgF_2
(2) Ag_2F (4) Ag_2F_2

Group 6 — Kinetics and Equilibrium

If you choose this group, be sure to answer questions 82–86.

82 Based on Reference Table M, which compound is less soluble in water than $PbCO_3$ at 298 K and 1 atmosphere?

(1) AgI (3) $CaSO_4$
(2) $AgCl$ (4) $BaSO_4$

83 Given the equilibrium reaction at constant pressure:

$$2HBr(g) + 17.4 \text{ kcal} \rightleftarrows H_2(g) + Br_2(g)$$

When the temperature is increased, the equilibrium will shift to the

(1) right, and the concentration of HBr(g) will decrease

(2) right, and the concentration of HBr(g) will increase

(3) left, and the concentration of HBr(g) will decrease

(4) left, and the concentration of HBr(g) will increase

84 A system is said to be in a state of dynamic equilibrium when the

(1) concentration of products is greater than the concentration of reactants

(2) concentration of products is the same as the concentration of reactants

(3) rate at which products are formed is greater than the rate at which reactants are formed

(4) rate at which products are formed is the same as the rate at which reactants are formed

85 Which reaction will occur spontaneously? [Refer to Reference Table G.]

(1) $\frac{1}{2} N_2(g) + \frac{1}{2} O_2(g) \rightarrow NO(g)$

(2) $\frac{1}{2} N_2(g) + O_2(g) \rightarrow NO_2(g)$

(3) $2C(s) + 3H_2(g) \rightarrow C_2H_6(g)$

(4) $2C(s) + 2H_2(g) \rightarrow C_2H_4(g)$

86 Which potential energy diagram represents the reaction $A + B \rightarrow C + $ energy?

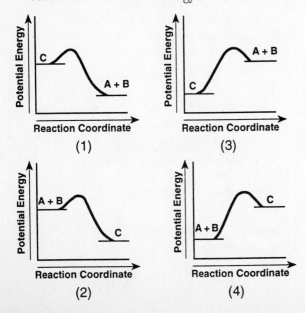

(1)   (3)

(2)   (4)

Group 7 — Acids and Bases

If you choose this group, be sure to answer questions 87–91.

87 Potassium chloride, KCl, is a salt derived from the neutralization of a

(1) weak acid and a weak base

(2) weak acid and a strong base

(3) strong acid and a weak base

(4) strong acid and a strong base

88 Given the reaction:

$$HSO_4^- + H_2O \rightleftarrows H_3O^+ + SO_4^{2-}$$

Which is a Brönsted-Lowry conjugate acid-base pair?

(1) HSO_4^- and H_3O^+ (3) H_2O and SO_4^{2-}

(2) HSO_4^- and SO_4^{2-} (4) H_2O and HSO_4^-

89 An aqueous solution that has a hydrogen ion concentration of 1.0×10^{-8} mole per liter has a pH of

(1) 6, which is basic   (3) 8, which is basic

(2) 6, which is acidic   (4) 8, which is acidic

90 The $[OH^-]$ of a solution is 1×10^{-6}. At 298 K and 1 atmosphere, the product $[H_3O^+][OH^-]$ is

(1) 1×10^{-2} (3) 1×10^{-8}

(2) 1×10^{-6} (4) 1×10^{-14}

91 Given the reaction:

$$KOH + HNO_3 \rightarrow KNO_3 + H_2O$$

Which process is taking place?

(1) neutralization   (3) substitution

(2) esterification   (4) addition

Group 8 — Redox and Electrochemistry

If you choose this group, be sure to answer questions 92–96.

92 Given the unbalanced equation:

$$\_MnO_2 + \_HCl \rightarrow \_MnCl_2 + \_H_2O + \_Cl_2$$

When the equation is correctly balanced using smallest whole-number coefficients, the coefficient of HCl is

(1) 1   (3) 3

(2) 2   (4) 4

93 Based on Reference Table N, which half-cell has a lower electrode potential than the standard hydrogen half-cell?

(1) $Au^{3+} + 3e^- \rightarrow Au(s)$
(2) $Hg^{2+} + 2e^- \rightarrow Hg(\ell)$
(3) $Cu^+ + e^- \rightarrow Cu(s)$
(4) $Pb^{2+} + 2e^- \rightarrow Pb(s)$

94 According to Reference Table N, which reaction will take place spontaneously?

(1) $Ni^{2+} + Pb(s) \rightarrow Ni(s) + Pb^{2+}$
(2) $Au^{3+} + Al(s) \rightarrow Au(s) + Al^{3+}$
(3) $Sr^{2+} + Sn(s) \rightarrow Sr(s) + Sn^{2+}$
(4) $Fe^{2+} + Cu(s) \rightarrow Fe(s) + Cu^{2+}$

95 Given the reaction:

$$Mg(s) + Zn^{2+}(aq) \rightarrow Mg^{2+}(aq) + Zn(s)$$

What is the cell voltage (E^0) for the overall reaction?

(1) +1.61 V   (3) +3.13 V
(2) –1.61 V   (4) –3.13 V

96 The diagram below represents a chemical cell at 298 K.

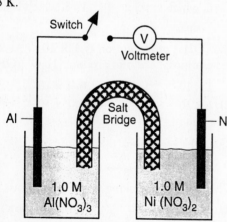

$$2\,Al(s) + 3Ni^{2+}(aq) \longrightarrow 2Al^{3+} + 3Ni(s)$$

When the switch is closed, electrons flow from

(1) $Al(s)$ to $Ni(s)$ (3) $Al^{3+}(aq)$ to $Ni^{2+}(aq)$
(2) $Ni(s)$ to $Al(s)$ (4) $Ni^{2+}(aq)$ to $Al^{3+}(aq)$

Group 9 — Organic Chemistry

If you choose this group, be sure to answer questions 97–101.

97 The compound C_4H_{10} belongs to the series of hydrocarbons with the general formula

(1) C_nH_{2n} (3) C_nH_{2n-2}
(2) C_nH_{2n+2} (4) C_nH_{2n-6}

98 Which is an isomer of H–C–C–OH?

(1) H–C–O–C–H   (3) H–C–C–H
(2) HO–C–C–H   (4) H–C–C–O–C–H

99 To be classified as a tertiary alcohol, the functional —OH group is bonded to a carbon atom that must be bonded to a total of how many additional carbon atoms?

(1) 1   (3) 3
(2) 2   (4) 4

100 Which substance is made up of monomers joined together in long chains?

(1) ketone   (3) ester
(2) protein   (4) acid

101 What is the total number of carbon atoms in a molecule of glycerol?

(1) 1   (3) 3
(2) 2   (4) 4

Group 10 — Applications of Chemical Principles

If you choose this group, be sure to answer questions 102–106.

102 Which type of reaction is occurring when a metal undergoes corrosion?

(1) oxidation-reduction
(2) neutralization
(3) polymerization
(4) saponification

103 Which process is used to separate the components of a petroleum mixture?

(1) addition polymerization
(2) condensation polymerization
(3) fractional distillation
(4) fractional crystallization

104 Which substance functions as the electrolyte in an automobile battery?

(1) PbO_2 (3) H_2SO_4
(2) $PbSO_4$ (4) H_2O

105 A battery consists of which type of cells?

(1) electrolytic   (3) electroplating
(2) electrochemical   (4) electromagnetic

106 Which element can be found in nature in the free (uncombined) state?

(1) Ca   (3) Au
(2) Ba   (4) Al

Group 11 — Nuclear Chemistry

If you choose this group, be sure to answer questions 107–111.

107 Which radioactive isotope is used in geological dating?

(1) uranium–238   (3) cobalt–60
(2) iodine–131   (4) technetium–99

108 Which equation represents a fusion reaction?

(1) $^3_1H + ^1_1H \rightarrow ^4_2He$

(2) $^{40}_{18}Ar + ^1_1H \rightarrow ^{40}_{19}K + ^1_0n$

(3) $^{234}_{91}Pa \rightarrow ^{234}_{92}U + ^0_1e$

(4) $^{226}_{88}Ra \rightarrow ^{226}_{86}Rn + ^4_2He$

109 Which substance is used as a coolant in a nuclear reactor?

(1) neutrons   (3) hydrogen
(2) plutonium   (4) heavy water

110 Which substance has chemical properties similar to those of radioactive ^{235}U?

(1) ^{235}Pa (3) ^{233}U
(2) ^{233}Pa (4) ^{206}Pb

111 Control rods in nuclear reactors are commonly made of boron and cadmium because these two elements have the ability to

(1) absorb neutrons
(2) emit neutrons
(3) decrease the speed of neutrons
(4) increase the speed of neutrons

Group 12 — Laboratory Activities

If you choose this group, be sure to answer questions 112–116.

Base your answers to questions 112 and 113 on the table below, which represents the production of 50 milliliters of CO_2 in the reaction of HCl with $NaHCO_3$. Five trials were performed under different conditions as shown. (The same mass of $NaHCO_3$ was used in each trial.)

Trial	Particle Size of $NaHCO_3$	Concentration of HCl	Temperature (°C) of HCl
A	small	1 M	20
B	large	1 M	20
C	large	1 M	40
D	small	2 M	40
E	large	2 M	40

112 Which two trials could be used to measure the effect of surface area?

(1) trials A and B   (3) trials A and D
(2) trials A and C   (4) trials B and D

113 Which trial would produce the fastest reaction?

(1) trial A   (3) trial C
(2) trial B   (4) trial D

114 A student determined the heat of fusion of water to be 88 calories per gram. If the accepted value is 80. calories per gram, what is the student's percent error?

(1) 8.0%   (3) 11%
(2) 10.%   (4) 90.%

115 Given: (52.6 cm) (1.214 cm)

What is the product expressed to the correct number of significant figures?

(1) 64 cm^2 (3) 63.86 cm^2
(2) 63.9 cm^2 (4) 63.8564 cm^2

116 The diagram below represents a metal bar and two centimeter rulers, A and B. Portions of the rulers have been enlarged to show detail.

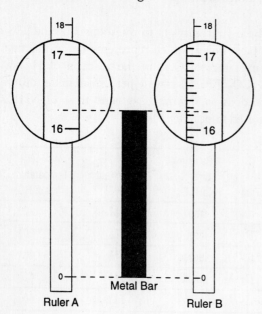

Ruler A   Metal Bar   Ruler B

What is the greatest degree of precision to which the metal bar can be measured by ruler A and by ruler B?

(1) to the nearest tenth by both rulers
(2) to the nearest hundredth by both rulers
(3) to the nearest tenth by ruler A and to the nearest hundredth by ruler B
(4) to the nearest hundredth by ruler A and to the nearest tenth by ruler B

CHEMISTRY
JUNE 1996

ANSWER SHEET

Student ....

Teacher ....

School ....

Record all of your answers on this answer sheet in accordance with the instructions on the front cover of the test booklet.

Part I (65 credits)

1 1 2 3 4	21 1 2 3 4	41 1 2 3 4	
2 1 2 3 4	22 1 2 3 4	42 1 2 3 4	
3 1 2 3 4	23 1 2 3 4	43 1 2 3 4	
4 1 2 3 4	24 1 2 3 4	44 1 2 3 4	
5 1 2 3 4	25 1 2 3 4	45 1 2 3 4	
6 1 2 3 4	26 1 2 3 4	46 1 2 3 4	
7 1 2 3 4	27 1 2 3 4	47 1 2 3 4	
8 1 2 3 4	28 1 2 3 4	48 1 2 3 4	
9 1 2 3 4	29 1 2 3 4	49 1 2 3 4	
10 1 2 3 4	30 1 2 3 4	50 1 2 3 4	
11 1 2 3 4	31 1 2 3 4	51 1 2 3 4	
12 1 2 3 4	32 1 2 3 4	52 1 2 3 4	
13 1 2 3 4	33 1 2 3 4	53 1 2 3	
14 1 2 3 4	34 1 2 3 4	54 1 2 3	
15 1 2 3 4	35 1 2 3 4	55 1 2 3	
16 1 2 3 4	36 1 2 3 4	56 1 2 3	
17 1 2 3 4	37 1 2 3 4		
18 1 2 3 4	38 1 2 3 4		
19 1 2 3 4	39 1 2 3 4		
20 1 2 3 4	40 1 2 3 4		

Part II (35 credits)

Answer the questions in only seven of the twelve groups in this part. Be sure to mark the answers to the groups of questions you choose in accordance with the instructions on the front cover of the test booklet. Leave blank the five groups of questions you do not choose to answer.

Group 1
Matter and Energy

57   1   2   3   4

58   1   2   3   4

59   1   2   3   4

60   1   2   3   4

61   1   2   3   4

Group 2
Atomic Structure

62   1   2   3   4

63   1   2   3   4

64   1   2   3   4

65   1   2   3   4

66   1   2   3   4

Group 3
Bonding

67   1   2   3   4

68   1   2   3   4

69   1   2   3   4

70   1   2   3   4

71   1   2   3   4

Group 4
Periodic Table

72   1   2   3   4

73   1   2   3   4

74   1   2   3   4

75   1   2   3   4

76   1   2   3   4

Group 5
Mathematics of Chemistry

77   1   2   3   4

78   1   2   3   4

79   1   2   3   4

80   1   2   3   4

81   1   2   3   4

Group 6
Kinetics and Equilibrium

82   1   2   3   4

83   1   2   3   4

84   1   2   3   4

85   1   2   3   4

86   1   2   3   4

Group 7
Acids and Bases

87   1   2   3   4

88   1   2   3   4

89   1   2   3   4

90   1   2   3   4

91   1   2   3   4

Group 8
Redox and Electrochemistry

92   1   2   3   4

93   1   2   3   4

94   1   2   3   4

95   1   2   3   4

96   1   2   3   4

Group 9
Organic Chemistry

97   1   2   3   4

98   1   2   3   4

99   1   2   3   4

100   1   2   3   4

101   1   2   3   4

Group 10
Applications of Chemical Principles

102   1   2   3   4

103   1   2   3   4

104   1   2   3   4

105   1   2   3   4

106   1   2   3   4

Group 11
Nuclear Chemistry

107   1   2   3   4

108   1   2   3   4

109   1   2   3   4

110   1   2   3   4

111   1   2   3   4

Group 12
Laboratory Activities

112   1   2   3   4

113   1   2   3   4

114   1   2   3   4

115   1   2   3   4

116   1   2   3   4

CHEMISTRY
JUNE 1997

Part I

Answer all 56 questions in this part. [65]

Directions (1–56): For *each* statement or question, select the word or expression that, of those given, best completes the statement or answers the question. Record your answer on the separate answer sheet in accordance with the directions on the front page of this booklet.

1 Which Kelvin temperature is equal to –73°C?

(1) 100 K   (3) 200 K
(2) 173 K   (4) 346 K

2 A substance that is composed only of atoms having the same atomic number is classified as

(1) a compound
(2) an element
(3) a homogeneous mixture
(4) a heterogeneous mixture

3 At which temperature will water boil when the external pressure is 17.5 torr?

(1) 14.5°C   (3) 20°C
(2) 16.5°C   (4) 100°C

4 At which point do a liquid and a solid exist at equilibrium?

(1) sublimation point
(2) vaporization point
(3) boiling point
(4) melting point

5 When 7.00 moles of gas *A* and 3.00 moles of gas *B* are combined, the total pressure exerted by the gas mixture is 760. mmHg. What is the partial pressure exerted by gas *A* in this mixture?

(1) 76.0 mmHg   (3) 532 mmHg
(2) 228 mmHg   (4) 760. mmHg

6 Which radioactive emanations have a charge of 2+?

(1) alpha particles   (3) gamma rays
(2) beta particles   (4) neutrons

7 Which symbols represent atoms that are isotopes of each other?

(1) ^{14}C and ^{14}N (3) ^{131}I and ^{131}I
(2) ^{16}O and ^{18}O (4) ^{222}Rn and ^{222}Ra

8 Which orbital notation correctly represents the outermost principal energy level of a nitrogen atom in the ground state?

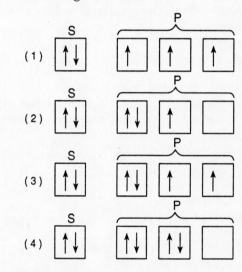

9 The atomic mass of an element is defined as the weighted average mass of that element's

(1) most abundant isotope
(2) least abundant isotope
(3) naturally occurring isotopes
(4) radioactive isotopes

10 When electrons in an atom in an excited state fall to lower energy levels, energy is

(1) absorbed, only
(2) released, only
(3) neither released nor absorbed
(4) both released and absorbed

11 A neutron has approximately the same mass as

(1) an alpha particle   (3) an electron
(2) a beta particle   (4) a proton

12 What is the formula for sodium oxalate?

(1) $NaClO$ (3) $Na_2C_2O_4$
(2) Na_2O (4) $NaC_2H_3O_2$

13 Given the unbalanced equation:

$$Al + O_2 \rightarrow Al_2O_3$$

When this equation is completely balanced using smallest whole numbers, what is the sum of the coefficients?

(1) 9   (3) 5
(2) 7   (4) 4

14 One mole of which substance contains a total of 6.02×10^{23} atoms?

(1) Li   (3) O_2
(2) NH_3 (4) CO_2

15 Which formula represents a molecular substance?

(1) CaO   (3) Li_2O
(2) CO   (4) Al_2O_3

16 In an aqueous solution of an ionic salt, the oxygen atom of the water molecule is attracted to the

(1) negative ion of the salt, due to oxygen's partial positive charge
(2) negative ion of the salt, due to oxygen's partial negative charge
(3) positive ion of the salt, due to oxygen's partial positive charge
(4) positive ion of the salt, due to oxygen's partial negative charge

17 What is the empirical formula of the compound whose molecular formula is P_4O_{10}?

(1) PO   (3) P_2O_5
(2) PO_2 (4) P_8O_{20}

18 Which sequence of Group 18 elements demonstrates a gradual *decrease* in the strength of the van der Waals forces?

(1) $Ar(\ell)$, $Kr(\ell)$, $Ne(\ell)$, $Xe(\ell)$
(2) $Kr(\ell)$, $Xe(\ell)$, $Ar(\ell)$, $Ne(\ell)$
(3) $Ne(\ell)$, $Ar(\ell)$, $Kr(\ell)$, $Xe(\ell)$
(4) $Xe(\ell)$, $Kr(\ell)$, $Ar(\ell)$, $Ne(\ell)$

19 In the ground state, atoms of the elements in Group 15 of the Periodic Table all have the same number of

(1) filled principal energy levels
(2) occupied principal energy levels
(3) neutrons in the nucleus
(4) electrons in the valence shell

20 Which elements have the most similar chemical properties?

(1) K and Na   (3) K and Ca
(2) K and Cl   (4) K and S

21 Which three groups of the Periodic Table contain the most elements classified as metalloids (semimetals)?

(1) 1, 2, and 13   (3) 14, 15, and 16
(2) 2, 13, and 14   (4) 16, 17, and 18

22 In which classification is an element placed if the outermost 3 sublevels of its atoms have a ground state electron configuration of $3p^6 3d^5 4s^2$?

(1) alkaline earth metals
(2) transition metals
(3) metalloids (semimetals)
(4) nonmetals

23 A diatomic element with a high first ionization energy would most likely be a

(1) nonmetal with a high electronegativity
(2) nonmetal with a low electronegativity
(3) metal with a high electronegativity
(4) metal with a low electronegativity

24 As the elements in Period 3 are considered from left to right, they tend to

(1) lose electrons more readily and increase in metallic character
(2) lose electrons more readily and increase in nonmetallic character
(3) gain electrons more readily and increase in metallic character
(4) gain electrons more readily and increase in nonmetallic character

25 An atom of an element has 28 innermost electrons and 7 outermost electrons. In which period of the Periodic Table is this element located?

(1) 5   (3) 3
(2) 2   (4) 4

26 Which solution is the most concentrated?

(1) 1 mole of solute dissolved in 1 liter of solution
(2) 2 moles of solute dissolved in 3 liters of solution
(3) 6 moles of solute dissolved in 4 liters of solution
(4) 4 moles of solute dissolved in 8 liters of solution

27 What is the gram formula mass of K_2CO_3?

(1) 138 g   (3) 99 g
(2) 106 g   (4) 67 g

28 What is the total number of atoms contained in 2.00 moles of nickel?

(1) 58.9   (3) 6.02×10^{23}
(2) 118   (4) 1.20×10^{24}

29 Given the reaction at STP:

$$2KClO_3(s) \rightarrow 2KCl(s) + 3O_2(g)$$

What is the total number of liters of $O_2(g)$ produced from the complete decomposition of 0.500 mole of $KClO_3(s)$?

(1) 11.2 L   (3) 44.8 L
(2) 16.8 L   (4) 67.2 L

30 What is the percent by mass of oxygen in magnesium oxide, MgO?

(1) 20%   (3) 50%
(2) 40%   (4) 60%

31 A solution in which the crystallizing rate of the solute equals the dissolving rate of the solute must be

(1) saturated   (3) concentrated
(2) unsaturated   (4) dilute

32 Which statement explains why the speed of some chemical reactions is increased when the surface area of the reactant is increased?

(1) This change increases the density of the reactant particles.
(2) This change increases the concentration of the reactant.
(3) This change exposes more reactant particles to a possible collision.
(4) This change alters the electrical conductivity of the reactant particles.

33 According to Reference Table G, which compound forms exothermically?

(1) hydrogen fluoride   (3) ethene
(2) hydrogen iodide   (4) ethyne

34 The potential energy diagram shown below represents the reaction $A + B \rightarrow AB$.

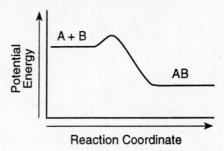

Which statement correctly describes this reaction?

(1) It is endothermic and energy is absorbed.
(2) It is endothermic and energy is released.
(3) It is exothermic and energy is absorbed.
(4) It is exothermic and energy is released.

35 Given the reaction at equilibrium:

$$N_2(g) + 3H_2(g) \rightleftarrows 2NH_3(g)$$

Increasing the concentration of $N_2(g)$ will increase the forward reaction rate due to

(1) a decrease in the number of effective collisions
(2) an increase in the number of effective collisions
(3) a decrease in the activation energy
(4) an increase in the activation energy

36 Based on Reference Table L, which of the following aqueous solutions is the best conductor of electricity?

(1) 0.1 M HF   (3) 0.1 M H_2SO_4
(2) 0.1 M H_2S (4) 0.1 M H_3PO_4

37 Which substance is classified as an Arrhenius base?

(1) HCl   (3) $LiNO_3$
(2) NaOH   (4) $KHCO_3$

38 The conjugate acid of the HS^- ion is

(1) H^+ (3) H_2O
(2) S^{2-} (4) H_2S

39 If 20. milliliters of 1.0 M HCl was used to completely neutralize 40. milliliters of an NaOH solution, what was the molarity of the NaOH solution?

(1) 0.50 M   (3) 1.5 M
(2) 2.0 M   (4) 4.0 M

40 According to Reference Table L, which species is amphoteric (amphiprotic)?

(1) HCl   (3) HSO_4^-
(2) HNO_2 (4) H_2SO_4

41 In the reaction $H_2O + CO_3^{2-} \rightleftarrows OH^- + HCO_3^-$, the two Brönsted-Lowry acids are

(1) H_2O and OH^- (3) CO_3^{2-} and OH^-
(2) H_2O and HCO_3^- (4) CO_3^{2-} and HCO_3^-

42 What happens to reducing agents in chemical reactions?

(1) Reducing agents gain protons.
(2) Reducing agents gain electrons.
(3) Reducing agents are oxidized.
(4) Reducing agents are reduced.

43 What is the oxidation number of carbon in $NaHCO_3$?

(1) +6   (3) −4
(2) +2   (4) +4

44 Which statement correctly describes a redox reaction?

(1) The oxidation half-reaction and the reduction half-reaction occur simultaneously.
(2) The oxidation half-reaction occurs before the reduction half-reaction.
(3) The oxidation half-reaction occurs after the reduction half-reaction.
(4) The oxidation half-reaction occurs spontaneously but the reduction half-reaction does not.

45 Given the redox reaction:

$Co(s) + PbCl_2(aq) \rightarrow CoCl_2(aq) + Pb(s)$

Which statement correctly describes the oxidation and reduction that occur?

(1) Co(s) is oxidized and $Cl^-(aq)$ is reduced.
(2) Co(s) is oxidized and $Pb^{2+}(aq)$ is reduced.
(3) Co(s) is reduced and $Cl^-(aq)$ is oxidized.
(4) Co(s) is reduced and $Pb^{2+}(aq)$ is oxidized.

46 Which half-reaction correctly represents reduction?

(1) $Cr^{3+} + 3e^- \rightarrow Cr(s)$

(2) $Cr^{3+} \rightarrow Cr(s) + 3e^-$

(3) $Cr(s) \rightarrow Cr^{3+} + 3e^-$

(4) $Cr(s) + 3e^- \rightarrow Cr^{3+}$

47 Which statement best describes how a salt bridge maintains electrical neutrality in the half-cells of an electrochemical cell?

(1) It prevents the migration of electrons.
(2) It permits the migration of ions.
(3) It permits the two solutions to mix completely.
(4) It prevents the reaction from occurring spontaneously.

48 What is the name of a compound that has the molecular formula C_6H_6?

(1) butane   (3) benzene
(2) butene   (4) butyne

49 The fermentation of $C_6H_{12}O_6$ will produce CO_2 and

(1) $C_3H_5(OH)_3$ (3) $Ca(OH)_2$
(2) C_2H_5OH (4) $Cr(OH)_3$

50 Which is the correct name for the substance below?

$$H-\overset{\overset{\displaystyle H}{|}}{C}=\overset{\overset{\displaystyle H}{|}}{C}-H$$

(1) ethanol   (3) ethane
(2) ethyne   (4) ethene

51 Which structural formula represents an organic acid?

52 In a molecule of CH_4, the hydrogen atoms are spatially oriented toward the corners of a regular

(1) pyramid   (3) square
(2) tetrahedron   (4) rectangle

Note that questions 53 through 56 have only three choices.

53 Given the reaction at equilibrium:

$$N_2(g) + O_2(g) \rightleftarrows 2NO(g)$$

As the concentration of $N_2(g)$ increases, the concentration of $O_2(g)$ will

(1) decrease
(2) increase
(3) remain the same

54 As the temperature of a sample of a radioactive element decreases, the half-life of the element will

(1) decrease
(2) increase
(3) remain the same

55 As ice cools from 273 K to 263 K, the average kinetic energy of its molecules will

(1) decrease
(2) increase
(3) remain the same

56 As the hydrogen ion concentration of an aqueous solution increases, the hydroxide ion concentration of this solution will

(1) decrease
(2) increase
(3) remain the same

Part II

This part consists of twelve groups, each containing five questions. Each group tests a major area of the course. Choose seven of these twelve groups. Be sure that you answer all five questions in each group chosen. Record the answers to these questions on the separate answer sheet in accordance with the directions on the front page of this booklet.   [35]

Group 1 — Matter and Energy

If you choose this group, be sure to answer questions 57–61.

57 The phase change represented by the equation $I_2(s) \rightarrow I_2(g)$ is called

(1) sublimation
(2) condensation
(3) melting
(4) boiling

58 The graph below represents the relationship between temperature and time as heat is added uniformly to a substance, starting when the substance is a solid below its melting point.

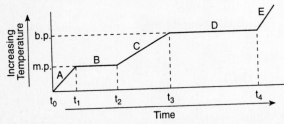

Which portions of the graph represent times when heat is absorbed and potential energy increases while kinetic energy remains constant?

(1) A and B
(2) B and D
(3) A and C
(4) C and D

59 The heat of fusion is defined as the energy required at constant temperature to change 1 unit mass of a

(1) gas to a liquid
(2) gas to a solid
(3) solid to a gas
(4) solid to a liquid

60 Given the equation:

$$2Na + 2H_2O \rightarrow 2NaOH + H_2$$

Which substance in this equation is a binary compound?

(1) Na
(2) H_2
(3) H_2O
(4) NaOH

61 At STP, 1 liter of $O_2(g)$ and 1 liter of $Ne(g)$ have the same

(1) mass
(2) density
(3) number of atoms
(4) number of molecules

Group 2 — Atomic Structure

If you choose this group, be sure to answer questions 62–66.

62 The diagram below represents radiation passing through an electric field.

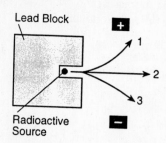

Which type of emanation is represented by the arrow labeled 2?

(1) alpha particle   (3) positron
(2) beta particle   (4) gamma radiation

63 Which sample will decay *least* over a period of 30 days? [Refer to Reference Table *H*.]

(1) 10 g of Au-198   (3) 10 g of P-32
(2) 10 g of I-131   (4) 10 g of Rn-222

64 A particle has a mass of 1.0 atomic mass unit. What is the approximate mass of this particle in grams?

(1) 1.0 g   (3) 1.7×10^{-24} g
(2) 2.0 g   (4) 6.0×10^{-23} g

65 Which equation represents nuclear disintegration resulting in release of a beta particle?

(1) $^{220}_{87}Fr + ^{4}_{2}He \rightarrow ^{224}_{89}Ac$

(2) $^{239}_{94}Pu \rightarrow ^{235}_{92}U + ^{4}_{2}He$

(3) $^{32}_{15}P + ^{0}_{-1}e \rightarrow ^{32}_{14}Si$

(4) $^{198}_{79}Au \rightarrow ^{198}_{80}Hg + ^{0}_{-1}e$

66 Which electron configuration represents a potassium atom in the excited state?

(1) $1s^2 2s^2 2p^6 3s^2 3p^3$
(2) $1s^2 2s^2 2p^6 3s^1 3p^4$
(3) $1s^2 2s^2 2p^6 3s^2 3p^6 4s^1$
(4) $1s^2 2s^2 2p^6 3s^2 3p^5 4s^2$

Group 3 — Bonding

If you choose this group, be sure to answer questions 67–71.

67 Which type of attraction is directly involved when KCl dissolves in water?

(1) molecule–molecule   (3) molecule–ion
(2) molecule–atom   (4) ion–ion

68 In which compound have electrons been transferred to the oxygen atom?

(1) CO_2 (3) N_2O
(2) NO_2 (4) Na_2O

69 A strontium atom differs from a strontium ion in that the atom has a greater

(1) number of electrons   (3) atomic number
(2) number of protons   (4) mass number

70 Which substance is an example of a network solid?

(1) nitrogen dioxide   (3) carbon dioxide
(2) sulfur dioxide   (4) silicon dioxide

71 Which combination of atoms can form a polar covalent bond?

(1) H and H   (3) N and N
(2) H and Br   (4) Na and Br

Group 4 — Periodic Table

If you choose this group, be sure to answer questions 72–76.

72 Which element has the highest first ionization energy?

(1) sodium   (3) calcium
(2) aluminum   (4) phosphorus

73 Which compound forms a colored aqueous solution?

(1) $CaCl_2$ (3) NaOH
(2) $CrCl_3$ (4) KBr

74 When a metal atom combines with a nonmetal atom, the nonmetal atom will

(1) lose electrons and decrease in size
(2) lose electrons and increase in size
(3) gain electrons and decrease in size
(4) gain electrons and increase in size

75 According to Reference Table *P*, which of the following elements has the smallest covalent radius?

(1) nickel   (3) calcium
(2) cobalt   (4) potassium

76 Which element's ionic radius is smaller than its atomic radius?

(1) neon   (3) sodium
(2) nitrogen   (4) sulfur

Group 5 — Mathematics of Chemistry

If you choose this group, be sure to answer questions 77–81.

77 What is the total number of moles of hydrogen gas contained in 9.03×10^{23} molecules?

(1) 1.50 moles   (3) 6.02 moles
(2) 2.00 moles   (4) 9.03 moles

78 At the same temperature and pressure, which gas will diffuse through air at the fastest rate?

(1) H_2 (3) CO
(2) O_2 (4) CO_2

79 How are the boiling and freezing points of a sample of water affected when a salt is dissolved in the water?

(1) The boiling point decreases and the freezing point decreases.
(2) The boiling point decreases and the freezing point increases.
(3) The boiling point increases and the freezing point decreases.
(4) The boiling point increases and the freezing point increases.

80 A sample of an unknown gas at STP has a density of 0.630 gram per liter. What is the gram molecular mass of this gas?

(1) 2.81 g   (3) 22.4 g
(2) 14.1 g   (4) 63.0 g

81 A compound is 86% carbon and 14% hydrogen by mass. What is the empirical formula for this compound?

(1) CH   (3) CH_3
(2) CH_2 (4) CH_4

Group 6 — Kinetics and Equilibrium

If you choose this group, be sure to answer questions 82–86.

82 In a chemical reaction, a catalyst changes the

(1) potential energy of the products
(2) potential energy of the reactants
(3) heat of reaction
(4) activation energy

83 Which statement describes characteristics of an endothermic reaction?

(1) The sign of ΔH is positive, and the products have less potential energy than the reactants.
(2) The sign of ΔH is positive, and the products have more potential energy than the reactants.
(3) The sign of ΔH is negative, and the products have less potential energy than the reactants.
(4) The sign of ΔH is negative, and the products have more potential energy than the reactants.

84 What is the K_{sp} expression for the salt PbI_2?

(1) $[Pb^{2+}][I^-]^2$ (3) $[Pb^{2+}][I_2]^2$
(2) $[Pb^{2+}][2I^-]$ (4) $[Pb^{2+}][2I^-]^2$

85 Given the equilibrium system:
$$PbCO_3(s) \rightleftarrows Pb^{2+}(aq) + CO_3^{2-}(aq)$$
Which changes occur as $Pb(NO_3)_2(s)$ is added to the system at equilibrium?

(1) The amount of $PbCO_3(s)$ decreases, and the concentration of $CO_3^{2-}(aq)$ decreases.
(2) The amount of $PbCO_3(s)$ decreases, and the concentration of $CO_3^{2-}(aq)$ increases.
(3) The amount of $PbCO_3(s)$ increases, and the concentration of $CO_3^{2-}(aq)$ decreases.
(4) The amount of $PbCO_3(s)$ increases, and the concentration of $CO_3^{2-}(aq)$ increases.

86 A chemical reaction will always occur spontaneously if the reaction has a negative

(1) ΔG (3) ΔS
(2) ΔH (4) T

Group 7 — Acids and Bases

If you choose this group, be sure to answer questions 87–91.

87 An acidic solution could have a pH of

(1) 7
(2) 10
(3) 3
(4) 14

88 What is the pH of a 0.00001 molar HCl solution?

(1) 1
(2) 9
(3) 5
(4) 4

89 According to the Brönsted-Lowry theory, an acid is any species that can

(1) donate a proton
(2) donate an electron
(3) accept a proton
(4) accept an electron

90 When the salt Na_2CO_3 undergoes hydrolysis, the resulting solution will be

(1) acidic with a pH less than 7
(2) acidic with a pH greater than 7
(3) basic with a pH less than 7
(4) basic with a pH greater than 7

91 In an aqueous solution, which substance yields hydrogen ions as the only positive ions?

(1) C_2H_5OH
(2) CH_3COOH
(3) KH
(4) KOH

Group 8 — Redox and Electrochemistry

If you choose this group, be sure to answer questions 92–96.

92 In which kind of cell are the redox reactions made to occur by an externally applied electrical current?

(1) galvanic cell
(2) chemical cell
(3) electrochemical cell
(4) electrolytic cell

93 According to Reference Table N, which metal will react spontaneously with Ag^+ ions, but not with Zn^{2+} ions?

(1) Cu
(2) Au
(3) Al
(4) Mg

94 Which atom forms an ion that would migrate toward the cathode in an electrolytic cell?

(1) F
(2) I
(3) Na
(4) Cl

95 Given the equations A, B, C, and D:

(A) $AgNO_3 + NaCl \rightarrow AgCl + NaNO_3$
(B) $Cl_2 + H_2O \rightarrow HClO + HCl$
(C) $CuO + CO \rightarrow CO_2 + Cu$
(D) $NaOH + HCl \rightarrow NaCl + H_2O$

Which two equations represent redox reactions?

(1) A and B
(2) B and C
(3) C and A
(4) D and B

96 Given the unbalanced equation:

$$\_NO_3^- + 4H^+ + \_Pb \rightarrow$$
$$\_Pb^{2+} + \_NO_2 + 2H_2O$$

What is the coefficient of NO_2 when the equation is correctly balanced?

(1) 1
(2) 2
(3) 3
(4) 4

Group 9 — Organic Chemistry

If you choose this group, be sure to answer questions 97–101.

97 Which polymers occur naturally?

(1) starch and nylon
(2) starch and cellulose
(3) protein and nylon
(4) protein and plastic

98 Which statement explains why the element carbon forms so many compounds?

(1) Carbon atoms combine readily with oxygen.
(2) Carbon atoms have very high electronegativity.
(3) Carbon readily forms ionic bonds with other carbon atoms.
(4) Carbon readily forms covalent bonds with other carbon atoms.

99 Which structural formula represents a primary alcohol?

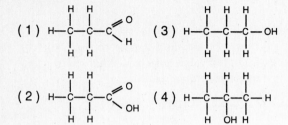

100 Which compounds are isomers?

(1) 1-propanol and 2-propanol
(2) methanoic acid and ethanoic acid
(3) methanol and methanal
(4) ethane and ethanol

101 Compared to the rate of inorganic reactions, the rate of organic reactions generally is

(1) slower because organic particles are ions
(2) slower because organic particles contain covalent bonds
(3) faster because organic particles are ions
(4) faster because organic particles contain covalent bonds

Group 10 — Applications of Chemical Principles

If you choose this group, be sure to answer questions 102–106.

102 Which products are obtained from the fractional distillation of petroleum?

(1) esters and acids
(2) alcohols and aldehydes
(3) soaps and starches
(4) kerosene and gasoline

103 Given the lead-acid battery reaction:

$$Pb + PbO_2 + 2H_2SO_4 \underset{\text{Charge}}{\overset{\text{Discharge}}{\rightleftarrows}} 2PbSO_4 + 2H_2O$$

Which species is oxidized during battery discharge?

(1) Pb
(2) PbO_2
(3) SO_4^{2-}
(4) H_2O

104 Given the reaction:

$$ZnO + X + \text{heat} \rightarrow Zn + XO$$

Which element, represented by X, is used industrially to reduce the ZnO to Zn?

(1) Cu
(2) C
(3) Sn
(4) Pb

105 Which metal is obtained commercially by the electrolysis of its salt?

(1) Zn
(2) K
(3) Fe
(4) Ag

106 The corrosion of aluminum (Al) is a less serious problem than the corrosion of iron (Fe) because

(1) Al does not oxidize
(2) Fe does not oxidize
(3) Al oxidizes to form a protective layer
(4) Fe oxidizes to form a protective layer

Group 11 — Nuclear Chemistry

If you choose this group, be sure to answer questions 107–111.

107 Fissionable uranium-233, uranium-235, and plutonium-239 are used in a nuclear reactor as

(1) coolants
(2) control rods
(3) moderators
(4) fuels

108 Which reaction illustrates fusion?

(1) $^2_1H + ^2_1H \rightarrow ^4_2He$
(2) $^1_0n + ^{27}_{13}Al \rightarrow ^{24}_{11}Na + ^4_2He$
(3) $^{27}_{13}Al + ^4_2He \rightarrow ^{30}_{15}P + ^1_0n$
(4) $^{14}_7N + ^4_2He \rightarrow ^1_1H + ^{17}_8O$

109 An accelerator can *not* be used to speed up

(1) alpha particles
(2) beta particles
(3) protons
(4) neutrons

110 Brain tumors can be located by using an isotope of

(1) carbon-14
(2) iodine-131
(3) technetium-99
(4) uranium-238

111 In the reaction $^9_4Be + X \rightarrow ^{12}_6C + ^1_0n$, the X represents

(1) an alpha particle
(2) a beta particle
(3) an electron
(4) a proton

Group 12 — Laboratory Activities

If you choose this group, be sure to answer questions 112–116.

112 Which piece of laboratory equipment should be used to remove a heated crucible from a ring-stand?

(1)

(2)

(3)

(4)

113 The following set of procedures was used by a student to determine the heat of solution of NaOH.

(A) Read the original temperature of the water.
(B) Read the final temperature of the solution.
(C) Pour the water into a beaker.
(D) Stir the mixture.
(E) Add the sodium hydroxide.

What is the correct order of procedures for making this determination?

(1) $A \rightarrow C \rightarrow E \rightarrow B \rightarrow D$
(2) $E \rightarrow D \rightarrow C \rightarrow A \rightarrow B$
(3) $C \rightarrow A \rightarrow E \rightarrow D \rightarrow B$
(4) $C \rightarrow E \rightarrow D \rightarrow A \rightarrow B$

114. In an experiment, a student found 18.6% by mass of water in a sample of $BaCl_2 \cdot 2H_2O$. The accepted value is 14.8%. What was the student's experimental percent error?

(1) $\frac{3.8}{18.6} \times 100$

(2) $\frac{3.8}{14.8} \times 100$

(3) $\frac{14.8}{18.6} \times 100$

(4) $\frac{18.6}{14.8} \times 100$

115 A student obtained the following data in a chemistry laboratory.

Trial	Temperature (°C)	Solubility (grams of KNO_3/100 g of H_2O)
1	25	40
2	32	50
3	43	70
4	48	60

Based on Reference Table D, which of the trials seems to be in error?

(1) 1
(2) 2
(3) 3
(4) 4

116 A student using a Styrofoam cup as a calorimeter added a piece of metal to distilled water and stirred the mixture as shown in the diagram below. The student's data is shown in the table below.

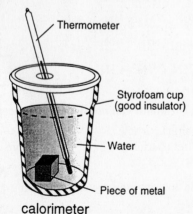

Thermometer

Styrofoam cup (good insulator)

Water

Piece of metal

calorimeter

DATA TABLE

Mass of H_2O ....50.0 g
Initial temperature of H_2O ....25.0°C
Mass of metal ....20.0 g
Initial temperature of metal..............100.°C
Final temperature of H_2O + metal.....32.0°C

Which statement correctly describes the heat flow in calories? [Ignore heat gained or lost by the calorimeter.]

(1) The water lost 1360 calories of heat and the metal gained 140. calories of heat.
(2) The water lost 350. calories of heat and the metal gained 350. calories of heat.
(3) The water gained 1360 calories of heat and the metal lost 140. calories of heat.
(4) The water gained 350. calories of heat and the metal lost 350. calories of heat.

CHEMISTRY
JUNE 1997

ANSWER SHEET

Student ....

Teacher ....

School ....

Record all of your answers on this answer sheet in accordance with the instructions on the front cover of the test booklet.

Part I (65 credits)

1	1 2 3 4		21	1 2 3 4		41	1 2 3 4
2	1 2 3 4		22	1 2 3 4		42	1 2 3 4
3	1 2 3 4		23	1 2 3 4		43	1 2 3 4
4	1 2 3 4		24	1 2 3 4		44	1 2 3 4
5	1 2 3 4		25	1 2 3 4		45	1 2 3 4
6	1 2 3 4		26	1 2 3 4		46	1 2 3 4
7	1 2 3 4		27	1 2 3 4		47	1 2 3 4
8	1 2 3 4		28	1 2 3 4		48	1 2 3 4
9	1 2 3 4		29	1 2 3 4		49	1 2 3 4
10	1 2 3 4		30	1 2 3 4		50	1 2 3 4
11	1 2 3 4		31	1 2 3 4		51	1 2 3 4
12	1 2 3 4		32	1 2 3 4		52	1 2 3 4
13	1 2 3 4		33	1 2 3 4		53	1 2 3
14	1 2 3 4		34	1 2 3 4		54	1 2 3
15	1 2 3 4		35	1 2 3 4		55	1 2 3
16	1 2 3 4		36	1 2 3 4		56	1 2 3
17	1 2 3 4		37	1 2 3 4		
18	1 2 3 4		38	1 2 3 4		
19	1 2 3 4		39	1 2 3 4		
20	1 2 3 4		40	1 2 3 4		

Part II (35 credits)

Answer the questions in only seven of the twelve groups in this part. Be sure to mark the answers to the groups of questions you choose in accordance with the instructions on the front cover of the test booklet. Leave blank the five groups of questions you do not choose to answer.

Group 1 Matter and Energy	Group 2 Atomic Structure	Group 3 Bonding	Group 4 Periodic Table
57 1 2 3 4	62 1 2 3 4	67 1 2 3 4	72 1 2 3 4
58 1 2 3 4	63 1 2 3 4	68 1 2 3 4	73 1 2 3 4
59 1 2 3 4	64 1 2 3 4	69 1 2 3 4	74 1 2 3 4
60 1 2 3 4	65 1 2 3 4	70 1 2 3 4	75 1 2 3 4
61 1 2 3 4	66 1 2 3 4	71 1 2 3 4	76 1 2 3 4

Group 5 Mathematics of Chemistry	Group 6 Kinetics and Equilibrium	Group 7 Acids and Bases	Group 8 Redox and Electrochemistry
77 1 2 3 4	82 1 2 3 4	87 1 2 3 4	92 1 2 3 4
78 1 2 3 4	83 1 2 3 4	88 1 2 3 4	93 1 2 3 4
79 1 2 3 4	84 1 2 3 4	89 1 2 3 4	94 1 2 3 4
80 1 2 3 4	85 1 2 3 4	90 1 2 3 4	95 1 2 3 4
81 1 2 3 4	86 1 2 3 4	91 1 2 3 4	96 1 2 3 4

Group 9 Organic Chemistry	Group 10 Applications of Chemical Principles	Group 11 Nuclear Chemistry	Group 12 Laboratory Activities
97 1 2 3 4	102 1 2 3 4	107 1 2 3 4	112 1 2 3 4
98 1 2 3 4	103 1 2 3 4	108 1 2 3 4	113 1 2 3 4
99 1 2 3 4	104 1 2 3 4	109 1 2 3 4	114 1 2 3 4
100 1 2 3 4	105 1 2 3 4	110 1 2 3 4	115 1 2 3 4
101 1 2 3 4	106 1 2 3 4	111 1 2 3 4	116 1 2 3 4

CHEMISTRY
JUNE 1998

Part I

Answer all 56 questions in this part. [65]

Directions (1–56): For *each* statement or question, select the word or expression that, of those given, best completes the statement or answers the question. Record your answer on the separate answer sheet in accordance with the directions on the front page of this booklet.

1 The diagrams below represent two solids and the temperature of each.

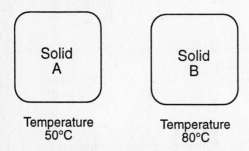

Temperature 50°C   Temperature 80°C

What occurs when the two solids are placed in contact with each other?

(1) Heat energy flows from solid *A* to solid *B*. Solid *A* decreases in temperature.
(2) Heat energy flows from solid *A* to solid *B*. Solid *A* increases in temperature.
(3) Heat energy flows from solid *B* to solid *A*. Solid *B* decreases in temperature.
(4) Heat energy flows from solid *B* to solid *A*. Solid *B* increases in temperature.

2 The particles of a substance are arranged in a definite geometric pattern and are constantly vibrating. This substance can be in

(1) the solid phase, only
(2) the liquid phase, only
(3) either the liquid or the solid phase
(4) neither the liquid nor the solid phase

3 What is the pressure of a mixture of CO_2, SO_2, and H_2O gases, if each gas has a partial pressure of 250 torr?

(1) 250 torr   (3) 750 torr
(2) 500 torr   (4) 1000 torr

4 Which substances can be decomposed chemically?

(1) CaO and Ca   (3) CO and Co
(2) MgO and Mg   (4) CaO and MgO

5 A gas sample has a volume of 25.0 milliliters at a pressure of 1.00 atmosphere. If the volume increases to 50.0 milliliters and the temperature remains constant, the new pressure will be

(1) 1.00 atm   (3) 0.250 atm
(2) 2.00 atm   (4) 0.500 atm

6 An atom with the electron configuration $1s^2 2s^2 2p^6 3s^2 3p^6 3d^5 4s^2$ has an incomplete

(1) 2*p* sublevel
(2) second principal energy level
(3) third principal energy level
(4) 4*s* sublevel

7 Which orbital notation represents a boron atom in the ground state?

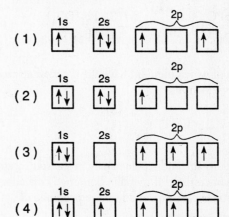

8 In the equation $^{234}_{90}Th \rightarrow ^{234}_{91}Pa + X$, the symbol *X* represents

(1) $^{0}_{+1}e$ (3) $^{1}_{0}n$

(2) $^{0}_{-1}e$ (4) $^{1}_{1}H$

9 Which subatomic particle is found in the nucleus of all isotopes of hydrogen?

(1) proton
(2) neutron
(3) electron
(4) positron

10 What is the highest principal quantum number (n) for an electron in an atom of sulfur in the ground state?

(1) 1
(2) 2
(3) 3
(4) 4

11 What is the total number of electrons in a completely filled fourth principal energy level?

(1) 8
(2) 10
(3) 16
(4) 32

12 What is the total number of hydrogen atoms required to form 1 molecule of $C_3H_5(OH)_3$?

(1) 1
(2) 5
(3) 3
(4) 8

13 Which element is found in both potassium chlorate and zinc nitrate?

(1) hydrogen
(2) oxygen
(3) potassium
(4) zinc

14 Which formula represents lead (II) phosphate?

(1) $PbPO_4$
(2) Pb_4PO_4
(3) $Pb_3(PO_4)_2$
(4) $Pb_2(PO_4)_3$

15 Atoms of which element have the *weakest* attraction for electrons?

(1) Na
(2) P
(3) Si
(4) S

16 The ability to conduct electricity in the solid state is a characteristic of metallic bonding. This characteristic is best explained by the presence of

(1) high ionization energies
(2) high electronegativities
(3) mobile electrons
(4) mobile protons

17 When ionic bonds are formed, metallic atoms tend to

lose electrons and become negative ions
lose electrons and become positive ions
gain electrons and become negative ions
gain electrons and become positive ions

18 The bond between hydrogen and oxygen in a water molecule is classified as

(1) ionic and nonpolar
(2) ionic and polar
(3) covalent and nonpolar
(4) covalent and polar

19 According to the Periodic Table, which element has more than one positive oxidation state?

(1) cadmium
(2) iron
(3) silver
(4) zinc

20 Which group contains a liquid that is a nonmetal at STP?

(1) 14
(2) 15
(3) 16
(4) 17

21 Which of these Group 14 elements has the most metallic properties?

(1) C
(2) Ge
(3) Si
(4) Sn

22 As the elements in Group 2 are considered in order of increasing atomic number, the atomic radius of each successive element increases. This increase is primarily due to an increase in the number of

(1) occupied principal energy levels
(2) electrons in the outermost shell
(3) neutrons in the nucleus
(4) unpaired electrons

23 Which element is classified as a metalloid (semimetal)?

(1) sulfur
(2) silicon
(3) barium
(4) bromine

24 Which element in Group 1 has the greatest tendency to lose an electron?

(1) cesium
(2) rubidium
(3) potassium
(4) sodium

25 The table below shows some properties of elements A, B, C, and D.

Element	Ionization Energy	Electronegativity	Conductivity of Heat and Electricity
A	low	low	low
B	low	low	high
C	high	high	low
D	high	high	high

Which element is most likely a nonmetal?

(1) A
(2) B
(3) C
(4) D

26 What is the gram formula mass of $Ca_3(PO_4)_2$?

(1) 135 g/mol (3) 278 g/mol
(2) 215 g/mol (4) 310. g/mol

27 The gram atomic mass of oxygen is 16.0 grams per mole. How many atoms of oxygen does this mass represent?

(1) 16.0 (3) 6.02×10^{23}
(2) 32.0 (4) $2(6.02 \times 10^{23})$

28 Given the *unbalanced* equation:

$$N_2(g) + H_2(g) \rightarrow NH_3(g)$$

When the equation is balanced using smallest whole-number coefficients, the ratio of moles of hydrogen consumed to moles of ammonia produced is

(1) 1:3 (3) 3:1
(2) 2:3 (4) 3:2

29 What is the concentration of a solution of 10. moles of copper (II) nitrate in 5.0 liters of solution?

(1) 0.50 M (3) 5.0 M
(2) 2.0 M (4) 10. M

30 Given the balanced equation:

$$Mg(s) + 2HCl(aq) \rightarrow MgCl_2(aq) + H_2(g)$$

At STP, what is the total number of liters of hydrogen gas produced when 3.00 moles of hydrochloric acid solution is completely consumed?

(1) 11.2 L (3) 33.6 L
(2) 22.4 L (4) 44.8 L

31 According to Reference Table *D*, which compound's solubility decreases most rapidly when the temperature increases from 50°C to 70°C?

(1) NH_3 (3) SO_2
(2) HCl (4) KNO_3

32 Given the reaction at equilibrium:

$$2CO(g) + O_2(g) \rightleftharpoons 2CO_2(g)$$

When the reaction is subjected to stress, a change will occur in the concentration of

(1) reactants, only
(2) products, only
(3) both reactants and products
(4) neither reactants nor products

33 An increase in the temperature of a system at equilibrium favors the

(1) endothermic reaction and decreases its rate
(2) endothermic reaction and increases its rate
(3) exothermic reaction and decreases its rate
(4) exothermic reaction and increases its rate

34 Based on Reference Table *L*, which compound, when in aqueous solution, is the best conductor of electricity?

(1) HF (3) H_2O
(2) H_2S (4) H_2SO_4

35 A compound that can act as an acid or a base is referred to as

(1) a neutral substance
(2) an amphoteric substance
(3) a monomer
(4) an isomer

Base your answers to questions 36 and 37 on the potential energy diagram of a chemical reaction shown below.

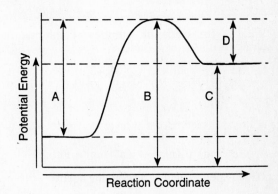

36 Which arrow represents the activation energy for the forward reaction?

(1) *A* (3) *C*
(2) *B* (4) *D*

37 The forward reaction is best described as an

(1) exothermic reaction in which energy is released
(2) exothermic reaction in which energy is absorbed
(3) endothermic reaction in which energy is released
(4) endothermic reaction in which energy is absorbed

38 In the reaction $HNO_3 + H_2O \rightleftharpoons H_3O^+ + NO_3^-$, the two Brönsted acids are

(1) H_2O and HNO_3
(3) H_2O and H_3O^+
(2) H_2O and NO_3^-
(4) HNO_3 and H_3O^+

39 Which substance can be classified as an Arrhenius acid?

(1) HCl
(3) LiOH
(2) NaCl
(4) KOH

40 How many milliliters of 0.20 M HCl are needed to exactly neutralize 40. milliliters of 0.40 M KOH?

(1) 20. mL
(3) 80. mL
(2) 40. mL
(4) 160 mL

41 Which 0.1 M solution will turn phenolphthalein pink?

(1) $HBr(aq)$
(3) $LiOH(aq)$
(2) $CO_2(aq)$
(4) $CH_3OH(aq)$

42 Which compound is an electrolyte?

(1) CH_3OH
(3) $C_3H_5(OH)_3$
(2) CH_3COOH
(4) $C_{12}H_{22}O_{11}$

43 What is the oxidation number of chlorine in $HClO_4$?

(1) +1
(3) +3
(2) +5
(4) +7

44 Given the redox reaction:

$$Fe^{2+}(aq) + Zn(s) \rightarrow Zn^{2+}(aq) + Fe(s)$$

Which species acts as a reducing agent?

(1) $Fe(s)$
(3) $Zn(s)$
(2) $Fe^{2+}(aq)$
(4) $Zn^{2+}(aq)$

45 Given the redox reaction:

$$2I^-(aq) + Br_2(\ell) \rightarrow 2Br^-(aq) + I_2(s)$$

What occurs during this reaction?

(1) The I^- ion is oxidized, and its oxidation number increases.
(2) The I^- ion is oxidized, and its oxidation number decreases.
   The I^- ion is reduced, and its oxidation number increases.
   The I^- ion is reduced, and its oxidation number decreases.

46 Given the reaction:

$$Zn(s) + 2HCl(aq) \rightarrow ZnCl_2(aq) + H_2(g)$$

Which equation represents the correct oxidation half-reaction?

(1) $Zn(s) \rightarrow Zn^{2+} + 2e^-$
(2) $2H^+ + 2e^- \rightarrow H_2(g)$
(3) $Zn^{2+} + 2e \rightarrow Zn(s)$
(4) $2Cl^- \rightarrow Cl_2(g) + 2e^-$

47 According to Reference Table N, which redox reaction occurs spontaneously?

(1) $Cu(s) + 2H^+ \rightarrow Cu^{2+} + H_2(g)$
(2) $Mg(s) + 2H^+ \rightarrow Mg^{2+} + H_2(g)$
(3) $2Ag(s) + 2H^+ \rightarrow 2Ag^+ + H_2(g)$
(4) $Hg(\ell) + 2H^+ \rightarrow Hg^{2+} + H_2(g)$

48 Which quantities are conserved in all oxidation-reduction reactions?

(1) charge, only
(2) mass, only
(3) both charge and mass
(4) neither charge nor mass

49 The reaction $CH_2CH_2 + H_2 \rightarrow CH_3CH_3$ is an example of

(1) substitution
(3) esterification
(2) addition
(4) fermentation

50 Given the compound:

Which structural formula represents an isomer?

51 In which pair of hydrocarbons does each compound contain only one double bond per molecule?

(1) C_2H_2 and C_2H_6
(3) C_4H_8 and C_2H_4
(2) C_2H_2 and C_3H_6
(4) C_6H_6 and C_7H_8

52 Which organic compound is classified as an acid?

(1) CH_3CH_2COOH (3) $C_{12}H_{22}O_{11}$

(2) CH_3CH_2OH (4) $C_6H_{12}O_6$

53 The products of the fermentation of a sugar are ethanol and

(1) water   (3) carbon dioxide

(2) oxygen   (4) sulfur dioxide

Note that questions 54 through 56 have only three choices.

54 As the temperature of $H_2O(\ell)$ in a closed system decreases, the vapor pressure of the $H_2O(\ell)$

(1) decreases

(2) increases

(3) remains the same

55 As the number of neutrons in the nucleus of a given atom of an element increases, the atomic number of that element

(1) decreases

(2) increases

(3) remains the same

56 Given the closed system at equilibrium:

$$CO_2(g) \rightleftharpoons CO_2(aq)$$

As the pressure on the system increases, the solubility of the $CO_2(g)$

(1) decreases

(2) increases

(3) remains the same

Part II

This part consists of twelve groups, each containing five questions. Each group tests a major area of the course. Choose seven of these twelve groups. Be sure that you answer all five questions in each group chosen. Record the answers to these questions on the separate answer sheet in accordance with the directions on the front page of this booklet. [35]

Group 1 — Matter and Energy

If you choose this group, be sure to answer questions 57–61.

57 The table below shows the temperature, pressure, and volume of five samples.

Sample	Substance	Temperature (K)	Pressure (atm)	Volume (L)
A	He	273	1	22.4
B	O_2	273	1	22.4
C	Ne	273	2	22.4
D	N_2	546	2	44.8
E	Ar	546	2	44.8

Which sample contains the same number of molecules as sample A?

(1) E   (3) C

(2) B   (4) D

58 The energy absorbed when ammonium chloride dissolves in water can be measured in

(1) degrees   (3) moles per liter

(2) kilocalories   (4) liters per mole

59 At 1 atmosphere of pressure, the steam-water equilibrium occurs at a temperature of

(1) 0 K   (3) 273 K

(2) 100 K   (4) 373 K

60 The graph below represents the uniform cooling of a substance, starting with the substance as a gas above its boiling point.

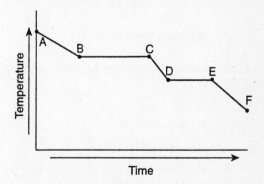

During which interval is the substance completely in the liquid phase?

(1) AB   (3) CD

(2) BC   (4) DE

61 Which two compounds readily sublime at room temperature (25°C)?

(1) $CO_2(s)$ and $I_2(s)$

(2) $CO_2(s)$ and $C_6H_{12}O_6(s)$

(3) $NaCl(s)$ and $I_2(s)$

(4) $NaCl(s)$ and $C_6H_{12}O_6(s)$

Group 2 — Atomic Structure

If you choose this group, be sure to answer questions 62–66.

62 Which electron configuration is possible for a nitrogen atom in the excited state?

(1) $1s^2 2s^2 2p^3$ (3) $1s^2 2s^2 2p^4$

(2) $1s^2 2s^2 2p^2 3s^1$ (4) $1s^2 2s^2 2p^2$

63 What is the total amount of energy required to remove the most loosely bound electron from each atom in a mole of gaseous Ca?

(1) 100 kcal/mol   (3) 141 kcal/mol

(2) 119 kcal/mol   (4) 176 kcal/mol

64 What is the total number of unpaired electrons in an atom of nickel in the ground state?

(1) 0   (3) 3

(2) 2   (4) 4

65 The characteristic bright-line spectrum of an element is produced when its electrons

(1) form a covalent bond
(2) form an ionic bond
(3) move to a higher energy state
(4) return to a lower energy state

66 Which emanation has *no* mass and *no* charge?

(1) alpha   (3) gamma

(2) beta   (4) neutron

Group 3 — Bonding

If you choose this group, be sure to answer questions 67–71.

67 Given the incomplete equation:

$$2N_2O_5 (g) \rightarrow$$

Which set of products completes and balances the incomplete equation?

(1) $2N_2(g) + 3H_2(g)$ (3) $4NO_2(g) + O_2(g)$

(2) $2N_2(g) + 2O_2(g)$ (4) $4NO(g) + 5O_2(g)$

68 Which structural formula represents a nonpolar molecule?

(1)   H — Cl   (3)   H — H

(2)   H — O   (4)   H — N — H
           | |
           H   H

69 Compared to the boiling point of H_2S, the boiling point of H_2O is relatively high. Which type of bonding causes this difference?

(1) covalent   (3) ionic

(2) hydrogen   (4) network

70 In which system do molecule-ion attractions exist?

(1) $NaCl(aq)$ (3) $C_6H_{12}O_6(aq)$

(2) $NaCl(s)$ (4) $C_6H_{12}O_6(s)$

71 An example of an empirical formula is

(1) C_4H_{10} (3) $HC_2H_3O_2$

(2) $C_6H_{12}O_6$ (4) CH_2O

Group 4 — Periodic Table

If you choose this group, be sure to answer questions 72–76.

72 The elements from which two groups of the Periodic Table are most similar in their chemical properties?

(1) 1 and 2   (3) 2 and 17

(2) 1 and 17   (4) 17 and 18

73 Which metal is most likely obtained by the electrolysis of its fused salt?

(1) Au   (3) Li

(2) Ag   (4) Zn

74 Which aqueous solution is colored?

(1) $CuSO_4(aq)$ (3) $KCl(aq)$

(2) $BaCl_2(aq)$ (4) $MgSO_4(aq)$

75 Because of its high reactivity, which element is *never* found free in nature?

(1) O   (3) N

(2) F   (4) Ne

76 Which Group 18 element is most likely to form a compound with the element fluorine?

(1) He   (3) Ar

(2) Ne   (4) Kr

Group 5 — Mathematics of Chemistry

If you choose this group, be sure to answer questions 77–81.

77 At STP, which gas will diffuse more rapidly than Ne?

(1) He   (3) Kr
(2) Ar   (4) Xe

78 The heat of fusion of a compound is 30.0 calories per gram. What is the total number of calories of heat that must be absorbed by a 15.0-gram sample to change the compound from solid to liquid at its melting point?

(1) 15.0 cal   (3) 150. cal
(2) 45.0 cal   (4) 450. cal

79 Which gas has a density of 1.70 grams per liter at STP?

(1) $F_2(g)$ (3) $N_2(g)$
(2) $He(g)$ (4) $SO_2(g)$

80 Given the reaction:

$$2C_2H_2(g) + 5O_2(g) \rightarrow 4CO_2(g) + 2H_2O(g)$$

What is the total number of grams of $O_2(g)$ needed to react completely with 0.50 mole of $C_2H_2(g)$?

(1) 10. g   (3) 80. g
(2) 40. g   (4) 160 g

81 Which statement describes KCl(aq)?

(1) KCl is the solute in a homogeneous mixture.
(2) KCl is the solute in a heterogeneous mixture.
(3) KCl is the solvent in a homogeneous mixture.
(4) KCl is the solvent in a heterogeneous mixture.

Group 6 — Kinetics and Equilibrium

If you choose this group, be sure to answer questions 82–86.

82 According to Reference Table *G*, which compound will form spontaneously from its elements?

(1) ethene   (3) nitrogen (II) oxide
(2) hydrogen iodide   (4) magnesium oxide

83 Given the equilibrium reaction:

$$AgCl(s) \rightleftharpoons Ag^+(aq) + Cl^-(aq)$$

At 25°C, the K_{sp} is equal to

(1) 6.0×10^{-23} (3) 1.0×10^{-7}
(2) 1.8×10^{-10} (4) 9.6×10^{-4}

84 Given the reaction:

$$2N_2(g) + O_2(g) \rightleftharpoons 2N_2O(g)$$

Which statement is true when this closed system reaches equilibrium?

(1) All of the $N_2(g)$ has been consumed.
(2) All of the $O_2(g)$ has been consumed.
(3) Pressure changes no longer occur.
(4) The forward reaction no longer occurs.

85 Which equation is used to determine the free energy change during a chemical reaction?

(1) $\Delta G = \Delta H - \Delta S$ (3) $\Delta G = \Delta H - T\Delta S$
(2) $\Delta G = \Delta H + \Delta S$ (4) $\Delta G = \Delta H + T\Delta S$

86 Which is the correct equilibrium expression for the reaction $2A(g) + 3B(g) \rightleftharpoons C(g) + 3D(g)$?

(1) $K = \dfrac{[2A]+[3B]}{[C]+[3D]}$ (3) $K = \dfrac{[A]^2[B]^3}{[C][D]^3}$

(2) $K = \dfrac{[C]+[3D]}{[2A]+[3B]}$ (4) $K = \dfrac{[C][D]^3}{[A]^2[B]^3}$

Group 7 — Acids and Bases

If you choose this group, be sure to answer questions 87–91.

87 According to Reference Table *L*, what is the conjugate acid of the hydroxide ion (OH^-)?

(1) O^{2-} (3) H_2O
(2) H^+ (4) H_3O^+

88 Which of the following is the *weakest* Brönsted acid?

(1) NH_4^+ (3) H_2SO_4
(2) HSO_4^- (4) HNO_3

89 Which compound is a salt?

(1) CH_3OH (3) $H_2C_2O_4$
(2) $C_6H_{12}O_6$ (4) $KC_2H_3O_2$

90 What is the pH of a solution with a hydronium ion concentration of 0.01 mole per liter?

(1) 1   (3) 10
(2) 2   (4) 14

91 Given the equation: $H^+ + OH^- \rightarrow H_2O$

Which type of reaction does the equation represent?

(1) esterification   (3) hydrolysis
(2) decomposition   (4) neutralization

Group 8 — Redox and Electricity

If you choose this group, be sure to answer questions 92–96.

92 Which reduction half-reaction has a standard electrode potential (E^0) of 1.50 volts?

(1) $Au^{3+} + 3e^- \rightarrow Au(s)$
(2) $Al^{3+} + 3e^- \rightarrow Al(s)$
(3) $Co^{2+} + 2e^- \rightarrow Co(s)$
(4) $Ca^{2+} + 2e^- \rightarrow Ca(s)$

93 Given the reaction:

$$2Li(s) + Cl_2(g) \rightarrow 2LiCl(s)$$

As the reaction takes place, the $Cl_2(g)$ will

(1) gain electrons   (3) gain protons
(2) lose electrons   (4) lose protons

94 The diagram below shows the electrolysis of fused KCl.

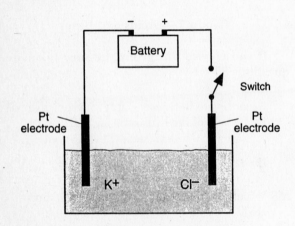

What occurs when the switch is closed?
(1) Positive ions migrate toward the anode, where they lose electrons.
(2) Positive ions migrate toward the anode, where they gain electrons.
(3) Positive ions migrate toward the cathode, where they lose electrons.
(4) Positive ions migrate toward the cathode, where they gain electrons.

95 The diagram below represents an electrochemical cell at 298 K and 1 atmosphere.

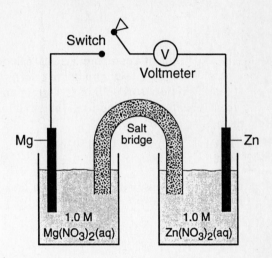

What is the maximum cell voltage (E^0) when the switch is closed?
(1) +1.61 V   (3) +3.13 V
(2) –1.61 V   (4) –3.13 V

96 Given the balanced equation:

$$2Al(s) + 6H^+(aq) \rightarrow 2Al^{3+}(aq) + 3H_2(g)$$

When 2 moles of Al(s) completely reacts, what is the total number of moles of electrons transferred from Al(s) to $H^+(aq)$?

(1) 5   (3) 3
(2) 6   (4) 4

Group 9 — Organic Chemistry

If you choose this group, be sure to answer questions 97–101.

97 A condensation polymerization reaction produces a polymer and

(1) H_2 (3) CO_2
(2) O_2 (4) H_2O

98 Which organic compound is classified as a primary alcohol?

(1) ethylene glycol   (3) glycerol
(2) ethanol   (4) 2-butanol

99 What is the structural formula for 1,2-ethanediol?

(1) H–C–C–OH (with H, OH on top; H, H on bottom)

(3) H–C–C–H (with OH, OH on top; H, H on bottom)

(2) H–C–C–C–OH (with H, H, OH on top; H, H, H on bottom)

(4) H–C–C–C–H (with H, OH, OH on top; H, H, H on bottom)

100 Given the structural formula for ethyne:

$$H-C \equiv C-H$$

What is the total number of electrons shared between the carbon atoms?

(1) 6   (3) 3
(2) 2   (4) 4

101 What is the name of the compound with the following formula?

H–C–C–C–H (with H, O(double bond), H on top; H, H on bottom)

(1) propanone   (3) propanal
(2) propanol   (4) propanoic acid

Group 10 — Applications of Chemical Principles

If you choose this group, be sure to answer questions 102–106.

102 Given the overall reaction for the lead-acid battery:

$$Pb + PbO_2 + 2H_2SO_4 \underset{\text{Charge}}{\overset{\text{Discharge}}{\rightleftharpoons}} 2PbSO_4 + 2H_2O$$

Which element changes oxidation state when electric energy is produced?

(1) hydrogen   (3) sulfur
(2) oxygen   (4) lead

103 Which substance is produced by the Haber process?

(1) aluminum   (3) nitric acid
(2) ammonia   (4) sulfuric acid

104 Iron corrodes more easily than aluminum and zinc because aluminum and zinc both

(1) are reduced
(2) are oxidizing agents
(3) form oxides that are self-protective
(4) form oxides that are very reactive

105 Which balanced equation represents a cracking reaction?

(1) $2C_3H_6 + 9O_2 \rightarrow 6H_2O + 6CO_2$
(2) $C_{14}H_{30} \rightarrow C_7H_{16} + C_7H_{14}$
(3) $C_{14}H_{28} + Cl_2 \rightarrow C_{14}H_{28}Cl_2$
(4) $C_2H_6 + Cl_2 \rightarrow C_2H_5Cl + HCl$

106 During fractional distillation, hydrocarbons are separated according to their

(1) boiling points   (3) triple points
(2) melting points   (4) saturation points

Group 11 — Nuclear Chemistry

If you choose this group, be sure to answer questions 107–111.

107 In a fusion reaction, reacting nuclei must collide. Collisions between two nuclei are difficult to achieve because the nuclei are

(1) both negatively charged and repel each other
(2) both positively charged and repel each other
(3) oppositely charged and attract each other
(4) oppositely charged and repel each other

108 A particle accelerator can increase the kinetic energy of

(1) an alpha particle and a beta particle
(2) an alpha particle and a neutron
(3) a gamma ray and a beta particle
(4) a neutron and a gamma ray

109 Which nuclide is a radioisotope used in the study of organic reaction mechanisms?

(1) carbon-12   (3) uranium-235
(2) carbon-14   (4) uranium-238

110 To make nuclear fission more efficient, which device is used in a nuclear reactor to slow the speed of neutrons?

(1) internal shield   (3) control rod
(2) external shield   (4) moderator

111 Which equation is an example of artificial transmutation?

(1) $^{238}_{92}U \rightarrow {}^{4}_{2}He + {}^{234}_{90}Th$

(2) $^{27}_{13}Al + {}^{4}_{2}He \rightarrow {}^{30}_{15}P + {}^{1}_{0}n$

(3) $^{14}_{6}C \rightarrow {}^{14}_{7}N + {}^{0}_{-1}e$

(4) $^{226}_{88}Ra \rightarrow {}^{4}_{2}He + {}^{222}_{86}Rn$

Group 12 — Laboratory Activities

If you choose this group, be sure to answer questions 112–116.

112 Which measurement contains three significant figures?

(1) 0.08 cm   (3) 800 cm
(2) 0.080 cm   (4) 8.08 cm

113 A student investigated the physical and chemical properties of a sample of an unknown gas and then identified the gas. Which statement represents a conclusion rather than an experimental observation?

(1) The gas is colorless.
(2) The gas is carbon dioxide.
(3) When the gas is bubbled into limewater, the liquid becomes cloudy.
(4) When placed in the gas, a flaming splint stops burning.

114 The table below shows properties of four solids, A, B, C, and D.

Substance	Melting Point	Conductivity in Solid State	Solubility in Water
A	high	no	soluble
B	high	yes	insoluble
C	high	no	insoluble
D	low	no	insoluble

Which substance could represent diamond, a network solid?

(1) A   (3) C
(2) B   (4) D

115 A student obtained the following data to determine the percent by mass of water in a hydrate.

Mass of empty crucible + cover	11.70 g
Mass of crucible + cover + hydrated salt before heating	14.90 g
Mass of crucible + cover + anhydrous salt after thorough heating	14.53 g

What is the approximate percent by mass of the water in the hydrated salt?

(1) 2.5%   (3) 88%
(2) 12%   (4) 98%

116 A student wishes to prepare approximately 100 milliliters of an aqueous solution of 6 M HCl using 12 M HCl. Which procedure is correct?

(1) adding 50 mL of 12 M HCl to 50 mL of water while stirring the mixture steadily
(2) adding 50 mL of 12 M HCl to 50 mL of water, and then stirring the mixture steadily
(3) adding 50 mL of water to 50 mL of 12 M HCl while stirring the mixture steadily
(4) adding 50 mL of water to 50 mL of 12 M HCl, and then stirring the mixture steadily

CHEMISTRY
JUNE 1998

ANSWER SHEET

Student ....

Teacher ....

School ....

Record all of your answers on this answer sheet in accordance with the instructions on the front cover of the test booklet.

Part I (65 credits)

1	1	2	3	4	21	1	2	3	4	41	1	2	3	4
2	1	2	3	4	22	1	2	3	4	42	1	2	3	4
3	1	2	3	4	23	1	2	3	4	43	1	2	3	4
4	1	2	3	4	24	1	2	3	4	44	1	2	3	4
5	1	2	3	4	25	1	2	3	4	45	1	2	3	4
6	1	2	3	4	26	1	2	3	4	46	1	2	3	4
7	1	2	3	4	27	1	2	3	4	47	1	2	3	4
8	1	2	3	4	28	1	2	3	4	48	1	2	3	4
9	1	2	3	4	29	1	2	3	4	49	1	2	3	4
10	1	2	3	4	30	1	2	3	4	50	1	2	3	4
11	1	2	3	4	31	1	2	3	4	51	1	2	3	4
12	1	2	3	4	32	1	2	3	4	52	1	2	3	4
13	1	2	3	4	33	1	2	3	4	53	1	2	3	4
14	1	2	3	4	34	1	2	3	4	54	1	2	3	
15	1	2	3	4	35	1	2	3	4	55	1	2	3	
16	1	2	3	4	36	1	2	3	4	56	1	2	3	
17	1	2	3	4	37	1	2	3	4					
18	1	2	3	4	38	1	2	3	4					
19	1	2	3	4	39	1	2	3	4					
20	1	2	3	4	40	1	2	3	4					

Part II (35 credits)

Answer the questions in only seven of the twelve groups in this part. Be sure to mark the answers to the groups of questions you choose in accordance with the instructions on the front cover of the test booklet. Leave blank the five groups of questions you do not choose to answer.

Group 1 Matter and Energy			
57	1	2	3	4
58	1	2	3	4
59	1	2	3	4
60	1	2	3	4
61	1	2	3	4

Group 2 Atomic Structure			
62	1	2	3	4
63	1	2	3	4
64	1	2	3	4
65	1	2	3	4
66	1	2	3	4

Group 3 Bonding			
67	1	2	3	4
68	1	2	3	4
69	1	2	3	4
70	1	2	3	4
71	1	2	3	4

Group 4 Periodic Table			
72	1	2	3	4
73	1	2	3	4
74	1	2	3	4
75	1	2	3	4
76	1	2	3	4

Group 5 Mathematics of Chemistry			
77	1	2	3	4
78	1	2	3	4
79	1	2	3	4
80	1	2	3	4
81	1	2	3	4

Group 6 Kinetics and Equilibrium			
82	1	2	3	4
83	1	2	3	4
84	1	2	3	4
85	1	2	3	4
86	1	2	3	4

Group 7 Acids and Bases			
87	1	2	3	4
88	1	2	3	4
89	1	2	3	4
90	1	2	3	4
91	1	2	3	4

Group 8 Redox and Electrochemistry			
92	1	2	3	4
93	1	2	3	4
94	1	2	3	4
95	1	2	3	4
96	1	2	3	4

Group 9 Organic Chemistry			
97	1	2	3	4
98	1	2	3	4
99	1	2	3	4
100	1	2	3	4
101	1	2	3	4

Group 10 Applications of Chemical Principles			
102	1	2	3	4
103	1	2	3	4
104	1	2	3	4
105	1	2	3	4
106	1	2	3	4

Group 11 Nuclear Chemistry			
107	1	2	3	4
108	1	2	3	4
109	1	2	3	4
110	1	2	3	4
111	1	2	3	4

Group 12 Laboratory Activities			
112	1	2	3	4
113	1	2	3	4
114	1	2	3	4
115	1	2	3	4
116	1	2	3	4